Traveling

in Italy

with

Henry James

E d i t e d   b y

F r e d   K a p l a n

•

William Morrow and

Company, Inc.

New York

Traveling

in Italy

with

Henry James

.

Essays

It is the policy of William Morrow and Company, Inc., and its imprints and affiliates, recognizing the importance of preserving what has been written, to print the books we publish on acid-free paper, and we exert our best efforts to that end.

Library of Congress Cataloging-in-Publication Data

James, Henry, 1843–1916
Traveling in Italy with Henry James / edited by Fred Kaplan.
p. cm.
Includes bibliographical references (p.   ).
ISBN 0-688-10901-2
1. Italy—Description and travel. 2. James, Henry, 1843–1916–
Journeys—Italy. 3. Authors, American—19th century—Journeys—
Italy. 4. Authors, American—20th century—Journeys—Italy.
I. Kaplan, Fred, 1937–   . II Title.
DG427.J3523   1994
914.504′84—dc20   93-21014
                                                        CIP

Printed in the United States of America

First Edition

1   2   3   4   5   6   7   8   9   10

Book design by Barbara M. Bachman

Title page photograph of Venice from
the collection of Thomas Nau.

Title page autograph from The Bettmann Archive

Contents

Florence 215

Bay of Naples 273

On the Road to and Within Italy 295

Introduction

....

To the modern visitor, Henry James's Italy seems both long ago and, at the same time, surprisingly contemporaneous. Actually, some of James's essays about Italy look back to an even earlier time than many of his visits, to the last days of papal Rome, which he experienced only once, during his first visit as a young man of twenty-six, a year before secular Italy was created and papal authority restricted to the Vatican. But, as James continued to visit and write about Italy, many of the essays also came to embody a personal retrospective, a comparison between what Italy had been like when he had most recently been there and what it was like now, during his present visit. James visited fourteen times over a period of almost forty years, often staying for six months or longer. His last visit was in 1907, when he was sixty-four years old.

When he first came to Italy, in 1869, his happiest local excursions were on horseback. When he last came, he and Italy had succumbed to the thrill of the automobile. The letters and essays about Italy inevitably, then, embody a record of James's changing tastes and interests. The man who found Italy a rapturous exaltation in 1869 found it, in 1907, a sober autumnal reminder of the passage of his own time.

Italy, though, was an enduring attraction, partly because for James it always fulfilled certain fantasies, certain needs. As a young man he felt compelled to experience the pagan and the Christian art of which Italy had the highest concentration. New York, Boston, London, even Paris—the frigid cultural capitals of North America and of northern Europe—had less to offer and made less satisfactory settings for the presentation of high art. Italy, and especially Rome, "was the æsthetic antidote to the ugliness of the rest of the world—that is, of

Anglo-Saxondom in especial." During his first decade of visits, he dutifully (and pleasurably) gave high priority to viewing Italian Renaissance art, Roman sculpture, and the remains of Roman architecture. He was a young American whose New York and Boston had little to offer in the way of important art collections or distinguished architecture, and to visit Italy was a great cultural adventure. His initial energy and enthusiasm as a traveler and museum visitor also had a practical purpose: He wrote most of his travel essays for money, to earn his keep, both the cost of his travels and the cost of sustaining himself as a professional writer whose only resource for much of his life was his pen. As an art critic, James needed to communicate with the general audiences of the magazines for which he wrote. His art criticism is impressionistic, humanistic, and sometimes commonplace. But it is often freshly phrased, and he hoped it would be useful to museum visitors or to armchair viewers who, in places distant from Italy, were looking at the photographic reproductions of masterpieces that were for the first time becoming available. His own avid museum-going gradually declined into occasional revisits and mostly memories. As he aged, he readily admitted that "the plastic arts may have less to say to us than in the hungry years of youth. . . ." Italy, though, continued to speak to him in many voices.

But that is hardly surprising. He had come to Italy initially to see great art in its original setting, and from the beginning the setting itself had major importance for him. After a while it became paramount, partly because Italy never lost for him its magical enchantment as an atmosphere, as a total environment, as a place in which air, light, landscape, and visual beauty of every kind seemed to him inseparable entities. Gradually, the presence of great art in his immediate surroundings became an enriching ambiance rather than a visual imperative: "It is always a comfort to know that they [the paintings at the Academy] are there, as the sense of them on the spot is part of the furniture of the mind. . . ." In every aspect of his Italian experience he retained, as part of the play of his experience, his constant awareness of the art that he had absorbed over the years. Life and art seemed interpenetrated in Italy as nowhere else: "All the splendour of light and colour, all the Venetian air and the Venetian history, are on the walls and ceilings of the palaces; and all the genius of the masters, all the images and visions they have left upon canvas, seem to tremble in the sunbeams and dance upon the waves." He assured his American readers that the totality of the Italian experience was best embodied in and represented not by single or even collected works of art but in the combination of the natural and the artistic. "The light here is in fact a mighty magician and, with all respect to Titian, Veronese and Tintoret, the greatest artist of them all."

When he stayed in Italy for long periods, he had difficulty working. For "Venice is not, in fair weather, a place for concentration of mind. The effort required for sitting down to a writing-table is heroic, and the brightest page of MS. looks dull beside the brilliancy of your *milieu*. All nature beckons you forth, and murmurs to you sophistically that such hours should be devoted to collecting impressions." He needed places like London for work. Its unattractive climate fostered a cocoon of writerly concentration. Italy, though, was a place whose beauty demanded constant attention, even for someone as single-minded as James in his discipline and devotion to his writing. Late in life, he affirmed a conviction he had held since his earliest visit: "Italy is so much the most beautiful country in the world . . . the incomparable wrought *fusion,* fusion of human history and mortal passion with the elements of earth and air, of colour, composition and form." Such compelling beauty had its dangers, especially for an American Victorian with an absolute dedication of principle and of economic necessity to the infamous work ethic of the world into which he had been born. Though he flirted numbers of times with taking, particularly in Venice, an apartment of his own to which he could return regularly, he always drew back from such a tempting prospect. Among other reasons, he did not feel regular residence in Italy to be compatible with his commitment to his vocation. He feared intellectual laxity, the wrong kind of aesthetic self-indulgence.

But he did flirt with it. From the beginning, Italy seemed to him to be feminine, luxuriant, sensual, and romantic. It did not seem to him really a Christian country, which did not distress him in the least. "One may call it singular," he remarked, "that in the capital of Christendom the portrait most suggestive of a Christian conscience is that of a pagan emperor" [Marcus Aurelius]. Italian attitudes seemed to him essentially pagan, especially in the appreciation of the sensual and the stoic acceptance of poverty. Vastly poorer (and much cheaper for the American and British visitor) than today, Italy did challenge James's social consciousness. But he easily met the challenge with the explicit recognition that he needed to and could make his awareness of the social realities secondary to his appreciation of the rich mixture of aesthetic and cultural attractions. Now and then he reminded himself that what he saw as grand opera other people experienced as bitter tragedy. But "one sees after all, however, even among the most palpable realities, very much what the play of one's imagination projects there."

As a young man, he brought to Italy the eyes of an American who felt himself victimized by a cultural Puritanism and aesthetic poverty for which Italy was one of the antidotes. He mostly kept his eyes on the aspects of Italy that most attracted him. He enjoyed the Mediterranean acceptance of nature, of human nature, and of the comparative elevation of means over ends; he enjoyed what seemed to him Italy's high regard for the experiences of daily life for themselves rather than for some moral message, commercial advantage, or theological finality. "Our picture" in Italy "is not of pondered finalities, but of happy processes, accidents, adventures, a generous acceptance of generous goodly appearances—all sufficient, in their order, unto the day." Italy was the place where he felt, to the extent that he ever did, free, expansive, and sensually fulfilled. It seemed the great magician whose erotic powers he could feel and respond to—they took the form of visual beauty in art, in architecture, in landscape, in light, in the gondoliers whose handsomeness he found inseparable from the totality of the Italian experience. All the elements were perfectly fused.

Italy itself, though, was far from perfect, and not every city equally attractive. When he initially looked for a temporary place of residence, he alternated between Florence and Rome, and selected each on different occasions, though Rome for the longer periods of time. Both cities had flourishing Anglo-

American colonies, which proved both an attraction and a disadvantage. He did not want extended periods of isolation, but he feared that too much of his time would be claimed by social obligations at the expense of his work and of gathering Italian impressions. Over the years of his visits both Florence and Rome changed substantially, especially the latter, and not for the better. When he first came, Florence seemed a late-Renaissance small city, Rome a medieval backwater, only distinguishable from other Italian towns by the concentration of its Roman heritage and the feudal pomp of papal self-satisfaction. In comparison to New York and London, Rome seemed tiny, premodern, and picturesque. On the one hand, James welcomed Italy's unification and modernization, at least to the extent that it embodied liberal political principles and an improved standard of life for many Italians. On the other, modernization meant that Italy would become more like America and Britain, that Rome would become more like New York, and that something quintessentially Italian would be diminished. Modernization would desecrate and dwarf the picturesque and the ancient. And the technology that made Italy more accessible and comfortable to non-Italians inevitably determined that tourism would flourish as it never had before. "The bark of Chicago" would be heard on the canals of Venice.

James was the epitome of the serious visitor. He would have preferred that other visitors be kept out or somehow be persuaded to stay away. Sometimes he felt resigned to the physical changes and to the crowds. Often he was nostalgic about what had been. "When I was first in Venice, in 1869, it was a very natural place, and there was only a rough lane across the little island from the landing-place to the beach. There was a bathing-place in those days, and a restaurant, which was very bad, but where, in the warm evenings, your dinner did not much matter as you sat letting it cool upon the wooden terrace that stretched out into the sea. Today the Lido is a part of united Italy, and has been made the victim of various improvements." More often than not, as he grew older, he felt that much though far from all of Italy, especially Rome, had been spoiled by "improvements" and by tourism. Increasingly, the city that most attracted and sustained him was Venice, primarily because it had changed the least. If Italy was the epitome of a nation-museum being modernized by a vulgar curator, Venice was the museum city whose natural features made change so difficult that important aspects of it seemed to him what they had always been. He returned regularly to Venice, with which he had fallen in love in the early 1880s, until he could no longer return to the country at all. It became to him an image of the magic of Italy.

James wrote about Italy in four distinctive ways and genres: in letters, in travel essays, in his 1903 biography of William Wetmore Story, an American sculptor who had lived most of his life in Rome, and in his fiction. From the moment of his first stepping onto Italian soil, he needed to express his feelings and share his impressions with his family and friends. A brilliant letter-writer, his epistolary impressions sparkle with immediacy, the spontaneous exultations of someone who feels that at last he is where he has for much of his life prepared himself to come. Since they too, like his essays, record his responses over a period of almost forty years, his letters also embody changes in attitude and tone that inevitably occured as James grew older. They move from frenzied excitement to autumnal nostalgia. But they always have the immediacy, the honesty, and the frankness of personal documents written to the moment and for the moment, the spontaneity of private conversations between people who have known each other and their subject for a very long time.

While the letters were for private ears only, the essays of course were public documents, self-conscious artifacts to serve an economic and a professional purpose. They are much more reflective than spontaneous, with the exception perhaps of "From a Roman Note-Book." Their quality varies: Mostly, as in the Venice essays and in "Italy Revisited," they are inspired; sometimes they seem here and there flat, tired, either too occasional or not sufficiently visually vivid. And they also reflect the larger pattern of changes in James's style as a writer. It may be all too easy to notice that some essays are written by the author of *Portrait of a Lady,* others by the author of *The Golden Bowl.* The latter have their own attractions, but they are less useful as Jamesian guides to Italy than as additional avenues into James's own inner territory. The letters were never meant to be read except to the chosen few to whom they were addressed; the essays, initially, were not meant to be read all at once, though James did eventually, in 1909, publish them in a single volume, in which he arranged them in chronological order of original publication. In *Traveling in Italy with Henry James* the letters and the essays (though not all of them) are brought together for the first time and arranged by topographical subject and then chronologically, with the notion that readers will not necessarily want to read all of James's writings about Italy at one go and simply for their own sake but in the context of some more localized interest. In Venice, or in anticipation of Venice, one is likely to want to read about Venice, and so on.

In Italy itself or on an airplane approaching Italy or in one's own home, before the proverbial New England fireplace, one may want to supplement reading James's essays about Italy with the imaginative adventure of reading some of his fiction set in and evocative of it. Considerations of length and their ready availability make it impractical to include here any of James's representations of Italy in his fiction. But a list of such stories and selections from his novels would certainly include "Travelling Companions" (1870), "At Isella" (1871), "The Madonna of the Future" (1873), "The Last of the Valerii" (1874), "Adina" (1874), "The Diary of a Man of Fifty" (1879), "The Aspern Papers" (1888), and portions of his second novel, *Roderick Hudson* (1875). The earliest story, "Travelling Companions," has much of the feel of a travel essay disguised as fiction. The last, "The Aspern Papers," is a brilliant transformation of Italy and Venice in particular into an expression of James's enduring fascination with the relationship between Americans and Italy and between place and art. Italy of course makes important contributions to James's last two novels, *Wings of the Dove* and *The Golden Bowl,* but in these the international theme and the Italian landscape of the earlier fiction have been fully absorbed into the imagery, symbols, and ambiance of those masterpieces.

In the variety of his ways of experiencing and imagining

Italy, James can serve to some extent and for some people as a guide to Italy now. For those with a historical perspective and to those with a literary sensibility, he provides both a way of touching and revitalizing the places that have changed only in what swirls around them—in their settings—though, indeed, as James granted, changes in setting result in changes in how we experience the things themselves. James's Rome is remarkably similar to and noticeably different from the Rome of today. Venice has changed less, though even the museum city has changed enough that we can notice the differences. But James himself provides the paradigmatic experience: He saw Italy mostly through his imagination, which was richly informed by what he had read; what he saw was inseparable from what he brought to the act of seeing. What James provides us with, among other things, in the letters and essays here, is the totality of his experience of Italy, which we can add to whatever other resources we bring to our own experience of the country. For some, *Traveling in Italy with Henry James* will be mostly an armchair adventure, an imaginative engagement with James's Italy; for others, it will also be an unusual guidebook, different from Baedeker and Frommer, one of a number of enriching companions to accompany your own Italian voyages, perhaps along with Stendhal, Byron, Thomas Mann, Mary McCarthy, and James Morris.

Textual Note

....

The excerpts from James's letters are printed courtesy of Mr. Alexander James and the following libraries: Houghton Library, Harvard University (7/28/1869, 9/25/1869, 10/6/1869, 10/13/1869, 10/30/1869, 11/7/1869, 11/11/1869, 11/21/1869, 12/25/1869, 12/28/1869, 1/1/1870, 1/17/1870, 1/20/1870, 12/25/1872, 1/8/1873, 1/26/1873, 2/10/1873, 3/28/1873, 3/31/1873, 4/9/1873, 4/25/1873, 7/17/1873, 12/10/1873, 1/14/1874, 12/15/1877, 3/31/1880, 4/9/1880, 4/18/1880, 6/12/1881, 6/13/1887, 5/18/1890, 5/20/1890, 6/30/1890, 7/3/1890, 12/13/1891, 7/4/1892, 5/25/1894, 6/24/1907); Dartmouth College Library (4/24/1887, 7/7/1890, 6/3/1894, 7/3/1894, 11/20/1899, 5/3/1900); Library of Congress (2/27/1887, 3/1/1887); New-York Historical Society (9/21/1869); Beinecke Library, Yale University (8/11/1907); Huntington Library (4/14/1887); British Library (5/29/1890); Henry Vaux (10/7/1887); Harvard University Press (4/24/1887, 5/30/1907, 9/13/1907).

James's essays on Italy are from a variety of sources, as follows, with the original place and date of publication in parentheses. From *Italian Hours* (1909): "Venice: An Early Impression" (originally "From Venice to Strasbourg," *Nation,* 3/6/1873); "Venice" (*Century Magazine,* 11/1882); "The Grand Canal" (*Scribner's Magazine,* 11/1892); "Two Old Houses and Three Young Women" (*Independent,* 9/7/1899); "Casa Alvisi" (*Cornhill Magazine,* 2/1902); "A Roman Holiday" (*Atlantic Monthly,* 7/1873); "Roman Rides" (*Atlantic Monthly,* 8/1873); "Roman Neighbourhoods" (*Atlantic Monthly,* 12/1873); "The After-Season in Rome" (*Nation,* 6/1873); "From a Roman Note-Book" (*Galaxy,* 11/1873); "A Few Other Roman Neighbourhoods" (*Italian Hours,* 1909); "The Spirit of Rome" (*William Wetmore Story and His Friends*), 1903; "The Autumn in Florence" (*Nation,* 1/1874); "Florentine Notes" (*Independent,*

4/1874); "Italy Revisited" (*Atlantic,* 4–5/1878); "The Saint's Afternoon and Others" (*The May Book,* 1901); "From Chambéry to Milan" (*Nation,* 11/1872); "The Old Saint-Gothard" (originally "An Autumn Journey," *Galaxy,* 4/1874); "A Chain of Cities" (originally "A Chain of Italian Cities," *Atlantic Monthly,* 2/1874); "The Shades of Siena" (*William Wetmore Story and His Friends),* 1903; "Sienna Early and Late" (originally Part I, "Siena," *Atlantic Monthly,* 6/1874, and Part II, *Italian Hours,* 1909); "Ravenna" (*Nation,* 7/1874); "Tuscan Cities" (*Nation,* 5/1874); "Other Tuscan Cities" (*Italian Hours,* 1909).

I have included only the portion of "Italy Revisited" that deals with Florence. James never published or even quite finished (and I have not included here) an essay called "Very Modern Rome" (edited by Richard C. Harrier, *Harvard Library Bulletin,* VIII, 1954). Two additional sections of James's *William Wetmore Story and His Friends* (1903), "The Roman Air and the Palazzo Barberini" and "Bagni di Lucca," do not lend themselves to inclusion here but also convey some of the flavor of James's Italy.

All explanatory notes in brackets and footnotes not indicated as James's are the editor's.

Recommended Reading

....

Honour, Hugh, and John Fleming. *The Venetian Hours of Henry James, Whistler and Sargent.* Boston: Bulfinch Press, 1991.

James, Henry. *Henry James, Collected Travel Writings, The Continent,* ed. Richard Howard. New York: Library of *America,* 1993.

MacDonald, Bonny. *Henry James's Italian Hours: Revelatory and Resistant Impressions.* Ann Arbor: UMI Research Press, 1990.

Maves, Carl. *Sensuous Pessimism: Italy in the Works of Henry James.* Bloomington: Indiana University Press, 1973.

Tuttleton, James, and Agostino Lombardo, eds. *The Sweetest Impression of Life: The James Family and Italy.* New York: New York University Press, 1990.

Vance, William L. *America's Rome,* 2 vols. New Haven: Yale University Press, 1989.

D *escent into Italy*

....

To Alice James* 8/31/1869. Hotel Belle-Vue, Cadenabbia, Lago di Como, Italy: I walked in two days . . . the greater part of the Swiss descent of the St. Gotthard . . . a most lovely journey with glorious weather . . . to the Rhone Glacier—a wondrous silent cataract of snow framed clean in the rocks . . . & expiring at your feet, at the inn door. . . . This day was somehow on the whole the pleasantest I have known in Switzerland. The superb weather—the clean unclouded views . . . & above all the sense of going down into Italy—the delight of seeing the north melt slowly into the south—of seeing Italy gradually crop up in bits & vaguely latently display itself—until finally at the little frontier village of Isella where I spent the night, it lay before me warm & living & palpable (*warm,* especially)—all these fine things bestowed upon the journey a delightful flavor of romance. . . . I was up betimes the next morning to catch the diligence on its way to the Domo d'Ossola (the terminus of the pass) & thence to the Lago Maggiore. I had a ride of six hours to Baveno on the shore of the Lake. Down, down—on, on into Italy we went—a rapturous progress thro' a wild luxuriance of corn & vines & olives & figs & mulberries & chestnuts & frescoed villages & clamorous beggars & all the good old Italianisms of tradition. At Baveno is a vast, cool, dim delicious hotel, with a great orange-haunted terrace on the lake. I had a cold bath in a great marble tank . . . & then as the afternoon began to wane, took a little boat at the terrace-stairs, lay out at my length beneath the striped awning & had myself pulled out to these delicious old Barromean Islands—the Isola Madre &

<hr>

* Henry James's sister (1848–1892).

the Isola Bella. . . . They're a quaint mixture of tawdry flummery & genuine beauty—a sort of tropical half-splendid, half slovenly Little Trianon & Hampton Court. The most striking feature of Italian scenery seems to be this same odd mingling of tawdriness & splendor—a generous profuse luxuriance of nature & the ludicrous gingerbread accessories of human contrivance. . . . So having slept at Baveno I took the early boat to Magadino at the head of the lake & thence walked (a sweltering ten miles) to Bellinzona, a charming dirty suffocating old town, where the St. Gothard & San Bernardino roads converge. Next morning I chose the latter. . . . The Bernardine is a lovely pass—but it turned out an awful grind. . . . I had underestimated the length of the ascent . . . & the result was a day of truly heroic fatigue. There is something strange & wild & curious in the sensation of great weariness in the midst of the lonely irridescent beauty of these Italian Alps. . . . I lay that night—(I unfortunately can't say I slept) at San Bernardino, a village on the Italian slope just below the summit & the next morning pursued my way (less than four hours) to the village of Splügen, where I was glad to halt & rest. . . . [At Thusis] I stopped at the inn & communed with my soul—to say nothing of my body. We all three had a little breakfast together & unanimously agreed that our poor old legs were very tired & had become conscious of an obstinate chronic aching. . . . So I gave up the Engadine, the Tyrol & all the rest of it & sadly took a vehicle back to Splügen. The next morning I entrusted my knapsack to the diligence & started off over the Splügen pass to Chiavenna—which I reached at about the end of eight hours. . . . At Chiavenna where I spent the night I was again in Italy—& met Italian beauty heat & dirt. I took the following morning the diligence to Colico—a woefully hot & dusty drive. Thence the steamer for two hours to this delicious spot. . . . It's too rapturous. Nothing is wanting but to feel fluttering at my side in the soft Italian breeze, some light muslin drapery of the sister of my soul. It's the place to enjoy *à deux* & it's a shame to be here in gross melancholy solitude. In its general presentment & contour the Lake of Como strikes me as hardly superior to the finest Swiss lakes—but it's when you come to the details—the swarming shimmering prodigality of the landscape—that you stand convinced & enchanted before Italy & summer. I may find it too hot here to stay, but I shall be glad to have had at least this glimpse of a potent southern August.

Venice

·

Letters

....

To John LaFarge,* 9/21/1869. Hotel Barbesi, Venice: Venice [is] perfectly *Italianissima*. . . . I have already eaten a good dish of the feast. I came over the Alps by Maggiore & Como, Milan, Pavia, Brescia, Verona & Vicenza; & I have been a week among these happy isles. I have seen a vast number of paintings, palaces and churches & received far more "impressions" than I know what to do with. . . . Venice is quite the Venice of one's dreams, but it remains strangely the Venice of dreams, more than of any appreciable reality. The mind is bothered with a constant sense of the exceptional character of the city; you can't quite reconcile it with common civilization. It's awfully sad too in its inexorable decay. Newport by the way is extremely like it in atmosphere & color; & the other afternoon on the sands at the Lido, looking out over the dazzling Adriatic, I fancied I was standing on Easton's beach. Its treasures of course are innumerable, & I have seen but a small fraction. I have been haunting chiefly the ducal palace & the Academy & putting off the churches. Tintoretto is omnipresent & well-nigh omnipotent. Titian I like less here than in London & elsewhere. He is strangely unequal. P. Veronese is great & J. Bellini greater. Perfect felicity I find nowhere but in the manner of the ducal palace, & bits of other palaces on the Grand Canal. . . . I wish I were a hereditary possessor of one of those old palazzi. I would make it over to you for a year's occupancy. The gondola by the way is a thing divine.

* American painter (1835–1910) whom James met in Newport in 1859 and who became a youthful influence and a lifelong friend.

To WILLIAM JAMES,* 9/25/1869. HOTEL BARBESI, VENICE: Venice is magnificently fair & quite, to my perception, the Venice of romance & fancy. . . . [But] it's as if I had been born in Boston: I can't for my life frankly surrender myself to the Genius of Italy, or the Spirit of the South—of whatever one may call the confounded thing; but I nevertheless *feel* it in all my pulses. . . . After you've been to the Ducal Palace & the Academy . . . you have not half so much been seeing paintings as *painters*. The accumulated mass of works by a few men drive each man home to your senses with extraordinary force. This is especially the case with the greatest of them all—Tintoretto—so much so that he ends by becoming an immense perpetual moral presence, brooding over the scene and worrying the mind into some species of response and acknowledgement. I have had more eyes & more thoughts for him than for anything else in Venice; & in future, I fancy, when I recall the place, I shall remember chiefly the full-streaming, dazzling light of the heavens, & Tintoretto's dark range of colour. . . . I should ask nothing better than his *Rape of Europa* in the Doge's Palace where a great rosy blond, gorgeous with brocade & pearls & bouncing with salubrity & a great mellow splendor of sea & sky & nymphs & flowers do their best to demoralize the world. . . . I have been abroad all day bidding farewell to Venice, for I think of leaving tomorrow or next day. . . . I took a gondola over to the Lido to look my last at the Adriatic. It was a glorious afternoon & I wandered for nearly two hours by the side of the murmuring sea. I was more than ever struck with the resemblance of Venice . . . to Newport. The same atmosphere, the same luminosity. . . . I have seen the Atlantic as blue & smooth & musical—almost! . . . I have spent a good deal of time in poking thro' the alleys which serve as streets & staring about in the *Campos*—the little squares formed about every church—some of them most sunnily desolate, the most grass-grown, the most cheerfully sad little reliquaries of a splendid past. Every one knows that the Grand Canal is a wonder; but really to feel in your heart the ancient wealth of Venice, you must have frequented these canalettos & camps &

* James's older brother (1842–1910), the psychologist and philosopher.

seen the number & splendor of the palaces that stand rotting & crumbling & abandoned to paupers. . . . How beautiful a thing this month in Italy has been & how my brain swarms with pictures & my bosom aches with memories. I should like in some neat formula to give you the *Italian feeling*—& tell you just how it is that one is conscious here of the aesthetic presence of the past. . . . What has fascinated me most here after Tintoretto & Co. are the two great buildings—the Ducal Palace & St. Mark's church. . . . St. Mark's, within, is a great hoary shadowy tabernacle of mosaic & marble, entrancing you with its remoteness, its picturesqueness & its chiaroscuro—an immense piece of Romanticism. But the Ducal Palace is as pure & perpetual as the facade of the Parthenon—& I think of all things in Venice, it's the one I should have been gladdest to achieve the one most worthy of civic affection & gratitude. When you're heated & weary to death with Tintoretto & his feverish Bible Stories, you can come out on the great Piazetta, between the marble columns, & grow comparatively cool & comfortable with gazing on this work of art which has so little to do with *persons*!

To Alice James, 10/6/1869. Hotel de l'Europe, Florence: Yes, Venice too has become a figment of the past—she lies like a great dazzling spot of yellow paint upon the backward path of my destiny. Now that I behold her no more I feel sadly as if I had done her wrong—as if I had been cold & insensible—that my eyes scowled & blinked at her brightness & that with more of self-oblivion I might have known her better & loved her more. Wherever we go we carry with us this heavy burden of our personal consciousness & wherever we stop we open it out over our heads like a great baleful cotton umbrella, to obstruct the prospect & obscure the light of heaven. Apparently it's in the nature of things. To come away vaguely dissatisfied with my Venetian sojourn is only one chapter in the lesson which this hardened old Europe is forever teaching—that you must rest content with the flimsiest knowledge of her treasures & the most superficial insight into her character. I feel sadly the lack of that intellectual outfit which is needful for seeing Italy properly & speaking of her in words which shall be more than

empty sounds—the lack of facts of all sorts—chiefly historical
& architectural. . . . Your only consolation is in the hope that
you may be able by hook or by crook to retain a few of the
impressions & confront them with the facts in the leisure of
subsequent years.—Well, Venice has gone, but Florence treads
fast on her heels. . . . Since leaving Venice I've transformed
Padua, Ferrara, Bologna & Parma from names into places—&
most interesting places too. At Padua I spent twenty-four hours
of immense felicity. . . . The great central treasure of Padua is
a certain edifice known unto men & angels as *Giotto's
Chapel*. . . . At Ferrara I spent some fine memorable hours
walking about the streets & tasting the exquisite quality of
Ferrarese desolation & decay. The city is immense in extent . . .
& peopled, I should say, to the tune of one individual to a dozen
houses. The streets are lined with mighty palaces & all coated
& muffled in silent grass. I got in particular a walk at sunset
upon the old ruined ramparts that enclose the town & melt
away in most pacific verdure into the great murmuring plain
of the Po. It was unique. . . . To Bologna I devoted three
days. . . . Bologna is rich in all great gifts. A mighty public
square, with the Middle Ages & the Renaissance all frowning
& smiling together about its margin—no end of fine churches
& palaces—a remarkable gallery of pictures. . . . From Bologna
I made a pilgrimmage to Parma (where I spent the night) in
order to see what is to be seen of Corregio. Parma was his
lifelong residence & possesses some of his best works. . . . I
reached Florence last evening—after a long journey thro' a
glorious country—the bosom of the Appenines. I have been
spending the day strolling about, thro' the streets & the two
Great Galleries—the Uffizi & the Pitti Palace. They are *incroy-
ables* [incredible]—& will give me work for many days. Florence strikes me very pleasantly & I should like to settle down
here for a series of weeks. . . . I have never seen a city which
took my fancy so fully & speedily. . . . I took a long long walk
this morning, as I didn't feel in the need for the Galleries. I
went out to Fiesole—'*my* Fiesole'—Mrs. Browning's, of course
that is,—& thence away into the hills beyond it. A lovely country—all pale olives and dark cypress—with beautiful views of

Florence lying in her circle of hills like—like what?—like a
chiselled jewel in a case of violet velvet!

To Grace Norton,* 6/12/1881. Vicenza: A greeting from this
quiet corner of old Italy. It is a bright, hot Sunday morning; I
have closed the shutters of my smartly-frescoed apartment, &
only a stray sunbeam rests on the cool *scagliola* [tile] floor. I wish
this rapid scrawl to carry a breath of the Italian summer, & of
sweet Vicenza, into your New England hills. . . . I had been sitting almost all the evening in the beautiful Square of this good
little city, in a flood of moonlight & amid a host of memories. (I
remembered among other things my first visit to this place, in
1869, & was pleased to find that on the whole I have not quite
lost my 'sensibility'—though it is as far from being as hysteri-
cally keen as it was at that time.) The great Palazzo della Ra-
gione was silvered by the moonlight, the tremendously tall &
slim campanile seemed to lose itself in the brightness of
night. . . . I went to Venice on the 25th March—where . . . I have
been ever since, & where I shall remain till July 1st. I came away
yesterday morning for a two or three days visit to this place &
to Padua—taking advantage of a perverse high wind, which had
prevailed for a week & blown much of the charm out of Venetian life. . . . The simplest thing to tell you of Venice is that
I adore it—have fallen deeply & desperately in love with it; in
spite of their having just begun to run an infamous *vaporino*
[steam ferry] on the Grand Canal. I had been there twice
before but each time only for a few days. This time I have
drunk deep, & the magic potion has entered into my blood.

To Katherine DeKay Bronson,† 7/19/1881. 3 Bolton St., London: I have been back in England a week. . . . My mind reverts, with a delicious pain, as the poets say, to Venice, & it

* One of James's oldest Cambridge friends (1834–1926) and the sister of
his friend and benefactor Charles Eliot Norton.

† A wealthy New York and Rhode Island socialite, Bronson (c. 1840–
1901) became James's friend and frequent hostess at Casa Alvisi, her home
in Venice.

serenades you every night beneath that balcony from which you waved me your last most friendly farewell. . . . I can't tell you with what affection I think of Venice, & how at this distance my whole stay there takes on the semblance of a beautiful dream. Happy you, to spend your life in such a dream. Fortunately, however, I dream of going back as well as of having been there. . . . Leaving Italy is always a heartbreak, but this time I bled more profusely than ever. If Italy looks lovely to you from the Grand Canal, you may fancy how it looks to me from Piccadilly.

To SARAH BUTLER WISTER,* 2/27/1887. PALAZZINO ALVISI, CANAL GRANDE, VENICE: Venice is wintry yet. . . . But it is Venice, none the less, & it is a ravishment to be here & to think that every week, at this season, will bring out a little more of the colour.

To SARAH BUTLER WISTER, 3/1/1887. PALAZZINO ALVISI, GRANDE CANAL, VENICE: The day is lovely—& the golden glow of Venice streams into my room.

To GRACE NORTON, 6/30/1890. PALAZZO BARBARO, VENICE: I am spending this splendid summer day in this beautiful empty house, under the care of the suavest & most obsequious of old Venetian butlers. . . . I go to Florence, first to stay four or five days . . . & then to go up (if I can find a perch at the inn) & spend the rest of July on the divine hilltop of Vallombrosa— which is high enough to be cool & lovely enough to be warm.

To ARIANA CURTIS,† 11/20/1899. LAMB HOUSE, RYE: Your report of your Venice autumn pulls on my heartstrings as only sounds & signs of Italy *can* pull: it is not to be *said* what a sorcery she wields over mind, memory, & hope.

---

* Daughter of the actress Fanny Kemble and mother of the novelist Owen Wister, Sarah Butler Wister (1835–1905) met James in Rome in 1872 and became his lifelong friend.

† Wealthy Bostonians Ariana Curtis (1833–1922) and her husband, Daniel (1825–1908), settled in 1881 in Venice at the Palazzo Barbaro, where James was their frequent guest.

To Jesse Allen,* 6/24/1907. Palazzo Barbaro, Canal Grande, Venice: I came here five days ago—from a week in Florence & previous month, almost, in Rome & Naples—all of which time Ariana [Curtis] was pulling hard at one end of my scant tether. I am now the only guest [at the Palazzo Barbaro]—the full-blown summer is divine (even if pretty torrid). . . . Venice is really (thanks to the glow & large ease of the season) more characteristically exquisite & loveable than I've *ever* known it. I have this vast cool upper floor—all scirocco draughts and easy undressedness quite to myself; I go out with Ariana at 5, in the cool (comparative), & then again by moonlight; so that if I'm not madly in love with her what influence is wanting? . . . Every note strikes true from the cool dim dawn, when the canal is a great curly floor of dark grim marble, to the still cooler blue night when I go forth with my Lady to be cradled by the plash outside the Giudecca. But of all this I must tell you—& of the new heartbreak it is just only to feel this enchantress (I allude now to the terrible old Venice herself!) weave her spell just again supremely to lose her. One dreams again so of some clutched perch of one's own here. But it's the most drivelling of dreams.

To Clare Benedict,† 9/13/1907. Lamb House, Rye: I did from Rome (with friends) a little wondrous *motoring*—down to Naples & back, by different ways etc., & that shows you the lovely land with an easy power that nothing does; but Venice was nevertheless the only place I feel—ever *shall* feel again—the *ache* of desire to go back to.

* An English friend of the Curtises, Jesse Allen (1845–1918) met James at the Palazzo Barbaro in 1899; they became close London friends thereafter.

† The niece (c. 1880–1961) of James's friend, the author Constance Fenimore Woolson.

*E*ssays

....

Venice: An Early Impression

There would be much to say about that golden chain of
historic cities which stretches from Milan to Venice, in which
the very names—Brescia, Verona, Mantua, Padua—are an ornament to one's phrase; but I should have to draw upon recollections now three years old and to make my short story a long
one. Of Verona and Venice only have I recent impressions, and
even to these I must do hasty justice. I came into Venice, just as
I had done before, toward the end of a summer's day, when the
shadows begin to lengthen and the light to glow, and found that
the attendant sensations bore repetition remarkably well. There
was the same last intolerable delay at Mestre, just before your
first glimpse of the lagoon confirms the already distinct sea-
smell which has added speed to the precursive flight of your
imagination; then the liquid level, edged afar off by its band of
undiscriminated domes and spires, soon distinguished and proclaimed, however, as excited and contentious heads multiply at
the windows of the train; then your long rumble on the immense
white railway-bridge, which, in spite of the invidious contrast
drawn, and very properly, by Mr. Ruskin* between the old and
the new approach, does truly, in a manner, shine across the
green lap of the lagoon like a mighty causeway of marble; then
the plunge into the station, which would be exactly similar to
every other plunge save for one little fact—that the keynote of
the great medley of voices borne back from the exit is not "Cab,
sir!" but "Barca, signore!"

---

* In John Ruskin (1819–1900), *The Stones of Venice* (1851).

I do not mean, however, to follow the traveller through every phase of his initiation, at the risk of stamping poor Venice beyond repair as the supreme bugbear of literature; though for my own part I hold that to a fine healthy romantic appetite the subject can't be too diffusely treated. Meeting in the Piazza on the evening of my arrival a young American painter who told me that he had been spending the summer just where I found him, I could have assaulted him for very envy. He was painting forsooth the interior of St. Mark's. To be a young American painter unperplexed by the mocking, elusive soul of things and satisfied with their wholesome light-bathed surface and shape; keen of eye; fond of colour, of sea and sky and anything that may chance between them; of old lace and old brocade and old furniture (even when made to order); of time-mellowed harmonies on nameless canvases and happy contours in cheap old engravings; to spend one's mornings in still, productive analysis of the clustered shadows of the Basilica, one's afternoons anywhere, in church or campo, on canal or lagoon, and one's evenings in starlight gossip at Florian's, feeling the sea-breeze throb languidly between the two great pillars of the Piazzetta and over the low black domes of the church—this, I consider, is to be as happy as is consistent with the preservation of reason.

The mere use of one's eyes in Venice is happiness enough, and generous observers find it hard to keep an account of their profits in this line. Everything the attention touches holds it, keeps playing with it—thanks to some inscrutable flattery of the atmosphere. Your brown-skinned, white-shirted gondolier, twisting himself in the light, seems to you, as you lie at contemplation beneath your awning, a perpetual symbol of Venetian "effect." The light here is in fact a mighty magician and, with all respect to Titian, Veronese and Tintoret, the greatest artist of them all. You should see in places the material with which it deals—slimy brick, marble battered and befouled, rags, dirt, decay. Sea and sky seem to meet half-way, to blend their tones into a soft iridescence, a lustrous compound of wave and cloud and a hundred nameless local reflections, and then to fling the clear tissue against every object of vision. You may see these elements at work everywhere, but to see them in their intensity you should choose the finest day in the month and have yourself rowed far away across the lagoon to Torcello. Without making this excursion you can hardly pretend to know Venice or to sympathise with that longing for pure radiance which animated her great colourists. It is a perfect bath of light, and I couldn't get rid of a fancy that we were cleaving the upper atmosphere on some hurrying cloud-skiff. At Torcello there is nothing but the light to see—nothing at least but a sort of blooming sand-bar intersected by a single narrow creek which does duty as a canal and occupied by a meagre cluster of huts, the dwellings apparently of market-gardeners and fishermen, and by a ruinous church of the eleventh century. It is impossible to imagine a more penetrating case of unheeded collapse. Torcello was the mother-city of Venice, and she lies there now, a mere mouldering vestige, like a group of weather-bleached parental bones left impiously un-buried. I stopped my gondola at the mouth of the shallow inlet and walked along the grass beside a hedge to the low-browed, crumbling cathedral. The charm of certain vacant grassy spaces, in Italy, overfrowned by masses of brickwork that are honeycombed by the suns of centuries, is something that I hereby renounce once for all the attempt to express; but you may be sure that whenever I mention such a spot enchantment lurks in it.

A delicious stillness covered the little campo at Torcello; I remember none so subtly audible save that of the Roman Campagna. There was no life but the visible tremor of the brilliant air and the cries of half-a-dozen young children who dogged our steps and clamoured for coppers. These children, by the way, were the handsomest little brats in the world, and each was furnished with a pair of eyes that could only have signified the protest of nature against the meanness of fortune. They were very nearly as naked as savages, and their little bellies protruded like those of infant cannibals in the illustrations of books of travel; but as they scampered and sprawled in the soft, thick grass, grinning like suddenly-translated cherubs and showing their hungry little teeth, they suggested forcibly that the best assurance of happiness in this world is to be found in the maximum of innocence and the minimum of wealth. One small urchin—framed, if ever a child was, to be the joy of an aristocratic mamma—was the most expressively beautiful creature I had ever looked upon. He had a smile to make Correggio sigh in his grave; and yet here he was running wild among the sea-stunted bushes, on the lonely margin of a decaying world, in prelude to how blank or to how dark a destiny? Verily nature is still at odds with propriety; though indeed if they ever really pull together I fear nature will quite lose her distinction. An infant citizen of our own republic, straight-haired, pale-eyed and freckled, duly darned and catechised, marching into a New England schoolhouse, is an object often seen and soon forgotten; but I think I shall always remember with infinite tender conjecture, as the years roll by, this little unlettered Eros of the Adriatic strand. Yet all youthful things at Torcello were not cheerful, for the poor lad who brought us the key of the cathedral was shaking with an ague, and his melancholy presence seemed to point the moral of forsaken nave and choir. The church, admirably primitive and curious, reminded me of the two or three oldest churches of Rome—St. Clement and St. Agnes. The interior is rich in grimly mystical mosaics of the twelfth century and the patchwork of precious fragments in the pavement not inferior to that of St. Mark's. But the terribly distinct Apostles are ranged against their dead gold backgrounds as stiffly as grenadiers presenting arms—intensely personal sentinels of a personal Deity. Their stony stare seems to wait forever vainly for some visible revival of primitive orthodoxy, and one may well wonder whether it finds much beguilement in idly-gazing troops of Western heretics—passionless even in their heresy.

I had been curious to see whether in the galleries and temples of Venice I should be disposed to transpose my old estimates—to burn what I had adored and adore what I had burned. It is a sad truth that one can stand in the Ducal Palace for the first time but once, with the deliciously ponderous sense of that particular half-hour's being an era in one's mental history; but I had the satisfaction of finding at least—a great comfort in a short stay—that none of my early memories were likely to change places and that I could take up my admirations where I had left them. I still found Carpaccio delightful,

Veronese magnificent, Titian supremely beautiful and Tintoret scarce to be appraised. I repaired immediately to the little church of San Cassano, which contains the smaller of Tintoret's two great Crucifixions; and when I had looked at it awhile I drew a long breath and felt I could now face any other picture in Venice with proper self-possession. It seemed to me I had advanced to the uttermost limit of painting; that beyond this another art—inspired poetry—begins, and that Bellini, Veronese, Giorgione, and Titian, all joining hands and straining every muscle of their genius, reach forward not so far but that they leave a visible space in which Tintoret alone is master. I well remember the exaltations to which he lifted me when first I learned to know him; but the glow of that comparatively youthful amazement is dead, and with it, I fear, that confident vivacity of phrase of which, in trying to utter my impressions, I felt less the magniloquence than the impotence. In his power there are many weak spots, mysterious lapses and fitful intermissions; but when the list of his faults is complete he still remains to me the most *interesting* of painters. His reputation rests chiefly on a more superficial sort of merit—his energy, his unsurpassed productivity, his being, as Théophile Gautier says, *le roi des fougueux* [the king of the high-spirited]. These qualities are immense, but the great source of his impressiveness is that his indefatigable hand never drew a line that was not, as one may say, a moral line. No painter ever had such breadth and such depth; and even Titian, beside him, scarce figures as more than a great decorative artist. Mr. Ruskin, whose eloquence in dealing with the great Venetians sometimes outruns his discretion, is fond of speaking even of Veronese as a painter of deep spiritual intentions. This, it seems to me, is pushing matters too far, and the author of "The Rape of Europa" is, pictorially speaking, no greater casuist than any other genius of supreme good taste. Titian was assuredly a mighty poet, but Tintoret—well, Tintoret was almost a prophet. Before his greatest works you are conscious of a sudden evaporation of old doubts and dilemmas, and the eternal problem of the conflict between idealism and realism dies the most natural of deaths. In his genius the problem is practically solved; the alternatives are so harmoniously interfused that I defy the keenest critic to say where one begins and the other ends. The homeliest prose melts into the most ethereal poetry—the literal and the imaginative fairly confound their identity.

This, however, is vague praise. Tintoret's great merit, to my mind, was his unequalled distinctness of vision. When once he had conceived the germ of a scene it defined itself to his imagination with an intensity, an amplitude, an individuality of expression, which make one's observation of his pictures seem less an operation of the mind than a kind of supplementary experience of life. Veronese and Titian are content with a much looser specification, as their treatment of any subject that the author of the Crucifixion at San Cassano has also treated abundantly proves. There are few more suggestive contrasts than that between the absence of a total character at all commensurate with its scattered variety and brilliancy in Veronese's "Marriage of Cana," at the Louvre, and the poignant, almost startling, completeness of Tintoret's illustration of the theme at the Salute church. To compare his "Presentation of the Virgin," at the Madonna dell' Orto, with Titian's at the Academy, or his "Annunication" with Titian's close at hand, is to measure the essential difference between observation and imagination. One has certainly not said all that there is to say for Titian when one has called him an observer. *Il y mettait du sien* [He put something of his own into it], and I use the term to designate roughly the artist whose apprehension, infinitely deep and strong when applied to the single figure or to easily balanced groups, spends itself vainly on great dramatic combinations—or rather leaves them ungauged. It was the whole scene that Tintoret seemed to have beheld in a flash of inspiration intense enough to stamp it ineffaceably on his perception; and it was the whole scene, complete, peculiar, individual, unprecedented, that he committed to canvas with all the vehemence of his talent. Compare his "Last Supper," at San Giorgio—its long, diagonally placed table, its dusky spaciousness, its scattered lamp-light and halo-light, its startled, gesticulating figures, its richly realistic foreground—with the customary formal, almost mathematical rendering of the subject, in which impressiveness seems to have been sought in elimination rather than comprehension. You get from Tintoret's work the impression that he *felt,* pictorially, the great, beautiful, terrible spectacle of human life very much as Shakespeare felt it poetically—with a heart that never ceased to beat a passionate accompaniment to every stroke of his brush. Thanks to this fact his works are signally grave, and their almost universal and rapidly increasing decay doesn't relieve their gloom. Nothing indeed can well be sadder than the great collection of Tintorets at San Rocco. Incurable blackness is settling fast upon all of them, and they frown at you across the sombre splendour of their great chambers like gaunt twilight phantoms of pictures. To our children's children Tintoret, as things are going, can be hardly more than a name; and such of them as shall miss the tragic beauty, already so dimmed and stained, of the great "Bearing of the Cross" in that temple of his spirit will live and die without knowing the largest eloquence of art. If you wish to add the last touch of solemnity to the place recall as vividly as possible while you linger at San Rocco the painter's singularly interesting portrait of himself, at the Louvre. The old man looks out of the canvas from beneath a brow as sad as a sunless twilight, with just such a stoical hopelessness as you might fancy him to wear if he stood at your side gazing at his rotting canvases. It isn't whimsical to read it as the face of a man who felt that he had given the world more than the world was likely to repay. Indeed before every picture of Tintoret you may remember this tremendous portrait with profit. On one side the power, the passion, the illusion of his art; on the other the mortal fatigue of his spirit. The world's knowledge of him is so small that the portrait throws a doubly precious light on his personality; and when we wonder vainly what manner of man he was, and what were his purpose, his faith and his method, we may find forcible assurance there that they were at any rate his life—one of the most intellectually passionate ever led.

Verona, which was my last Italian stopping-place, is in any conditions a delightfully interesting city; but the kindness of my own memory of it is deepened by a subsequent ten days' experience of Germany. I rose one morning at Verona, and went to bed at night at Botzen! The statement needs no comment, and the two places, though but fifty miles apart, are as

painfully dissimilar as their names. I had prepared myself for
your delectation with a copious tirade on German manners,
German scenery, German art and the German stage—on the
lights and shadows of Innsbrück, Munich, Nuremberg and
Heidelberg; but just as I was about to put pen to paper I
glanced into a little volume* on these very topics lately published by that famous novelist and moralist, M. Ernest Fey-
deau, the fruit of a summer's observation at Homburg. This
work produced a reaction; and if I chose to follow M. Fey-
deau's own example when he wishes to qualify his approbation
I might call his treatise by any vile name known to the speech
of man. But I content myself with pronouncing it superficial. I
then reflect that my own opportunities for seeing and judging
were extremely limited, and I suppress my tirade, lest some
more enlightened critic should come and hang me with the
same rope. Its sum and substance was to have been that—
superficially—Germany is ugly; that Munich is a nightmare,
Heidelberg a disappointment (in spite of its charming castle)
and even Nuremberg not a joy for ever. But comparisons are
odious, and if Munich is ugly Verona is beautiful enough. You
may laugh at my logic, but will probably assent to my meaning.
I carried away from Verona a precious mental picture upon
which I cast an introspective glance whenever between Botzen
and Strassburg the oppression of external circumstance became
painful. It was a lovely August afternoon in the Roman
arena—a ruin in which repair and restoration have been so
watchfully and plausibly practised that it seems all of one
harmonious antiquity. The vast stony oval rose high against the
sky in a single clear, continuous line, broken here and there
only by strolling and reclining loungers. The massive tiers
inclined in solid monotony to the central circle, in which a
small open-air theatre was in active operation. A small quarter
of the great slope of masonry facing the stage was roped off
into an auditorium, in which the narrow level space between
the foot-lights and the lowest step figured as the pit. Foot-lights
are a figure of speech, for the performance was going on in the

* *L' Allemagne en 1871* (1872).

broad glow of the afternoon, with a delightful and apparently by no means misplaced confidence in the good-will of the spectators. What the piece was that was deemed so superbly able to shift for itself I know not—very possibly the same drama that I remember seeing advertised during my former visit to Verona; nothing less than *La Tremenda Giustizia di Dio* [*The Terrible Judgment of God*]. If titles are worth anything this product of the melodramatist's art might surely stand upon its own legs. Along the tiers above the little group of regular spectators was gathered a free-list of unauthorised observers, who, although beyond ear-shot, must have been enabled by the generous breadth of Italian gesture to follow the tangled thread of the piece. It was all deliciously Italian—the mixture of old life and new, the mountebank's booth (it was hardly more) grafted on the antique circus, the dominant presence of a mighty architecture, the loungers and idlers beneath the kindly sky and upon the sun-warmed stones. I never felt more keenly the difference between the background to life in very old and very new civilisations. There are other things in Verona to make it a liberal education to be born there, though that it *is* one for the contemporary Veronese I don't pretend to say. The Tombs of the Scaligers, with their soaring pinnacles, their high-poised canopies, their exquisite refinement and concentration of the Gothic idea, I can't profess, even after much worshipful gazing, to have fully comprehended and enjoyed. They seemed to me full of deep architectural meanings, such as must drop gently into the mind one by one, after infinite tranquil contemplation. But even to the hurried and preoccupied traveller the solemn little chapel-yard in the city's heart, in which they stand girdled by their great swaying curtain of linked and twisted iron, is one of the most impressive spots in Italy. Nowhere else is such a wealth of artistic achievement crowded into so narrow a space; nowhere else are the daily comings and goings of men blessed by the presence of *manlier* art. Verona is rich furthermore in beautiful churches—several with beautiful names: San Fermo, Santa Anastasia, San Zenone. This last is a structure of high antiquity and of the most impressive loveliness. The nave terminates in a double choir, that is a sub-choir or crypt into which you descend and where you wander among primitive columns whose variously grotesque capitals rise hardly higher than your head, and an upper choral plane reached by broad stairways of the bravest effect. I shall never forget the impression of majestic chastity that I received from the great nave of the building on my former visit. I then decided to my satisfaction that every church is from the devotional point of view a solecism that has not something of a similar absolute felicity of proportion; for strictly formal beauty seems best to express our conception of spiritual beauty. The nobly serious character of San Zenone is deepened by its single picture—a masterpiece of the most serious of painters, the severe and exquisite Mantegna.

[1873]

Venice

It is a great pleasure to write the word; but I am not sure there is not a certain impudence in pretending to add anything to it. Venice has been painted and described many thousands of times, and of all the cities of the world it is the easiest to visit without going there. Open the first book and you will find a rhapsody about it; step into the first picture-dealer's and you will find three or four high-coloured "views" of it. There is nothing more to be said about it. Every one has been there, and every one has brought back a collection of photographs. There is as little mystery about the Grand Canal as about our local thoroughfare; and the name of St. Mark is as familiar as the postman's ring. It is not forbidden, however, to speak of familiar things, and I believe that, for the true Venice-lover, Venice is always in order. There is nothing new to be said about it certainly, but the old is better than any novelty. It would be a sad day, indeed, when there should be something new to say. I write these lines with the full consciousness of having no information whatever to offer. I do not pretend to enlighten the reader; I pretend only to give a fillip to his memory; and I hold any writer sufficiently justified who is himself in love with his topic.

i

Mr. Ruskin has given it up, that is very true; but it is only after extracting half a life-time of pleasure and an immeasurable quantity of fame from it. We all may do the same, after it has served our turn, which it probably will not cease to do for many a year to come. Meantime, it is Mr. Ruskin who, beyond any one, helps us to enjoy. He has, indeed, lately produced several aids to depression in the shape of certain little humorous—ill-humorous—pamphlets (the series of *St. Mark's Rest*), which embody his latest reflections on the subject of Venice and describe the latest atrocities that have been perpetrated there. These latter are numerous and deeply to be deplored; but to admit that they have spoiled Venice would be to admit that Venice may be spoiled—an admission pregnant, as it seems to us, with disloyalty. Fortunately, one reacts against the Ruskinian contagion, and one hour of the lagoon is worth a hundred pages of demoralised prose. This queer, late-coming prose of Mr. Ruskin (including the revised and condensed issue of the *Stones of Venice,* only one little volume of which has appeared or, perhaps, will ever appear) is all to be read, though much of it seems to be addressed to children of tender age. It is pitched in the nursery-key, and might be supposed to emanate from an angry governess. It is, however, all suggestive, and much of it is delightfully just. There is an inconceivable want of form in it, though the author has spent his life in laying down the principles of form, and scolding people for departing from them; but it throbs and flashes with the love of his subject—a love disconcerted and abjured, but which has still some of the force of inspiration. Among the many strange things that have befallen Venice, she has had the good fortune to become the object of a passion to a man of splendid genius, who has made her his own, and, in doing so, has made her the world's. There is no better reading at Venice, therefore, as I say, than Ruskin, for every true Venice-lover can separate the wheat from the chaff. The narrow theological spirit, the moralism *à tout propos* [everywhere], the queer provincialities and pruderies, are mere wild weeds in a mountain of flowers. One may doubtless be very happy in Venice without reading at all—without criticising or analysing or thinking a strenuous thought. It is a city in which, I suspect, there is very little strenuous thinking, and yet it is a city in which there must be almost as much happiness as misery. The misery of Venice stands there for all the world to see; it is part of the spectacle—a thorough-going devotee of local colour might consistently say it is part of the pleasure. The Venetian people have little to call their own—little more than the bare privilege of leading their lives in the most beautiful of towns. Their habitations are decayed; their taxes heavy; their pockets light; their opportunities few. One receives an impression, however, that life presents itself to them with attractions not accounted for in this meagre train of advantages, and that they are on better terms with it than many people who have made a better bargain. They lie in the sunshine; they dabble in the sea; they wear bright rags; they fall into attitudes and harmonies; they assist at an eternal *conversazione.* It is not easy to say that one would have them other than they are, and it certainly would make an immense difference should they be better fed. The number of persons in Venice who evidently never have enough to eat is painfully large; but it would be more painful if we did not equally perceive that the rich Venetian temperament may bloom upon a dog's allowance. Nature has been kind to it, and sunshine and leisure and conversation and beautiful views form the greater part of its sustenance. It takes a great deal to make a successful American; but to make a happy Venetian takes only a handful of quick sensibility. The Italian people have, at once, the good and evil fortune to be conscious of few wants; so that if the civilisation of a society is measured by the number of its needs, as seems to be the common opinion to-day, it is to be feared that the children of the lagoon would make but a poor figure in a set of comparative tables. Not their misery, doubtless, but the way they elude their misery, is what pleases the sentimental tourist, who is gratified by the sight of a beautiful race that lives by the aid of its imagination. The way to enjoy Venice is to follow the example of these people and make the most of simple pleasures. Almost all the pleasures of the place are simple; this may be maintained even under the imputation of ingenious paradox. There is no simpler pleasure than looking at a fine Titian—unless it be looking at a fine Tintoret, or strolling into St. Mark's—it is abominable, the way one falls into the habit—and resting one's light-wearied eyes upon the windowless gloom; or than floating in a gondola, or hanging over a balcony, or taking one's coffee at Florian's. It is of these superficial pastimes that a Venetian day is composed, and the pleasure of the matter is in the emotions to which they minister. These, fortunately, are of the finest; otherwise, Venice would be insufferably dull. Reading Ruskin is good; reading the old records is, perhaps, better; but the best thing of all is simply staying on. The only way to care for Venice as she deserves it, is to give her a chance to touch you often—to linger and remain and return.

····· *i i* . ······

The danger is that you will not linger enough—a danger of which the author of these lines had known something. It is possible to dislike Venice, and to entertain the sentiment in a responsible and intelligent manner. There are travellers who think the place odious, and those who are not of this opinion often find themselves wishing that the others were only more numerous. The sentimental tourist's only quarrel with his Venice is that he has too many competitors there. He likes to be alone; to be original; to have (to himself, at least) the air of making discoveries. The Venice of to-day is a vast museum where the little wicket that admits you is perpetually turning and creaking, and you march through the institution with a herd of fellow-gazers. There is nothing left to discover or describe, and originality of attitude is completely impossible. This is often very annoying; you can only turn your back on your impertinent playfellow and curse his want of delicacy. But this is not the fault of Venice; it is the fault of the rest of the world. The fault of Venice is that, though it is easy to admire it, it is not so easy to live in it. After you have been there a week, and the bloom of novelty has rubbed off, you wonder whether you can accommodate yourself to the peculiar conditions. Your old habits become impracticable, and you find yourself obliged to form new ones of an undesirable and unprofitable character. You are tired of your gondola (or you think you are), and you have seen all the principal pictures and heard the names of the palaces announced a dozen times by your gondolier, who brings them out almost as impressively as if he were an English butler bawling titles into a drawing-room. You have walked several hundred times round the Piazza, and bought several bushels of photographs. You have visited the antiquity-mongers whose horrible sign-boards dishonour some of the grandest vistas in the Grand Canal; you have tried the opera and found it very bad; you have bathed at the Lido and found the water flat. You have begun to have a shipboard-feeling—to regard the Piazza as an enormous saloon and the Riva degli Schiavoni as a promenade-deck. You are obstructed and encaged; your desire for space is unsatisfied; you miss your usual exercise. You try to take a walk, and you fail, and meantime, as I say, you have come to regard your gondola as a sort of magnified baby's cradle. You have no desire to be rocked to sleep, though you are sufficiently kept awake by the irritation produced, as you gaze across the shallow lagoon, by the attitude of the perpetual gondolier, with his turned-out toes, his protruded chin, his absurdly unscientific stroke. The canals have a horrible smell, and the everlasting Piazza, where you have looked repeatedly at every article in every shop-window and found them all rubbish, where the young Venetians who sell bead-bracelets and "panoramas" are perpetually thrusting their wares at you, where the same tightly-buttoned officers are for ever sucking the same black weeds, at the same empty tables, in front of the same *caffès*—the Piazza, as I say, has resolved itself into a sort of magnificent tread-mill. This is the state of mind of those shallow inquirers who find Venice all very well for a week; and if in such a state of mind you take your departure, you act with fatal rashness. The loss is your own, moreover; it is not—with all deference to your personal attractions—that of your companions who remain behind; for though there are some disagreeable things in Venice, there is nothing so disagreeable as the visitors. The conditions are peculiar, but your intolerance of them evaporates before it has had time to become a prejudice. When you have called for the bill to go, pay it and remain, and you will find on the morrow that you are deeply attached to Venice. It is by living there from day to day that you feel the fulness of its charm; that you invite its exquisite influence to sink into your spirit. The place is as changeable as a nervous woman, and you know it only when you know all the aspects of its beauty. It has high spirits or low, it is pale or red, gray or pink, cold or warm, fresh or wan, according to the weather or the hour. It is always interesting and almost always sad; but it has a thousand occasional graces and is always liable to happy accidents. You become extraordinarily fond of these things; you count upon them; they make part of your life. Tenderly fond you become; there is something indefinable in those depths of personal acquaintance that gradually establish themselves. The place seems to personify itself, to become human and sentient, and conscious of your affection. You desire to embrace it, to caress it, to possess it; and finally, a soft sense of possession grows up, and your visit becomes a perpetual love-affair. It is very true that if you go there, like the author of these lines, about the middle of March, a certain amount of disappointment is possible. He had not been there for several years, and in the interval the beautiful and helpless city had suffered an increase of injury. The barbarians are in full possession, and you tremble for what they may do. You are reminded, from the moment of your arrival, that Venice scarcely exists any more as a city at all; that it exists only as a battered peep-show and bazaar. There was a horde of savage Germans encamped in the Piazza, and they filled the Ducal Palace and the Academy with their uproar. The English and Americans came a little later. They came in good time, with a great many French, who were discreet enough to make very long repasts at the Caffè Quadri, during which they were out of the way. The months of April and May of the year 1881 were not, as a general thing, a favourable season for visiting the Ducal Palace and the Academy. The valet-de-place had marked them for his own, and held triumphant possession of them. He celebrates his triumphs in a terrible brassy voice, which resounds all over the place, and has, whatever language he be speaking, the accent of some other idiom. During all the spring months in Venice these gentry abound in the great resorts, and they lead their helpless captives through churches and galleries in dense irresponsible groups. They infest the Piazza; they pursue you along the Riva; they hang about the bridges and the doors of the *caffès*. In saying just now that I was disappointed at first, I had chiefly in mind the impression that assails me to-day in the whole precinct of St. Mark's. The condition of this ancient sanctuary is surely a great scandal. The pedlars and commissioners ply their trade—often a very unclean one—at the very door of the temple; they follow you across the threshold, into the sacred dusk, and pull your sleeve, and hiss into your ear, scuffling with each other for customers. There is a great deal of dishonour about St. Mark's altogether, and if Venice, as I say, has become a great bazaar, this exquisite edifice is now the biggest booth.

····· *i i i* . ······

It is treated as a booth in all ways, and if it had not, some-how, a great spirit of solemnity within it, the traveller would soon have little warrant for regarding it as a religious affair. The restoration of the outer walls, which has lately been so much attacked and defended, is certainly a great shock. Of the necessity of the work only an expert is, I suppose, in a position to judge; but there is no doubt that, if a necessity it be, it is one that is deeply to be regretted. To no more distressing necessity have people of taste lately had to resign themselves. Wherever the hand of the restorer has been laid all semblance of beauty has vanished; which is a sad fact, considering that the external loveliness of St. Mark's has been for ages less impressive only than that of the still comparatively uninjured interior. I know not what is the measure of necessity in such a case, and it appears indeed to be a very delicate question. To-day, at any rate, that admirable harmony of faded mosaic and marble, which, to the eye of the traveller emerging from the narrow streets that lead to the Piazza, filled all the farther end of it with a sort of dazzling, silvery presence—to-day this lovely vision is in a way to be completely reformed and, indeed, well-nigh abolished. The old softness and mellowness of colour—the work of the quiet centuries and of the breath of the salt sea—is giving way to large crude patches of new ma-terial, which have the effect of a monstrous malady rather than of a restoration to health. They look like blotches of red and white paint and dishonourable smears of chalk on the cheeks of a noble matron. The face toward the Piazzetta is in especial the newest-looking thing conceivable—as new as a new pair of boots, or as the morning's paper. We do not profess, however, to undertake a scientific quarrel with these changes; we admit that our complaint is a purely sentimental one. The march of industry in united Italy must doubtless be looked at as a whole, and one must endeavour to believe that it is through innumerable lapses of taste that this deeply interesting country is groping her way to her place among the nations. For the present, it is not to be denied, certain odd phases of the process are more visible than the result, to arrive at which it seems necessary that, as she was of old a passionate votary of the beautiful, she should to-day burn everything that she has adored. It is, doubtless, too soon to judge her, and there are moments when one is willing to forgive her even the restoration of St. Mark's. Inside, as well, there has been a considerable attempt to make the place more tidy; but the general effect, as yet, has not seriously suffered. What I chiefly remember is the straightening out of that dark and rugged old pavement—those deep undulations of primitive mosaic, in which the wondering tourist was thought to perceive an intended resemblance to the waves of the ocean. Whether intended or not, the analogy was an image the more in a treasure-house of images; but from a considerable portion of the church it has now disappeared. Throughout the greater part, indeed, the pavement remains as recent generations have known it—dark, rich, cracked, uneven, spotted with porphyry and time-blackened malachite, and polished by the knees of innumerable worshippers; but in other large sections the idea imitated by the restorers is that of the ocean in a dead calm, and the model they have taken, the floor of a London club-house or of a New York hotel. I think no Venetian and scarcely any Italian cares much for such differences; and when, a year ago, people in England were writing to the *Times* about the whole business, and holding meetings to protest against it, the dear children of the lagoon (so far as they heard, or heeded, the rumour) thought them partly busy-bodies and partly asses. Busy-bodies they doubtless were, but they took a good deal of disinterested trouble. It never occurs to the Venetian mind of to-day that such trouble may be worth taking; the Venetian mind vainly endeavours to conceive a state of existence in which personal questions are so insipid that people have to look for grievances in the wrongs of brick and marble. I must not, however, speak of St. Mark's as if I had the pretension of giving a description of it, or as if the reader desired one. The reader has been too well served already. It is surely the best-described building in the world. Open the *Stones of Venice,* open Théophile Gautier's *Italia,* and you will see. These writers take it very seriously, and it is only because there is another way of taking it that I venture to speak of it; the way that offers itself after you have been in Venice a couple of months, and the light is hot in the great Square, and you pass in under the pictured porticoes with a feeling of habit and friendliness, and a desire for something cool and dark. There are moments, after all, when the church is comparatively quiet and empty, when you may sit there with an easy consciousness of its beauty. From the moment, of course, that you go into any Italian church for any purpose but to say your prayers or look at the ladies, you rank yourself among the trooping barbarians I just spoke of; you treat the place like an orifice in the peep-show. Still, it is almost a spiritual function—or, at the worst, an amorous one—to feed one's eyes on the moulten colour that drops from the hollow vaults and thickens the air with its richness. It is all so quiet and sad and faded; and yet it is all so brilliant and living. The strange figures in the mosaic pictures, bending with the curve of niche and vault, stare down through the glowing dimness; and the burnished gold that stands behind them catches the light on its little uneven cubes. St. Mark's owes nothing of its character to the beauty of proportion or perspective; there is nothing grandly balanced or far-arching; there are no long lines nor triumphs of the perpendicular. The church arches indeed; but it arches like a dusky cavern. Beauty of surface, of tone, of detail, of things near enough to touch and kneel upon and lean against—it is from this the effect proceeds. In this sort of beauty the place is incredibly rich, and you may go there every day and find afresh some lurking pictorial nook. It is a treasury of bits, as the painters say; and there are usually three or four painters, with their easels set up in uncertain equilibrium on the undulating floor. It is not easy to catch the real complexion of St. Mark's, and these laudable attempts at portraiture are apt to look either lurid or livid. But, if you cannot paint the old loose-looking marble slabs, the great panels of basalt and jasper, the crucifixes, of which the lonely anguish looks deeper in the vertical light, the tabernacles whose open doors disclose a dark Byzantine image, spotted with dull, crooked gems—if you cannot paint these things, you can at least grow fond of them. You grow fond even of the old benches of red marble, partly worn away by the breeches of many generations, and attached to the base of those wide pilasters, of which the precious plating, delightful in its faded brownness, with a faint gray bloom upon it, bulges and yawns a little with honourable age.

····· *i v* . ······

Even at first, when the vexatious sense of the city of the Doges having been reduced to earning its living as a curiosity-shop was in its keenness, there was a great deal of entertainment to be got from lodging on the Riva degli Schiavoni and looking out at the far-shimmering lagoon. There was entertainment indeed in simply getting into the place and observing the queer incidents of a Venetian installation. A great many persons contribute indirectly to this undertaking, and it is surprising how they spring out at you during your novitiate to remind you that they are bound up in some mysterious manner with the constitution of your little establishment. It was an interesting problem, for instance, to trace the subtle connection existing between the niece of the landlady and the occupancy of the fourth floor. Superficially, it was not easily visible, as the young lady in question was a dancer at the Fenice theatre—or, when that was closed, at the Rossini—and might have been supposed to be absorbed by her professional duties. It proved to be necessary, however, that she should hover about the premises in a velvet jacket and a pair of black kid gloves, with one little white button; as also, that she should apply a thick coating of powder to her face, which had a charming oval and a sweet, weak expression, like that of most of the Venetian maidens, who, as a general thing (it was not a peculiarity of the landlady's niece), are fond of besmearing themselves with flour. It soon became plain that it is not only the many-twinkling lagoon that you behold from a habitation on the Riva; you see a little of everything Venetian. Straight across, before my windows, rose the great pink mass of San Giorgio Maggiore, which, for an ugly Palladian church, has a success beyond all reason. It is a success of position, of colour, of the immense detached Campanile, tipped with a tall gold angel. I know not whether it is because San Giorgio is so grandly conspicuous, and because it has a great deal of worn, faded-looking brick-work; but for many persons the whole place has a kind of suffusion of rosiness. If we were asked what is the leading colour at Venice we should say pink, and yet, after all, we cannot remember that this elegant tint occurs very often. It is a faint, shimmering, airy, watery pink; the bright sea-light seems to flush with it, and the pale whitish-green of lagoon and canal to drink it in. There is, indeed, in Venice a great deal of very evident brickwork, which is never fresh or loud in colour, but always burnt out, as it were, always exquisitely mild. There are certain little mental pictures that rise before the sentimental tourist at the simple mention, written or spoken, of the places he has loved. When I hear, when I see, the magical name I have written above these pages, it is not of the great Square that I think, with its strange basilica and its high arcades, nor of the wide mouth of the Grand Canal, with the stately steps and the well-poised dome of the Salute; it is not of the low lagoon, nor the sweet Piazzetta, nor the dark chambers of St. Mark's. I simply see a narrow canal in the heart of the city—a patch of green water and a surface of pink wall. The gondola moves slowly; it gives a great, smooth swerve, passes under a bridge, and the gondolier's cry, carried over the quiet water, makes a kind of splash in the stillness. A girl is passing over the little bridge, which has an arch like a camel's back, with an old shawl on her head, which makes her look charming; you see her against the sky as you float beneath. The pink of the old wall seems to fill the whole place; it sinks even into the opaque water. Behind the wall is a garden, out of which the long arm of a white June rose—the roses of Venice are splendid—has flung itself by way of spontaneous ornament. On the other side of this small water-way is a great shabby façade of Gothic windows and balconies—balconies on which dirty clothes are hung and under which a cavernous-looking doorway opens from a low flight of slimy water-steps. It is very hot and still, the canal has a queer smell, and the whole place is enchanting. It is poor work, however, talking about the colour of things in

Venice. The sentimental tourist is perpetually looking at it from his window, when he is not floating about with that delightful sense of being for the moment a part of it, which any gentleman in a gondola is free to entertain. Venetian windows and balconies are a dreadful lure, and while you rest your elbows on these cushioned ledges the precious hours fly away. But, in truth, Venice is not, in fair weather, a place for concentration of mind. The effort required for sitting down to a writing-table is heroic, and the brightest page of MS. looks dull beside the brilliancy of your *milieu*. All nature beckons you forth, and murmurs to you sophistically that such hours should be devoted to collecting impressions. Afterward, in ugly places, at unprivileged times, you can convert your impressions into prose. Fortunately for the present proser, the weather was not always fine; the first month was wet and windy, and it was better to look at the lagoon from an open casement than to respond to the advances of persuasive gondoliers. Even then, however, there was a constant entertainment in the view. It was all cold colour, and the steel-gray floor of the lagoon was stroked the wrong way by the wind. Then there were charming cool intervals, when the churches, the houses, the anchored fishing-boats, the whole gently-curving line of the Riva, seemed to be washed with a pearly white. Later it all turned warm— warm to the eye as well as to other senses. After the middle of May the whole place was in a glow. The sea took on a thousand shades, but they were only infinite variations of blue, and those rosy walls I just spoke of began to flush in the thick sunshine. Every patch of colour, every yard of weather-stained stucco, every glimpse of nestling garden or daub of sky above a *calle* [narrow alley], began to shine and sparkle—began, as the painters say, to "compose." The lagoon was streaked with odd currents, which played across it like huge, smooth finger-marks. The gondolas multiplied and spotted it all over; every gondola and every gondolier looking, at a distance, precisely like every other. There is something strange and fascinating in this mysterious impersonality of the gondola. It has an identity when you are in it, but, thanks to their all being of the same size, shape, and colour, and of the same deportment and gait, it has none, or as little as possible, as you see it pass before you.

From my windows on the Riva there was always the same silhouette—the long, black, slender skiff, lifting its head and throwing it back a little, moving yet seeming not to move, with the grotesquely-graceful figure on the poop. This figure inclines, as may be, more to the graceful or to the grotesque— standing in the "second position" of the dancing-master, but indulging, from the waist upward, in a freedom of movement which that functionary would deprecate. One may say, as a general thing, that there is something rather awkward in the movement of even the most graceful gondolier, and something graceful in the movement of the most awkward. In the graceful men of course the grace predominates, and nothing can be finer than the large firm way in which, from their point of vantage, they throw themselves over their tremendous oar. It has the boldness of a plunging bird, and the regularity of a pendulum. Sometimes, as you see this movement in profile, in a gondola that passes you—see, as you recline on your own low cushions, the arching body of the gondolier lifted up against the sky—it has a kind of nobleness which suggests an image on a Greek frieze. The gondolier at Venice is your very good friend—if you choose him happily—and on the quality of the personage depends a good deal that of your impressions. He is a part of your daily life, your double, your shadow, your complement. Most people, I think, either like their gondolier or hate him; and if they like him, like him very much. In this case they take an interest in him after his departure; wish him to be sure of employment, speak of him as the gem of gondoliers, and tell their friends to be certain to "secure" him. There is usually no difficulty in securing him; there is nothing elusive or reluctant about a gondolier. They are, for the most part, excellent fellows, and the sentimental tourist must always have a kindness for them. More than the rest of the population, of course, they are the children of Venice; they are associated with its idiosyncrasy, with its essence, with its silence, with its melancholy. When I say they are associated with its silence, I should immediately add that they are associated also with its sound. Among themselves they are an extraordinarily talkative company. They chatter at the *traghetti* [ferries], where they always have some sharp point under discussion; they bawl across the canals; they bespeak your commands as you approach; they defy each other from afar. If you happen to have a *traghetto* under your window, you are well aware that they are a vocal race. I should go even farther than I went just now, and say that the voice of the gondolier is, in fact, the sound of Venice. There is scarcely any other, and that, indeed, is part of the interest of the place. There is no noise there save distinctly human noise; no rumbling, no vague uproar, nor rattle of wheels and hoofs. It is all articulate, personal sound. One may say, indeed, that Venice is, emphatically, the city of conversation; people talk all over the place, because there is nothing to interfere with their being heard. Among the populace it is a kind of family party. The still water carries the voice, and good Venetians exchange confidences at a distance of half a mile. It saves a world of trouble, and they don't like trouble. Their delightful garrulous language helps them to make Venetian life a long *conversazione*. This language, with its soft elisions, its odd transpositions, its kindly contempt for consonants and other disagreeables, has in it something peculiarly human and accommodating. If your gondolier had no other merit, he would have the merit that he speaks Venetian. This may rank as a merit, even—some people perhaps would say especially— when you don't understand what he says. But he adds to it other graces which make him an agreeable feature in your life. The price he sets on his services is touchingly small, and he has a happy art of being obsequious, without being, or, at least, without seeming, abject. For occasional liberalities he evinces an almost lyrical gratitude. In short, he has delightfully good manners, a merit which he shares, for the most part, with Venetians at large. One grows very fond of these people, and the reason of one's fondness is the frankness and sweetness of their address. That of the Italian people, in general, has much to recommend it; but in the Venetian manner there is something peculiarly ingratiating. One feels that the race is old, that it has a long and rich civilisation in its blood, and that if it has not been blessed by fortune, it has at least been polished by time. It has not a genius for morality, and indeed makes few pretensions in that direction. It scruples not to represent the false as the true, and is liable to confusion in the attribution of property. It is peculiarly susceptible to the tender sentiment, which it cultivates with a graceful disregard of the more rigid formalities. I am not sure that it is very brave, and was not struck with its being very industrious. But it has an unfailing sense of the amenities of life; the poorest Venetian is a natural man of the world. He is better company than persons of his class are apt to be among the nations of industry and virtue— where people are also, sometimes, perceived to lie and steal. He has a great desire to please and to be pleased.

· · · · · *v* · · · · · ·

In this latter point the cold-blooded stranger begins at last to imitate him; he begins to lead a life that is, before all things, good-humoured: unless, indeed, he allow himself, like Mr. Ruskin, to be put out of his good-humour by Titian and Tiepolo. The hours he spends among the pictures are his best hours in Venice, and I am ashamed of myself to have written so much of common things when I might have been making festoons of the names of the masters. But, when we have covered our page with such festoons, what more is left to say? When one has said Carpaccio and Bellini, the Tintoret and the Veronese, one has struck a note that must be left to resound at will. Everything has been said about the mighty painters, and it is of little importance to record that one traveller the more has found them to his taste. "Went this morning to the Academy; was very much pleased with Titian's 'Assumption.' " That honest phrase has doubtless been written in many a traveller's diary, and was not indiscreet on the part of its author. But it appeals little to the general reader, and we must, moreover, not expose our deepest feelings. Since I have mentioned Titian's "Assumption," I must say that there are some people who have been less pleased with it than the gentleman we have just imagined. It is one of the possible disappointments of Venice, and you may, if you like, take advantage of your privilege of not caring for it. It imparts a look of great richness to the side of the beautiful room of the Academy on which it hangs; but the same room contains two or three works less known to fame which are equally capable of inspiring a passion. "The 'Annunciation' struck me as coarse and superficial":

that was once written in a simple-minded traveller's note-book. At Venice, strange to say, Titian is altogether a disappointment; the city of his adoption is far from containing the best of him. Madrid, Paris, London, Florence, Dresden, Munich—these are the homes of his greatness. There are other painters who have but a single home, and the greatest of these is the Tintoret. Close beside him sit Carpaccio and Bellini, who make with him the dazzling Venetian trio. The Veronese may be seen and measured in other places; he is most splendid in Venice, but he shines in Paris and in Dresden. You may walk out of the noon-day dusk of Trafalgar Square in November, and in one of the chambers of the National Gallery see the family of Darius rustling and pleading and weeping at the feet of Alexander. Alexander is a beautiful young Venetian in crimson pantaloons, and the picture sends a glow into the cold London twilight. You may sit before it for an hour, and dream you are floating to the water-gate of the Ducal Palace, where a certain old beggar, with one of the handsomest heads in the world—he has sat to a hundred painters for Doges, and for personages more sacred—has a prescriptive right to pretend to pull your gondola to the steps and to hold out a greasy, immemorial cap. But you must go to Venice, in fact, to see the other masters, who form part of your life while you are there, and illuminate your view of the universe. It is difficult to express one's relation to them; for the whole Venetian art-world is so near, so familiar, so much an extension and adjunct of the actual world, that it seems almost invidious to say one owes more to one of them than to another. Nowhere (not even in Holland, where the correspondence between the real aspects and the little polished canvases is so constant and so exquisite) do art and life seem so interfused and, as it were, so consanguineous. All the splendour of light and colour, all the Venetian air and the Venetian history, are on the walls and ceilings of the palaces; and all the genius of the masters, all the images and visions they have left upon canvas, seem to tremble in the sunbeams and dance upon the waves. That is the perpetual interest of the place—that you live in a certain sort of knowledge as in a rosy cloud. You don't go into the churches and galleries by way of a change from the streets; you go into them because they offer you an exquisite reproduction of the things that surround you. All Venice was both model and painter, and life was so pictorial that art could not help becoming so. With all diminutions life is pictorial still, and this fact gives an extraordinary freshness to one's perception of the great Venetian works. You judge of them not as a connoisseur, but as a man of the world, and you enjoy them because they are so social and so actual. Perhaps, of all works of art that are equally great, they demand least reflection on the part of the spectator—they make least of a mystery of being enjoyed. Reflection only confirms your admiration but it is almost ashamed to show its head. These things speak so frankly and benignantly to the sense that we feel there is reason as well in such an address. But it is hard, as I say, to express all this, and it is painful as well to attempt it—painful, because in the memory of vanished hours so filled with beauty the sense of present loss is overwhelming. Exquisite hours, enveloped in light and silence, to have known them once is to have always a terrible standard of enjoyment. Certain lovely mornings of May and June come back with an ineffaceable fairness. Venice is not smothered in flowers at this season, in the manner of Florence and Rome; but the sea and sky themselves seem to blossom and rustle. The gondola waits at the wave-washed steps, and if you are wise you will take your place beside a discriminating companion. Such a companion, in Venice, should, of course, be of the sex that discriminates most finely. An intelligent woman who knows her Venice seems doubly intelligent, and it makes no woman's perceptions less keen to be aware that she cannot help looking graceful as she glides over the waves. The handsome Pasquale, with uplifted oar, awaits your command, knowing, in a general way, from observation of your habits, that your intention is to go to see a picture or two. It perhaps docs not immensely matter what picture you choose: the whole affair is so charming. It is charming to wander through the light and shade of intricate canals, with perpetual architecture above you and perpetual fluidity beneath. It is charming to disembark at the polished steps of a little empty *campo*—a sunny, shabby square, with an old well in the middle, an old church on one side, and tall Venetian windows looking down. Sometimes the windows are tenantless; sometimes a lady in a faded dressing-gown is leaning vaguely on the sill. There is always an old man holding out his hat for coppers; there are always three or four small boys dodging possible umbrella-pokes while they precede you, in the manner of custodians, to the door of the church.

· · · · · · *v i* · · · · · · ·

The churches of Venice are rich in pictures, and many a masterpiece lurks in the unaccommodating gloom of side-chapels and sacristies. Many a noble work is perched behind the dusty candles and muslin roses of a scantily-visited altar; some of them, indeed, are hidden behind the altar, in a dark-ness that can never be explored. The facilities offered you for approaching the picture, in such cases, are a kind of mockery of your irritated desire. You stand on tip-toe on a three-legged stool, you climb a rickety ladder, you almost mount upon the shoulders of the *custode*. You do everything but see the picture. You see just enough to perceive that it is beautiful. You catch a glimpse of a divine head, of a fig-tree against a mellow sky; but the rest is impenetrable mystery. You renounce all hope, for instance, of approaching the magnificent Cima da Coneg-liano in San Giovanni in Bragora; and bethinking yourself of the immaculate purity that dwells in the works of this master, you renounce it with chagrin and pain. Behind the high altar, in that church, there hangs a Baptism of Christ, by Cima, which, I believe, has been more or less repainted. You can make the thing out in spots; you can see that it has a fulness of perfection. But you turn away from it with a stiff neck, and promise yourself consolation in the Academy and at the Ma-donna dell' Orto, where two noble pictures, by the same hand—pictures as clear as a summer twilight—present them-selves in better circumstances. It may be said, as a general thing, that you never see the Tintoret. You admire him, you adore him, you think him the greatest of painters, but, in the great majority of cases, you don't see him. This is partly his own fault; so many of his works have turned to blackness and are positively rotting in their frames. At the Scuola di San

Rocco, where there are acres of the Tintoret, there is scarcely anything at all adequately visible save the immense "Crucifixion" in the upper story. It is true that in looking at this huge composition you look at many pictures; it has not only a multitude of figures, but a wealth of episodes; and you pass from one of these to the other as if you were "doing" a gallery. Surely, no single picture in the world contains more of human life; there is everything in it, including the most exquisite beauty. It is one of the greatest things of art; it is always interesting. There are pictures by the Tintoret which contain touches more exquisite, revelations of beauty more radiant, but there is no other vision of so intense a reality and an execution so splendid. The interest, the impressiveness, of that whole corner of Venice, however melancholy the effect of its gorgeous and ill-lighted chambers, gives a strange importance to a visit to the Scuola. Nothing that all travellers go to see appears to suffer less from the incursions of travellers. It is one of the loneliest booths of the bazaar, and the author of these lines has always had the good fortune, which he wishes to every other traveller, of having it to himself. I think most visitors find the place rather alarming and wicked-looking. They walk about a while among the fitful figures that gleam here and there out of the great tapestry (as it were) with which the painter has hung all the walls, and then, depressed and bewildered by the portentous solemnity of these objects, by strange glimpses of unnatural scenes, by the echo of their lonely footsteps on the vast stone floors, they take a hasty departure, and find themselves again, with a sense of release from danger, and of the *genius loci* having been a sort of mad white-washer, who worked with a bad mixture, in the bright light of the *campo,* among the beggars, the orange-vendors, and the passing gondolas. Solemn, indeed, is the place, solemn and strangely suggestive, for the simple reason that we shall scarcely find four walls elsewhere that inclose within a like area an equal quantity of genius. The air is thick with it, and dense and difficult to breathe; for it was genius that was not happy, inasmuch as it lacked the art to fix itself for ever. It is not immortality that we breathe at the Scuola di San Rocco, but conscious, reluctant mortality. Fortunately, however, we have the Ducal Palace, where everything is so brilliant and splendid that the poor dusky Tintoret is lifted in spite of himself into the concert. This deeply original building is, of course, the loveliest thing in Venice, and a morning's stroll there is a wonderful illumination. Cunningly select your hour—half the enjoyment of Venice is a question of dodging—and go at about one o'clock, when the tourists have gone to lunch and the echoes of the charming chambers have gone to sleep among the sunbeams. There is no brighter place in Venice; by which I mean that, on the whole, there is none half so bright. The reflected sunshine plays up through the great windows from the glittering lagoon, and shimmers and twinkles over gilded walls and ceilings. All the history of Venice, all its splendid, stately past, glows around you in a strong sea-light. Every one here is magnificent, but the great Veronese is the most magnificent of all. He swims before you in a silver cloud; he thrones in an eternal morning. The deep blue sky burns behind him, streaked across with milky bars; the white colonnades sustain the richest canopies, under which the first gentlemen and ladies in the world both render homage and receive it. Their glorious garments rustle in the air of the sea, and their sun-lighted faces are the very complexion of Venice. The mixture of pride and piety, of politics and religion, of art and patriotism, gives a magnificent dignity to every scene. Never was a painter more nobly joyous, never did an artist take a greater delight in life, seeing it all as a kind of breezy festival and feeling it through the medium of perpetual success. He revels in the gold-framed ovals of the ceilings, with the fluttering movement of an embroidered banner that tosses itself into the blue. He was the happiest of painters, and he produced the happiest picture in the world. The "Rape of Europe" surely deserves this title; it is impossible to look at it without aching with envy. Nowhere else in art is such a temperament revealed; never did inclination and opportunity combine to express such enjoyment. The mixture of flowers and gems and brocade, of blooming flesh and shining sea and waving groves, of youth, health, movement, desire—all this is the brightest vision that ever descended upon the soul of a painter.

Happy the artist who could entertain such a vision; happy the artist who could paint it as the "Rape of Europa" is painted. The Tintoret's visions were not so bright as that; but he had several that were radiant enough. In the room that contains the "Rape of Europa" are several smaller canvases by the greatly more complex genius of the Scuola di San Rocco, which are almost simple in their loveliness, almost happy in their simplicity. They have kept their brightness through the centuries, and they shine with their neighbours in those golden rooms. There is a piece of painting in one of them which is one of the sweetest things in Venice, and which reminds one afresh of those wild flowers of execution that bloom so profusely and so unheeded in the dark corners of all of the Tintoret's work. "Pallas chasing away Mars" is, I believe, the name that is given to the picture; and it represents in fact a young woman of noble appearance administering a gentle push to a fine young man in armour, as if to tell him to keep his distance. It is of the gentleness of this push that I speak, the charming way in which she puts out her arm, with a single bracelet on it, and rests her young hand, with its rosy fingers parted, upon his dark breast-plate. She bends her enchanting head with the effort—a head which has all the strange fairness that the Tintoret always sees in women—and the soft, living, flesh-like glow of all these members, over which the brush has scarcely paused in its course, is as pretty an example of genius as all Venice can show. But why speak of the Tintoret when I can say nothing of the great "Paradise," which unfolds its somewhat smoky splendour, and the wonder of its multitudinous circles, in one of the other chambers? If it were not one of the first pictures in the world, it would be about the biggest, and it must be confessed that at first the spectator gets from it chiefly an impression of quantity. Then he sees that this quantity is really wealth; that the dim confusion of faces is a magnificent composition, and that some of the details of this composition are supremely beautiful. It is impossible, however, in a retrospect of Venice, to specify one's happiest hours, though, as one looks backward, certain ineffaceable moments start here and there into vividness. How is it possible to forget one's visits to the sacristy of the Frari, however frequent they may have been, and the great work of John Bellini which forms the treasure of that apartment?

····· *v i i* . ······

Nothing in Venice is more perfect than this, and we know of no work of art more complete. The picture is in three compartments: the Virgin sits in the central division with her child; two venerable saints, standing close together, occupy each of the others. It is impossible to imagine anything more finished or more ripe. It is one of those things that sum up the genius of a painter, the experience of a life, the teaching of a school. It seems painted with molten gems, which have only been clarified by time, and it is as solemn as it is gorgeous, and as simple as it is deep. John Bellini is, more or less, everywhere in Venice, and wherever he is, he is almost certain to be first— first, I mean, in his own line; he paints little else than the Madonna and the saints; he has not Carpaccio's care for human life at large, nor the Tintoret's, nor that of the Veronese. Some of his greater pictures, however, where several figures are clustered together, have a richness of sanctity that is almost profane. There is one of them on the dark side of the room at the Academy, containing Titian's "Assumption," which, if we could only see it—its position is an inconceivable scandal— would evidently be one of the mightiest of so-called sacred pictures. So, too, is the Madonna of San Zaccaria, hung in a cold, dim, dreary place, ever so much too high, but so mild and serene, and so grandly disposed and accompanied, that the proper attitude for even the most critical amateur, as he looks at it, seems to be the bended knee. There is another noble John Bellini, one of the very few in which there is no Virgin, at San Giovanni Crisostomo—a St. Jerome, in a red dress, sitting aloft upon the rocks, with a landscape of extraordinary purity behind him. The absence of the peculiarly erect Madonna makes it an interesting surprise among the works of the painter, and gives it a somewhat less strenuous air. But it has brilliant beauty, and the St. Jerome is a delightful old personage. The same church contains another great picture, for which he must find a shrine apart in his memory; one of the most interesting things he will have seen, if not the most brilliant. Nothing appeals more to him than three figures of Venetian ladies which occupy the foreground of a smallish canvas of Sebastian del Piombo, placed above the high altar of San Giovanni Crisostomo. Sebastian was a Venetian by birth, but few of his productions are to be seen in his native place; few, indeed, are to be seen anywhere. The picture represents the patron-saint of the church, accompanied by other saints, and by the worldly votaries I have mentioned. These ladies stand together on the left, holding in their hands little white caskets; two of them are in profile, but the foremost turns her face to the spectator. This face and figure are almost unique among the beautiful things of Venice, and they leave the susceptible observer with the impression of having made, or rather having missed, a strange, a dangerous, but a most valuable, acquaintance. The lady, who is superbly handsome, is the typical Venetian of the sixteenth century, and she remains in the mind as the perfect flower of that society. Never was there a greater air of breeding, a deeper expression of tranquil superiority. She walks like a goddess—as if she trod, without sinking, the waves of the Adriatic. It is impossible to conceive a more perfect expression of the aristo-cratic spirit, either in its pride or in its benignity. This mag-nificent creature is so strong and secure that she is gentle, and so quiet that, in comparison, all minor assumptions of calmness suggest only a vulgar alarm. But for all this, there are depths of possible disorder in her light-coloured eye. I had meant, however, to say nothing about her, for it is not right to speak of Sebastian when one has not found room for Carpaccio. These visions come to one, and one can neither hold them nor brush them aside. Memories of Carpaccio, the magnificent, the delightful—it is not for want of such visitations, but only for want of space, that I have not said of him what I would. There is little enough need of it for Carpaccio's sake, his fame being brighter to-day—thanks to the generous lamp Mr. Ruskin has held up to it—than it has ever been. Yet there is something ridiculous in talking of Venice without making him, almost, the refrain. He and the Tintoret are the two great realists, and it is hard to say which is the more human, the more various. The Tintoret had the mightier temperament, but Carpaccio, who had the advantage of more newness and more responsibility, sailed nearer to perfection. Here and there he quite touches it, as in the enchanting picture, at the Academy, of St. Ursula asleep in her little white bed, in her high, clean room, where the angel visits her at dawn; or in the noble St. Jerome in his study, at S. Giorgio degli Schiavoni. This latter work is a pearl of sentiment, and I may add, without being fantastic, a ruby of colour. It unites the most masterly finish with a kind of universal largeness of feeling, and he who has it well in his memory will never hear the name of Carpaccio without a throb of almost personal affection. This, indeed, is the feeling that descends upon you in that wonderful little chapel of St. George of the Slaves, where this most personal and sociable of artists has expressed all the sweetness of his imagination. The place is small and incommodious, the pictures are out of sight and ill-lighted, the custodian is rapacious, the visitors are mutually intolerable, but the shabby little chapel is a palace of art. Mr. Ruskin has written a pamphlet about it which is a real aid to enjoyment, though I cannot but think the generous artist, with his keen senses and his just feeling, would have suffered at hearing his eulogist declare that one of his other productions—in the Museo Civico in Palazzo Correr, a delightful portrait of two Venetian ladies, with pet animals—is the "finest picture in the world." It has no need of that to be thought admirable; and what more can a painter desire?

····· *v i i i .* ······

May in Venice is better than April, but June is best of all. Then the days are hot, but not too hot, and the nights are more beautiful than the days. Then Venice is rosier than ever in the morning, and more golden than ever as the day descends. It seems to expand and evaporate, to multiply all its reflections and iridescences. Then the life of its people and the strangeness of its constitution become a perpetual comedy, or, at least, a perpetual drama. Then the gondola is your sole habitation, and you spend days between sea and sky. You go to the Lido, though the Lido has been spoiled. When I was first in Venice, in 1869, it was a very natural place, and there was only a rough lane across the little island from the landing-place to the beach. There was a bathing-place in those days, and a restaurant, which was very bad, but where, in the warm evenings, your dinner did not much matter as you sat letting it cool upon the wooden terrace that stretched out into the sea. To-day the Lido is a part of united Italy, and has been made the victim of villainous improvements. A little cockney village has sprung up on its rural bosom, and a third-rate boulevard leads from Santa Elisabetta to the Adriatic. There are bitumen walls and gas-lamps, lodging-houses, shops, and a *teatro diurno* [theater with an afternoon performance]. The bathing-establishment is bigger than before, and the restaurant as well; but it is a compensation, perhaps, that the cuisine is no better. Such as it is, however, you will not scorn occasionally to partake of it on the breezy platform under which bathers dart and splash, and which looks out to where the fishing-boats, with sails of orange and crimson, wander along the darkening horizon. The beach at the Lido is still lonely and beautiful, and you can easily walk away from the cockney village. The return to Venice in the sunset is classical and indispensable, and those who, at that glowing hour, have floated toward the towers that rise out of the lagoon, will not easily part with the impression. But you indulge in larger excursions—you go to Burano and Torcello, to Malamocco and Chioggia. Torcello, like the Lido, has been improved; the deeply interesting little cathedral of the eighth century, which stood there on the edge of the sea, as touching in its ruin, with its grassy threshold and its primitive mosaics, as the bleached bones of a human skeleton washed ashore by the tide, has now been restored and made cheerful, and the charm of the place, its strange and suggestive desolation, has well-nigh departed. It will still serve you as a pretext, however, for a day on the lagoon, especially as you will disembark at Burano and admire the wonderful fisher-folk, whose good looks—and bad manners, I am sorry to say—can scarcely be exaggerated. Burano is celebrated for the beauty of its women and the rapacity of its children, and it is a fact that though some of the ladies are rather bold about it, every one of them shows you a handsome face. The children assail you for coppers, and, in their desire to be satisfied, pursue your gondola into the sea. Chioggia is a larger Burano, and you carry away from either place a half-sad, half-cynical, but altogether pictorial impression; the impression of bright-coloured hovels, of bathing in stagnant canals, of young girls with faces of a delicate shape and a susceptible expression, with splendid heads of hair and complexions smeared with powder, faded yellow shawls that hang like old Greek draperies, and little wooden shoes that click as they go up and down the steps of the convex bridges; of brown-checked matrons with lustrous tresses and high tempers, massive throats encased with gold beads, and eyes that meet your own with a certain traditional defiance. The men throughout the islands of Venice are almost as handsome as the women; I have never seen so many good-looking fellows. At Burano and Chioggia they sit mending their nets, or lounge at the street corners, where conversation is always high-pitched, or clamour to you to take a boat; and everywhere they decorate the scene with their splendid colour—cheeks and throats as richly brown as the sails of their fishing-smacks— their sea-faded tatters which are always a "costume"—their soft Venetian jargon, and the gallantry with which they wear their hats—an article that nowhere sits so well as on a mass of dense Venetian curls. If you are happy, you will find yourself, after a June day in Venice (about ten o'clock), on a balcony that overhangs the Grand Canal, with your elbows on the broad ledge, a cigarette in your teeth, and a little good company beside you. The gondolas pass beneath, the watery surface gleams here and there from their lamps, some of which are coloured lanterns that move mysteriously in the darkness. There are some evenings in June when there are too many gondolas, too many lanterns, too many serenades in front of the hotels. The serenading (in particular) is overdone; but on such a balcony as I speak of you needn't suffer from it, for in the apartment behind you—an accessible refuge—there is more good company, there are more cigarettes. If you are wise you will step back there presently.

[1882]

The Grand Canal

The honour of representing the plan and the place at their best might perhaps appear, in the City of St. Mark, properly to belong to the splendid square which bears the patron's name and which is the centre of Venetian life so far (this is pretty well all the way indeed) as Venetian life is a matter of strolling and chaffering, of gossiping and gaping, of circulating without a purpose, and of staring—too often with a foolish one—through the shop-windows of dealers whose hospitality makes their doorsteps dramatic, at the very vulgarest rubbish in all the modern market. If the Grand Canal, however, is not quite technically a "street," the perverted Piazza is perhaps even less normal; and I hasten to add that I am glad not to find myself studying my subject under the international arcades, or yet (I will go the length of saying) in the solemn presence of the church. For indeed in that case I foresee I should become still more confoundingly conscious of the stumbling-block that inevitably, even with his first few words, crops up in the path of the lover of Venice who rashly addresses himself to expression. "Venetian life" is a mere literary convention, though it be an indispensable figure. The words have played an effective part in the literature of sensibility; they constituted thirty years ago the title of Mr. Howells's delightful volume of impressions*; but in using them to-day one owes some frank amends to one's own lucidity. Let me carefully premise therefore that so often

---

* A good friend of James's, William Dean Howells (1837–1920), the American novelist, essayist, and editor of the *Atlantic Monthly,* published a volume on Venice, *Venetian Life* (1866), based on his residence as American consul from 1861 to 1865.

as they shall again drop from my pen, so often shall I beg to be regarded as systematically superficial.

Venetian life, in the large old sense, has long since come to an end, and the essential present character of the most melancholy of cities resides simply in its being the most beautiful of tombs. Nowhere else has the past been laid to rest with such tenderness, such a sadness of resignation and remembrance. Nowhere else is the present so alien, so discontinuous, so like a crowd in a cemetery without garlands for the graves. It has no flowers in its hands, but, as a compensation perhaps—and the thing is doubt-less more to the point—it has money and little red books. The everlasting shuffle of these irresponsible visitors in the Piazza is contemporary Venetian life. Everything else is only a reverber-ation of that. The vast mausoleum has a turnstile at the door, and a functionary in a shabby uniform lets you in, as per tariff, to see how dead it is. From this *constatation* [testimony], this cold curiosity, proceed all the industry, the prosperity, the vitality of the place. The shopkeepers and gondoliers, the beggars and the models, depend upon it for a living; they are the custodians and the ushers of the great museum—they are even themselves to a certain extent the objects of exhibition. It is in the wide vestibule of the square that the polyglot pilgrims gather most densely; Pi-azza San Marco is the lobby of the opera in the intervals of the performance. The present fortune of Venice, the lamentable dif-ference, is most easily measured there, and that is why, in the effort to resist our pessimism, we must turn away both from the purchasers and from the vendors of *ricordi* [souvenirs]. The *ri-cordi* that we prefer are gathered best where the gondola glides—best of all on the noble waterway that begins in its glory at the Salute and ends in its abasement at the railway station. It is, however, the cockneyfied Piazzetta (forgive me, shade of St. Theodore—has not a brand new café begun to glare there, elec-trically, this very year?) that introduces us most directly to the great picture by which the Grand Canal works its first spell, and to which a thousand artists, not always with a talent apiece, have paid their tribute. We pass into the Piazzetta to look down the great throat, as it were, of Venice, and the vision must console us for turning our back on St. Mark's.

We have been treated to it again and again, of course, even

if we have never stirred from home; but that is only a reason the more for catching at any freshness that may be left in the world of photography. It is in Venice above all that we hear the small buzz of this vulgarising voice of the familiar; yet perhaps it is in Venice too that the picturesque fact has best mastered the pious secret of how to wait for us. Even the classic Salute waits like some great lady on the threshold of her saloon. She is more ample and serene, more seated at her door, than all the copyists have told us, with her domes and scrolls, her scolloped buttresses and statues forming a pompous crown, and her wide steps disposed on the ground like the train of a robe. This fine air of the woman of the world is carried out by the well-bred assurance with which she looks in the direction of her old-fashioned Byzantine neighbour; and the juxtaposition of two churches so distinguished and so different, each splendid in its sort, is a sufficient mark of the scale and range of Venice. However, we ourselves are looking away from St. Mark's—we must blind our eyes to that dazzle; without it indeed there are brightnesses and fascinations enough. We see them in abundance even while we look away from the shady steps of the Salute. These steps are cool in the morning, yet I don't know that I can justify my excessive fondness for them any better than I can explain a hundred of the other vague infatuations with which Venice sophisticates the spirit. Under such an influence fortunately one needn't explain—it keeps account of nothing but perceptions and affections. It is from the Salute steps perhaps, of a summer morning, that this view of the open mouth of the city is most brilliantly amusing. The whole thing composes as if composition were the chief end of human institutions. The charming architectural promontory of the Dogana stretches out the most graceful of arms, balancing in its hand the gilded globe on which revolves the delightful satirical figure of a little weathercock of a woman. This Fortune, this Navigation, or whatever she is called—she surely needs no name—catches the wind in the bit of drapery of which she has divested her rotary bronze loveliness. On the other side of the Canal twinkles and glitters the long row of the happy palaces which are mainly expensive hotels. There is a little of everything everywhere, in the bright Venetian air, but to these

better example of the roving i[...]
vision, a real spirit of adventur[...]
always a cluster of accidents; not a[...]
peopled and agitated chapter of li[...]
submissive pictorial notes. These [...]
beauty and heterogeneity, and if [...]
make the principle of selection [...]
the sense of "composition" ir [...]
exist—reaches out to the p[...]
must be the spirit of the w[...]
with that particular ques[...]
the eternal problem the[...]

If the long reach [...]
bridge which discha[...]
more comprehensi[...]
noble Palazzo Fo[...]
one point as a v[...]
as it were, of [...]
has the liker[...]
our passage a [...]
sketcher's sense, and[...]
our intensely Venetian fata[...]
It is the early palaces, of course, a[...]
late, if we could take them one by one,[...]
best of its grand air. The fairest are often c[...]
the foulest, and there are few, alas, so fair as t[...]
completely protected by their beauty. The ages and the [...]
ations have worked their will on them, and the wind and the[...]
weather have had much to say; but disfigured and dishonoured
as they are, with the bruises of their marbles and the patience
of their ruin, there is nothing like them in the world, and the
long succession of their faded, conscious faces makes of the
quiet water-way they overhang a *promenade historique* of which
the lesson, however often we read it, gives, in the depth of its
interest, an incomparable dignity to Venice. We read it in the
Romanesque arches, crooked to-day in their very curves, of
the early middle-age, in the exquisite individual Gothic of the
splendid time, and in the cornices and columns of a decadence
almost as proud. These things at present are almost equally

houses belongs especially the app[...]
water, at the receipt of custom, o[...]
ical loveliness for the stranger an[...]
happy, because even their sordid uses[...]
melt somehow, with their vague sea-stab[...]
into that strange gaiety of light and colour[...]
of the reflection of superannuated things. The a[...]
over them like a laugh, they are of the essence [...]
joke. They are almost as charming from other pla[...]
are from their own balconies, and share fully in that [...]
privilege of Venetian objects which consists of being bo[...]
picture and the point of view.
This double character, which is particularly strong in th[...]
Grand Canal, adds a difficulty to any control of one's notes.
The Grand Canal may be practically, as an impression, the[...]
cushioned balcony of a high and well-loved palace—the memory of irresistible evenings; or it may evoke the restlessness of a
lingering and looking, of the sociable elbow, of endless
fresh curiosity, in a gondola piled with
references. There are no references, I ought to mention, in the
present remarks, which sacrifice to accident, not to completeness. A rhapsody on Venice is always in order, but I think here the
catalogues are finished. I should not attempt to write here the
names of all the palaces, even if the number of those I find
myself able to remember in the immense array were less insignificant. There are many I delight in that I don't know, or
at least don't keep apart. Then there are the bad reasons for
preference that are better than the good, and all the sweet
bribery of association and recollection. These things, as one
stands on the Salute steps, are so many delicate fingers to pick
straight out of the row a dear little featureless house which
with its pale green shutters, looks straight across at the chu[...]
door and through the very keyhole, as it were, of the gre[...]
and which I needn't call by a name—a pleasant Am[...]
name—that every one in Venice, these many years, ha[...]
grateful lips. It is the very friendliest house in all[...]
world, and it has, as it deserves to have, the m[...]
position. It is a real *porto di mare*, as the gondoli[...]
within a port; it sees everything that comes an[...]

good faith; they have each in their degree so ...rted with their pride. They have lived on as they ... lasted as they might, and we hold them to no ac... ... of their infirmities, for even those of them whose blank ...es to-day meet criticism with most submission are far less vulgar than the uses we have mainly managed to put them to. We have botched them and patched them and covered them with sordid signs; we have restored and improved them with a merciless taste, and the best of them we have made over to the pedlars. Some of the most striking objects in the finest vistas at present are the huge advertisements of the curiosity-shops.

The antiquity-mongers in Venice have all the courage of their opinion, and it is easy to see how well they know they can confound you with an unanswerable question. What is the whole place but a curiosity-shop, and what are you here for yourself but to pick up odds and ends? "We pick them up *for* you," say these honest Jews, whose prices are marked in dollars, "and who shall blame us if, the flowers being pretty well plucked, we add an artificial rose or two to the composition of the bouquet?" They take care in a word that there be plenty of relics, and their establishments are huge and active. They administer the antidote to pedantry, and you can complain of them only if you never cross their thresholds. If you take this step you are lost, for you have parted with the correctness of your attitude. Venice becomes frankly from such a moment the big depressing dazzling joke in which after all our sense of her contradictions sinks to rest—the grimace of an over-strained philosophy. It's rather a comfort, for the curiosity-shops are amusing. You have bad moments indeed as you stand in their halls of humbug and, in the intervals of haggling, hear through the high windows the soft plash of the sea on the old water-steps, for you think with anger of the noble homes that are laid waste in such scenes, of the delicate lives that must have been, that might still be, led there. You reconstruct the admirable house according to your own needs; leaning on a back balcony, you drop your eyes into one of the little green gardens with which, for the most part, such establishments are exasperatingly blessed, and end by feeling it a shame that you yourself are not in possession. (I take for granted, of course, that as you go and come you are, in imagination, perpetually lodging yourself and setting up your gods; for if this innocent pastime, this borrowing of the mind, be not your favourite sport there is a flaw in the appeal that Venice makes to you.) There may be happy cases in which your envy is tempered, or perhaps I should rather say intensified, by real participation. If you have had the good fortune to enjoy the hospitality of an old Venetian home and to lead your life a little in the painted chambers that still echo with one of the historic names, you have entered by the shortest step into the inner spirit of the place. If it didn't savour of treachery to private kindness I should like to speak frankly of one of these delightful, even though alienated, structures, to refer to it as a splendid example of the old palatial type. But I can only do so in passing, with a hundred precautions, and, lifting the curtain at the edge, drop a commemorative word on the success with which, in this particularly happy instance, the cosmopolite habit, the modern sympathy, the intelligent, flexible attitude, the latest fruit of time, adjust themselves to the great gilded, relinquished shell and try to fill it out. A Venetian palace that has not too grossly suffered and that is not overwhelming by its mass makes almost any life graceful that may be led in it. With cultivated and generous contemporary ways it reveals a pre-established harmony. As you live in it day after day its beauty and its interest sink more deeply into your spirit; it has its molds and its hours and its mystic voices and its shifting expressions. If in the absence of its masters you have happened to have it to yourself for twenty-four hours you will never forget the charm of its haunted stillness, late on the summer afternoon for instance, when the call of playing children comes in behind from the campo, nor the way the old ghosts seemed to pass on tip-toe on the marble floors. It gives you practically the essence of the matter that we are considering, for beneath the high balconies Venice comes and goes, and the particular stretch you command contains all the characteristics. Everything has its turn, from the heavy barges of merchandise, pushed by long poles and the patient shoulder, to the floating pavilions of the great serenades, and you may study at your leisure the admirable Venetian arts of managing a boat and organising a spectacle. Of the beautiful free stroke with which the gondola, especially when there are two oars, is impelled, you never, in the Venetian scene, grow weary; it is always in the picture, and the large profiled action that lets the standing rowers throw themselves forward to a constant recovery has the double value of being, at the fag-end of greatness, the only energetic note. The people from the hotels are always afloat, and, at the hotel pace, the solitary gondolier (like the solitary horseman of the old-fashioned novel) is, I confess, a somewhat melancholy figure. Perched on his poop without a mate, he re-enacts perpetually, in high relief, with his toes turned out, the comedy of his odd and charming movement. He always has a little the look of an absent-minded nursery-maid pushing her small charges in a perambulator.

But why should I risk too free a comparison, where this picturesque and amiable class are concerned? I delight in their sun-burnt complexions and their childish dialect; I know them only by their merits, and I am grossly prejudiced in their favour. They are interesting and touching, and alike in their virtues and their defects human nature is simplified as with a big effective brush. Affecting above all is their dependence on the stranger, the whimsical stranger who swims out of their ken, yet whom Providence sometimes restores. The best of them at any rate are in their line great artists. On the swarming feast-days, on the strange feast-night of the Redentore,* their steering is a miracle of ease. The master-hands, the celebrities and winners of prizes—you may see them on the private gondolas in spotless white, with brilliant sashes and ribbons, and often with very handsome persons—take the right of way with a pardonable insolence. They penetrate the crush of boats with an authority of their own. The crush of boats, the universal sociable bumping and squeezing, is great when, on the summer nights, the ladies shriek with alarm, the city pays the fiddlers and the illuminated barges, scattering music and song, lead a

---

* A holiday in July to celebrate the deliverance of the city from a plague in which a temporary bridge is built across the Giudecca Canal to the Church of the Redentore.

long train down the Canal. The barges used to be rowed in rhythmic strokes, but now they are towed by the steamer. The coloured lamps, the vocalists before the hotels, are not to my sense the greatest seduction of Venice; but it would be an uncandid sketch of the Canalazzo that shouldn't touch them with indulgence. Taking one nuisance with another, they are probably the prettiest in the world, and if they have in general more magic for the new arrival than for the old Venice-lover, they in any case, at their best, keep up the immemorial tradition. The Venetians have had from the beginning of time the pride of their processions and spectacles, and it's a wonder how with empty pockets they still make a clever show. The Carnival is dead, but these are the scraps of its inheritance. Vauxhall* on the water is of course more Vauxhall than ever, with the good fortune of home-made music and of a mirror that reduplicates and multiplies. The feast of the Redeemer—the great popular feast of the year—is a wonderful Venetian Vauxhall. All Venice on this occasion takes to the boats for the night and loads them with lamps and provisions. Wedged together in a mass it sups and sings; every boat is a floating arbour, a private *café-concert*. Of all Christian commemorations it is the most ingenuously and harmlessly pagan. Toward morning the passengers repair to the Lido, where, as the sun rises, they plunge, still sociably, into the sea. The night of the Redentore has been described, but it would be interesting to have an account, from the domestic point of view, of its usual morrow. It is mainly an affair of the Giudecca, however, which is bridged over from the Zattere to the great church. The pontoons are laid together during the day—it is all done with extraordinary celerity and art—and the bridge is prolonged across the Canalazzo (to Santa Maria Zobenigo), which is my only warrant for glancing at the occasion. We glance at it from our palace windows; lengthening our necks a little, as we look up toward the Salute, we see all Venice, on the July afternoon, so serried as to move slowly, pour across the temporary footway. It is a flock of very good children, and the bridged Canal

* A popular eighteenth- and early nineteenth-century garden and pleasure resort in London.

is their toy. All Venice on such occasions is gentle and friendly; not even all Venice pushes any one into the water.

But from the same high windows we catch without any stretching of the neck a still more indispensable note in the picture, a famous pretender eating the bread of bitterness. This repast is served in the open air, on a neat little terrace, by attendants in livery, and there is no indiscretion in our seeing that the pretender dines. Ever since the table d'hôte in "Candide" Venice has been the refuge of monarchs in want of thrones—she wouldn't know herself without her *rois en exil*. The exile is agreeable and soothing, the gondola lets them down gently. Its movement is an anodyne, its silence a philtre, and little by little it rocks all ambitions to sleep. The proscript has plenty of leisure to write his proclamations and even his memoirs, and I believe he has organs in which they are published; but the only noise he makes in the world is the harmless splash of his oars. He comes and goes along the Canalazzo, and he might be much worse employed. He is but one of the interesting objects it presents, however, and I am by no means sure that he is the most striking. He has a rival, if not in the iron bridge, which, alas, is within our range, at least—to take an immediate example—in the Montecuculi Palace. Far-descended and weary, but beautiful in its crooked old age, with its lovely proportions, its delicate round arches, its carvings and its disks of marble, is the haunted Montecuculi. Those who have a kindness for Venetian gossip like to remember that it was once for a few months the property of Robert Browning, who, however, never lived in it, and who died in the splendid Rezzonico, the residence of his son and a wonderful cosmopolite "document," which, as it presents itself, in an admirable position, but a short way further down the Canal, we can almost see, in spite of the curve, from the window at which we stand. This great seventeenth-century pile, throwing itself upon the water with a peculiar florid assurance, a certain upward toss of its cornice which gives it the air of a rearing sea-horse, decorates immensely—and within, as well as without—the wide angle that it commands.

There is a more formal greatness in the high square Gothic Foscari, just below it, one of the noblest creations of the fifteenth century, a masterpiece of symmetry and majesty. Dedicated to-day to official uses—it is the property of the State—it looks conscious of the consideration it enjoys, and is one of the few great houses within our range whose old age strikes us as robust and painless. It is visibly "kept up"; perhaps it is kept up too much; perhaps I am wrong in thinking so well of it. These doubts and fears course rapidly through my mind—I am easily their victim when it is a question of architecture—as they are apt to do to-day, in Italy, almost anywhere, in the presence of the beautiful, of the desecrated or the neglected. We feel at such moments as if the eye of Mr. Ruskin were upon us; we grow nervous and lose our confidence. This makes me inevitably, in talking of Venice, seek a pusillanimous safety in the trivial and the obvious. I am on firm ground in rejoicing in the little garden directly opposite our windows—it is another proof that they really show us everything—and in feeling that the gardens of Venice would deserve a page to themselves. They are infinitely more numerous than the arriving stranger can suppose; they nestle with a charm all their own in the complications of most back-views. Some of them are exquisite, many are large, and even the scrappiest have an artful understanding, in the interest of colour, with the waterways that edge their foundations. On the small canals, in the hunt for amusement, they are the prettiest surprises of all. The tangle of plants and flowers crowds over the battered walls, the greenness makes an arrangement with the rosy sordid brick. Of all the reflected and liquefied things in Venice, and the number of these is countless, I think the lapping water loves them most. They are numerous on the Canalazzo, but wherever they occur they give a brush to the picture and in particular, it is easy to guess, give a sweetness to the house. Then the elements are complete—the trio of air and water and of things that grow. Venice without them would be too much a matter of the tides and the stones. Even the little trellises of the *traghetti* count charmingly as reminders, amid so much artifice, of the woodland nature of man. The vine-leaves, trained on horizontal poles, make a roof of chequered shade for the gondoliers and ferrymen, who doze there according to opportunity, or chatter or hail the approaching "fare." There is no "hum" in Venice, so that their voices travel far; they enter your windows and mingle even with your dreams. I beg the reader to believe that if I had time to go into everything, I would go into the *traghetti,* which have their manners and their morals, and which used to have their piety. This piety was always a *madonnina,* the protectress of the passage—a quaint figure of the Virgin with the red spark of a lamp at her feet. The lamps appear for the most part to have gone out, and the images doubtless have been sold for *bric-à-brac.* The ferrymen, for aught I know, are converted to Nihilism—a faith consistent happily with a good stroke of business. One of the figures has been left, however—the Madonnetta which gives its name to a *traghetto* near the Rialto. But this sweet survivor is a carven stone inserted ages ago in the corner of an old palace and doubtless difficult of removal. *Pazienza,* the day will come when so marketable a relic will also be extracted from its socket and purchased by the devouring American. I leave that expression, on second thought, standing; but I repent of it when I remember that it is a devouring American—a lady long resident in Venice and whose kindnesses all Venetians, as well as her country-people, know, who has rekindled some of the extinguished tapers, setting up especially the big brave Gothic shrine, of painted and gilded wood, which, on the top of its stout *palo* [stake], sheds its influence on the place of passage opposite the Salute.

If I may not go into those of the palaces this devious discourse has left behind, much less may I enter the great galleries of the Academy, which rears its blank wall, surmounted by the lion of St. Mark, well within sight of the windows at which we are still lingering. This wondrous temple of Venetian art—for all it promises little from without—overhangs, in a manner, the Grand Canal, but if we were so much as to cross its threshold we should wander beyond recall. It contains, in some of the most magnificent halls—where the ceilings have all the glory with which the imagination of Venice alone could over-arch a room—some of the noblest pictures in the world; and whether or not we go back to them on any particular occasion for another look, it is always a comfort to know that they are there, as the sense of them on the spot is a part of the furniture of the mind—the sense of them close at hand, behind every wall and under every cover, like the inevitable reverse of a medal, of the side exposed to the air that reflects, intensifies, completes the scene. In other words, as it was the inevitable destiny of Venice to be painted, and painted with passion, so the wide world of picture becomes, as we live there, and however much we go about our affairs, the constant habitation of our thoughts. The truth is, we are in it so uninterruptedly, at home and abroad, that there is scarcely a pressure upon us to seek it in one place more than in another. Choose your standpoint at random and trust the picture to come to you. This is manifestly why I have not, I find myself conscious, said more about the features of the Canalazzo which occupy the reach between the Salute and the position we have so obstinately taken up. It is still there before us, however, and the delightful little Palazzo Dario, intimately familiar to English and American travellers, picks itself out in the foreshortened brightness. The Dario is covered with the loveliest little marble plates and sculptured circles; it is made up of exquisite pieces—as if there had been only enough to make it small—so that it looks, in its extreme antiquity, a good deal like a house of cards that hold together by a tenure it would be fatal to touch. An old Venetian house dies hard indeed, and I should add that this delicate thing, with submission in every feature, continues to resist the contact of generations of lodgers. It is let out in floors (it used to be let as a whole) and in how many eager hands—for it is in great requisition—under how many fleeting dispensations have we not known and loved it? People are always writing in advance to secure it, as they are to secure the Jenkins's gondolier, and as the gondola passes we see strange faces at the windows—though it's ten to one we recognise them—and the millionth artist coming forth with his traps at the water-gate. The poor little patient Dario is one of the most flourishing booths at the fair.

The faces at the window look out at the great Sansovino—the splendid pile that is now occupied by the Prefect. I feel decidedly that I don't object as I ought to the palaces of the sixteenth and seventeenth centuries. Their pretensions impose upon me, and the imagination peoples them more freely than it can people the interiors of the prime. Was not moreover this masterpiece of Sansovino once occupied by the Venetian post-office, and thereby intimately connected with an ineffaceable first impression of the author of these remarks? He had arrived, wondering, palpitating, twenty-three years ago, after nightfall, and, the first thing on the morrow, had repaired to the post-office for his letters. They had been waiting a long time and were full of delayed interest, and he returned with them to the gondola and floated slowly down the Canal. The mixture, the rapture, the wonderful temple of the *poste restante,* the beautiful strangeness, all humanised by good news—the memory of this abides with him still, so that there always proceeds from the splendid water-front I speak of a certain secret appeal, something that seems to have been uttered first in the sonorous chambers of youth. Of course this association falls to the ground—or rather splashes into the water—if I am the victim of a confusion. *Was* the edifice in question twenty-three years ago the post-office, which has occupied since, for many a day, very much humbler quarters? I am afraid to take the proper steps for finding out, lest I should learn that during these years I have misdirected my emotion. A better reason for the sentiment, at any rate, is that such a great house has surely, in the high beauty of its tiers, a refinement of its own. They make one think of colosseums and aqueducts and bridges, and they constitute doubtless, in Venice, the most pardonable specimen of the imitative. I have even a timid kindness for the huge Pesaro, far down the Canal, whose main reproach, more even than the coarseness of its forms, is its swaggering size, its want of consideration for the general picture, which the early examples so reverently respect. The Pesaro is as far out of the frame as a modern hotel, and the Cornaro, close to it, oversteps almost equally the modesty of art. One more thing they and their kindred do, I must add, for which, unfortunately, we can patronise them less. They make even the most elaborate material civilisation of the present day seem woefully shrunken and *bourgeois,* for they simply—I allude to the biggest palaces—can't be lived in as they were intended to be. The modern tenant may take in all the magazines, but he bends not the bow of Achilles. He occupies the place, but he doesn't fill it, and he has guests from the neighbouring inns with ulsters and

Baedekers. We are far at the Pesaro, by the way, from our attaching window, and we take advantage of it to go in rather a melancholy mood to the end. The long straight vista from the Foscari to the Rialto, the great middle stretch of the Canal, contains, as the phrase is, a hundred objects of interest, but it contains most the bright oddity of its general Deluge air. In all these centuries it has never got over its resemblance to a flooded city; for some reason or other it is the only part of Venice in which the houses look as if the waters had overtaken them. Everywhere else they reckon with them—have chosen them; here alone the lapping seaway seems to confess itself an accident.

There are persons who hold this long, gay, shabby, spotty perspective, in which, with its immense field of confused reflection, the houses have infinite variety, the dullest expanse in Venice. It was not dull, we imagine, for Lord Byron, who lived in the midmost of the three Mocenigo palaces, where the writing-table is still shown at which he gave the rein to his passions. For other observers it is sufficiently enlivened by so delightful a creation as the Palazzo Loredan, once a masterpiece and at present the Municipio, not to speak of a variety of other immemorial bits whose beauty still has a degree of freshness. Some of the most touching relics of early Venice are here—for it was here she precariously clustered—peeping out of a submersion more pitiless than the sea. As we approach the Rialto indeed the picture falls off and a comparative commonness suffuses it. There is a wide paved walk on either side of the Canal, on which the waterman—and who in Venice is not a waterman?—is prone to seek repose. I speak of the summer days—it is the summer Venice that is the visible Venice. The big tarry barges are drawn up at the *fondamenta* [stone foundations], and the bare-legged boatmen, in faded blue cotton, lie asleep on the hot stones. If there were no colour anywhere else there would be enough in their tanned personalities. Half the low doorways open into the warm interior of waterside drinking-shops, and here and there, on the quay, beneath the bush that overhangs the door, there are rickety tables and chairs. Where in Venice is there not the amusement of character and of detail? The tone in this part is very vivid, and is largely that of the brown plebeian faces looking out of the patchy miscellaneous houses—the faces of fat undressed women and of other simple folk who are not aware that they enjoy, from balconies once doubtless patrician, a view the knowing ones of the earth come thousands of miles to envy them. The effect is enhanced by the tattered clothes hung to dry in the windows, by the sun-faded rags that flutter from the polished balustrades—these are ivory-smooth with time; and the whole scene profits by the general law that renders decadence and ruin in Venice more brilliant than any prosperity. Decay is in this extraordinary place golden in tint and misery *couleur de rose*. The gondolas of the correct people are unmitigated sable, but the poor market-boats from the islands are kaleidoscopic.

The Bridge of the Rialto is a name to conjure with, but, honestly speaking, it is scarcely the gem of the composition. There are of course two ways of taking it—from the water or from the upper passage, where its small shops and booths abound in Venetian character; but it mainly counts as a feature of the Canal when seen from the gondola or even from the awful *vaporetto*. The great curve of its single arch is much to be commended, especially when, coming from the direction of the railway-station, you see it frame with its sharp compass-line the perfect picture, the reach of the Canal on the other side. But the backs of the little shops make from the water a graceless collective hump, and the inside view is the diverting one. The big arch of the bridge—like the arches of all the bridges—is the waterman's friend in wet weather. The gondolas, when it rains, huddle beside the peopled barges, and the young ladies from the hotels, vaguely fidgeting, complain of the communication of insect life. Here indeed is a little of everything, and the jewellers of this celebrated precinct—they have their immemorial row—make almost as fine a show as the fruiterers. It is a universal market, and a fine place to study Venetian types. The produce of the islands is discharged there, and the fish-mongers announce their presence. All one's senses indeed are vigorously attacked; the whole place is violently hot and bright, all odorous and noisy. The churning of the screw of the *vaporetto* mingles with the other sounds—not indeed that this offensive note is confined to one part of the Canal. But just here the little piers of the resented steamer are particularly near together, and it seems somehow to be always kicking up the water. As we go further down we see it stopping exactly beneath the glorious windows of the Ca' d' Oro. It has chosen its position well, and who shall gainsay it for having put itself under the protection of the most romantic façade in Europe? The companionship of these objects is a symbol; it expresses supremely the present and the future of Venice. Perfect, in its prime, was the marble Ca' d' Oro, with the noble recesses of its *loggie* [balconies] but even then it probably never "met a want," like the successful *vaporetto*. If, however, we are not to go into the Museo Civico—the old Museo Correr, which rears a staring renovated front far down on the left, near the station, so also we must keep out of the great vexed question of steam on the Canalazzo, just as a while since we prudently kept out of the Accademia. These are expensive and complicated excursions. It is obvious that if the *vaporetti* have contributed to the ruin of the gondoliers, already hard pressed by fate, and to that of the palaces, whose foundations their waves undermine, and that if they have robbed the Grand Canal of the supreme distinction of its tranquillity, so on the other hand they have placed "rapid transit," in the New York phrase, in everybody's reach, and enabled everybody—save indeed those who wouldn't for the world—to rush about Venice as furiously as people rush about New York. The suitability of this consummation needn't be pointed out.

Even we ourselves, in the irresistible contagion, are going so fast now that we have only time to note in how clever and costly a fashion the Museo Civico, the old Fondaco dei Turchi, has been reconstructed and restored. It is a glare of white marble without, and a series of showy majestic halls within, where a thousand curious mementos and relics of old Venice are gathered and classified. Of its miscellaneous treasures I fear I may perhaps frivolously prefer the series of its remarkable living Longhis, an illustration of manners more copious than the celebrated Carpaccio, the two ladies with their little animals and their long sticks. Wonderful indeed to-day are the museums of Italy, where the renovations and the *belle ordon-*

nance [attractive arrangement] speak of funds apparently un-
limited, in spite of the fact that the numerous custodians
frankly look starved. What is the pecuniary source of all this
civic magnificence—it is shown in a hundred other ways—and
how do the Italian cities manage to acquit themselves of ex-
penses that would be formidable to communities richer and
doubtless less æsthetic? Who pays the bills for the expressive
statues alone, the general exuberance of sculpture, with which
every *piazzetta* of almost every village is patriotically decorated? Let us not seek an answer to the puzzling question, but
observe instead that we are passing the mouth of the populous
Canareggio, next widest of the water-ways, where the race of
Shylock abides, and at the corner of which the big colourless
church of San Geremia stands gracefully enough on guard.
The Canareggio, with its wide lateral footways and hump-
backed bridges, makes on the feast of St. John an admirable
noisy, tawdry theatre for one of the prettiest and the most
infantile of the Venetian processions.

The rest of the course is a reduced magnificence, in spite of
interesting bits, of the battered pomp of the Pesaro and the
Cornaro, of the recurrent memories of royalty in exile which
cluster about the Palazzo Vendramin Calergi, once the residence of the Comte de Chambord and still that of his half-
brother, in spite too of the big Papadopoli gardens, opposite the
station, the largest private grounds in Venice, but of which
Venice in general mainly gets the benefit in the usual form of
irrepressible greenery climbing over walls and nodding at water. The rococo church of the Scalzi is here, all marble and
malachite, all a cold, hard glitter and a costly, curly ugliness,
and here too, opposite, on the top of its high steps, is San
Simeone Profeta, I won't say immortalised, but unblushingly
misrepresented, by the perfidious Canaletto. I shall not stay to
unravel the mystery of this prosaic painter's malpractices; he
falsified without fancy, and as he apparently transposed at will
the objects he reproduced, one is never sure of the particular
view that may have constituted his subject. It would look exactly like such and such a place if almost everything were not
different. San Simeone Profeta appears to hang there upon the
wall; but it is on the wrong side of the Canal and the other

elements quite fail to correspond. One's confusion is the greater because one doesn't know that everything may not really have changed, even beyond all probability—though it's only in America that churches cross the street or the river—and the mixture of the recognisable and the different makes the ambiguity maddening, all the more that the painter is almost as attaching as he is bad. Thanks at any rate to the white church, domed, and porticoed, on the top of its steps, the traveller emerging for the first time upon the terrace of the railroad-station seems to have a Canaletto before him. He speedily discovers indeed even in the presence of this scene of the final accents of the Canalazzo—there is a charm in the old pink warehouses on thc hot *fondamenta*—that he has something much better. He looks up and down at the gathered gondolas; he has his surprise after all, his little first Venetian thrill; and as the terrace of the station ushers in these things we shall say no harm of it, though it is not lovely. It is the beginning of his experience, but it is the end of the Grand Canal.

[1892]

....

Two Old Houses and Three Young Women

There are times and places that come back yet again, but that, when the brooding tourist puts out his hand to them, meet it a little slowly, or even seem to recede a step, as if in slight fear of some liberty he may take. Surely they should know by this time that he is capable of taking none. He has his own way—he makes it all right. It now becomes just a part of the charming solicitation that it presents precisely a problem—that of *giving* the particular thing as much as possible without at the same time giving it, as we say, away. There are considerations, proprieties, a necessary indirectness—he must use, in short, a little art. No necessity, however, more than this, makes him warm to his work, and thus it is that, after all, he hangs his three pictures.

..... *i* ......

The evening that was to give me the first of them was by no means the first occasion of my asking myself if that inveterate "style" of which we talk so much be absolutely conditioned—in dear old Venice and elsewhere—on decrepitude. Is it the style that has brought about the decrepitude, or the decrepitude that has, as it were, intensified and consecrated the style? There is an ambiguity about it all that constantly haunts and beguiles. Dear old Venice has lost her complexion, her figure, her reputation, her self-respect; and yet, with it all, has so puzzlingly not lost a shred of her distinction. Perhaps indeed the case is simpler than it seems, for the poetry of misfortune is familiar to us all, whereas, in spite of a stroke here and there of some happy justice

that charms, we scarce find ourselves anywhere arrested by the
poetry of a run of luck. The misfortune of Venice being, accordingly, at every point, what we most touch, feel and see, we
end by assuming it to be of the essence of her dignity; a consequence, we become aware, by the way, sufficiently discouraging
to the general application or pretension of style, and all the more
that, to make the final felicity deep, the original greatness must
have been something tremendous. If it be the ruins that are noble we have known plenty that were not, and moreover there are
degrees and varieties; certain monuments, solid survivals, hold
up their heads and decline to ask for a grain of your pity. Well,
one knows of course when to keep one's pity to oneself; yet one
clings, even in the face of the colder stare, to one's prized Venetian privilege of making the sense of doom and decay a part
of every impression. Cheerful work, it may be said of course; and
it is doubtless only in Venice that you gain more by such a trick
than you lose. What was most beautiful is gone; what was next
most beautiful is, thank goodness, going—that, I think, is the
monstrous description of the better part of your thought. Is it
really your fault if the place makes you want so desperately to
read history into everything?

You do that wherever you turn and wherever you look, and
you do it, I should say, most of all at night. It comes to you there
with longer knowledge, and with all deference to what flushes
and shimmers, that the night is the real time. It perhaps even
wouldn't take much to make you award the palm to the nights
of winter. This is certainly true for the form of progression that
is most characteristic, for every question of departure and arrival
by gondola. The little closed cabin of this perfect vehicle, the
movement, the darkness and the plash, the indistinguishable
swerves and twists, all the things you don't see and all the things
you do feel—each dim recognition and obscure arrest is a possible throb of your sense of being floated to your doom, even
when the truth is simply and sociably that you are going out to
tea. Nowhere else is anything as innocent so mysterious, nor
anything as mysterious so pleasantly deterrent to protest. These
are the moments when you are most daringly Venetian, most
content to leave cheap trippers and other aliens the high light of
the mid-lagoon and the pursuit of pink and gold. The splendid

day is good enough for *them;* what is best for you is to stop at last, as you are now stopping, among clustered *pali* [poles] and softly-shifting poops and prows, at a great flight of water-steps that play their admirable part in the general effect of a great entrance. The high doors stand open from them to the paved chamber of a basement tremendously tall and not vulgarly lighted, from which, in turn, mounts the slow stone staircase that draws you further on. The great point is, that if you are worthy of this impression at all, there isn't a single item of it of which the association isn't noble. Hold to it fast that there is no other such dignity of arrival as arrival by water. Hold to it that to float and slacken and gently bump, to creep out of the low, dark *felze* [gondola cabin] and make the few guided movements and find the strong crooked and offered arm, and then, beneath lighted palace-windows, pass up the few damp steps on the precautionary carpet—hold to it that these things constitute a preparation of which the only defect is that it may sometimes perhaps really prepare too much. It's so stately that what can come after?—it's so good in itself that what, upstairs, as we comparative vulgarians say, can be better? Hold to it, at any rate, that if a lady, in especial, scrambles out of a carriage, tumbles out of a cab, flops out of a tram-car, and hurtles, projectile-like, out of a "lightning-elevator," she alights from the Venetian conveyance as Cleopatra may have stepped from her barge. Upstairs—whatever may be yet in store for her—her entrance shall still advantageously enjoy the support most opposed to the "momentum" acquired. The beauty of the matter has been in the absence of all momentum—elsewhere so scientifically applied to us, from behind, by the terrible life of our day—and in the fact that, as the elements of slowness, the felicities of deliberation, doubtless thus all hang together, the last of calculable dangers is to enter a great Venetian room with a rush.

Not the least happy note, therefore, of the picture I am trying to frame is that there was absolutely no rushing; not only in the sense of a scramble over marble floors, but, by reason of something dissuasive and distributive in the very air of the place, a suggestion, under the fine old ceilings and among types of face and figure abounding in the unexpected, that here were many things to consider. Perhaps the simplest rendering of a scene into

the depths of which there are good grounds of discretion for not
sinking would be just this emphasis on the value of the unexpected for such occasions—with due qualification, naturally, of
its degree. Unexpectedness pure and simple, it is needless to say,
may easily endanger any social gathering, and I hasten to add
moreover that the figures and faces I speak of were probably not
in the least unexpected to each other. The stage they occupied
was a stage of variety—Venice has ever been a garden of strange
social flowers. It is only as reflected in the consciousness of the
visitor from afar—brooding tourist even call him, or sharp-eyed
bird on the branch—that I attempt to give you the little drama;
beginning with the felicity that most appealed to him, the visible, unmistakable fact that he was the only representative of his
class. The whole of the rest of the business was but what he saw
and felt and fancied—what he was to remember and what he
was to forget. Through it all, I may say distinctly, he clung to his
great Venetian clue—the explanation of everything by the historic idea. It was a high historic house, with such a quantity of
recorded past twinkling in the multitudinous candles that one
grasped at the idea of something waning and displaced, and
might even fondly and secretly nurse the conceit that what one
was having was just the very last. Wasn't it certainly, for instance, no mere illusion that there is no appreciable future left
for such manners—an urbanity so comprehensive, a form so
transmitted, as those of such a hostess and such a host? The future is for a different conception of the graceful altogether—so
far as it's for a conception of the graceful at all. Into that com-
putation I shall not attempt to enter; but these representative
products of an antique culture, at least, and one of which the
secret seems more likely than not to be lost, were not common,
nor indeed was any one else—in the circle to which the picture
most insisted on restricting itself.

Neither, on the other hand, was any one either very beautiful
or very fresh: which was again, exactly, a precious "value" on an
occasion that was to shine most, to the imagination, by the complexity of its references. Such old, old women with such old, old
jewels; such ugly, ugly ones with such handsome, becoming
names; such battered, fatigued gentlemen with such inscrutable
decorations; such an absence of youth, for the most part, in either

sex—of the pink and white, the "bud" of new worlds; such a
general personal air, in fine, of being the worse for a good deal
of wear in various old ones. It was not a society—that was
clear—in which little girls and boys set the tune; and there was
that about it all that might well have cast a shadow on the path
of even the most successful little girl. Yet also—let me not be
rudely inexact—it was in honour of youth and freshness that we
had all been convened. The *fiançailles* [betrothal] of the last—
unless it were the last but one—unmarried daughter of the
house had just been brought to a proper climax; the contract had
been signed, the betrothal rounded off—I'm not sure that the
civil marriage hadn't, that day, taken place. The occasion then
had in fact the most charming of heroines and the most ingenuous of heroes, a young man, the latter, all happily suffused with
a fair Austrian blush. The young lady had had, besides other
more or less shining recent ancestors, a very famous paternal
grandmother, who had played a great part in the political history of her time and whose portrait, in the taste and dress of
1830, was conspicuous in one of the rooms. The granddaughter
of this celebrity, of royal race, was strikingly like her and, by a
fortunate stroke, had been habited, combed, curled in a manner
exactly to reproduce the portrait. These things were charming
and amusing, as indeed were several other things besides. The
great Venetian beauty of our period was there, and nature had
equipped the great Venetian beauty for her part with the prop-
erest sense of the suitable, or in any case with a splendid generosity—since on the ideally suitable *character* of so brave a
human symbol who shall have the last word? This responsible
agent was at all events the beauty in the world about whom
probably, most, the absence of question (an absence never
wholly propitious) would a little smugly and monotonously
flourish: the one thing wanting to the interest she inspired was
thus the possibility of ever discussing it. There were plenty of
suggestive subjects round about, on the other hand, as to which
the exchange of ideas would by no means necessarily have
dropped. You profit to the full at such times by all the old voices,
echoes, images—by that element of the history of Venice which
represents all Europe as having at one time and another revelled
or rested, asked for pleasure or for patience there; which gives

you the place supremely as the refuge of endless strange secrets, broken fortunes and wounded hearts.

····· *i i* . ······

There had been, on lines of further or different speculation, a young Englishman to luncheon, and the young Englishman had proved "sympathetic"; so that when it was a question afterwards of some of the more hidden treasures, the browner depths of the old churches, the case became one for mutual guidance and gratitude—for a small afternoon tour and the wait of a pair of friends in the warm little *campi,* at locked doors for which the nearest urchin had scurried off to fetch the keeper of the key. There are few brown depths to-day into which the light of the hotels doesn't shine, and few hidden treasures about which pages enough, doubtless, haven't already been printed: my business, accordingly, let me hasten to say, is not now with the fond renewal of any discovery—at least in the order of impressions most usual. Your discovery may be, for that matter, renewed every week; the only essential is the good luck—which a fair amount of practice has taught you to count upon—of not finding, for the particular occasion, other discoverers in the field. Then, in the quiet corner, with the closed door—then in the presence of the picture and of your companion's sensible emotion—not only the original happy moment, but everything else, is renewed. Yet once again it can all come back. The old *custode,* shuffling about in the dimness, jerks away, to make sure of his tip, the old curtain that isn't much more modern than the wonderful work itself. He does his best to create light where light can never be; but you have your practised groping gaze, and in guiding the young eyes of your less confident associate, moreover, you feel you possess the treasure. These are the most refined pleasures that Venice has still to give, these odd happy passages of communication and response.

But the point of my reminiscence is that there were other communications that day, as there were certainly other responses. I have forgotten exactly what it was we were looking for—without much success—when we met the three Sisters. Nothing requires more care, as a long knowledge of Venice works in, than not to lose the useful faculty of getting lost. I had so successfully done my best to preserve it that I could at that moment conscientiously profess an absence of any suspicion of where we might be. It proved enough that, wherever we were, we were where the three sisters found us. This was on a little bridge near a big *campo,* and a part of the charm of the matter was the theory that it was very much out of the way. They took us promptly in hand—they were only walking over to San Marco to match some coloured wool for the manufacture of such belated cushions as still bloom with purple and green in the long leisures of old palaces; and that mild errand could easily open a parenthesis. The obscure church we had feebly imagined we were looking for proved, if I am not mistaken, that of the sisters' parish; as to which I have but a confused recollection of a large grey void and of admiring for the first time a fine work of art of which I have now quite lost the identity. This was the effect of the charming beneficence of the three sisters, who presently were to give our adventure a turn in the emotion of which everything that had preceded seemed as nothing. It actually strikes me even as a little dim to have been told by them, as we all fared together, that a certain low, wide house, in a small square as to which I found myself without particular association, had been in the far-off time the residence of George Sand. And yet this was a fact that, though I could then only feel it must be for another day, would in a different connection have set me richly reconstructing.

Madame Sand's famous Venetian year has been of late immensely in the air—a tub of soiled linen which the muse of history, rolling her sleeves well up, has not even yet quite ceased energetically and publicly to wash. The house in question must have been the house to which the wonderful lady betook herself when, in 1834, after the dramatic exit of Alfred de Musset, she enjoyed that remarkable period of rest and refreshment with the so long silent, the but recently rediscovered, reported, extinguished, Doctor Pagello.* As an old Sandist—not exactly indeed of the *première heure,* but of the fine

* Pietro Pagello (1807–1898) succeeded Alfred de Musset (1810–1857) as George Sand's (1804–1876) lover. James was an avid reader of a series of recent books on the subject.

high noon and golden afternoon of the great career—I had been, though I confess too inactively, curious as to a few points in the topography of the eminent adventure to which I here allude; but had never got beyond the little public fact, in itself always a bit of a thrill to the Sandist, that the present Hotel Danieli had been the scene of its first remarkable stages. I am not sure indeed that the curiosity I speak of has not at last, in my breast, yielded to another form of wonderment—truly to the rather rueful question of why we have so continued to concern ourselves, and why the fond observer of the footprints of genius is likely so to continue attentive to an altercation neither in itself and in its day, nor in its preserved and attested records, at all positively edifying. The answer to such an inquiry would doubtless reward patience, but I fear we can now glance at its possibilities only long enough to say that interesting persons—so they be of a sufficiently approved and established interest—render in some degree interesting whatever happens to them, and give it an importance even when very little else (as in the case I refer to) may have operated to give it a dignity. Which is where I leave the issue of further identifications.

For the three sisters, in the kindest way in the world, had asked us if we already knew their sequestered home and whether, in case we didn't, we should be at all amused to see it. My own acquaintance with them, though not of recent origin, had hitherto lacked this enhancement, at which we both now grasped with the full instinct, indescribable enough, of what it was likely to give. But how, for that matter, either, can I find the right expression of what was to remain with us of this episode? It is the fault of the sad-eyed old witch of Venice that she so easily puts more into things that can pass under the common names that do for them elsewhere. Too much for a rough sketch was to be seen and felt in the home of the three sisters, and in the delightful and slightly pathetic deviation of their doing us so simply and freely the honours of it. What was most immediately marked was their resigned cosmopolite state, the effacement of old conventional lines by foreign contact and example; by the action, too, of causes full of a special interest, but not to be emphasised perhaps—granted indeed they be named at all—without a certain sadness of sympathy. If "style," in Venice, sits among ruins, let us always lighten our tread when we pay her a visit.

Our steps were in fact, I am happy to think, almost soft enough for a death-chamber as we stood in the big, vague *sala* of the three sisters, spectators of their simplified state and their beautiful blighted rooms, the memories, the portraits, the shrunken relics of nine Doges. If I wanted a first chapter it was here made to my hand; the painter of life and manners, as he glanced about, could only sigh—as he so frequently has to— over the vision of so much more truth than he can use. What on earth is the need to "invent," in the midst of tragedy and comedy that never cease? Why, with the subject itself, all round, so inimitable, condemn the picture to the silliness of trying not to be aware of it? The charming lonely girls, carrying so simply their great name and fallen fortunes, the de-spoiled *decaduta* [impoverished] house, the unfailing Italian grace, the space so out of scale with actual needs, the absence of books, the presence of ennui, the sense of the length of the hours and the shortness of everything else—all this was a matter not only for a second chapter and a third, but for a whole volume, a *dénoûment* and a sequel.

This time, unmistakably, it *was* the last—Wordsworth's stately "shade of that which once was great";* and it was almost as if our distinguished young friends had consented to pass away slowly in order to treat us to the vision. Ends are only ends in truth, for the painter of pictures, when they are more or less conscious and prolonged. One of the sisters had been to London, whence she had brought back the impression of having seen at the British Museum a room exclusively filled with books and documents devoted to the commemoration of her family. She must also then have encountered at the National Gallery the exquisite specimen of an early Venetian master in which one of her ancestors, then head of the State, kneels with so sweet a dignity before the Virgin and Child. She was perhaps old enough, none the less, to have seen this precious work taken down from the wall of the room in which we

* From "On the Extinction of the Venetian Republic" (1807).

sat and—on terms so far too easy—carried away for ever; and not too young, at all events, to have been present, now and then, when her candid elders, enlightened too late as to what their sacrifice might really have done for them, looked at each other with the pale hush of the irreparable. We let ourselves note that these were matters to put a great deal of old, old history into sweet young Venetian faces.

····· *iii.* ·······

In Italy, if we come to that, this particular appearance is far from being only in the streets, where we are apt most to observe it—in countenances caught as we pass and in the objects marked by the guide-books with their respective stellar allowances. It is behind the walls of the houses that old, old history is thick and that the multiplied stars of Baedeker might often best find their application. The feast of St. John the Baptist is the feast of the year in Florence, and it seemed to me on that night that I could have scattered about me a handful of these signs. I had the pleasure of spending a couple of hours on a signal high terrace that overlooks the Arno, as well as in the galleries that open out to it, where I met more than ever the pleasant curious question of the disparity between the old conditions and the new manners. Make our manners, we moderns, as good as we can, there is still no getting over it that they are not good enough for many of the great places. This was one of those scenes, and its greatness came out to the full into the hot Florentine evening, in which the pink and golden fires of the pyrotechnics arranged on Ponte Carraja—the occasion of our assembly—lighted up the large issue. The "good people" beneath were a huge, hot, gentle, happy family; the fireworks on the bridge, kindling river as well as sky, were delicate and charming; the terrace connected the two wings that give bravery to the front of the palace, and the close-hung pictures in the rooms, open in a long series, offered to a lover of quiet perambulation an alternative hard to resist.

Wherever he stood—on the broad loggia, in the cluster of company, among bland ejaculations and liquefied ices, or in the presence of the mixed masters that led him from wall to wall—such a seeker for the spirit of each occasion could only turn it over that in the first place this was an intenser, finer little Florence than ever, and that in the second the testimony was again wonderful to former fashions and ideas. What did they do, in the other time, the time of so much smaller a society, smaller and fewer fortunes, more taste perhaps as to some particulars, but fewer tastes, at any rate, and fewer habits and wants—what did they do with chambers so multitudinous and so vast? Put their "state" at its highest—and we know of many ways in which it must have broken down—how did they live in them without the aid of variety? How did they, in minor communities in which every one knew every one, and every one's impression and effect had been long, as we say, discounted, find representation and emulation sufficiently amusing? Much of the charm of thinking of it, however, is doubtless that we are not able to say. This leaves us with the conviction that does them most honour: the old generations built and arranged greatly for the simple reason that they liked it, and they could bore themselves—to say nothing of each other, when it came to that—better in noble conditions than in mean ones.

It was not, I must add, of the far-away Florentine age that I most thought, but of periods more recent and of which the sound and beautiful house more directly spoke. If one had always been homesick for the Arno-side of the seventeenth and eighteenth centuries, here was a chance, and a better one than ever, to taste again of the cup. Many of the pictures—there was a charming quarter of an hour when I had them to myself— were bad enough to have passed for good in those delightful years. Shades of Grand-Dukes encompassed me—Dukes of the pleasant later sort who weren't really grand. There was still the sense of having come too late—yet not too late, after all, for this glimpse and this dream. My business was to people the place— its own business had never been to save us the trouble of understanding it. And then the deepest spell of all was perhaps that just here I was supremely out of the way of the so terribly actual Florentine question. This, as all the world knows, is a battle-ground, to-day, in many journals, with all Italy practically pulling on one side and all England, America and Germany pulling on the other: I speak of course of the more or less

articulate opinion. The "improvement," the rectification of Florence is in the air, and the problem of the particular ways in
which, given such desperately delicate cases, these matters
should be understood. The little treasure-city is, if there ever
was one, a delicate case—more delicate perhaps than any other
in the world save that of our taking on ourselves to persuade
the Italians that they mayn't do as they like with their own.
They so absolutely may that I profess I see no happy issue from
the fight. It will take more tact than our combined tactful
genius may at all probably muster to convince them that their
own is, by an ingenious logic, much rather *ours*. It will take
more subtlety still to muster for them that truly dazzling show
of examples from which they may learn that what in general is
"ours" shall appear to them as a rule a sacrifice to beauty and
a triumph of taste. The situation, to the truly analytic mind,
offers in short, to perfection, all the elements of despair; and I
am afraid that if I hung back, at the Corsini palace, to woo
illusions and invoke the irrelevant, it was because I could think,
in the conditions, of no better way to meet the acute responsibility of the critic than just to shirk it.

   [1899]

Casa Alvisi

Invited to "introduce" certain pages of cordial and faithful reminiscence from another hand,* in which a frankly predominant presence seems to live again, I undertook that office with an interest inevitably somewhat sad—so passed and gone today is so much of the life suggested. Those who fortunately knew Mrs. Bronson will read into her notes still more of it— more of her subject, more of herself too, and of many things— than she gives, and some may well even feel tempted to do for her what she has done here for her distinguished friend. In Venice, during a long period, for many pilgrims, Mrs. Arthur Bronson, originally of New York, was, so far as society, hospitality, a charming personal welcome were concerned, almost in sole possession; she had become there, with time, quite the prime representative of those private amenities which the Anglo-Saxon abroad is apt to miss just in proportion as the place visited is publicly wonderful, and in which he therefore finds a value twice as great as at home. Mrs. Bronson really earned in this way the gratitude of mingled generations and races. She sat for twenty years at the wide mouth, as it were, of the Grand Canal, holding out her hand, with endless good-nature, patience, charity, to all decently accredited petitioners, the incessant troop of those either bewilderedly making or fondly renewing acquaintance with the dazzling city.

Casa Alvisi is directly opposite the high, broad-based florid church of S. Maria della Salute—so directly that from the bal-

* "Browning in Venice," being Recollections of the late Katharine De Kay Bronson, with a Prefatory Note by H. J. (*Cornhill Magazine,* February 1902). [James's footnote.]

cony over the water-entrance your eye, crossing the canal, seems
to find the key-hole of the great door right in a line with it; and
there was something in this position that for the time made all
Venice-lovers think of the genial *padrona* as thus levying in the
most convenient way the toll of curiosity and sympathy. Every
one passed, every one was seen to pass, and few were those not
seen to stop and to return. The most generous of hostesses died
a year ago at Florence; her house knows her no more—it had
ceased to do so for some time before her death; and the long,
pleased procession—the charmed arrivals, the happy sojourns at
anchor, the reluctant departures that made Ca' Alvisi, as was
currently said, a social *porto di mare* [haven]—is, for remembrance and regret, already a possession of ghosts; so that, on the
spot, at present, the attention ruefully averts itself from the dear
little old faded but once familiarly bright façade, overtaken at
last by the comparatively vulgar uses that are doing their best to
"paint out" in Venice, right and left, by staring signs and other
vulgarities, the immemorial note of distinction. The house, in a
city of palaces, was small, but the tenant clung to her perfect, her
inclusive position—the one right place that gave her a better
command, as it were, than a better house obtained by a harder
compromise; not being fond, moreover, of spacious halls and
massive treasures, but of compact and familiar rooms, in which
her remarkable accumulation of minute and delicate Venetian
objects could show. She adored—in the way of the Venetian, to
which all her taste addressed itself—the small, the domestic and
the exquisite; so that she would have given a Tintoretto or two,
I think, without difficulty, for a cabinet of tiny gilded glasses or
a dinner-service of the right old silver.

The general receptacle of these multiplied treasures played
at any rate, through the years, the part of a friendly private-box
at the constant operatic show, a box at the best point of the best
tier, with the cushioned ledge of its front raking the whole
scene and with its withdrawing rooms behind for more detached conversation; for easy—when not indeed slightly difficult—polyglot talk, artful *bibite* [drinks], artful cigarettes too,
straight from the hand of the hostess, who could do all that
belonged to a hostess, place people in relation and keep them
so, take up and put down the topic, cause delicate tobacco and

little gilded glasses to circulate, without ever leaving her sofa-cushions or intermitting her good-nature. She exercised in these conditions, with never a block, as we say in London, in the traffic, with never an admission, an acceptance of the least social complication, her positive genius for easy interest, easy sympathy, easy friendship. It was as if, at last, she had taken the human race at large, quite irrespective of geography, for her neighbours, with neighbourly relations as a matter of course. These things, on her part, had at all events the greater appearance of ease from their having found to their purpose—and as if the very air of Venice produced them—a cluster of forms so light and immediate, so pre-established by picturesque custom. The old bright tradition, the wonderful Venetian legend had appealed to her from the first, closing round her house and her well-plashed water-steps, where the waiting gondolas were thick, quite as if, actually, the ghost of the defunct Carnival—since I have spoken of ghosts—still played some haunting part.

Let me add, at the same time, that Mrs. Bronson's social facility, which was really her great refuge from importunity, a defence with serious thought and serious feeling quietly cherished behind it, had its discriminations as well as its inveteracies, and that the most marked of all these, perhaps, was her attachment to Robert Browning. Nothing in all her beneficent life had probably made her happier than to have found herself able to minister, each year, with the returning autumn, to his pleasure and comfort. Attached to Ca' Alvisi, on the land side, is a somewhat melancholy old section of a Giustiniani palace, which she had annexed to her own premises mainly for the purpose of placing it, in comfortable guise, at the service of her friends. She liked, as she professed, when they were the real thing, to have them under her hand; and here succeeded each other, through the years, the company of the privileged and the more closely domesticated, who liked, harmlessly, to distinguish between themselves and outsiders. Among visitors partaking of this pleasant provision Mr. Browning was of course easily first. But I must leave her own pen to show him as her best years knew him. The point was, meanwhile, that if her charity was great even for the outsider, this was by reason of the inner essence of it—her perfect tenderness for Venice, which she always recognised as a link. That was the true principle of fusion, the key to communication. She communicated in proportion—little or much, measuring it as she felt people more responsive or less so; and she expressed herself, or in other words her full affection for the place, only to those who had most of the same sentiment. The rich and interesting form in which she found it in Browning may well be imagined—together with the quite independent quantity of the genial at large that she also found; but I am not sure that his favour was not primarily based on his paid tribute of such things as "Two in a Gondola" and "A Toccata of Galuppi." He had more ineffaceably than any one recorded his initiation from of old.

She was thus, all round, supremely faithful; yet it was perhaps after all with the very small fork, those to the manner born, that she made the easiest terms. She loved, she had from the first enthusiastically adopted, the engaging Venetian people, whose virtues she found touching and their infirmities but such as appeal mainly to the sense of humour and the love of anecdote; and she befriended and admired, she studied and spoiled them. There must have been a multitude of whom it would scarce be too much to say that her long residence among them was their settled golden age. When I consider that they have lost her now I fairly wonder to what shifts they have been put and how long they may not have to wait for such another messenger of Providence. She cultivated their dialect, she renewed their boats, she piously relighted—at the top of the tide-washed *pali* of traghetto or lagoon—the neglected lamp of the tutelary Madonnetta; she took cognisance of the wives, the children, the accidents, the troubles, as to which she became, perceptibly, the most prompt, the established remedy. On lines where the amusement was happily less one-sided she put together in dialect many short comedies, dramatic proverbs, which, with one of her drawing-rooms permanently arranged as a charming diminutive theatre, she caused to be performed by the young persons of her circle—often, when the case lent itself, by the wonderful small offspring of humbler friends, children of the Venetian lower class, whose aptitude, teachability, drollery, were her constant delight. It was certainly true that an impression of Venice as humanly sweet might easily found itself on the frankness and quickness and amiability of these little people. They were at least so much to the good; for the philosophy of their patroness was as Venetian as everything else; helping her to accept experience without bitterness and to remain fresh, even in the fatigue which finally overtook her, for pleasant surprises and proved sincerities. She was herself sincere to the last for the place of her predilection; inasmuch as though she had arranged herself, in the later time—and largely for the love of "Pippa Passes"*—an alternative refuge at Asolo, she absented herself from Venice with continuity only under coercion of illness.

At Asolo, periodically, the link with Browning was more confirmed than weakened, and there, in old Venetian territory, and with the invasion of visitors comparatively checked, her preferentially small house became again a setting for the pleasure of talk and the sense of Italy. It contained again its own small treasures, all in the pleasant key of the homelier Venetian spirit. The plain beneath it stretched away like a purple sea from the lower cliffs of the hills, and the white *campanili* [bell towers] of the villages, as one was perpetually saying, showed on the expanse like scattered sails of ships. The rumbling carriage, the old-time, rattling, red-velveted carriage of provincial, rural Italy, delightful and quaint, did the office of the gondola; to Bassano, to Treviso, to high-walled Castelfranco, all pink and gold, the home of the great Giorgione. Here also memories cluster; but it is in Venice again that her vanished presence is most felt, for there, in the real, or certainly the finer, the more sifted Cosmopolis, it falls into its place among the others evoked, those of the past seekers of poetry and dispensers of romance. It is a fact that almost every one interesting, appealing, melancholy, memorable, odd, seems at one time or another, after many days and much life, to have gravitated to Venice by a happy instinct, settling in it and treating it, cherishing it, as a sort of repository of consolations; all of which to-day, for the conscious mind, is mixed with its air and constitutes its unwritten history. The deposed, the defeated, the disenchanted, the

* Robert Browning's dramatic poem (1846) set in Asolo.

wounded, or even only the bored, have seemed to find there something that no other place could give. But such people came for themselves, as we seem to see them—only with the egotism of their grievances and the vanity of their hopes. Mrs. Bronson's case was beautifully different—she had come altogether for others.

[1902]

Rome

•

L*etters*

....

To William James, 10/30/1869. Hotel d'Angleterre, Rome: Here I am then in the Eternal City. It was easy to leave Florence; the cold had become intolerable & the rain perpetual. I started last night, & at 10½ o'clock & after a bleak & fatiguing journey of twelve hours found myself here with the morning light. . . . From midday to dusk I have been roaming the streets. . . . At last—for the first time—I live! It beats everything: it leaves the Rome of your fancy—your education—nowhere. It makes Venice—Florence—Oxford—London—seem like little cities of pasteboard. I went reeling & moaning thro' the streets, in a fever of enjoyment. In the course of four or five hours I traversed almost the whole of Rome & got a glimpse of everything—the Forum, the Coliseum (stupendissimo!), the Pantheon, the Capitol, St. Peter's, the Column of Trajan, the Castle of St. Angelo—all the Piazzas & ruins & monuments. The effect is something indescribable. For the first time I know what the picturesque is.—In St. Peter's I stayed some time. It's even beyond its reputation. It was filled with foreign ecclesiastics—great armies encamped in prayer on the marble plains of its pavement—an inexhaustible physiognomical study. To crown my day, on my way home, I met his Holiness in person—driving in prodigious purple state—sitting dim within the shadows of his coach with two uplifted benedictory fingers—like some dusky Hindoo idol in the depths of its shrine. Even if I should leave Rome tonight I should feel that I have caught the keynote of its operations on the senses. I have looked along the grassy vista of the Appian way & seen the topmost stone-work of the Coliseum sitting shrouded in the light of heaven, like the edge of an Alpine chain. I've trod the Forum & I have scaled the Capitol. I've seen the Tiber hurrying along, as swift & dirty as history! From the high tribune of a great chapel of St. Peter's I have heard in the papal choir a strange old man sing in a shrill unpleasant soprano. I've seen troops of little tonsured neophytes clad in scarlet, marching & countermarching & ducking & flopping, like poor little raw recruits for the heavenly host. In fine I've seen Rome, & I shall go to bed a wiser man than I last rose— yesterday morning.

To Alice James, 11/7/1869. Hotel de Rome: The excitement of the first hour has passed away & I have recovered the healthy mental equilibrium of the sober practical tourist. Nevertheless Rome is still Rome at the end of a week or rather is more thoroughly Rome than ever. . . . It seems a sadly vain ambition to attempt to give you any idea of its affect upon the mind. It's so vast, so heavy, so multitudinous that you seem to require all your energy simply to bear up against it. Your foremost feeling is that of your own ignorance. . . . It's a place in which you needn't in the least feel ashamed of a perpetual reference to *Murray:** a place in which you feel emphatically the value of *culture*. . . . In the morning I have regularly gone to the Vatican, & in the afternoon have strolled about at hazard. . . . In spite of an immense deal of dove-tailing and intermingling, Pagan & Christian Rome keeps tolerably distinct & the ancient city is a fact that you can appreciate more or less in its purity. Appreciate, but not express! No words can reproduce the eloquence of a Roman block of blunted marble or a mass of eternal brickwork. . . . Last Sunday, the Vatican being closed, I went down & had a long lounge in the Coliseum. The day was magnificent & the sun seemed to shine on purpose to illumine its crevices & set off its immensity. I climbed over the accessible portions of the summit & communed with the genius of the spot. . . . The Coliseum is a thing about which it's useless to talk: it must be seen & felt. But as a piece of the picturesque—a province of it—it is thoroughly & simply delightful. The grassy arena with its circle of tarnished shrines & praying

* The London publisher John Murray issued a popular series of travel guides.

strollers—the sky between the arches & above the oval—the weeds & flowers against the sky etc.—are as charming as anything in Rome. The next day in the afternoon I betook myself to the almost equal ruins of the Baths of Caracalla. It was the hour of sunset & I had them all to myself. They are a collection of perfectly mountainous masses of brickwork, to the right of the Appian Way. Even more than the Coloseum I think they give you a notion of the Roman *scale*. Imagine a good second class mountain in reduced circumstances—perforated & honeycombed by some terrestrial cataclysm—& you'll have an idea of these terrific ruins. Through a modern staircase in one of the columns I ascended to the roof (or what remains of it) & saw the Campagna bathed in the sunset. At this giddy elevation the effect is more mountainous than ever. The aged masonry seems all compacted & condensed into natural stratifications & a great wilderness of trees & thickets sits blooming over the abyss.—By far the most beautiful piece of ancientry in Rome is that simple & unutterable Pantheon to which I repeated my devotions yesterday afternoon. It makes you profoundly regret that you are not a pagan suckled in the creed outworn that produced it. It's the most conclusive example I have yet seen of the simple sublime. Imagine simply a vast cupola with its drum, set directly on the earth & fronted with a porch of columns & a triangular summit: the interior lighted by a hole in the apex of the cupola & the circumference furnished with a series of altars. The effect within is the very *delicacy* of grandeur—& more worshipful to my perception than the most mysterious & aspiring Gothic. St. Peter's, beside it, is absurdly vulgar. Taken absolutely however St. Peter's is extremely interesting—not quite so much so as it pretends to be—but quite enough so to give you a first class sensation. . . . You stand at the heart & centre of modern ecclesiasticism: you are watching the heartbeats of the church. The past week has been a season of great performances; but the combined absence of a dress-suit & an aversion to a crowd has prevented me from going to the Sistine Chapel, where the best of the fun has been going on. Before I leave Rome, however, I mean to get a glimpse. A glimpse indeed I had some three days since, when the Pope came in state to say mass at a church opposite this hotel. I made no

attempt to enter the church: but I saw tolerably well the arrival
of the cardinals & ambassadors etc & finally of the Gran Llama
in person. The whole spectacle was very handsome, but it was
precisely like a leaf out of the Middle-Ages. . . . Broadly, until
you've trod these glorious halls [of the Vatican] you don't know
what sculpture is. They are immense in content & crowded
with different specimens. . . . The innumerable busts & statues
of the Roman emperor hold a foremost place. I find a particular fascination in a magnificent statue of Augustus, excavated
only some five years since, in a marvelous state of preservation.
Also in a ravishing little bust of Augustus as a boy, as clear &
fresh in quality as if it dated from yesterday. . . . I saw yesterday at the Capitol the dying Gladiator, the Lydian Apollo, the
Amazon etc—all of them unspeakably simple & noble & eloquent of the breadth of human genius. . . . Out of the high
windows of the Vatican you get glimpses of all kinds of delicious Italian courts & gardens. You even surprise the secrets of
the papal household. I am sure I saw one of the pontifical
petticoats hanging out to dry. In the corridors & stairways you
likewise see the Swiss Guard—glorious medieval warriors clad
in splendid fantastic trappings of red & yellow. Indeed the
human picturesque in Rome is quite as rich as the architectural
. . . in the innumerable host of soldiers & priests—of whom
there is about an equal swarm. You may meet in any half
hour's walk a dozen as genuine squalid friars of the early
church—or a dozen pale ascetics of as good a quality—as the
imagination could possibly desire. . . . I have changed my hotel—much for the better. I suffered so from the cold in Florence that I made a point of taking a room *with sun*. . . . If I
were surer of my health & the duration of my stay I would take
a private room or a couple of them. Prices, this winter, however are so high in Rome. . . . Here, I live for about eighty
[francs a week]—dining to suit myself at a very good restaurant. It's not cheap—but for Rome, apparently (and for comfort) it's not dear.

To Grace Norton, 11/11/1869. Rome: I've been too perpetually
tired to take up a pen. After roaring through the city all day I
have generally in the evening collapsed into languor & stupe-

faction. . . . It's poor work writing from Rome, if you pretend in the least to write up to the level of your impressions. . . . I find Rome—*interesting:* I can't say more. In this quality it exceeds everything I have yet seen & falls not a whit below my preconceptions. Other places are pleasing, picturesque, pretty, charming; but Rome is thoroughly serious. Heaven knows its picturesque enough: but it has in this respect a depth of tone which makes it differ not only in degree but even in kind from Florence & Venice. . . . My mind swarms with *effects* of all kinds—to be introduced into realistic novels yet unwritten. . . . I came hither . . . by the night express. . . . After going to my hotel & a hasty 'wash' & breakfast I set myself loose on the city. It was decidedly one of the days of my life. I roamed about in every direction from noon till dusk & when I came home to dinner had pretty well taken the cream off of Rome. My senses being a great deal quickened by excitement I think that if I had been compelled to depart that evening I should have felt myself to have got a good . . . impression of the subject. . . . I *do* find Rome "*rubbishy*"—magnificently, sublimely so. Amid many of the heaps of rubbish I have lingered & gloated with the fondest fascination. I spent a long dreamy morning (besides various secondary visits) lounging & meandering & murmuring in the Coliseum; & an afternoon very much in the same fashion in the Baths of Caracalla. I enjoyed a magnificent lunch there, on the summit, quite by [my]self; & I think I never had quite so intimate a *tête à tête* with the glories of the past. We were literally face to face—& eye to eye. Another long sunny cloudy breezy morning at the Palace of the Caesars which (since you were here probably) has been under the auspices of Napoleon III excavated & revealed in the most wondrous manner. Much too have I loafed & lingered in the Forum. Two great long stares have I had at those *unutterably* manly sculptures which adorn the arch of Constantine. Few things tell so well the Roman tale. Decidedly I veto female suffrage. Again & again have I taken the measure of that noblest & simplest & sweetest of statues—the kind old Marcus Aurelius at the Capitol. It makes even Roman bronze mild & humane & pathetic. At the Pantheon I have said at least a dozen good round Pagan prayers. It seems to me *exquisitely* sublime & I don't believe I

shall ever get from architecture a purer cleaner sensation. As
for St. Peter's, I decidedly go in for it—tho' indeed as you
suggest I am extremely glad "it ain't no bigger." But it *is* big
without a doubt & furnishes the mind with a perfectly satisfactory standard & example of vastness. . . . The glorious whole
swallows up the inglorious parts & you get one rich transcendent effect. To the Vatican I have of course paid many visits &
almost feel as if I have seen a fair portion of it. Its richness &
interest are even greater than I supposed. The great things are
more numerous & greater. That there *are* such things is certainly a great comfort to the feeble conscientious mind. I had
finally got into a wretched muddle in the Florentine galleries
with regard to pictures & painters & my likes & dislikes. . . . I
have seen today one really great picture—one of those works
which draw heavily on your respect, & make you feel the richer
for the loss: the portrait of Innocent X, by Velasquez at the
Doria Palace. Also a Correggio—a mere sketch, but most divinely touched—& a glorious Claude which leaves Turner nowhere. . . . I do wish I could put into my poor pale words some
faint reflection of the color & beauty of this glorious old world,
but you have it all in memory.

To GRACE NORTON, 11/18/1869. ROME: But it is not only these
special marvels & localities that enchant my soul—it is all the
chance beauties & delights of one's wanderings here—the very
air & light & colour of the Roman landscape—the sky that
seems to reflect the unseen campagna—the great grassy waste
skirted with cement walls & dotted with lounging soldiers or a
wandering monk—the cypresses, the olives, the little pallid
stunted oaks—the silence & idleness of the scene—the perpetual presence of the past. . . . Did I say anything in my last letter
about the Sistine Chapel? Possibly I hadn't seen it. But I have
seen it now—& tho' I am not sure that I have learned anything
new about the reach of human genius I think I like M. A.* the
better for it. That is, the Last Judgment strikes me as being a
good deal of an error, but the ceiling, as ceilings go, is decidedly
great. . . . Rome as yet is by no means crowded—As if Rome

* Marcus Aurelius.

were ever anything else but crowded! "Crowded" is just the word. It's not the dear light atmosphere of Florence—but an air thick with the presence of invisible ghosts.

To Mrs. Henry James, Sr.,* 11/21/1869. Hotel de Rome: Mrs. Ward . . . arranged with me to accompany her to the Vesper Service (3 o'clock) at the little Church of St. Cecilia away over in the Trastevere. . . . The music & singing on this occasion draws great crowds & is most divinely beautiful. Much of it was immensely florid & profane in tone—as far at least as I could judge; but in spite of the crowded & fetid church & the revolt provoked in my mind by the spectacular catholicism (if you don't love it here, here in Rome you must hate it: there is no middle path) I truly enjoyed the performance. . . . I don't at all agree with the people who assume that Rome is the place to disgust & disenchant you with the Church. On the contrary, a faint impulse once received (an essential premise) Rome makes the rest of the journey all down-hill work. The sense you get here of the great collective Church must be far more potent than elsewhere to swallow up & efface all the vile & flagrant offenses to the soul & the senses. Once *in* the Church you can be perfectly indifferent to the debased & stultified priests & the grovelling peasantry: out of it you certainly can't. But enough on this chapter. There is a better Rome than all this—a Rome in the lingering emanation of whose genius & energy I have spent many a memorable hour. It makes all this modern ec-clesiasticism . . . seem sadly hollow & vulgar. The ruins & relics & chance wayside reminders of this ancient strength are far more numerous & absorbing that I supposed. You come upon them in some form at every step & when once encountered, they fix & fascinate the mind. . . . It's hard to say, however, what are the choicest spots. Each one at the moment seems richer in suggestion, more eloquent & thought-provoking than the last & you surrender yourself to the absolute spell of its melancholy charm. I betook myself one glorious morning a number of days since to the mighty Baths of Caracalla . . . & spent a long time alternately quaking among their damp cold

* Mary James (1810–1822), Henry James's mother.

shadows & roasting in the sunshine which floods their crumbling summits, as they gaze out across the Campagna. From there I went to certain *Columbaria* in the same quarter—a series of subterranean vaults recently discovered, in which the Romans *pigeon-holed* or deposited on small concave shelves the vases containing the ashes of their dead. They stand in a great sunny rubbishy Italian vineyard, whence you descend into the dead moist air & the dim mildewed light of these strange funeral wells. Few things transport you so forcibly into the past. . . . I took a drive along the Appian Way, as far as the tomb of Cecilia Metella. . . . The great violet Campagna . . . stretching its idle breadth to the horizon known of Roman eyes—a wilderness of sunny decay & vacancy. . . . I went into . . . that divine little protestant Cemetery where Shelley & Keats lie buried—a place most lovely & solemn & exquisitely full of the traditional Roman quality—with a vast grey pyramid inserted into the sky on one side & the dark cold cypresses on the other, & the light bursting out between them. . . . Another emotion of equal value was the fruit some three nights since of a moonlight visit to the Coliseum. I started off by myself on foot, about 8 o'clock, beneath a radiant evening sky. The Coliseum itself was all very well; but it was not that that repaid me, but my halt in the square before the Capitol, beneath the great transfigured statue of M[arcus]. Aurelius. . . . It massed itself up before me in the magical moonlight with a truly appalling reality. . . . At the Corsini Palace the other day I got myself let into the Gardens where I spent a delicious hour. I did the same at the Vatican & went strolling about the sunny terraces like a wicked old Cardinal.

To Henry James, Sr.,* 12/25/1872. 33 Via Gregorian, Rome: I came through in twenty-four hours to Turin, rested there a day; proceeded in another to Florence; spent a lovely day in that lovely place & came hither by day on the 24th. I have therefore been here but one complete day; long enough, however, to recognize Rome—& its changes. These are numer-

---

* The writer and Swedenborgian theologian, Henry James's father (1811–1882).

ous—almost painful; & consist not so much in special alterations as in a kind of modernized air in the streets, a multiplication of shops, carts, newspaper-stalls etc., & an obscuration of cardinals' carriages & general picturesqueness. It all promises me great pleasure, however, & I shan't prejudge. The vast sunshine is divine, & I walked about yesterday thinking my summer coat would be better on my back than in my trunk.

To WILLIAM JAMES, 1/8/1873. HOTEL DE ROME: What I find Rome & am likely to find it, it is hard to say in a few words. Much less simply & sensuously & satisfyingly picturesque than before, but on the whole immensely interesting. It is a strange jumble now of its old inalterable self & its new Italian assumptions—a most disturbing one for sentimentalists, such as generally all educated strangers are, here. It is an impossible modern city & will be a lugubrious modern capital, such as Victor Emmanuel is trying to make it. It has for this purpose both too many virtues & too many vices. It is too picturesque to spoil & too inconvenient to remedy. . . . But every now & then there come to you great gusts of largely-mingled delight such as no other place can give. Generally, what one feels & inhales, naturally & easily, with every breath, is the importunate presence of tradition of *every* kind—the influence of an atmosphere electrically charged with historic intimation & whisperings.

To MRS. HENRY JAMES, SR., 1/26/1873. ROME: Rain in Rome brings out the dirt as darkness does a photographer's negative, & makes the streets impassable to the fastidious. I am not fastidious, but I hankered for exercise & walked down the Corso to the Forum & thence to the mouldy Temple of Vesta by the Tiber & thence along to the Gate of St. Paul, the Pyramid of Caius Cestius and the Protestant Cemetery which holds Shelley & Keats so picturesquely. I don't recite these fine names to aggravate you, for I regard the places far less gushingly than when I was here before & they often seem to me so shabby & rubbishy, too stale & *exploités* to deserve another thought. Today, however, under a beautiful cool light, (in which the sun made warm enough shadows however), it was all picturesque enough & satisfactorily Roman.—The days are passing terribly fast, the daisies & wild flowers are already starring the colorless grass, & though in places you are cool without your overcoat you are everywhere over-warm with it.

TO ALICE JAMES, 2/10/1873. ROME: Rome doesn't amaze—it quietly, profoundly, intensely delights & satisfies. As the weeks pass by I find myself settling down to it, morally, with less & less reluctance & more & more devotion. It is partly the inevitable attachment one forms for any place one tries to *live* in . . . but chiefly of course the fact that taking bad & good together Rome abounds in interest & ever-varying charm. The first month I was here I was acutely homesick for the high civilization of Paris—especially in the evening, at the hour the theatres go in—when I groped homeward from my dinner through a narrow black alley lighted by a single lamp, in which, here & there, in a dusky caffé a lot of frugal Romans were huddled round a lot of empty tables. But there are compensations—& one by one I am learning them. I mingle enough in society to give a flavor of magnificence to my life—am moreover getting fond—which is the only footing on which you can acquire any sense of permanence here—of the very barbarisms & miseries & uncleanesses of Rome.

TO HENRY JAMES, SR., 3/28/1873. 101 CORSO, ROME: I have just changed my quarters. My hotel, with the increase of the mild weather, had become insufferably warm & suffocating; & living in one small room, especially at night, on the terms one has to be on with one's window in Rome, an uncomfortable affair. . . . No news—save that Rome grows every day more divine.

TO CHARLES ELIOT NORTON,* 3/31/1873. 101 CORSO, ROME: I am growing daily fonder of Rome, & Rome at this season is growing daily more loveable. My only complaint is of the climate, which takes a good deal more strength from you than it gives. But Rome with a *snap* in the air would not be Rome.

---

* A professor of art history at Harvard and editor of the *North American Review,* Norton (1827–1908) was an early influential supporter and friend of James.

To WILLIAM JAMES, 4/9/1873. 101 CORSO, ROME: When I first came & the winter gave it a certain freshness, I felt nothing but [Rome's] lovely mildness; but for the past eight or ten weeks I have been in a state of ineffable languefaction. The want of 'tone' in the air is altogether indescribable: it makes it mortally flat & dead & relaxing. The great point is that it is all excessively pleasant & you succumb to languor with a perfectly demoralized conscience. But it is languor (for me at least) . . . perpetual & irresistible. My struggles with sleep have been heroic, but utterly vain. . . . It seems to me that I have slept in these three months more than in my whole life beside. The soft divine, enchanting days of spring have of course made matters worse. . . . Of Rome itself, otherwise, I have grown very fond, in spite of the inevitable fits of distaste that one has here. . . . I often hanker for the high culture & high finish of Paris. . . . But the atmosphere is nevertheless weighted—to infinitude—with a something that forever stirs & feeds & fills the mind & makes the sentient being feel that on the whole he can lead as complete a life here as elsewhere.—Then there is the something— the myriad somethings—that one grows irresistably & tenderly fond of—the unanalysable *loveableness* of Italy.

To ALICE JAMES, 4/25/1873. ALBERGO DI PARIGI, ALBANO: I came hither three days since & behold me established at the top of this wondrous old ex-palazzo, now an inn, with two great windows sweeping the whole expanse of the mist-bathed Campagna. Mist-bathed is a flattering epithet; rain-washed would be true; for I have fallen upon evil weather & today promises ill. But I don't despair of getting a walk in this afternoon. This rural seclusion is a great change from life in Rome, which I see distinctly with all the domes & spires from the edge of the town. I felt that I should be the better for change of air. . . . Besides I wanted to see Albano. . . . It is in truth an enchanting spot. . . . The walks are innumerable, the views divine. Half an hour away is the Alban lake—hidden in the woody cup of the most exquisite rotundity; & half an hour thence the lake of Nemi, deep down in a smaller & boskier oval, & flanked with its little high-perched black-walled towns, Genzano & Nemi. All the roads hereabouts, plunge down on one side into the

Campagna which lies out as blue & vast & iridescent as the sea, or on the other into one of these little high-rimmed lakes; & they are all so grassy to the feet & bordered with such great arching greenery of twisted oak & stunted elm, & ilex & olive, & so haunted with throbbing nightingales & so adorned all along . . . with these dark little mouldy villages. . . . Rome, in all ways, has been growing more & more charming with the advance of the spring, which brings out its individuality with tenfold distinctness. Everything interesting, suggestive, pictur-esque seems to become a hundred times more intensely itself, in the atmosphere of April. The place is born again & your old resorts & walks put on a new fascination. The Villas (Doria, Borghese & Ludovici) become most strangely fair, & you can hardly keep out of them.

To Grace Norton, 7/17/1873. Homburg bei Frankfort: I think a great deal about Italy & seem to myself to love it better than anything in the world. Altogether why, I don't think I could say, but I believe that is always the case in a great *tendresse* [fondness]. . . . Rome is such an infernal compound of seduc-tions & repulsions.

To Elizabeth Boott,* 12/10/1873. 101 Corso, Rome: We came hither about a fortnight since, & owing to a good deal of troublesome delay in getting domiciled it is only lately that I am beginning to feel shaken down & settled. . . . I am back in the room I occupied last spring. They are excellent quarters & I am very comfortable. I had been some two months in Flo-rence when I left & [had] . . . grown so very fond of it that it was not at all easy to depart. If I had been alone, I am sure I should have staid, for there is something about the whole constitution & nature of Florence that suits me wonderfully well. I had drunk deep of Rome last winter, & was quite willing to let it serve for the present. . . . My winter here how-ever promises to be of a much tamer pattern than the last. . . .

---

* An American musician and painter, Elizabeth Boott (1846–1888) was James's longtime friend whom he visited regularly at her Bellosguardo (Florence) residence.

Rome itself is unchanged of course, & has been putting forth her characteristic charms through the lovely weather of the past fortnight. But I feel here always the importunate *muchness* of the place—all the memories & materials & elements which one can't assimilate & do justice to.

To Grace Norton, 1/14/1874. Florence: I have been jerked away from Rome, where I had been expecting to spend the winter, just as I was warming to the feast, & Florence, tho' very well in itself, doesn't go so far as it might as a substitute for Rome. It's like having a great plum-pudding set down on the table before you, & then seeing it whisked away & finding yourself served with wholesome tapioca. . . . I oughtn't to speak light words of Florence to you. . . . They are really words from my pen's end simply & not from my heart. I have an inextinguishable relish for Florence & now that I have been back here for a fortnight this early love is beginning to shake off timidly the ponderous shadow of Rome. But the truth is that when one has come to know Rome well & feel its vast & various charm, & depend on it for one's daily impression, it is impossible for any other human habitation not to seem pale & tame & meagre. I have never felt its charm more than during this past December. It was empty, the weather was divine. . . . One's wanderings in Rome, during the mild sunny afternoons of midwinter are a most prodigious intellectual dissipation. The whole place keeps playing such everlasting tunes on one's imagination.

To Grace Norton, 12/15/1877. Paris: I went directly to Rome some seven weeks since, & came directly back; but I spent a few days in Florence on my way down. Italy was still more her irresistible old self than ever, & getting away from Rome was really no joke. In spite of the "changes"—& they are very perceptible—the old enchantment of Rome, taking its own good time, steals over you & possesses you, till it becomes really almost a nuisance & an importunity. That is, it keeps you from working, from staying indoors, etc. To do those things in sufficient measure, one must live in an ugly country; & that is why, instead of lingering in that golden climate, I am going back to poor, smutty, dusky, Philistine London.

To Sarah Butler Wister, 10/7/1887. De Vere Gardens, London: I went abroad the 1st December last—& came back only at midsummer—spending all my time in Italy & dividing it only between Florence & Venice. I hadn't even a look at our unspeakable old Rome—& indeed I think it isn't "ours" any more. It has become unspeakable—not to say damnable. What I hear of the way it is pulled about undermines my interest & profanes my reminiscences—which were the most sacred things I possessed. The Villa Ludovici is devoured—that gives you the measure of the sort of thing. Besides, I went abroad in some hope of quieter days than one gets in London & I knew that Rome wasn't likely to give them to me. I am trying as hard to get out of society as many people try to get into it—or are supposed to. Fortunately it isn't really difficult from the moment one really endeavours. The trouble one is prepared to take is much greater than that the world is prepared to take to keep you. I spent between three or four months in Florence & upward of the same time in Venice; but it wasn't so very much to me that I was in either place as that I was in *Italy*. Thank heaven that charm still holds, & I think it always will, surviving the support given by religion, the domestic affections, the loss of fame, the hope of glory, the desire of fortune & various other squeezed oranges. I have always loved Florence tenderly, but it has a vulgar little vicinity which I don't love. . . . Venice is much more socially adulterated than Florence—one may possess one's soul there; & I adored it & came near taking a little cheap permanent pied a terre there (which was offered me) as an occasional asylum: but didn't—for all sorts of reasons—mainly the fear that if I had a link my love would turn to hate.

To Mr. & Mrs. William James, 5/28/1894. Grand Hotel, Rome: I find Rome deliciously cool & empty & still very pleasing in spite of the 'ruining' which has been going on so long & of which one has heard so much—i.e., the redemption & cocknefication of the ruins. It is 'changed' immensely—as everyone says; but I find myself, I am afraid, so much *more* changed—since I first knew & rhapsodised over it, that I am bound in justice to hold Rome the less criminal of the two.

To Ariana Curtis, 6/3/1894. Grand Hotel, Rome: I came to Rome for 5 days & I am staying & probably on Tuesday going for 3 or 4 to Naples. The exquisite charm of this place at this moment is responsible for these aberrations. Delightfully empty & delightfully cool, Rome has breathed almost all its old enchantment on me—& I can scarcely tear myself away. I almost don't mind the "alterations" & am conscious of nothing but the sweetness. The weather has been delicious & almost too cool; that has had much to do with it.

To William James, Jr.,* 5/30/1907. Hotel de Russie, Rome: The Season is warm (& not too warm—the nights delicious for coolness after the good Roman sort—till late in the summer); & the great sense of the old place is still more or less with one; but the abatements & changes & modernisms & vulgarities, the crowd & the struggle & the frustration (of real communion with what one wanted) are quite dreadful—& I really quite revel in the thought that I shall never come to Italy *at all* again—in *all* probability. However I am as glad to have come as I am impatient to turn my face homeward now—& am only at present waiting (to get on to a very brief dealing with Florence and Venice).

To Mr. & Mrs. Edward Wharton,† 8/12/1907. Lamb House, Rye: I remained in Rome—for myself—a goodish while after last writing you & there were charming moments, faint reverberations of the old-time refrains—with a happy tendency of the superfluous, the incongruous crew [of tourists] to take its departure as the summer came on; yet I feel that I shouldn't care if I never saw the perverted place again, were it not for the memory of four or five adorable occasions—charming chances—enjoyed by the bounty of the Filippis [Caroline and Philippo de Filippi]. . . . They carried me in their wondrous car

* Henry James's nephew (1882–1961), the second son of his brother William.

† The writer Edith Wharton (1862–1937) and her husband, Teddy (1850–1928).

. . . first to 2 or 3 adorable Roman excursions—to Fiumincino, e.g., where we crossed the Tiber on a mediaeval raft & then had tea—out of a Piccadilly tea-basket—on the cool sea-sand, & for a divine day to Subiaco, the unutterable, where I had never been; & then, second, down to Naples (where we spent 2 days) & back; going by the mountains (the valleys really) & Monte Cassino, & returning by the sea—i.e. by Gaeta, Terracina, the Pontine Marshes & the Castelli—quite an ineffable experience. This brought home to me with an intimacy & a penetration unprecedented how incomparably the old *coquine* [whore] of an Italy is the most beautiful country in the world—of a beauty (& an interest & complexity of beauty) so far beyond any other that none other is worth talking about. The day we came down from Posilippo in the early June morning (getting out of Naples & roundabout by that end—the road from Capua on, coming, is *archi*-damnable) is a memory of splendour & style & heroic elegance I never shall lose—& never shall renew! . . . The Italian driving is *crapulous,* & the roads mostly not good enough. . . . But I mustn't expatiate. I wish I were younger. . . . I spent at the last 2 divine weeks in Venice—at the Barbaro. I don't care, frankly, if I never see the vulgarized Rome or Florence again, but Venice never seemed to me more loveable—though the vaporetto rages. They keep their cars at Mestre!

E ssays

....

A Roman Holiday

It is certainly sweet to be merry at the right moment; but the right moment hardly seems to me the ten days of the Roman Carnival. It was my rather cynical suspicion perhaps that they wouldn't keep to my imagination the brilliant promise of legend; but I have been justified by the event and have been decidedly less conscious of the festal influences of the season than of the inalienable gravity of the place. There was a time when the Carnival was a serious matter—that is a heartily joyous one; but, thanks to the seven-league boots the kingdom of Italy has lately donned for the march of progress in quite other directions, the fashion of public revelry has fallen woefully out of step. The state of mind and manners under which the Carnival was kept in generous good faith I doubt if an American can exactly conceive: he can only say to himself that for a month in the year there must have been things—things considerably of humiliation—it was comfortable to forget. But now that Italy is made the Carnival is unmade; and we are not especially tempted to envy the attitude of a population who have lost their relish for play and not yet acquired to any striking extent an enthusiasm for work. The spectacle on the Corso has seemed to me, on the whole, an illustration of that great breach with the past of which Catholic Christendom felt the somewhat muffled shock in September 1870. A traveller acquainted with the fully papal Rome, coming back any time during the past winter, must have immediately noticed that something momentous had happened—something hostile to the elements of picture and colour and "style." My first warning was that ten minutes after my arrival I found myself face to face with a newspaper stand. The impossibility in the other days of having anything in the journalistic line but the *Osservatore Romano* and the *Voce della Verità** used to seem to me much connected with the extraordinary leisure of thought and stillness of mind to which the place admitted you. But now the slender piping of the Voice of Truth is stifled by the raucous note of eventide vendors of the *Capitale,* the *Libertà* and the *Fanfulla*; and Rome reading unexpurgated news is another Rome indeed. For every subscriber to the *Libertà* there may well be an antique masker and reveller less. As striking a sign of the new régime is the extraordinary increase of population. The Corso was always a well-filled street, but now it's a perpetual crush. I never cease to wonder where the new-comers are lodged, and how such spotless flowers of fashion as the gentlemen who stare at the carriages can bloom in the atmosphere of those *camere mobiliate* [furnished rooms] of which I have had glimpses. This, however, is their own question, and bravely enough they meet it. They proclaimed somehow, to the first freshness of my wonder, as I say, that by force of numbers Rome had been secularised. An Italian dandy is a figure visually to reckon with, but these goodly throngs of them scarce offered compensation for the absent monsignori, treading the streets in their purple stockings and followed by the solemn servants who returned on their behalf the bows of the meaner sort; for the mourning gear of the cardinals' coaches that formerly glittered with scarlet and swung with the weight of the footmen clinging behind; for the certainty that you'll not, by the best of traveller's luck, meet the Pope† sitting deep in the shadow of his great chariot with uplifted fingers like some inaccessible idol in his shrine. You may meet the King‡ indeed, who is as ugly, as imposingly ugly, as some idols, though not so inaccessible. The other day as I passed the Quirinal he drove up in a low carriage with a single attendant; and a group of men

* Conservative Catholic newspapers.

† Pius IX (1792–1878) was pope from 1846 to 1878. His pontificate was the longest in history.

‡ Victor Emmanuel II (1820–1878).

and women who had been waiting near the gate rushed at him with a number of folded papers. The carriage slackened pace and he pocketed their offerings with a business-like air—that of a good-natured man accepting hand-bills at a street-corner. Here was a monarch at his palace gate receiving petitions from his subjects—being adjured to right their wrongs. The scene ought to have thrilled me, but somehow it had no more intensity than a woodcut in an illustrated newspaper. Homely I should call it at most; admirably so, certainly, for there were lately few sovereigns standing, I believe, with whom their people enjoyed these filial hand-to-hand relations. The King this year, however, has had as little to do with the Carnival as the Pope, and the innkeepers and Americans have marked it for their own.

It was advertised to begin at half-past two o'clock of a certain Saturday, and punctually at the stroke of the hour, from my room across a wide court, I heard a sudden multiplication of sounds and confusion of tongues in the Corso. I was writing to a friend for whom I cared more than for any mere romp; but as the minutes elapsed and the hubbub deepened curiosity got the better of affection, and I remembered that I was really within eye-shot of an affair the fame of which had ministered to the day-dreams of my infancy. I used to have a scrap-book with a coloured print of the starting of the bedizened wild horses, and the use of a library rich in keepsakes and annuals with a frontispiece commonly of a masked lady in a balcony, the heroine of a delightful tale further on. Agitated by these tender memories I descended into the street; but I confess I looked in vain for a masked lady who might serve as a frontispiece, in vain for any object whatever that might adorn a tale. Masked and muffled ladies there were in abundance; but their masks were of ugly wire, perfectly resembling the little covers placed upon strong cheese in German hotels, and their drapery was a shabby water-proof with the hood pulled over their chignons. They were armed with great tin scoops or funnels, with which they solemnly shovelled lime and flour out of bushel-baskets and down on the heads of the people in the street. They were packed into balconies all the way along the straight vista of the Corso, in which their calcareous shower maintained a dense, gritty, unpalatable fog. The crowd was compact in the street, and the Americans in it were tossing back confetti out of great satchels hung round their necks. It was quite the "you're another" sort of repartee, and less seasoned than I had hoped with the airy mockery tradition hangs about this festival. The scene was striking, in a word; but somehow not as I had dreamed of its being. I stood regardful, I suppose, but with a peculiarly tempting blankness of visage, for in a moment I received half a bushel of flour on my too-philosophic head. Decidedly it was an ignoble form of humour. I shook my ears like an emergent diver, and had a sudden vision of how still and sunny and solemn, how peculiarly and undisturbedly themselves, how secure from any intrusion less sympathetic than one's own, certain outlying parts of Rome must just then be. The Carnival had received its death-blow in my imagination; and it has been ever since but a thin and dusky ghost of pleasure that has flitted at intervals in and out of my consciousness.

I turned my back accordingly on the Corso and wandered away to the grass-grown quarters delightfully free even from the possibility of a fellow-countryman. And so having set myself an example I have been keeping Carnival by strolling perversely along the silent circumference of Rome. I have doubtless lost a great deal. The Princess Margaret has occupied a balcony opposite the open space which leads into Via Condotti and, I believe, like the discreet princess she is, has dealt in no missiles but bonbons, bouquets and white doves. I would have waited half an hour any day to see the Princess Margaret hold a dove on her forefinger; but I never chanced to notice any preparation for that effect. And yet do what you will you can't really elude the Carnival. As the days elapse it filters down into the manners of the common people, and before the week is over the very beggars at the church-doors seem to have gone to the expense of a domino. When you meet these specimens of dingy drollery capering about in dusky back-streets at all hours of the day and night, meet them flitting out of black doorways between the greasy groups that cluster about Roman thresholds, you feel that a love of "pranks," the more vivid the better, must from far back have been implanted in the Roman temperament with a strong hand. An unsophisticated American is wonderstruck at the number of persons, of every age and various conditions, whom it costs nothing in the nature of an ingenuous blush to walk up and down the streets in the costume of a theatrical supernumerary. Fathers of families do it at the head of an admiring progeniture; aunts and uncles and grandmothers do it; all the family does it, with varying splendour but with the same good conscience. "A pack of babies!" the doubtless too self-conscious alien pronounces it for its pains, and tries to imagine himself strutting along Broadway in a battered tin helmet and a pair of yellow tights. Our vices are certainly different; it takes those of the innocent sort to be so ridiculous. A self-consciousness lapsing so easily, in fine, strikes me as so near a relation to amenity, urbanity and general gracefulness that, for myself, I should be sorry to lay a tax on it, lest these other commodities should also cease to come to market.

I was rewarded, when I had turned away with my ears full of flour, by a glimpse of an intenser life than the dingy foolery of the Corso. I walked down by the back streets to the steps mounting to the Capitol—that long inclined plane, rather, broken at every two paces, which is the unfailing disappointment, I believe, of tourists primed for retrospective raptures. Certainly the Capitol seen from this side isn't commanding. The hill is so low, the ascent so narrow, Michael Angelo's architecture in the quadrangle at the top so meagre, the whole place somehow so much more of a mole-hill than a mountain, that for the first ten minutes of your standing there Roman history seems suddenly to have sunk through a trap-door. It emerges however on the other side, in the Forum; and here meanwhile, if you get no sense of the sublime, you get gradually a sense of exquisite composition. Nowhere in Rome is more colour, more charm, more sport for the eye. The mild incline, during the winter months, is always covered with lounging sun-seekers, and especially with those more constantly obvious members of the Roman population—beggars, soldiers, monks and tourists. The beggars and peasants lie kicking their heels along that grandest of loafing-places the great steps of the Ara Coeli. The dwarfish look of the Capitol is intensified, I think, by the neighbourhood of this huge blank staircase, mouldering away in disuse, the weeds thick in its crevices, and climbing to the rudely solemn façade of the church. The sunshine glares on this great unfinished wall only to light up its featureless despair, its expression of conscious, irremediable incompleteness. Sometimes, massing its rusty screen against the deep blue sky, with the little cross and the sculptured porch casting a clear-cut shadow on the bricks, it seems to have even more than a Roman desolation, it confusedly suggests Spain and Africa— lands with no latent *risorgimenti*, with absolutely nothing but a fatal past. The legendary wolf of Rome has lately been accommodated with a little artificial grotto, among the cacti and the palms, in the fantastic triangular garden squeezed between the steps of the church and the ascent to the Capitol, where she holds a perpetual levee and "draws" apparently as powerfully as the Pope himself. Above, in the piazzetta before the stuccoed palace which rises so jauntily on a basement of thrice its magnitude, are more loungers and knitters in the sun, seated round the massively inscribed base of the statue of Marcus Aurelius. Hawthorne has perfectly expressed the attitude of this admirable figure in saying that it extends its arm with "a command which is in itself a benediction." I doubt if any statue of king or captain in the public places of the world has more to commend it to the general heart. Irrecoverable simplicity—residing so in irrecoverable Style—has no sturdier representative. Here is an impression that the sculptors of the last three hundred years have been laboriously trying to reproduce; but contrasted with this mild old monarch their prancing horsemen suggest a succession of riding-masters taking out young ladies' schools. The admirably human character of the figure survives the rusty decomposition of the bronze and the slight "debasement" of the art; and one may call it singular that in the capital of Christendom the portrait most suggestive of a Christian conscience is that of a pagan emperor.

You recover in some degree your stifled hopes of sublimity as you pass beyond the palace and take your choice of either curving slope to descend into the Forum. Then you see that the little stuccoed edifice is but a modern excrescence on the mighty cliff of a primitive construction, whose great squares of porous tufa, as they underlie each other, seem to resolve themselves back into the colossal cohesion of unhewn rock. There are prodigious strangenesses in the union of this airy and comparatively fresh-faced superstructure and these deep-plunging, hoary foundations; and few things in Rome are more entertaining to the eye than to measure the long plumb-line which drops from the inhabited windows of the palace, with their little over-peeping balconies, their muslin curtains and their bird-cages, down to the rugged constructional work of the Republic. In the Forum proper the sublime is eclipsed again, though the late extension of the excavations gives a chance for it.

Nothing in Rome helps your fancy to a more vigorous backward flight than to lounge on a sunny day over the railing which guards the great central researches. It "says" more things to you than you can repeat to see the past, the ancient world, as you stand there, bodily turned up with the spade and transformed from an immaterial, inaccessible fact of time into a matter of soils and surfaces. The pleasure is the same—in kind—as what you enjoy at Pompeii, and the pain the same. It wasn't here, however, that I found my compensation for forfeiting the spectacle on the Corso, but in a little church at the end of the narrow byway which diverges up the Palatine from just beside the Arch of Titus. This byway leads you between high walls, then takes a bend and introduces you to a long row of rusty, dusty little pictures of the stations of the cross. Beyond these stands a small church with a front so modest that you hardly recognise it till you see the leather curtain. I never see a leather curtain without lifting it; it is sure to cover a constituted *scene* of some sort—good, bad or indifferent. The scene this time was meagre—whitewash and tarnished candlesticks and mouldy muslin flowers being its principal features. I shouldn't have remained if I hadn't been struck with the attitude of the single worshipper—a young priest kneeling before one of the side-altars, who, as I entered, lifted his head and gave me a sidelong look so charged with the languor of devotion that he immediately became an object of interest. He was visiting each of the altars in turn and kissing the balustrade beneath them. He was alone in the church, and indeed in the whole region. There were no beggars even at the door; they were plying their trade on the skirts of the Carnival. In the entirely deserted place he alone knelt for religion, and as I sat respectfully by it seemed to me I could hear in the perfect silence the far-away uproar of the maskers. It was my late impression of these frivolous people, I suppose, joined with the extraordinary gravity of the young priest's face—his pious fatigue, his droning prayer and his isolation—that gave me just then and there a supreme vision of the religious passion, its privations and resignations and exhaustions and its terribly small share of amusement. He was young and strong and evidently of not too refined a fibre to enjoy the Carnival; but, planted there with his face pale with fasting and his knees stiff with praying, he seemed so stern a satire on it and on the crazy thousands who were preferring it to *his* way, that I half expected to see some heavenly portent out of a monastic legend come down and confirm his choice. Yet I confess that though I wasn't enamoured of the Carnival myself his seemed a grim preference and this forswearing of the world a terrible game—a gaining one only if your zeal never falters; a hard fight when it does. In such an hour, to a stout young fellow like the hero of my anecdote, the smell of incense must seem horribly stale and the muslin flowers and gilt candlesticks to figure no great bribe. And it wouldn't have helped him much to think that not so very far away, just beyond the Forum, in the Corso, there was sport for the million, and for nothing. I doubt on the other hand whether my young priest had thought of this. He had made himself a temple out of the very elements of his innocence, and his prayers followed each other too fast for the tempter to slip in a whisper. And so, as I say, I found a solider fact of human nature than the love of *coriandoli* [confetti].

One of course never passes the Colosseum without paying it one's respects—without going in under one of the hundred portals and crossing the long oval and sitting down awhile, generally at the foot of the cross in the centre. I always feel, as I do so, as if I were seated in the depths of some Alpine valley. The upper portions of the side toward the Esquiline look as remote and lonely as an Alpine ridge, and you raise your eyes to their rugged sky-line, drinking in the sun and silvered by the blue air, with much the same feeling with which you would take in a grey cliff on which an eagle might lodge. This roughly mountainous quality of the great ruin is its chief interest; beauty of detail has pretty well vanished, especially since the high-growing wild-flowers have been plucked away by the new government, whose functionaries, surely, at certain points of their task, must have felt as if they shared the dreadful trade of those who gather samphire. Even if you are on your way to the Lateran you won't grudge the twenty minutes it will take you, on leaving the Colosseum, to turn away under the Arch of Constantine, whose noble battered bas-reliefs, with the chain of tragic statues—fettered, dropping barbarians—round its summit, I assume you to have profoundly admired, toward the piazzetta of the church of San Giovanni e Paolo, on the slope of Cælian. No spot in Rome can show a cluster of more charming accidents. The ancient brick apse of the church peeps down into the trees of the little wooded walk before the neighbouring church of San Gregorio, intensely venerable beneath its excessive modernisation; and a series of heavy brick buttresses, flying across to an opposite wall, overarches the short, steep, paved passage which leads into the small square. This is flanked on one side by the long mediæval portico of the church of the two saints, sustained by eight time-blackened columns of granite and marble. On another rise the great scarce-windowed walls of a Passionist convent, and on the third the portals of a grand villa, whose tall porter, with his cockade and silver-topped staff, standing sublime behind his grating, seems a kind of mundane St. Peter, I suppose, to the beggars who sit at the church door or lie in the sun along the farther slope which leads to the gate of the convent. The place always seems to me the perfection of an out-of-the-way corner—a place you would think twice before telling people about, lest you should find them there the next time you were to go. It is such a group of objects, singly and in their happy combination, as one must come to Rome to find at one's house door; but what makes it peculiarly a picture is the beautiful dark red campanile of the church, which stands embedded in the mass of the convent. It begins, as so many things in Rome begin, with a stout foundation of antique travertine, and rises high, in delicately quaint mediæval brickwork—little tiers and apertures sustained on miniature columns and adorned with small cracked slabs of green and yellow marble, inserted almost at random. When there are three or four brown-breasted contadini sleeping in the sun before the convent doors, and a departing monk leading his shadow down over them, I think you will not find anything in Rome more *sketchable*.

If you stop, however, to observe everything worthy of your water-colours you will never reach St. John Lateran. My business was much less with the interior of that vast and empty, that cold clean temple, which I have never found peculiarly interesting, than with certain charming features of its surrounding precinct—the crooked old court beside it, which admits you to the Baptistery and to a delightful rear-view of the queer architectural odds and ends that may in Rome compose a florid ecclesiastical façade. There are more of these, a stranger jumble of chance detail, of lurking recesses and wanton projections and inexplicable windows, than I have memory or phrase for; but the gem of the collection is the oddly perched peaked turret, with its yellow travertine welded upon the rusty brickwork, which was not meant to be suspected, and the brickwork retreating beneath and leaving it in the odd position of a tower *under* which you may see the sky. As to the great front of the church overlooking the Porta San Giovanni, you are not admitted behind the scenes; the term is quite in keeping, for the architecture has a vastly theatrical air. It is extremely imposing—that of St. Peter's alone is more so; and when from far off on the Campagna you see the colossal images of the mitred saints along the top standing distinct against the sky, you forget their coarse construction and their inflated draperies. The view from the great space which stretches from the church steps to the city wall is the very prince of views. Just beside you, beyond the great alcove of mosaic, is the Scala Santa, the marble staircase which (says the legend) Christ descended under the weight of Pilate's judgment, and which all Christians must forever ascend on their knees; before you is the city gate which opens upon the Via Appia Nuova, the long gaunt file of arches of the Claudian aqueduct, their jagged ridge stretching away like the vertebral column of some monstrous mouldering skeleton, and upon the blooming brown and purple flats and dells of the

Campagna and the glowing blue of the Alban Mountains, spotted with their white, high-nestling towns; while to your left is the great grassy space, lined with dwarfish mulberry-tress, which stretches across to the damp little sister-basilica of Santa Croce in Gerusalemme. During a former visit to Rome I lost my heart to this idle tract,* and wasted much time in sitting on the steps of the church and watching certain white-cowled friars who were sure to be passing there for the delight of my eyes. There are fewer friars now, and there are a great many of the king's recruits, who inhabit the ex-conventual barracks adjoining Santa Croce and are led forward to practise their goose-step on the sunny turf. Here too the poor old cardinals who are no longer to be seen on the Pincio descend from their mourning-coaches and relax their venerable knees. These members alone still testify to the traditional splendour of the princes of the Church; for as they advance the lifted black petticoat reveals a flash of scarlet stockings and makes you groan at the victory of civilisation over colour.

If St. John Lateran disappoints you internally, you have an easy compensation in pacing the long lane which connects it with Santa Maria Maggiore and entering the singularly perfect nave of that most delightful of churches. The first day of my stay in Rome under the old dispensation I spent in wandering at random through the city, with accident for my *valet-de-place* [tourist guide]. It served me to perfection and introduced me to the best things; among others to an immediate happy relation with Santa Maria Maggiore. First impressions, memorable impressions, are generally irrecoverable; they often leave one the wiser, but they rarely return in the same form. I remember, of my coming uninformed and unprepared into the place of worship and of curiosity that I have named, only that I sat for half an hour on the edge of the base of one of the marble columns of the beautiful nave and enjoyed a perfect revel of—what shall I call it?—taste, intelligence, fancy, perceptive emotion? The place proved so endlessly suggestive that perception became a throbbing confusion of images, and I departed with a sense of knowing a good deal that is not set down in Murray. I have

* Utterly overbuilt and gone—1909. [James's footnote.]

seated myself more than once again at the base of the same
column; but you live your life only once, the parts as well as the
whole. The obvious charm of the church is the elegant grandeur of the nave—its perfect shapeliness and its rich simplicity,
its long double row of white marble columns and its high flat
roof, embossed with intricate gildings and mouldings. It opens
into a choir of an extraordinary splendour of effect, which I
recommend you to look out for of a fine afternoon. At such a
time the glowing western light, entering the high windows of
the tribune, kindles the scattered masses of colour into sombre
brightness, scintillates on the great solemn mosaic of the vault,
touches the porphyry columns of the superb baldachino with
ruby lights, and buries its shining shafts in the deep-toned
shadows that hang about frescoes and sculptures and mouldings. The deeper charm even than in such things, however, is
the social or historic note or tone or atmosphere of the
church—I fumble, you see, for my right expression; the sense
it gives you, in common with most of the Roman churches, and
more than any of them, of having been prayed in for several
centuries by an endlessly curious and complex society. It takes
no great attention to let it come to you that the authority of
Italian Catholicism has lapsed not a little in these days; not less
also perhaps than to feel that, as they stand, these deserted
temples were the fruit of a society leavened through and
through by ecclesiastical manners, and that they formed for
ages the constant background of the human drama. They are,
as one may say, the *churchiest* churches in Europe—the fullest
of gathered memories, of the experience of their office. There's
not a figure one has read of in old-world annals that isn't to be
imagined on proper occasion kneeling before the lamp-decked
Confession beneath the altar of Santa Maria Maggiore. One
sees after all, however, even among the most palpable realities,
very much what the play of one's imagination projects there;
and I present my remarks simply as a reminder that one's
constant excursions into these places are not the least interesting episodes of one's walks in Rome.

I had meant to give a simple illustration of the church-habit,
so to speak, but I have given it at such a length as leaves scant
space to touch on the innumerable topics brushed by the pen

that begins to take Roman notes. It is by the aimless *flânerie* [strolling] which leaves you free to follow capriciously every hint of entertainment that you get to know Rome. The greater part of the life about you goes on in the streets; and for an observer fresh from a country in which town scenery is at the least monotonous incident and character and picture seem to abound. I become conscious with compunction, let me hasten to add, that I have launched myself thus on the subject of Roman churches and Roman walks without so much as a preliminary allusion to St. Peter's. One is apt to proceed thither on rainy days with intentions of exercise—to put the case only at that—and to carry these out body and mind. Taken as a walk not less than as a church, St. Peter's of course reigns alone. Even for the profane "constitutional" it serves where the Boulevards, where Piccadilly and Broadway, fall short, and if it didn't offer to our use the grandest area in the world it would still offer the most diverting. Few great works of art last longer to the cùriosity, to the perpetually transcended attention. You think you have taken the whole thing in, but it expands, it rises sublime again, and leaves your measure itself poor. You never let the ponderous leather curtain bang down behind you—your weak lift of a scant edge of whose padded vastness resembles the liberty taken in folding back the parchment corner of some mighty folio page—without feeling all former visits to have been but missed attempts at apprehension and the actual to achieve your first real possession. The conventional question is ever as to whether one hasn't been "disappointed in the size," but a few honest folk here and there, I hope, will never cease to say no. The place struck me from the first as the hugest thing conceivable—a real exaltation of one's idea of space; so that one's entrance, even from the great empty square which either glares beneath the deep blue sky or makes of the cool far-cast shadow of the immense front something that resembles a big slate-coloured country on a map, seems not so much a going in somewhere as a going out. The mere man of pleasure in quest of new sensations might well not know where to better his encounter there of the sublime shock that brings him, within the threshold, to an immediate gasping pause. There are days when the vast nave looks mysteriously vaster than on others and the gorgeous baldachino a longer journey beyond the far-spreading tessellated plain of the pavement, and when the light has yet a quality, which lets things loom their largest, while the scattered figures—I mean the human, for there are plenty of others—mark happily the scale of items and parts. Then you have only to stroll and stroll and gaze and gaze; to watch the glorious altar-canopy lift its bronze architecture, its colossal embroidered contortions, like a temple within a temple, and feel yourself, at the bottom of the abysmal shaft of the dome, dwindle to a crawling dot.

Much of the constituted beauty resides in the fact that it is all general beauty, that you are appealed to by no specific details, or that these at least, practically never importunate, are as taken for granted as the lieutenants and captains are taken for granted in a great standing army—among whom indeed individual aspects may figure here the rather shifting range of decorative dignity in which details, when observed, often prove poor (though never not massive and substantially precious) and sometimes prove ridiculous. The sculptures, with the sole exception of Michael Angelo's ineffable "Pietà," which lurks obscurely in a side-chapel—this indeed to my sense the rarest artistic *combination* of the greatest things the hand of man has produced—are either bad or indifferent; and the universal incrustation of marble, though sumptuous enough, has a less brilliant effect than much later work of the same sort, that for instance of St. Paul's without the Walls. The supreme beauty is the splendidly sustained simplicity of the whole. The thing represents a prodigious imagination extraordinarily strained, yet strained, at its happiest pitch, without breaking. Its happiest pitch I say, because this is the only creation of its strenuous author in presence of which you are in presence of serenity. You may invoke the idea of ease at St. Peter's without a sense of sacrilege—which you can hardly do, if you are at all spiritually nervous, in Westminster Abbey or Notre Dame. The vast enclosed clearness has much to do with the idea. There are no shadows to speak of, no marked effects of shade; only effects of light innumerable—points at which this element seems to mass itself in airy density and scatter itself in enchanting gradations and cadences. It performs the office of gloom or of mystery in Gothic churches; hangs like a rolling mist along the gilded vault of the nave, melts into bright interfusion the mosaic scintillations of the dome, clings and clusters and lingers, animates the whole huge and otherwise empty shell. A good Catholic, I suppose, is the same Catholic anywhere, before the grandest as well as the humblest altars; but to a visitor not formally enrolled St. Peter's speaks less of aspiration than of full and convenient assurance. The soul infinitely expands there, if one will, but all on its quite human level. It marvels at the reach of our dream and the immensity of our resources. To be so impressed and put in our place, we say, is to be sufficiently "saved"; we can't be more than that in heaven itself; and what specifically celestial beauty such a show or such a substitute may lack it makes up for in certainty and tangibility. And yet if one's hours on the scene are not actually spent in praying, the spirit seeks it again as for the finer comfort, for the blessing, exactly, of its example, its protection and its exclusion. When you are weary of the swarming democracy of your fellow-tourists, of the unremunerative aspects of human nature on Corso and Pincio, of the oppressively frequent combination of coronets on carriage panels and stupid faces in carriages, of addled brains and lacquered boots, of ruin and dirt and decay, of priests and beggars and takers of advantage, of the myriad tokens of a halting civilisation, the image of the great temple depresses the balance of your doubts, seems to rise above even the highest tide of vulgarity and make you still believe in the heroic will and the heroic act. It's a relief, in other words, to feel that there's nothing but a cab-fare between your pessimism and one of the greatest of human achievements.

This might serve as a Lenten peroration to these remarks of mine which have strayed so woefully from their jovial text, save that I ought fairly to confess that my last impression of the Carnival was altogether Carnivalesque. The merry-making of Shrove Tuesday had life and felicity; the dead letter of tradition broke out into nature and grace. I pocketed my scepticism and spent a long afternoon on the Corso. Almost every one was a masker, but you had no need to conform; the pelting rain of confetti effectually disguised you. I can't say I found it all very exhilarating; but here and there I noticed a brighter episode—a capering clown inflamed with contagious jollity, some finer humourist forming a circle every thirty yards to crow at his indefatigable sallies. One clever performer so especially pleased me that I should have been glad to catch a glimpse of the natural man. You imagined for him that he was taking a prodigious intellectual holiday and that his gaiety was in inverse ratio to his daily mood. Dressed as a needy scholar, in an ancient evening-coat and with a rusty black hat and gloves fantastically patched, he carried a little volume carefully under his arm. His humours were in excellent taste, his whole manner the perfection of genteel comedy. The crowd seemed to relish him vastly, and he at once commanded a gleefully attentive audience. Many of his sallies I lost; those I caught were excellent. His trick was often to begin by taking some one urbanely and caressingly by the chin and complimenting him on the *intelligenza della sua fisionomia* [intelligence of his visage]. I kept near him as long as I could; for he struck me as a real ironic artist, cherishing a disinterested, and yet at the same time a motived and a moral, passion for the grotesque. I should have liked, however—if indeed I shouldn't have feared—to see him the next morning, or when he unmasked that night over his hard-earned supper in a smoky *trattoria*. As the evening went on the cloud thickened and became a motley press of shouting, pushing, scrambling, everything but squabbling, revellers. The rain of missiles ceased at dusk, but the universal deposit of chalk and flour was trampled into a cloud made lurid by flaring pyramids of the gas-lamps that replaced for the occasion the stingy Roman luminaries. Early in the evening came off the classic exhibition of the *moccoletti* [tapers], which I but half saw, like a languid reporter resigned beforehand to be cashiered for want of enterprise. From the mouth of a side-street, over a thousand heads, I caught a huge slow-moving illuminated car, from which blue-lights and rockets and Roman candles were in course of discharge, meeting all in a dim fuliginous glare far above the house-tops. It was like a glimpse of some public orgy in ancient Babylon. In the small hours of the morning, walking homeward from a private entertainment, I found Ash-Wednesday still kept at bay. The Corso, flaring with light, smelt like a circus. Every one was taking

friendly liberties with every one else and using up the dregs of
his festive energy in convulsive hootings and gymnastics. Here
and there certain indefatigable spirits, clad all in red after the
manner of devils and leaping furiously about with torches,
were supposed to affright you. But they shared the universal
geniality and bequeathed me no midnight fears as a pretext for
keeping Lent, the *carnevale dei preti* [the priests' carnival: a
derisive term], as I read in that profanely radical sheet the
Capitale. Of this too I have been having glimpses. Going lately
into Santa Francesca Romana, the picturesque church near the
Temple of Peace, I found a feast for the eyes—a dim crimson-
toned light through curtained windows, a great festoon of
tapers round the altar, a bulging girdle of lamps before the
sunken shrine beneath, and a dozen white-robed Dominicans
scattered in the happiest composition on the pavement. It was
better than the *moccoletti*.

    [1873]

Roman Rides

I shall always remember the first I took: out of the Porta del Popolo, to where the Ponte Molle, whose single arch sustains a weight of historic tradition, compels the sallow Tiber to flow between its four great-mannered ecclesiastical statues, over the crest of the hill and along the old posting-road to Florence. It was mild midwinter, the season peculiarly of colour on the Roman Campagna; and the light was full of that mellow purple glow, that tempered intensity, which haunts the after-visions of those who have known Rome like the memory of some supremely irresponsible pleasure. An hour away I pulled up and at the edge of a meadow gazed away for some time into remoter distances. Then and there, it seemed to me, I measured the deep delight of knowing the Campagna. But I saw more things in it than I can easily tell. The country rolled away around me into slopes and dells of long-drawn grace, chequered with purple and blue and blooming brown. The lights and shadows were at play on the Sabine Mountains—an alternation of tones so exquisite as to be conveyed only by some fantastic comparison to sapphire and amber. In the foreground a contadino in his cloak and peaked hat jogged solitary on his ass; and here and there in the distance, among blue undulations, some white village, some gray tower, helped deliciously to make the picture the typical "Italian landscape" of old-fashioned art. It was so bright and yet so sad, so still and yet so charged, to the supersensuous ear, with the murmur of an extinguished life, that you could only say it was intensely and adorably strange, could only impute to the whole overarched scene an unsurpassed secret for bringing tears of appreciation to no matter how ignorant—archeologically ignorant—eyes. To ride once, in these conditions, is of course to ride again and to allot to the Campagna a generous share of the time one spends in Rome.

It is a pleasure that doubles one's horizon, and one can scarcely say whether it enlarges or limits one's impression of the city proper. It certainly makes St. Peter's seem a trifle smaller and blunts the edge of one's curiosity in the Forum. It must be the effect of the experience, at all extended, that when you think of Rome afterwards you will think still respectfully and regretfully enough of the Vatican and the Pincio, the streets and the picture-making street life; but will even more wonder, with an irrepressible contraction of the heart, when again you shall feel yourself bounding over the flower-smothered turf, or pass from one framed picture to another beside the open arches of the crumbling aqueducts. You look back at the City so often from some grassy hill-top—hugely compact within its walls, with St. Peter's overtopping all things and yet seeming small, and the vast girdle of marsh and meadow receding on all sides to the mountains and the sea—that you come to remember it at last as hardly more than a respectable parenthesis in a great sweep of generalisation. Within the walls, on the other hand, you think of your intended ride as the most romantic of all your possibilities; of the Campagna generally as an illimitable experience. One's rides certainly give Rome an inordinate scope for the reflective—by which I suppose I mean after all the æsthetic and the "esoteric"—life. To dwell in a city which, much as you grumble at it, is after all very fairly a modern city; with crowds and shops and theatres and cafés and balls and receptions and dinner-parties and all the modern confusion of social pleasures and pains; to have at your door the good and evil of it all; and yet to be able in half an hour to gallop away and leave it a hundred miles, a hundred years, behind, and to look at the tufted broom glowing on a lonely tower-top in the still blue air, and the pale pink asphodels trembling none the less for the stillness, and the shaggy-legged shepherds leaning on their sticks in motionless brotherhood with the heaps of ruin, and the scrambling goats and staggering little kids treading out wild desert smells from the top of hollow-sounding mounds; and then to come back through one of the great gates and a couple of hours later find yourself in the "world," dressed, introduced, entertained, inquiring, talking about "Middlemarch"* to a young English lady or listening to Neapolitan songs from a gentleman in a very low-cut shirt—all this is to lead in a manner a double life and to gather from the hurrying hours more impressions than a mind of modest capacity quite knows how to dispose of.

I touched lately upon this theme with a friend who, I fancied, would understand me, and who immediately assured me that he had just spent a day that this mingled diversity of sensation made to the days one spends elsewhere what an uncommonly good novel may be to the daily paper. "There was an air of idleness about it, if you will," he said, "and it was certainly pleasant enough to have been wrong. Perhaps, being after all unused to long stretches of dissipation, this was why I had a half-feeling that I was reading an odd chapter in the history of a person very much more of a *héros de roman* [hero in a novel] than myself." Then he proceeded to relate how he had taken a long ride with a lady whom he extremely admired. "We turned off from the Tor di Quinto Road to that castellated farm-house you know of—once a Ghibelline fortress—whither Claude Lorrain used to come to paint pictures of which the surrounding landscape is still so artisitcally, so compositionally, suggestive. We went into the inner court, a cloister almost, with the carven capitals of its loggia columns, and looked at a handsome child swinging shyly against the half-opened door of a room whose impenetrable shadow, behind her, made her, as it were, a sketch in bituminous water-colours. We talked with the farmer, a handsome, pale, fever-tainted fellow with a well-to-do air that didn't in the least deter his affability from a turn compatible with the acceptance of small coin; and then we galloped away and away over the meadows which stretch with hardly a break to Veii. The day was strangely delicious, with a cool grey sky and just a touch of moisture in the air stirred by our rapid motion. The Campagna, in the colourless even light, was more solemn and romantic than ever; and a ragged shepherd, driving a meagre straggling flock, whom we stopped to ask our way of, was a

* George Eliot's novel (1872).

perfect type of pastoral, weather-beaten misery. He was precisely the shepherd for the foreground of a scratchy etching. There were faint odours of spring in the air, and the grass here and there was streaked with great patches of daisies; but it was spring with a foreknowledge of autumn, a day to be enjoyed with a substrain of sadness, the foreboding of regret, a day somehow to make one feel as if one had seen and felt a great deal—quite, as I say, like a *héros de roman*. Touching such characters, it was the illustrious Pelham,* I think, who, on being asked if he rode, replied that he left those violent exercises to the ladies. But under such a sky, in such an air, over acres of daisied turf, a long, long gallop is certainly a supersubtle joy. The elastic bound of your horse is the poetry of motion; and if you are so happy as to add to it not the prose of companionship riding comes almost to affect you as a spiritual exercise. My gallop, at any rate," said my friend, "threw me into a mood which gave an extraordinary zest to the rest of the day." He was to go to a dinner-party at a villa on the edge of Rome, and Madame X——, who was also going, called for him in her carriage. "It was a long drive," he went on, "through the Forum, past the Colosseum. She told me a long story about a most interesting person. Toward the end my eyes caught through the carriage window a slab of rugged sculptures. We were passing under the Arch of Constantine. In the hall pavement of the villa is a rare antique mosaic—one of the largest and most perfect; the ladies on their way to the drawing-room trail over it the flounces of Worth.† We drove home late, and there's my day."

On your exit from most of the gates of Rome you have generally half-an-hour's progress through winding lanes, many of which are hardly less charming than the open meadows. On foot the walls and high hedges would vex you and spoil your walk; but in the saddle you generally overtop them, to an endless peopling of the minor vision. Yet a Roman wall in the springtime is for that matter almost as interesting as anything

* In *Pelham; or, the Adventures of a Gentleman* (1828), a novel by Edward Bulwer-Lytton.

† A Paris dressmaking firm.

it conceals. Crumbling grain by grain, coloured and mottled to a hundred tones by sun and storm, with its rugged structure of brick extruding through its coarse complexion of peeling stucco, its creeping lacework of wandering ivy starred with miniature violets, and its wild fringe of stouter flowers against the sky—it is as little as possible a blank partition; it is practically a luxury of landscape. At the moment at which I write, in mid-April, all the ledges and cornices are wreathed with flaming poppies, nodding there as if they knew so well what faded greys and yellows are an offset to their scarlet. But the best point in a dilapidated enclosing surface of vineyard or villa is of course the gateway, lifting its great arch of cheap rococo scroll-work, its balls and shields and mossy dish-covers—as they always perversely figure to me—and flanked with its dusky cypresses. I never pass one without taking out my mental sketch-book and jotting it down as a vignette in the insubstantial record of my ride. They are as sad and dreary as if they led to the moated grange where Mariana waited in desperation for something to happen; and it's easy to take the usual inscription over the porch as a recommendation to those who enter to renounce all hope of anything but a glass of more or less agreeably acrid *vino romano* [Roman wine]. For what you chiefly see over the walls and at the end of the straight short avenue of rusty cypresses are the appurtenances of a *vigna*—a couple of acres of little upright sticks blackening in the sun, and a vast sallow-faced, scantily windowed mansion, whose expression denotes little of the life of the mind beyond what goes to the driving of a hard bargain over the tasted hogsheads. If Mariana is there she certainly has no pile of old magazines to beguile her leisure. The life of the mind, if the term be in any application here not ridiculous, appears to any asker of curious questions, as he wanders about Rome, the very thinnest deposit of the past. Within the rococo gateway, which itself has a vaguely æsthetic self-consciousness, at the end of the cypress walk, you will probably see a mythological group in rusty marble—a Cupid and Psyche, a Venus and Paris, an Apollo and Daphne—the relic of an age when a Roman proprietor thought it fine to patronise the arts. But I imagine you are safe in supposing it to constitute the only allusion savouring of culture that has been made on the premises for three or four generations.

There is a franker cheerfulness—though certainly a proper amount of that forlornness which lurks about every object to which the Campagna forms a background—in the primitive little taverns where, on the homeward stretch, in the waning light, you are often glad to rein up and demand a bottle of their best. Their best and their worst are indeed the same, though with a shifting price, and plain *vino bianco* or *vino rosso* (rarely both) is the sole article of refreshment in which they deal. There is a ragged bush over the door, and within, under a dusky vault, on crooked cobble-stones, sit half-a-dozen conta-dini [peasants] in their indigo jackets and goatskin breeches and with their elbows on the table. There is generally a rabble of infantile beggars at the door, pretty enough in their dusty rags, with their fine eyes and intense Italian smile, to make you forget your private vow of doing your individual best to make these people, whom you like so much, unlearn their old vices. Was Porta Pia bombarded three years ago* that Peppino should still grow up to whine for a copper? But the Italian shells had no direct message for Peppino's stomach—and you are going to a dinner-party at a villa. So Peppino "points" an instant for the copper in the dust and grows up a Roman beggar. The whole little place represents the most primitive form of hos-telry; but along any of the roads leading out of the city you may find establishments of a higher type, with Garibaldi, superbly mounted and foreshortened, painted on the wall, or a lady in a low-necked dress opening a fictive lattice with irresistible hospitality, and a yard with the classic vine-wreathed arbour casting thin shadows upon benches and tables draped and cush-ioned with the white dust from which the highways from the gates borrow most of their local colour. None the less, I say, you avoid the highroads, and, if you are a person of taste, don't grumble at the occasional need of following the walls of the city. City walls, to a properly constituted American, can never be an object of indifference; and it is emphatically "no end of

---

* In the successful attempt by the newly united Kingdom of Italy to wrest Rome away from papal rule.

a sensation" to pace in the shadow of this massive cincture
of Rome. I have found myself, as I skirted its base, talking of
trivial things, but never without a sudden reflection on the
deplorable impermanence of first impressions. A twelvemonth
ago the raw plank fences of a Boston suburb, inscribed with the
virtues of healing drugs, bristled along my horizon: now I
glance with idle eyes at a compacted antiquity in which a more
learned sense may read portentous dates and signs—Servius,
Aurelius, Honorius.* But even to idle eyes the prodigious, the
continuous thing bristles with eloquent passages. In some
places, where the huge brickwork is black with time and certain strange square towers look down at you with still blue
eyes, the Roman sky peering through lidless loopholes, and
there is nothing but white dust in the road and solitude in the
air, I might take myself for a wandering Tartar touching on
the confines of the Celestial Empire. The wall of China must
have very much such a gaunt robustness. The colour of the
Roman ramparts is everywhere fine, and their rugged patchwork has been subdued by time and weather into a mellow
harmony that the brush only asks to catch up. On the northern
side of the city, behind the Vatican, St. Peter's and the Trastevere, I have seen them glowing in the late afternoon with the
tones of ancient bronze and rusty gold. Here at various points
they are embossed with the Papal insignia, the tiara with its
flying bands and crossed keys; to the high style of which the
grace that attaches to almost any lost cause—even if not quite
the "tender" grace of a day that is dead—considerably adds a
style. With the dome of St. Peter's resting on their cornice and
the hugely clustered architecture of the Vatican rising from
them as from a terrace, they seem indeed the valid bulwark of
an ecclesiastical city. Vain bulwark, alas! sighs the sentimental
tourist, fresh from the meagre entertainment of this latter Holy
Week. But he may find monumental consolation in this neighbourhood at a source where, as I pass, I never fail to apply for
it. At half-an-hour's walk beyond Porta San Pancrazio, beneath the wall of the Villa Doria, is a delightfully pompous
ecclesiastical gateway of the seventeenth century, erected by

* Ancient Roman emperors.

Paul V to commemorate his restoration of the aqueducts through which the stream bearing his name flows towards the fine florid portico protecting its clear-sheeted outgush on the crest of the Janiculan. It arches across the road in the most ornamental manner of the period, and one can hardly pause before it without seeming to assist at a ten minutes' revival of old Italy—without feeling as if one were in a cocked hat and sword and were coming up to Rome, in another mood than Luther's, with a letter of recommendation to the mistress of a cardinal.

The Campagna differs greatly on the two sides of the Tiber; and it is hard to say which, for the rider, has the greater charm. The half-dozen rides you may take from Porta San Giovanni possess the perfection of traditional Roman interest and lead you through a far-strewn wilderness of ruins—a scattered maze of tombs and towers and nameless fragments of antique masonry. The landscape here has two great features; close before you on one side is the long, gentle swell of the Alban Hills, deeply, fantastically blue in most weathers, and marbled with the vague white masses of their scattered towns and villas. It would be difficult to draw the hard figure to a softer curve than that with which the heights sweep from Albano to the plain; this a perfect example of the classic beauty of line in the Italian landscape—that beauty which, when it fills the background of a picture, makes us look in the foreground for a broken column couched upon flowers and a shepherd piping to dancing nymphs. At your side, constantly, you have the broken line of the Claudian Aqueduct, carrying its broad arches far away into the plain. The meadows along which it lies are not the smoothest in the world for a gallop, but there is no pleasure greater than to wander near it. It stands knee-deep in the flower-strewn grass, and its rugged piers are hung with ivy as the columns of a church are draped for a festa. Every archway is a picture, massively framed, of the distance beyond—of the snow-tipped Sabines and lonely Soracte. As the spring advances the whole Campagna smiles and waves with flowers; but I think they are nowhere more rank and lovely than in the shifting shadow of the aqueducts, where they muffle the feet of the columns and smother the half-dozen brooks which wander in and out like silver meshes between the legs of a file of giants. They make a niche for themselves too in every crevice and tremble on the vault of the empty conduits. The ivy hereabouts in the springtime is peculiarly brilliant and delicate; and though it cloaks and muffles these Roman fragments far less closely than the castles and abbeys of England it hangs with the light elegance of all Italian vegetation. It is partly doubtless because their mighty outlines are still unsoftened that the aqueducts are so impressive. They seem the very source of the solitude in which they stand; they look like architectural spectres and loom through the light mists of their grassy desert, as you recede along the line, with the same insubstantial vastness as if they rose out of Egyptian sands. It is a great neighbourhood of ruins, many of which, it must be confessed, you have applauded in many an album. But station a peasant with sheep-skin coat and bandaged legs in the shadow of a tomb or tower best known to drawing-room art, and scatter a dozen goats on the mound above him, and the picture has a charm which has not yet been sketched away.

The other quarter of the Campagna has wider fields and smoother turf and perhaps a greater number of delightful rides; the earth is sounder, and there are fewer pitfalls and ditches. The land for the most part lies higher and catches more wind, and the grass is here and there for great stretches as smooth and level as a carpet. You have no Alban Mountains before you, but you have in the distance the waving ridge of the nearer Apennines, and west of them, along the course of the Tiber, the long seaward level of deep-coloured fields, deepening as they recede to the blue and purple of the sea itself. Beyond them, of a very clear day, you may see the glitter of the Mediterranean. These are the occasions perhaps to remember most fondly, for they lead you to enchanting nooks, and the landscape has details of the highest refinement. Indeed when my sense reverts to the lingering impressions of so blest a time, it seems a fool's errand to have attempted to express them, and a waste of words to do more than recommend the reader to go citywards at twilight of the end of March, making for Porta Cavalleggieri, and note what he sees. At this hour the Cam-

pagna is to the last point its melancholy self, and I remember
roadside "effects" of a strange and intense suggestiveness. Certain mean, mouldering villas behind grass-grown courts have
an indefinably sinister look; there was one in especial of which
it was impossible not to argue that a despairing creature must
have once committed suicide there, behind bolted door and
barred window, and that no one has since had the pluck to go
in and see why he never came out. Every wayside mark of
manners, of history, every stamp of the past in the country
about Rome, touches my sense to a thrill, and I may thus
exaggerate the appeal of very common things. This is the more
likely because the appeal seems ever to rise out of heaven
knows what depths of ancient trouble. To delight in the aspects
of *sentient* ruin might appear a heartless pastime, and the pleasure, I confess, shows the note of perversity. The sombre and
the hard are as common an influence from southern things as
the soft and the bright, I think; sadness rarely fails to assault a
northern observer when he misses what he takes for comfort.
Beauty is no compensation for the loss, only making it more
poignant. Enough beauty of climate hangs over these Roman
cottages and farm-houses—beauty of light, of atmosphere and
of vegetation; but their charm for the maker-out of the stories
in things is the way the golden air shows off their desolation.
Man lives more with Nature in Italy than in New or than in
Old England; she does more work for him and gives him more
holidays than in our short-summered climes, and his home is
therefore much more bare of devices for helping him to do
without her, forget her and forgive her. These reflections are
perhaps the source of the character you find in a moss-coated
stone stairway climbing outside of a wall; in a queer inner
court, befouled with rubbish and drearily bare of convenience;
in an ancient quaintly carven well, worked with infinite labour
from an overhanging window; in an arbour of time-twisted
vines under which you may sit with your feet in the dirt and
remember as a dim fable that there are races for which the type
of domestic allurement is the parlour hearth-rug. For reasons
apparent or otherwise these things amuse me beyond expression, and I am never weary of staring into gateways, of lin-

gering by dreary, shabby, half-barbaric farm-yards, of feasting a foolish gaze on sun-cracked plaster and unctuous indoor shadows.

I mustn't forget, however, that it's not for wayside effects that one rides away behind St. Peter's, but for the strong sense of wandering over boundless space, of seeing great classic lines of landscape, of watching them dispose themselves into pictures so full of "style" that you can think of no painter who deserves to have you admit that they suggest him—hardly knowing whether it is better pleasure to gallop far and drink deep of air and grassy distance and the whole delicious opportunity, or to walk and pause and linger, and try and grasp some ineffaceable memory of sky and colour and outline. Your pace can hardly help falling into a contemplative measure at the time, everywhere so wonderful, but in Rome so persuasively divine, when the winter begins palpably to soften and quicken. Far out on the Campagna, early in February, you feel the first vague earthly emanations, which in a few weeks come wandering into the heart of the city and throbbing through the close, dark streets. Springtime in Rome is an immensely poetic affair; but you must stand often far out in the ancient waste, between grass and sky, to measure its deep, full, steadily accelerated rhythm. The winter has an incontestable beauty, and is pre-eminently the time of colour—the time when it is no affectation, but homely verity, to talk about the "purple" tone of the atmosphere. As February comes and goes your purple is streaked with green and the rich, dark bloom of the distance begins to lose its intensity. But your loss is made up by other gains; none more precious than that inestimable gain to the ear—the disembodied voice of the lark. It comes with the early flowers, the white narcissus and the cyclamen, the half-buried violets and the pale anemones, and makes the whole atmosphere ring like a vault of tinkling glass. You never see the source of the sound, and are utterly unable to localise his note, which seems to come from everywhere at once, to be some hundred-throated voice of the air. Sometimes you fancy you just catch him, a mere vague spot against the blue, an intenser throb in the universal pulsation of light. As the weeks go on the flowers multiply and the deep blues and purples of the hills, turning to azure and violet, creep higher toward the narrowing snow-line of the Sabines. The temperature rises, the first hour of your ride you feel the heat, but you beguile it with brushing the hawthorn-blossoms as you pass along the hedges, and catching at the wild rose and honeysuckle; and when you get into the meadows there is stir enough in the air to lighten the dead weight of the sun. The Roman air, however, is not a tonic medicine, and it seldom suffers exercise to be all exhilarating. It has always seemed to me indeed part of the charm of the latter that your keenest consciousness is haunted with a vague languor. Occasionally when the sirocco blows that sensation becomes strange and exquisite. Then, under the grey sky, before the dim distances which the south-wind mostly brings with it, you seem to ride forth into a world from which all hope has departed and in which, in spite of the flowers that make your horse's footfalls soundless, nothing is left save some queer probability that your imagination is unable to measure, but from which it hardly shrinks. This quality in the Roman element may now and then "relax" you almost to ecstasy; but a season of sirocco would be an overdose of morbid pleasure. You may at any rate best feel the peculiar beauty of the Campagna on those mild days of winter when the mere quality and temper of the sunshine suffice to move the landscape to joy, and you pause on the brown grass in the sunny stillness and, by listening long enough, almost fancy you hear the shrill of the midsummer cricket. It is detail and ornament that vary from month to month, from week to week even, and make your returns to the same places a constant feast of unexpectedness; but the great essential features of the prospect preserve throughout the year the same impressive serenity. Soracte, be it January or May, rises from its blue horizon like an island from the sea and with an elegance of contour which no mood of the year can deepen or diminish. You know it well; you have seen it often in the mellow backgrounds of Claude; and it has such an irresistibly classic, academic air that while you look at it you begin to take your saddle for a faded old arm-chair in a palace gallery. A month's rides in different directions will show you a dozen prime Claudes. After I had seen them all I went piously to the Doria gallery to refresh my memory of its two famous specimens and to enjoy to the utmost their delightful air of reference to something that had become a part of my personal experience. Delightful it certainly is to feel the common element in one's own sensibility and those of a genius whom that element has helped to do great things. Claude must have haunted the very places of one's personal preference and adjusted their divine undulations to his splendid scheme of romance, his view of the poetry of life. He was familiar with aspects in which there wasn't a single uncompromising line. I saw a few days ago a small finished sketch from his hand, in the possession of an American artist, which was almost startling in its clear reflection of forms unaltered by the two centuries that have dimmed and cracked the paint and canvas.

This unbroken continuity of the impressions I have tried to indicate is an excellent example of the intellectual background of all enjoyment in Rome. It effectually prevents pleasure from becoming vulgar, for your sensation rarely begins and ends with itself; it reverberates—it recalls, commemorates, resuscitates something else. At least half the merit of everything you enjoy must be that it suits you absolutely; but the larger half here is generally that it has suited some one else and that you can never flatter yourself you have discovered it. It has been addressed to some use a million miles out of your range, and has had great adventures before ever condescending to please you. It was in admission of this truth that my discriminating friend who showed me the Claudes found it impossible to designate a certain delightful region which you enter at the end of an hour's riding from Porta Cavalleggieri as anything but Arcadia. The exquisite correspondence of the term in this case altogether revived its faded bloom; here veritably the oaten pipe must have stirred the windless air and the satyrs have laughed among the brookside reeds. Three or four long grassy dells stretch away in a chain between low hills over which delicate trees are so discreetly scattered that each one is a resting place for a shepherd. The elements of the scene are simple enough, but the composition has extraordinary refinement. By one of those happy chances which keep observation in Italy always in her best humour a shepherd had thrown himself down under one of the trees in the very attitude of

Melibœus. He had been washing his feet, I suppose, in the neighbouring brook, and had found it pleasant afterwards to roll his short breeches well up on his thighs. Lying thus in the shade, on his elbow, with his naked legs stretched out on the turf and his soft peaked hat over his long hair crushed back like the veritable bonnet of Arcady, he was exactly the figure of the background of this happy valley. The poor fellow, lying there in rustic weariness and ignorance, little fancied that he was a symbol of old-world meanings to new-world eyes.

Such eyes may find as great a store of picturesque meanings in the cork-woods of Monte Mario, tenderly loved of all equestrians. These are less severely pastoral than our Arcadia, and you might more properly lodge there a damosel of Ariosto than a nymph of Theocritus. Among them is strewn a lovely wilderness of flowers and shrubs, and the whole place has such a charming woodland air, that, casting about me the other day for a compliment, I declared that it reminded me of New Hampshire. My compliment had a double edge, and I had no sooner uttered it than I smiled—or sighed—to perceive in all the undiscriminated botany about me the wealth of detail, the idle elegance and grace of Italy alone, the natural stamp of the land which has the singular privilege of making one love her unsanctified beauty all but as well as those features of one's own country toward which nature's small allowance doubles that of one's own affection. For this effect of casting a spell no rides have more value than those you take in Villa Doria or Villa Borghese; or don't take, possibly, if you prefer to reserve these particular regions—the latter in especial—for your walking hours. People do ride, however, in both villas, which deserve honourable mention in this regard. Villa Doria, with its noble site, its splendid views, its great groups of stone-pines, so clustered and yet so individual, its lawns and flowers and fountains, its altogether princely disposition, is a place where one may pace, well mounted, of a brilliant day, with an agreeable sense of its being rather a more elegant pastime to balance in one's stirrups than to trudge on even the smoothest gravel. But at Villa Borghese the walkers have the best of it; for they are free of those adorable outlying corners and bosky byways which the rumble of barouches never reaches. In March the place becomes a perfect epitome of the spring. You cease to care much for the melancholy greenness of the disfeatured statues which has been your chief winter's intimation of verdure; and before you are quite conscious of the tender streaks and patches in the great quaint grassy arena round which the Propaganda students, in their long skirts, wander slowly, like dusky seraphs revolving the gossip of Paradise, you spy the brave little violets uncapping their azure brows beneath the high-stemmed pines. One's walks here would take us too far, and one's pauses detain us too long, when in the quiet parts under the wall one comes across a group of charming small school-boys in full-dress suits and white cravats, shouting over their play in clear Italian, while a grave young priest, beneath a tree, watches them over the top of his book. It sounds like nothing, but the force behind it and the frame round it, the setting, the air, the chord struck, make it a hundred wonderful things.

[1873]

....

Roman Neighbourhoods

I made a note after my first stroll at Albano to the effect that I had been talking of the "picturesque" all my life, but that now for a change I beheld it. I had been looking all winter across the Campagna at the free-flowing outline of the Alban Mount, with its half-dozen towns shining on its purple side even as vague sun-spots in the shadow of a cloud, and thinking it simply an agreeable incident in the varied background of Rome. But now that during the last few days I have been treating it as a fore-ground, have been suffering St. Peter's to play the part of a small mountain on the horizon, with the Campagna swimming mist-ily through the ambiguous lights and shadows of the interval, I find the interest as great as in the best of the by-play of Rome. The walk I speak of was just out of the village, to the south, toward the neighbouring town of L'Ariccia, neighbouring these twenty years, since the Pope* (the late Pope, I was on the point of calling him) threw his superb viaduct across the deep ravine which divides it from Albano. At the risk of seeming to fan-tasticate I confess that the Pope's having built the viaduct—in this very recent antiquity—made me linger there in a pensive posture and marvel at the march of history and at Pius the Ninth's beginning already to profit by the sentimental allow-ances we make to vanished powers. An ardent *nero* [a "black," or papal supporter] then would have had his own way with me and obtained a frank admission that the Pope was indeed a fa-ther to his people. Far down into the charming valley which slopes out the ancestral woods of the Chigis into the level Cam-

* Pius IX. See footnote on p. 128.

pagna winds the steep stone-paved road at the bottom of which, in the good old days, tourists in no great hurry saw the mules and oxen tackled to their carriage for the opposite ascent. And indeed even an impatient tourist might have been content to lounge back in his jolting chaise and look out at the mouldy foundations of the little city plunging into the verdurous flank of the gorge. Questioned, as a cherisher of quaintness, as to the best "bit" hereabouts, I should certainly name the way in which the crumbling black houses of these ponderous villages plant their weary feet on the flowery edges of all the steepest chasms. Before you enter one of them you invariably find yourself lingering outside its pretentious old gateway to see it clutched and stitched to the stony hillside by this rank embroidery of the wildest and bravest things that grow. Just at this moment nothing is prettier than the contrast between their dusky ruggedness and the tender, the yellow and pink and violet fringe of that mantle. All this you may observe from the viaduct at the Ariccia; but you must wander below to feel the full force of the eloquence of our imaginary *papalino* [advocate for the papacy]. The pillars and arches of pale grey peperino arise in huge tiers with a magnificent spring and solidity. The older Romans built no better; and the work has a deceptive air of being one of their sturdy bequests which help one to drop another sigh over the antecedents the Italians of to-day are so eager to repudiate. Will those *they* give their descendants be as good?

At the Ariccia, in any case, I found a little square with a couple of mossy fountains, occupied on one side by a vast dusky-faced Palazzo Chigi and on the other by a goodly church with an imposing dome. The dome, within, covers the whole edifice and is adorned with some extremely elegant stucco-work of the seventeenth century. It gave a great value to this fine old decoration that preparations were going forward for a local festival and that the village carpenter was hanging certain mouldy strips of crimson damask against the piers of the vaults. The damask might have been of the seventeenth century too, and a group of peasant-women were seeing it unfurled with evident awe. I regarded it myself with interest—it seemed so the tattered remnant of a fashion that had gone out for ever. I thought again of the poor disinherited Pope, wondering whether, when such venerable frippery will no longer bear the carpenter's nails, any more will be provided. It was hard to fancy anything but shreds and patches in that musty tabernacle. Wherever you go in Italy you receive some such intimation as this of the shrunken proportions of Catholicism, and every church I have glanced into on my walks hereabouts has given me an almost pitying sense of it. One finds one's self at last—without fatuity, I hope—feeling sorry for the solitude of the remaining faithful. It's as if the churches had been made so for the world, in its social sense, and the world had so irrevocably moved away. They are in size out of all modern proportion to the local needs, and the only thing at all alive in the melancholy waste they collectively form is the smell of stale incense. There are pictures on all the altars by respectable third-rate painters; pictures which I suppose once were ordered and paid for and criticised by worshippers who united taste with piety. At Genzano, beyond the Ariccia, rises on the grey village street a pompous Renaissance temple whose imposing nave and aisles would contain the population of a capital. But where is the *taste* of the Ariccia and Genzano? Where are the choice spirits for whom Antonio Raggi modelled the garlands of his dome and a hundred clever craftsmen imitated Guido and Caravaggio? Here and there, from the pavement, as you pass, a dusky crone interlards her devotions with more profane importunities, or a grizzled peasant on rusty-jointed knees, tilted forward with his elbows on a bench, reveals the dimensions of the patch in his blue breeches. But where is the connecting link between Guido and Caravaggio and those poor souls for whom an undoubted original is only a something behind a row of candlesticks, of no very clear meaning save that you must bow to it? You find a vague memory of it at best in the useless grandeurs about you, and you seem to be looking at a structure of which the stubborn earth-scented foundations alone remain, with the carved and painted shell that bends above them, while the central substance has utterly crumbled away.

I shall seem to have adopted a more meditative pace than befits a brisk constitutional if I say that I also fell a-thinking before the shabby façade of the old Chigi Palace. But it seemed somehow in its grey forlornness to respond to the sadly superannuated expression of the opposite church; and indeed in any condition what self-respecting cherisher of quaintness can for-bear to do a little romancing in the shadow of a provincial palazzo? On the face of the matter, I know, there is often no very salient peg to hang a romance on. A sort of dusky blank-ness invests the establishment, which has often a rather imbe-cile old age. But a hundred brooding secrets lurk in this inexpressive mask, and the Chigi Palace did duty for me in the suggestive twilight as the most haunted of houses. Its basement walls sloped outward like the beginning of a pyramid, and its lower windows were covered with massive iron cages. Within the doorway, across the court, I saw the pale glimmer of flow-ers on a terrace, and I made much, for the effect of the roof, of a great covered loggia or belvedere with a dozen window-panes missing or mended with paper. Nothing gives one a stronger impression of old manners than an ancestral palace towering in this haughty fashion over a shabby little town; you hardly stretch a point when you call it an impression of feu-dalism. The scene may pass for feudal to American eyes, for which a hundred windows on a façade mean nothing more exclusive than a hotel kept (at the most invidious) on the European plan. The mouldy grey houses on the steep crooked street, with their black cavernous archways pervaded by bad smells, by the braying of asses and by human intonations hardly more musical, the haggard and tattered peasantry staring at you with hungry-heavy eyes, the brutish-looking monks (there are still enough to point a moral), the soldiers, the mounted con-stables, the dirt, the dreariness, the misery, and the dark over-grown palace frowning over it all from barred window and guarded gateway—what more than all this do we dimly descry in a mental image of the dark ages? For all his desire to keep the peace with the vivid image of things if it be only vivid enough, the votary of this ideal may well occasionally turn over such val-ues with the wonder of what one takes them as paying for. They pay sometimes for such sorry "facts of life." At Genzano, out of the very midst of the village squalor, rises the Palazzo Cesarini, separated from its gardens by a dirty lane. Between peasant and prince the contact is unbroken, and one would suppose Italian good-nature sorely taxed by their mutual allowances; that the prince in especial must cultivate a firm impervious shell. There are no comfortable townsfolk about him to remind him of the blessings of a happy mediocrity of fortune. When he looks out of his window he sees a battered old peasant against a sunny wall sawing off his dinner from a hunch of black bread.

I must confess, however, that "feudal" as it amused me to find the little piazza of the Ariccia, it appeared to threaten in no manner an exasperated rising. On the contrary, the afternoon being cool, many of the villagers were contentedly muffled in those ancient cloaks, lined with green baize, which, when tossed over the shoulder and surmounted with a peaked hat, form one of the few lingering remnants of "costume" in Italy; others were tossing wooden balls light-heartedly enough on the grass outside the town. The egress on this side is under a great stone archway thrown out from the palace and surmounted with the family arms. Nothing could better confirm your theory that the townsfolk are groaning serfs. The road leads away through the woods, like many of the roads hereabouts, among trees less remarkable for their size than for their picturesque contortions and posturings. The woods, at the moment at which I write, are full of the raw green light of early spring, a *jour* vastly becoming to the various complexions of the wild flowers that cover the waysides. I have never seen these untended parterres in such lovely exuberance; the sturdiest pedestrian becomes a lingering idler if he allows them to catch his eye. The pale purple cyclamen, with its hood thrown back, stands up in masses as dense as tulip-beds; and here and there in the duskier places great sheets of forget-me-not seem to exhale a faint blue mist. These are the commonest plants; there are dozens more I know no name for—a rich profusion in especial of a beautiful five-petalled flower whose white texture is pencilled with hair-strokes certain fair copyists I know of would have to hold their breath to imitate. An Italian oak has neither the girth nor the height of its English brothers, but it contrives in proportion to be perhaps even more effective. It crooks its back and twists its arms and clinches its hundred fists with the queerest extravagance, and wrinkles its bark into strange rugosities from which its first scattered sprouts of yellow green seem to break out like a morbid fungus. But the tree which has the greatest charm to northern eyes is the cold grey-green ilex, whose clear crepuscular shade drops against a Roman sun a veil impenetrable, yet not oppressive. The ilex has even less colour than the cypress, but it is much less funereal, and a landscape in which it is frequent may still be said to smile faintly, though by no means to laugh. It abounds in old Italian gardens, where the boughs are trimmed and interlocked into vaulted corridors in which, from point to point, as in the niches of some dimly frescoed hall, you see mildewed busts stare at you with a solemnity which the even grey light makes strangely intense. A humbler relative of the ilex, though it does better things than help broken-nosed emperors to look dignified, is the olive, which covers many of the neighbouring hillsides with its little smoky puffs of foliage. A stroke of composition I never weary of is that long blue stretch of the Campagna which makes a high horizon and rests on this vaporous base of olive-tops. A reporter intent upon a simile might liken it to the ocean seen above the smoke of watch-fires kindled on the strand.

To do perfect justice to the wood-walk away from the Ariccia I ought to touch upon the birds that were singing vespers as I passed. But the reader would find my rhapsody as poor entertainment as the programme of a concert he had been unable to attend. I have no more learning about bird-music than would help me to guess that a dull dissyllabic refrain in the heart of the wood came from the cuckoo; and when at moments I heard a twitter of fuller tone, with a more suggestive modulation, I could only *hope* it was the nightingale. I have listened for the nightingale more than once in places so charming that his song would have seemed but the articulate expression of their beauty, and have never heard much beyond a provoking snatch or two—a prelude that came to nothing. In spite of a natural grudge, however, I generously believe him a great artist or at least a great genius—a creature who despises any prompting short of absolute inspiration. For the rich, the multitudinous melody around me seemed but the offering to my ear of the prodigal spirit of tradition. The wood was ringing with sound because it was twilight, spring and Italy. It was also because of these good things and various others besides that I relished so keenly my visit to the Capuchin convent upon

which I emerged after half-an-hour in the wood. It stands
above the town, on the slope of the Alban Mount, and its wild
garden climbs away behind it and extends its melancholy influence. Before it is a small stiff avenue of trimmed live-oaks
which conducts you to a grotesque little shrine beneath the
staircase ascending to the church. Just here, if you are apt to
grow timorous at twilight, you may take a very pretty fright;
for as you draw near you catch behind the grating of the shrine
the startling semblance of a gaunt and livid monk. A sickly
lamplight plays down upon his face, and he stares at you from
cavernous eyes with a dreadful air of death in life. Horror of
horrors, you murmur, is this a Capuchin penance? You discover of course in a moment that it is only a Capuchin joke,
that the monk is a pious dummy and his spectral visage a
matter of the paintbrush. You resent his intrusion on the surrounding loveliness; and as you proceed to demand entertainment at their convent you pronounce the Capuchins very
foolish fellows. This declaration, as I made it, was supported by
the conduct of the simple brother who opened the door of the
cloister in obedience to my knock and, on learning my errand,
demurred about admitting me at so late an hour. If I would
return on the morrow morning he'd be most happy. He broke
into a blank grin when I assured him that this was the very
hour of my desire and that the garish morning light would do
no justice to the view. These were mysteries beyond his ken,
and it was only his good-nature (of which he had plenty) and
not his imagination that was moved. So that when, passing
through the narrow cloister and out upon the grassy terrace, I
saw another cowled brother standing with folded hands profiled against the sky, in admirable harmony with the scene, I
questioned his knowing the uses for which he is still most
precious. This, however, was surely too much to ask of him,
and it was cause enough for gratitude that, though he was
there before me, he was not a fellow-tourist with an opera-glass
slung over his shoulder. There was support to my idea of the
convent in the expiring light, for the scene was in its way
unsurpassable. Directly below the terrace lay the deep-set circle
of the Alban Lake, shining softly through the light mists of
evening. This beautiful pool—it is hardly more—occupies the

crater of a prehistoric volcano, a perfect cup, shaped and smelted by furnace-fires. The rim of the cup, rising high and densely wooded round the placid stone-blue water, has a sort of natural artificiality. The sweep and contour of the long circle are admirable; never was a lake so charmingly lodged. It is said to be of extraordinary depth; and though stone-blue water seems at first a very innocent substitute for boiling lava it has a sinister look which betrays its dangerous antecedents. The winds never reach it and its surface is never ruffled; but its deep-bosomed placidity seems to cover guilty secrets, and you fancy it in communication with the capricious and treacherous forces of nature. Its very colour is of a joyless beauty, a blue as cold and opaque as a solidified sheet of lava. Streaked and wrinkled by a mysterious motion of its own, it affects the very type of a legendary pool, and I could easily have believed that I had only to sit long enough into the evening to see the ghosts of classic nymphs and naiads cleave its sullen flood and beckon me with irresistible arms. Is it because its shores are haunted with these vague Pagan influences that two convents have risen there to purge the atmosphere? From the Capuchin terrace you look across at the grey Franciscan monastery of Palazzuola, which is not less romantic certainly than the most obstinate myth it may have exorcised. The Capuchin garden is a wild tangle of great trees and shrubs and clinging, trembling vines which in these hard days are left to take care of themselves; a weedy garden, if there ever was one, but none the less charming for that, in the deepening dusk, with its steep grassy vistas struggling away into impenetrable shadow. I braved the shadow for the sake of climbing upon certain little flat-roofed crumbling pavilions that rise from the corners of the further wall and give you a wider and lovelier view of lake and hills and sky.

I have perhaps justified to the reader the mild proposition with which I started—convinced him, that is, that Albano is worth a walk. It may be a different walk each day, moreover, and not resemble its predecessors save by its keeping in the shade. "Galleries" the roads are prettily called, and with the justice that they are vaulted and draped overhead and hung with an immense succession of pictures. As you follow the few miles from Genzano to Frascati you have perpetual views of the Campagna framed by clusters of trees; the vast iridescent expanse of which completes the charm and comfort of your verdurous dusk. I compared it just now to the sea, and with a good deal of truth, for it has the same incalculable lights and shades, the same confusion of glitter and gloom. But I have seen it at moments—chiefly in the misty twilight—when it resembled less the waste of waters than something more portentous, the land itself in fatal dissolution. I could believe the fields to be dimly surging and tossing and melting away into quicksands, and that one's very last chance of an impression was taking place. A view, however, which has the merit of being really as interesting as it seems, is that of the Lake of Nemi; which the enterprising traveller hastens to compare with its sister sheet of Albano. Comparison in this case is particularly odious, for in order to prefer one lake to the other you have to discover faults where there are none. Nemi is a smaller circle, but lies in a deeper cup, and if with no grey Franciscan pile to guard its woody shores, at least, in the same position, the little high-perched black town to which it gives its name and which looks across at Genzano on the opposite shore as Palazzuola regards Castel Gandolfo. The walk from the Ariccia to Genzano is charming, most of all when it reaches a certain grassy piazza from which three public avenues stretch away under a double row of stunted and twisted elms. The Duke Cesarini has a villa at Genzano—I mentioned it just now—whose gardens overhang the lake; but he has also a porter in a faded rakish-looking livery who shakes his head at your proffered franc unless you can reinforce it with a permit countersigned at Rome. For this annoying complication of dignities he is justly to be denounced; but I forgive him for the sake of that ancestor who in the seventeenth century planted this shady walk. Never was a prettier approach to a town than by these low-roofed light-chequered corridors. Their only defect is that they prepare you for a town of rather more rustic coquetry than Genzano exhibits. It has quite the usual allowance, the common cynicism, of accepted decay, and looks dismally as if its best families had all fallen into penury together and lost the means of keeping anything better than donkeys in their great dark, vaulted basements and mending their broken window-panes with anything better than paper. It was on the occasion of this drear Genzano that I had a difference of opinion with a friend who maintained that there was nothing in the same line so pretty in Europe as a pretty New England village. The proposition seemed to a cherisher of quaintness on the face of it inacceptable; but calmly considered it has a measure of truth. I am not fond of chalk-white painted planks, certainly; I vastly prefer the dusky tones of ancient stucco and peperino; but I succumb on occasion to the charms of a vine-shaded porch, of tulips and dahlias glowing in the shade of high-arching elms, of heavy-scented lilacs bending over a white paling to brush your cheek.

"I prefer Siena to Lowell," said my friend; "but I prefer Farmington to such a thing as this."* In fact an Italian village is simply a miniature Italian city, and its various parts imply a town of fifty times the size. At Genzano are neither dahlias nor lilacs, and no odours but foul ones. Flowers and other graces are all confined to the high-walled precincts of Duke Cesarini, to which you must obtain admission twenty miles away. The houses on the other hand would generally lodge a New England cottage, porch and garden and high-arching elms included, in one of their cavernous basements. These vast grey dwellings are all of a fashion denoting more generous social needs than any they serve nowadays. They speak of better days and of a fabulous time when Italy was either not shabby or could at least "carry off" her shabbiness. For what follies are they doing penance? Through what melancholy stages have their fortunes ebbed? You ask these questions as you choose the shady side of the long blank street and watch the hot sun glare upon the dust-coloured walls and pause before the fetid gloom of open doors.

I should like to spare a word for mouldy little Nemi, perched upon a cliff high above the lake, at the opposite side; but after all, when I had climbed up into it from the water-side, passing beneath a great arch which I suppose once topped a gateway, and counted its twenty or thirty apparent inhabitants peeping

* Lowell, Massachusetts; Farmington, Connecticut.

at me from black doorways, and looked at the old round tower at whose base the village clusters, and declared that it was all queer, queer, desperately queer, I had said all that is worth saying about it. Nemi has a much better appreciation of its lovely position than Genzano, where your only view of the lake is from a dunghill behind one of the houses. At the foot of the round tower is an overhanging terrace, from which you may feast your eyes on the only freshness they find in these dusky human hives—the blooming seam, as one may call it, of strong wild-flowers which binds the crumbling walls to the face of the cliff. Of Rocca di Papa I must say as little. It consorted generally with the bravery of its name; but the only object I made a note of as I passed through it on my way to Monte Cavo, which rises directly above it, was a little black house with a tablet in its face setting forth that Massimo d'Azeglio had dwelt there. The story of his sojourn is not the least attaching episode in his delightful *Ricordi*. From the summit of Monte Cavo is a prodigious view, which you may enjoy with whatever good-nature is left you by the reflection that the modern Passionist convent occupying this admirable site was erected by the Cardinal of York (grandson of James II) on the demolished ruins of an immemorial temple of Jupiter: the last foolish act of a foolish race. For me I confess this folly spoiled the convent, and the convent all but spoiled the view; for I kept thinking how fine it would have been to emerge upon the old pillars and sculptures from the lava pavement of the Via Triumphalis, which wanders grass-grown and untrodden through the woods. A convent, however, which nothing spoils is that of Palazzuola, to which I paid my respects on this same occasion. It rises on a lower spur of Monte Cavo, on the edge, as we have seen, of the Alban Lake, and though it occupies a classic site, that of early Alba Longa, it displaced nothing more precious than memories and legends so dim that the antiquarians are still quarrelling about them. It has a meagre little church and the usual sham Perugino with a couple of tinsel crowns for the Madonna and the Infant inserted into the canvas; and it has also a musty old room hung about with faded portraits and charts and queer ecclesiastical knick-knacks, which borrowed a mysterious interest from the sudden assurance of the simple

Franciscan brother who accompanied me that it was the room of the Son of the King of Portugal. But my peculiar pleasure was the little thick-shaded garden which adjoins the convent and commands from its massive artificial foundations an enchanting view of the lake. Part of it is laid out in cabbages and lettuce, over which a rubicund brother, with his frock tucked up, was bending with a solicitude which he interrupted to remove his skull-cap and greet me with the unsophisticated sweet-humoured smile that every now and then in Italy does so much to make you forget the ambiguities of monachism. The rest is occupied by cypresses and other funereal umbrage, making a dank circle round an old cracked fountain black with water-moss. The parapet of the terrace is furnished with good stone seats where you may lean on your elbows to gaze away a sunny half-hour and, feeling the general charm of the scene, declare that the best mission of such a country in the world has been simply to produce, in the way of prospect and picture, these masterpieces of mildness. Mild here as a dream the whole attained effect, mild as resignation, mild as one's thoughts of another life. Such a session wasn't surely an experience of the irritable flesh; it was the deep degustation, on a summer's day, of something immortally expressed by a man of genius.

From Albano you may take your way through several ancient little cities to Frascati, a rival centre of *villeggiatura* [country homes], the road following the hillside for a long morning's walk and passing through alternations of denser and clearer shade—the dark vaulted alleys of ilex and the brilliant corridors of fresh-sprouting oak. The Campagna is beneath you continually, with the sea beyond Ostia receiving the silver arrows of the sun upon its chased and burnished shield, and mighty Rome, to the north, lying at no great length in the idle immensity around it. The highway passes below Castel Gandolfo, which stands perched on an eminence behind a couple of gateways surmounted with the Papal tiara and twisted cordon; and I have more than once chosen the roundabout road for the sake of passing beneath these pompous insignia. Castel Gandolfo is indeed an ecclesiastical village and under the peculiar protection of the Popes, whose huge summer-palace rises in the midst of it like a rural Vatican. In speaking of the road to

Frascati I necessarily revert to my first impressions, gathered on the occasion of the feast of the Annunziata, which falls on the 25th of March and is celebrated by a peasants' fair. As Murray strongly recommends you to visit this spectacle, at which you are promised a brilliant exhibition of all the costumes of modern Latium, I took an early train to Frascati and measured, in company with a prodigious stream of humble pedestrians, the half-hour's interval to Grotta Ferrata, where the fair is held. The road winds along the hillside, among the silver-sprinkled olives and through a charming wood where the ivy seemed tacked upon the oaks by women's fingers and the birds were singing to the late anemones. It was covered with a very jolly crowd of vulgar pleasure-takers, and the only creatures not in a state of manifest hilarity were the pitiful little overladen, overbeaten donkeys (who surely deserve a chapter to themselves in any description of these neighbourhoods) and the horrible beggars who were thrusting their sores and stumps at you from under every tree. Every one was shouting, singing, scrambling, making light of dust and distance and filling the air with that childlike jollity which the blessed Italian temperament never goes roundabout to conceal. There is no crowd surely at once so jovial and so gentle as an Italian crowd, and I doubt if in any other country the tightly packed third-class car in which I went out from Rome would have introduced me to so much smiling and so little swearing. Grotta Ferrata is a very dirty little village, with a number of raw new houses baking on the hot hillside and nothing to charm the fond gazer but its situation and its old fortified abbey. After pushing about among the shabby little booths and declining a number of fabulous bargains in tinware, shoes and pork, I was glad to retire to a comparatively uninvaded corner of the abbey and divert myself with the view. This grey ecclesiastical stronghold is a thoroughly scenic affair, hanging over the hillside on plunging foundations which bury themselves among the dense olives. It has massive round towers at the corners and a grass-grown moat, enclosing a church and a monastery. The forecourt, within the abbatial gateway, now serves as the public square of the village and in fair-time of course witnesses the best of the fun. The best of the fun was to be found in certain great vaults and cellars of the abbey, where wine was in free flow from gigantic hogsheads. At the exit of these trickling grottos shady trellises of bamboo and gathered twigs had been improvised, and under them a grand guzzling proceeded. All of which was so in the fine old style that I was roughly reminded of the wedding-feast of Gamacho.* The banquet was far less substantial of course, but it had a note as of immemorial manners that couldn't fail to suggest romantic analogies to a pilgrim from the land of no cooks. There was a feast of reason close at hand, however, and I was careful to visit the famous frescoes of Domenichino in the adjoining church. It sounds rather brutal perhaps to say that, when I came back into the clamorous little piazza, the sight of the peasants swilling down their sour wine appealed to me more than the masterpieces—Murray calls them so—of the famous Bolognese. It amounts after all to saying that I prefer Teniers† to Domenichino; which I am willing to let pass for the truth. The scene under the rickety trellises was the more suggestive of Teniers that there were no costumes to make it too Italian. Murray's attractive statement on this point was, like many of his statements, much truer twenty years ago than today. Costume is gone or fast going; I saw among the women not a single crimson bodice and not a couple of classic head-cloths. The poorer sort, dressed in vulgar rags of no fashion and colour, and the smarter ones in calico gowns and printed shawls of the vilest modern fabric, had honoured their dusky tresses but with rich applications of grease. The men are still in jackets and breeches, and, with their slouched and pointed hats and open-breasted shirts and rattling leather leggings, may remind one sufficiently of the Italian peasant as he figured in the woodcuts familiar to our infancy. After coming out of the church I found a delightful nook—a queer little terrace before a more retired and tranquil drinking-shop—where I called for a bottle of wine to help me to guess why I "drew the line" at Domenichino.

This little terrace was a capricious excrescence at the end of the piazza, itself simply a greater terrace; and one reached it,

* A lavish wedding feast, in Cervantes' *Don Quixote* (1605).
† The Flemish painter David Teniers the Elder (1582–1649), who lived and worked for a long period in Rome.

picturesquely, by ascending a short inclined plane of grass-grown cobble-stones and passing across a little dusky kitchen through whose narrow windows the light of the mighty landscape beyond touched up old earthen pots. The terrace was oblong and so narrow that it held but a single small table, placed lengthwise; yet nothing could be pleasanter than to place one's bottle on the polished parapet. Here you seemed by the time you had emptied it to be swinging forward into immensity—hanging poised above the Campagna. A beautiful gorge with a twinkling stream wandered down the hill far below you, beyond which Marino and Castel Gandolfo peeped above the trees. In front you could count the towers of Rome and the tombs of the Appian Way. I don't know that I came to any very distinct conclusion about Domenichino; but it was perhaps because the view was perfection that he struck me as more than ever mediocrity. And yet I don't think it was one's bottle of wine, either, that made one after all maudlin about him; it was the sense of the foolishly usurped in his tenure of fame, of the derisive in his ever having been put forward. To say so indeed savours of flogging a dead horse, but it is surely an unkind stroke of fate for him that Murray assures ten thousand Britons every winter in the most emphatic manner that his Communion of St. Jerome is the "second finest picture in the world." If this were so one would certainly here in Rome, where such institutions are convenient, retire into the very nearest convent; with such a world one would have a standing quarrel. And yet this sport of destiny is an interesting case, in default of being an interesting painter, and I would take a moderate walk, in most moods, to see one of his pictures. He is so supremely good an example of effort detached from inspiration and school-merit divorced from spontaneity, that one of his fine frigid performances ought to hang in a conspicuous place in every academy of design. Few things of the sort contain more urgent lessons or point a more precious moral; and I would have the headmaster in the drawing-school take each ingenuous pupil by the hand and lead him up to the Triumph of David or the Chase of Diana or the red-nosed Persian Sibyl and make him some such little speech as the following: "This great picture, my son, was hung here to show

you how you must *never* paint; to give you a perfect specimen
of what in its boundless generosity the providence of nature
created for our fuller knowledge—an artist whose development was a negation. The great thing in art is charm, and the
great thing in charm is spontaneity. Domenichino, having talent, is here and there an excellent model—he was devoted,
conscientious, observant, industrious; but now that we've seen
pretty well what can simply be learned do its best, these things
help him little with us, because his imagination was cold. It
loved nothing, it lost itself in nothing, its efforts never gave it
the heartache. It went about trying this and that, concocting
cold pictures after cold receipts, dealing in the second-hand, in
the ready-made, and putting into its performances a little of
everything but itself. When you see so many things in a composition you might suppose that among them all some charm
might be born; yet they're really but the hundred mouths
through which you may hear the unhappy thing murmur 'I'm
dead!' It's by the simplest thing it has that a picture lives—by
its temper. Look at all the great talents, Domenichino as well
as at Titian; but think less of dogma than of plain nature, and
I can almost promise you that yours will remain true." This is
very little to what the æsthetic sage I have imagined *might* say;
and we are after all unwilling to let our last verdict be an
unkind one on any great bequest of human effort. The faded
frescoes in the chapel at Grotta Ferrata leave us a memory the
more of man's effort to dream beautifully; and they thus mingle harmoniously enough with our multifold impressions of
Italy, where dreams and realities have both kept such pace and
so strangely diverged. It was absurd—that was the truth—to
be critical at all among the appealing old Italianisms round me
and to treat the poor exploded Bolognese more harshly than,
when I walked back to Frascati, I treated the charming old
water-works of the Villa Aldobrandini. I confound these various products of antiquated art in a genial absolution, and
should like especially to tell how fine it was to watch this
prodigious fountain come tumbling down its channel of
mouldy rock-work, through its magnificent vista of ilex, to the
fantastic old hemicycle where a dozen tritons and naiads sit
posturing to receive it. The sky above the ilexes was incredibly

blue and the ilexes themselves incredibly black; and to see the young white moon peeping above the trees you could easily have fancied it was midnight. I should like furthermore to expatiate on Villa Mondragone, the most grandly impressive hereabouts, of all such domestic monuments. The great Casino in the midst is as big as the Vatican, which it strikingly resembles, and it stands perched on a terrace as vast as the parvise of St. Peter's, looking straight away over black cypress-tops into the shining vastness of the Campagna. Everything somehow seemed immense and solemn; there was nothing small but certain little nestling blue shadows on the Sabine Mountains, to which the terrace seems to carry you wonderfully near. The place has been for some time lost to private uses, since it figures fantastically in a novel of George Sand—*La Daniella*—and now, in quite another way, as a Jesuit college for boys. The afternoon was perfect, and as it waned it filled the dark alleys with a wonderful golden haze. Into this came leaping and shouting a herd of little collegians with a couple of long-skirted Jesuits striding at their heels. We all know—I make the point for my antithesis—the monstrous practices of these people; yet as I watched the group I verily believe I declared that if I had a little son he should go to Mondragone and receive their crooked teachings for the sake of the other memories, the avenues of cypress and ilex, the view of the Campagna, the atmosphere of antiquity. But doubtless when a sense of "mere character," shameless incomparable character, has brought one to this it is time one should pause.

[1873]

The After-Season in Rome

One may at the blest end of May say without injustice to anybody that the state of mind of many a *forestiero* [foreign visitor] in Rome is one of intense impatience for the moment when all other *forestieri* shall have taken themselves off. One may confess to this state of mind and be no misanthrope. The place has passed so completely for the winter months into the hands of the barbarians that that estimable character the passionate pilgrim finds it constantly harder to keep his passion clear. He has a rueful sense of impressions perverted and adulterated; the all-venerable visage disconcerts us by a vain eagerness to see itself mirrored in English, American, German eyes. It isn't simply that you are never first or never alone at the classic or historic spots where you have dreamt of persuading the shy *genius loci* into confidential utterance; it isn't simply that St. Peter's, the Vatican, the Palatine, are forever ringing with the false note of the languages without style: it is the general oppressive feeling that the city of the soul has become for the time a monstrous mixture of watering-place and curiosity-shop and that its most ardent life is that of the tourists who haggle over false intaglios and yawn through palaces and temples. But you are told of a happy time when these abuses begin to pass away, when Rome becomes Rome again and you may have her all to yourself. "You may like her more or less now," I was assured at the height of the season; "but you must wait till the month of May, when she'll give you *all* she has, to love her. Then the foreigners, or the excess of them, are gone; the galleries and ruins are empty, and the place," said my informant, who was a happy Frenchman of the Académie de France, "*renaît à elle-même* [returns to herself]." Indeed I was haunted all winter by an irresistible prevision of what Rome *must* be in declared spring. Certain charming places seemed to murmur: "Ah, this is nothing! Come back at the right weeks and see the sky above us almost black with its excess of blue, and the new grass already deep, but still vivid, and the white roses tumble in odorous spray and the warm radiant air distil gold for the smelting-pot that the *genius loci* then dips his brush into before making play with it, in his inimitable way, for the general effect of complexion."

A month ago I spent a week in the country, and on my return, the first time I approached the Corso, became conscious of a change. Something delightful had happened, to which at first I couldn't give a name, but which presently shone out as the fact that there were but half of many people present and that these were chiefly the natural or the naturalised. We had been docked of half our irrelevance, our motley excess, and now physically, morally, æsthetically there was elbow-room. In the afternoon I went to the Pincio, and the Pincio was almost dull. The band was playing to a dozen ladies who lay in landaus poising their lace-fringed parasols; but they had scarce more than a light-gloved dandy apiece hanging over their carriage doors. By the parapet to the great terrace that sweeps the city stood but three or four interlopers looking at the sunset and with their Baedekers only just showing in their pockets— the sunsets not being down among the tariffed articles in these precious volumes. I went so far as to hope for them that, like myself, they were, under every precaution, taking some amorous intellectual liberty with the scene.

Practically I violate thus the instinct of monopoly, since it's a shame not to publish that Rome in May is indeed exquisitely worth your patience. I have just been so gratified at finding myself in undisturbed possession for a couple of hours of the Museum of the Lateran that I can afford to be magnanimous. It's almost as if the old all-papal paradise had come back. The weather for a month has been perfect, the sky an extravagance of blue, the air lively enough, the nights cool, nippingly cool, and the whole ancient greyness lighted with an irresistible smile. Rome, which in some moods, especially to new-comers, seems a place of almost sinister gloom, has an occasional art, as one knows her better, of brushing away care by the grand gesture with which some splendid impatient mourning matron—just the Niobe of Nations, surviving, emerging and looking about her again—might pull off and cast aside an oppression of muffling crape. This admirable power still temperamentally to react and take notice lurks in all her darkness and dirt and decay—a something more careless and hopeless that our thrifty northern cheer, and yet more genial and urbane than the Parisian spirit of *blague* [banter]. The collective Roman nature is a healthy and hearty one, and you feel it abroad in the streets even when the sirocco blows and the medium of life seems to proceed more or less from the mouth of a furnace. But who shall analyse even the simplest Roman impression? It is compounded of so many things, it says so much, it involves so much, it so quickens the intelligence and so flatters the heart, that before we fairly grasp the case the imagination has marked it for her own and exposed us to a perilous likelihood of talking nonsense about it.

The smile of Rome, as I have called it, and its insidious message to those who incline to ramble irresponsibly and take things as they come, is ushered in with the first breath of spring, and then grows and grows with the advancing season till it wraps the whole place in its tenfold charm. As the process develops you can do few better things than go often to Villa Borghese and sit on the grass—on a stout bit of drapery—and watch its exquisite stages. It has a frankness and a sweetness beyond any relenting of *our* clumsy climates even when ours leave off their damnable faces and begin. Nature departs from every reserve with a confidence that leaves one at a loss where, as it were, to look—leaves one, as I say, nothing to do but to lay one's head among the anemones at the base of a high-stemmed pine and gaze up crestward and skyward along its slanting silvery column. You may watch the whole business from a dozen of these choice standpoints and have a different villa for it every day in the week. The Doria, the Ludovisi, the Medici, the Albani, the Wolkonski, the Chigi, the Mellini, the Massimo—there are more of them, with all their sights and sounds and odours and memories, than you have senses for. But I prefer none of them to the Borghese, which is free to all the world at all times and yet never crowded; for when the whirl of carriages is great in the middle regions you may find a hundred untrodden spots and silent corners, tenanted at the worst by a group of those long-skirted young Propagandists who stalk about with solemn angularity, each with a book under his arm, like silhouettes from a mediæval missal, and "compose" so extremely well with the still more processional cypresses and with stretches of golden-russet wall overtopped by ultramarine. And yet if the Borghese is good the Medici is strangely charming, and you may stand in the little belvedere which rises with such surpassing oddity out of the dusky heart of the Boschetto at the latter establishment—a miniature presentation of the wood of the Sleeping Beauty—and look across at the Ludovisi pines lifting their crooked parasols into a sky of what a painter would call the most morbid blue, and declare that the place where *they* grow is the most delightful in the world. Villa Ludovisi has been all winter the residence of the lady familiarly known in Roman society as "Rosina," Victor Emmanuel's morganatic wife, the only familiarity, it would seem, that she allows, for the grounds were rigidly closed, to the inconsolable regret of old Roman sojourners. Just as the nightingales began to sing, however, the quasi-august *padrona* departed, and the public, with certain restrictions, have been admitted to hear them. The place takes, where it lies, a princely ease, and there could be no better example of the expansive tendencies of ancient privilege than the fact that its whole vast extent is contained by the city walls. It has in this respect very much the same enviable air of having got up early that marks the great intramural demesne of Magdalen College at Oxford. The stern old ramparts of Rome form the outer enclosure of the villa, and hence a series of "striking scenic effects" which it would be unscrupulous flattery to say you can imagine. The grounds are laid out in the formal last century manner; but nowhere do the straight black cypresses lead off the gaze into vistas of a melancholy more charged with associations—poetic, romantic, historic; nowhere are there grander smoother walls of laurel and myrtle.

I recently spent an afternoon hour at the little Protestant cemetery close to St. Paul's Gate, where the ancient and the modern world are insidiously contrasted. They make between them one of the solemn places of Rome—although indeed when funereal things are so interfused it seems ungrateful to call them sad. Here is a mixture of tears and smiles, of stones and flowers, of mourning cypresses and radiant sky, which gives us the impression of our looking back at death from the brighter side of the grave. The cemetery nestles in an angle of the city wall, and the older graves are sheltered by a mass of ancient brickwork, through whose narrow loopholes you peep at the wide purple of the Campagna. Shelley's grave is here, buried in roses—a happy grave every way for the very type and figure of the Poet. Nothing could be more impenetrably tranquil than this little corner in the bend of the protecting rampart, where a cluster of modern ashes is held tenderly in the rugged hand of the Past. The past is tremendously embodied in the hoary pyramid of Caius Cestius, which rises hard by, half within the wall and half without, cutting solidly into the solid blue of the sky and casting its pagan shadow upon the grass of English graves—that of Keats, among them—with an effect of poetic justice. It is a wonderful confusion of mortality and a grim enough admonition of our helpless promiscuity in the crucible of time. But the most touching element of all is the appeal of the pious English inscriptions among all these Roman memories; touching because of their universal expression of that trouble within trouble, misfortune in a foreign land. Something special stirs the heart through the fine Scriptural language in which everything is recorded. The echoes of massive Latinity with which the atmosphere is charged suggest nothing more majestic and monumental. I may seem unduly to refine, but the injunction to the reader in the monument to Miss Bathurst, drowned in the Tiber in 1824, "If thou art young and lovely, build not thereon, for she who lies beneath thy feet in death was the loveliest flower ever cropt in its bloom," affects us irresistibly as a case for tears on the spot. The whole elaborate inscription indeed says something over and beyond all it does say. The English have the reputation of being the most reticent people in the world, and as there is no smoke without fire I suppose they have done something to deserve it; yet who can say that one doesn't constantly meet the most startling examples of the insular faculty to "gush?" In this instance the mother of the deceased takes the public into her confidence with surprising frankness and omits no detail, seizing the opportunity to mention by the way that she had already lost her husband by a most mysterious visitation. The appeal to one's attention and the confidence in it are withal most moving. The whole record has an old-fashioned gentility that makes its frankness tragic. You seem to hear the garrulity of passionate grief.

To be choosing these positive commonplaces of the Roman tone for a theme when there are matters of modern moment going on may seem none the less to require an apology. But I make no claim to your special correspondent's faculty for getting an "inside" view of things, and I have hardly more than a pictorial impression of the Pope's illness and of the discussion of the Law of the Convents. Indeed I am afraid to speak of the Pope's illness at all, lest I should say something egregiously heartless about it, recalling too forcibly that unnatural husband who was heard to wish that his wife would "either" get well—! He had his reasons, and Roman tourists have theirs in the shape of a vague longing for something spectacular at St. Peter's. If it takes the sacrifice of somebody to produce it let somebody then be sacrificed. Meanwhile we have been having a glimpse of the spectacular side of the Religious Corporations Bill.* Hearing one morning a great hubbub in the Corso I stepped forth upon my balcony. A couple of hundred men were strolling slowly down the street with their hands in their pockets, shouting in unison "Abbasso il ministero!" and huzzaing in chorus. Just beneath my window they stopped and began to murmur "Al Quirinale, al Quirinale!"† The crowd surged a moment gently and then drifted to the Quirinal, where it scuffled harmlessly with half-a-dozen of the king's soldiers. It ought to have been impressive, for what was it, strictly, unless the seeds of revolution? But its carriage was too gentle and its cries too musical to send the most timorous tourist to packing his trunk. As I began with saying: in Rome, in May, everything has an amiable side, even popular uprisings.

[1873]

---

* A controversial bill that attempted to provide greater freedom of religion than was acceptable to the Church; it disestablished religious orders and put Catholic hospitals and schools under civil authority.

† Palazzo del Quirinale, the residence of Victor Emmanuel II.

....

From a Roman Note-Book

December 28, 1872. —In Rome again for the last three days—
that second visit which, when the first isn't followed by a fatal
illness in Florence, the story goes that one is doomed to pay. I
didn't drink of the Fountain of Trevi on the eve of departure the
other time; but I feel as if I had drunk of the Tiber itself. Nevertheless as I drove from the station in the evening I wondered
what I should think of it at this first glimpse hadn't I already
known it. All manner of evil perhaps. Paris, as I passed along the
Boulevards three evenings before to take the train, was swarming and glittering as befits a great capital. Here, in the black,
narrow, crooked, empty streets, I saw nothing I would fain regard as eternal. But there were new gas-lamps round the spout-
ing Triton in Piazza Barberini and a newspaper stall on the
corner of the Condotti and the Corso—salient signs of the
emancipated state. An hour later I walked up to Via Gregoriana
by Piazza di Spagna. It was all silent and deserted, and the great
flight of steps looked surprisingly small. Everything seemed
meagre, dusky, provincial. Could Rome after all really *be* a
world-city? That queer old rococo garden gateway at the top of
the Gregoriana stirred a dormant memory; it awoke into a consciousness of the delicious mildness of the air, and very soon, in
a little crimson drawing-room, I was reconciled and re-
initiated. . . . Everything is dear (in the way of lodgings) but it
hardly matters, as everything is taken and some one else paying
for it. I must make up my mind to a bare perch. But it seems
poorly perverse here to aspire to an "interior" or to be conscious
of the economic side of life. The æsthetic is so intense that you
feel you should live on the taste of it, should extract the nutritive

essence of the atmosphere. For positively it's *such* an atmosphere! The weather is perfect, the sky as blue as the most exploded tradition fames it, the whole air glowing and throbbing with lovely colour. . . . The glitter of Paris is now all gaslight. And oh the monotonous miles of rain-washed asphalt!

December 30th.—I have had nothing to do with the "ceremonies." In fact I believe there have hardly been any—no midnight mass at the Sistine chapel, no silver trumpets at St. Peter's. Everything is remorselessly clipped and curtailed—the Vatican in deepest mourning. But I saw it in its superbest scarlet in '69* . . . I went yesterday with L. to the Colonna gardens—an adventure that would have reconverted me to Rome if the thing weren't already done. It's a rare old place—rising in mouldy bosky terraces and mossy stairways and winding walks from the back of the palace to the top of the Quirinal. It's the grand style of gardening, and resembles the present natural manner as a chapter of Johnsonian rhetoric resembles a piece of clever contemporary journalism. But it's a better style in horticulture than in literature; I prefer one of the long-drawn blue-green Colonna vistas, with a maimed and mossy-coated garden goddess at the end, to the finest possible quotation from a last-century classic. Perhaps the best thing there is the old orangery with its trees in fantastic terra-cotta tubs. The late afternoon light was gilding the monstrous jars and suspending golden chequers among the golden-fruited leaves. Or perhaps the best thing is the broad terrace with its mossy balustrade and its benches; also its view of the great naked Torre di Nerone (I think) which might look stupid if the rosy brickwork didn't take such a colour in the blue air. Delightful, at any rate, to stroll and talk there in the afternoon sunshine.

January 2nd, 1873.—Two or three drives with A.—one to St. Paul's without the Walls and back by a couple of old churches on the Aventine. I was freshly struck with the rare distinction of the little Protestant cemetery† at the Gate, lying in the shadow of the black sepulchral Pyramid and the thick-growing

---

* Before Rome had become part of a united Italy and the rule of the pope was reduced to the territory of the Vatican.

† The cemetery where Keats and Shelley are buried.

black cypresses. Bathed in the clear Roman light the place is heartbreaking for what it asks you—in such a world as *this*—to renounce. If it should "make one in love with death to lie there," that's only if death should be conscious. As the case stands the weight of a tremendous past presses upon the flowery sod, and the sleeper's mortality feels the contact of all the mortality with which the brilliant air is tainted. . . . The restored Basilica is incredibly splendid. It seems a last pompous effort of formal Catholicism, and there are few more striking emblems of later Rome—the Rome foredoomed to see Victor Emmanuel in the Quirinal, the Rome of abortive councils and unheeded anathemas. It rises there, gorgeous and useless, on its miasmatic site, with an air of conscious bravado—a florid advertisement of the superabundance of faith. Within it's magnificent, and its magnificence has no shabby spots—a rare thing in Rome. Marble and mosaic, alabaster and malachite, lapis and porphyry, incrust it from pavement to cornice and flash back their polished lights at each other with such a splendour of effect that you seem to stand at the heart of some immense prismatic crystal. One has to come to Italy to know marbles and love them. I remember the fascination of the first great show of them I met in Venice—at the Scalzi and Gesuiti. Colour has in no other form so cool and unfading a purity and lustre. Softness of tone and hardness of substance—isn't that the sum of the artist's desire? G., with his beautiful caressing, open-lipped Roman utterance, so easy to understand and, to my ear, so finely suggestive of genuine Latin, not our horrible Anglo-Saxon and Protestant kind, urged upon us the charms of a return by the Aventine and the sight of a couple of old churches. The best is Santa Sabina, a very fine old structure of the fifth century, mouldering in its dusky solitude and consuming its own antiquity. What a massive heritage Christianity and Catholicism are leaving here! What a substantial fact, in all its decay, this memorial Christian temple outliving its uses among the sunny gardens and vineyards! It has a noble nave, filled with a stale smell which (like that of the onion) brought tears to my eyes, and bordered with twenty-four fluted marble columns of Pagan origin. The crudely primitive little mosaics along the entablature are extremely curious. A Dominican monk, still young, who showed us the church, seemed a creature generated from its musty shadows and odours. His physiognomy was wonderfully *de l'emploi* [appropriate to the occasion], and his voice, most agreeable, had the strangest jaded humility. His lugubrious salute and sanctimonious impersonal appropriation of my departing franc would have been a master-touch on the stage. While we were still in the church a bell rang that he had to go and answer, and as he came back and approached us along the nave he made with his white gown and hood and his cadaverous face, against the dark church background, one of those pictures which, thank the Muses, have not yet been reformed out of Italy. It was the exact illustration, for insertion in a text, of heaven knows how many old romantic and conventional literary Italianisms—plays, poems, mysteries of Udolpho.* We got back into the carriage and talked of profane things and went home to dinner—drifting recklessly, it seemed to me, from æsthetic luxury to social.

On the 31st we went to the musical vesper-service at the Gesù—hitherto done so splendidly before the Pope and the cardinals. The manner of it was eloquent of change—no Pope, no cardinals, and indifferent music; but a great *mise-en-scène* nevertheless. The church is gorgeous; late Renaissance, of great proportions, and full, like so many others, but in a preeminent degree, of seventeenth and eighteenth century Romanism. It doesn't impress the imagination, but richly feeds the curiosity, by which I mean one's sense of the curious; suggests no legends, but innumerable anecdotes à la Stendhal. There is a vast dome, filled with a florid concave fresco of tumbling foreshortened angels, and all over the ceilings and cornices a wonderful outlay of dusky gildings and mouldings. There are various Bernini saints and seraphs in stucco-sculpture, astride of the tablets and door-tops, backing against their rusty machinery of coppery *nimbi* and egg-shaped cloudlets. Marble, damask and tapers in gorgeous profusion. The high altar a great screen of twinkling chandeliers. The choir perched in a little loft high up in the right transept, like a balcony in a side-scene at the opera, and indulging in surprising roulades and flourishes. . . . Near

* *The Mysteries of Udolpho* (1794), a Gothic novel by the English novelist Ann Radcliffe.

me sat a handsome, opulent-looking nun—possibly an abbess or prioress of noble lineage. Can a holy woman of such a complexion listen to a fine operatic barytone in a sumptuous temple and receive none but ascetic impressions? What a cross-fire of influences does Catholicism provide!

January 4th.—A drive with A. out of Porta San Giovanni and along Via Appia Nuova. More and more beautiful as you get well away from the walls and the great view opens out before you—the rolling green-brown dells and flats of the Campagna, the long, disjointed arcade of the aqueducts, the deep-shadowed blue of the Alban hills, touched into pale lights by their scattered towns. We stopped at the ruined basilica of San Stefano, an affair of the fifth century, rather meaningless without a learned companion. But the perfect little sepulchral chambers of the Pancratii,* disinterred beneath the church, tell their own tale—in their hardly dimmed frescoes, their beautiful sculptured coffin and great sepulchral slab. Better still the tomb of the Valerii adjoining it—a single chamber with an arched roof, covered with stucco mouldings perfectly intact, exquisite figures and arabesques as sharp and delicate as if the plasterer's scaffold had just been taken from under them. Strange enough to think of these things—so many of them as there are—surviving their immemorial eclipse in this perfect shape and coming up like long-lost divers from the sea of time.

January 16th.—A delightful walk last Sunday with F. to Monte Mario. We drove to Porta Angelica, the little gate hidden behind the right wing of Bernini's colonnade, and strolled thence up the winding road to the Villa Mellini, where one of the greasy peasants huddled under the wall in the sun admits you for half a franc into the finest old ilex-walk in Italy. It is all vaulted grey-green shade with blue Campagna stretches in the interstices. The day was perfect; the still sunshine, as we sat at the twisted base of the old trees, seemed to have the drowsy hum of midsummer—with that charm of Italian vegetation that comes to us as its confession of having scenically served, to weariness at last, for some pastoral these many centuries a classic. In a certain cheapness and thinness of substance—as compared

---

* An ancient Roman burial society.

with the English stoutness, never left athirst—it reminds me of our own, and it is relatively dry enough and pale enough to explain the contempt of many unimaginative Britons. But it has an idle abundance and wantonness, a romantic shabbiness and dishevelment. At the Villa Mellini is the famous lonely pine which "tells" so in the landscape from other points, bought off from the axe by (I believe) Sir George Beaumont, commemorated in a like connection in Wordsworth's great sonnet.* He at least was not an unimaginative Briton. As you stand under it, its far-away shallow dome, supported on a single column almost white enough to be marble, seems to dwell in the dizziest depths of the blue. Its pale grey-blue boughs and its silvery stem make a wonderful harmony with the ambient air. The Villa Mellini is full of the elder Italy of one's imagination—the Italy of Boccaccio and Ariosto. There are twenty places where the Florentine story-tellers might have sat round on the grass. Outside the villa walls, beneath the over-crowding orange-boughs, straggled old Italy as well—but not in Boccaccio's velvet: a row of ragged and livid contadini, some simply stupid in their squalor, but some downright brigands of romance, or of reality, with matted locks and terribly sullen eyes.

A couple of days later I walked for old acquaintance sake over to San Onofrio on the Janiculan. The approach is one of the dirtiest adventures in Rome, and though the view is fine from the little terrace, the church and convent are of a meagre and musty pattern. Yet here—almost like pearls in a dunghill—are hidden mementos of two of the most exquisite of Italian minds. Torquato Tasso spent the last months of his life here, and you may visit his room and various warped and faded relics. The most interesting is a cast of his face taken after death—looking, like all such casts, almost more than mortally gallant and distinguished. But who should look all ideally so if not he? In a little shabby, chilly corridor adjoining is a fresco of Leonardo, a Virgin and Child with the *donatorio*. It is very small, simple and faded, but it has all the artist's magic, that mocking, illusive refinement and hint of a vague *arrière-pensée* [mental reservation] which mark every stroke of

* "The Pine of Monte Mario at Rome" (1837).

Leonardo's brush. Is it the perfection of irony or the perfection of tenderness? What does he mean, what does he affirm, what does he deny? Magic wouldn't be magic, nor the author of such things stand so absolutely alone, if we were ready with an explanation. As I glanced from the picture to the poor stupid little red-faced brother at my side I wondered if the thing mightn't pass for an elegant epigram on monasticism. Certainly, at any rate, there is more intellect in it than under all the monkish tonsures it has seen coming and going these three hundred years.

January 21st.—The last three or four days I have regularly spent a couple of hours from noon baking myself in the sun of the Pincio to get rid of a cold. The weather perfect and the crowd (especially to-day) amazing. Such a staring, lounging, dandified, amiable crowd! Who does the vulgar stay-at-home work of Rome? All the grandees and half the foreigners are there in their carriages, the *bourgeoisie* on foot staring at them and the beggars lining all the approaches. The great difference between public places in America and Europe is in the number of unoccupied people of every age and condition sitting about early and late on benches and gazing at you, from your hat to your boots, as you pass. Europe is certainly the continent of the practised stare. The ladies on the Pincio have to run the gauntlet; but they seem to do so complacently enough. The European woman is brought up to the sense of having a definite part in the way of manners or manner to play in public. To lie back in a barouche alone, balancing a parasol and seeming to ignore the extremely immediate gaze of two serried ranks of male creatures on each side of her path, save here and there to recognise one of them with an imperceptible nod, is one of her daily duties. The number of young men here who, like the cœnobites of old, lead the purely contemplative life is enormous. They muster in especial force on the Pincio, but the Corso all day is thronged with them. They are well-dressed, good-humoured, good-looking, polite; but they seem never to do a harder stroke of work than to stroll from the Piazza Colonna to the Hôtel de Rome or *vice versâ* Some of them don't even stroll, but stand leaning by the hour against the doorways, sucking the knobs of their canes, feeling their back hair and settling their shirt-cuffs. At my cafe in the morning several stroll in already (at nine o'clock) in light, in "evening" gloves. But they order nothing, turn on their heels, glance at the mirrors and stroll out again. When it rains they herd under the *portes-cochères* and in the smaller cafes. . . . Yesterday Prince Humbert's little *primogenito** was on the Pincio in an open landau with his governess. He's a sturdy blond little man and the image of the King. They had stopped to listen to the music, and the crowd was planted about the carriage-wheels, staring and criticising under the child's snub little nose. It appeared bold cynical curiosity, without the slightest manifestation of "loyalty," and it gave me a singular sense of the vulgarisation of Rome under the new régime. When the Pope drove abroad it was a solemn spectacle; even if you neither kneeled nor uncovered you were irresistibly impressed. But the Pope never stopped to listen to opera tunes, and he had no little popelings, under the charge of superior nurse-maids, whom you might take liberties with. The family at the Quirinal make something of a merit, I believe, of their modest and inexpensive way of life. The merit is great; yet, representationally, what a change for the worse from an order which proclaimed stateliness a part of its essence! The divinity that doth hedge a king must be pretty well on the wane. But how many more fine old traditions will the extremely sentimental traveller miss in the Italians over whom that little jostled prince in the landau will have come into his kinghood? . . . The Pincio continues to beguile; it's a great resource. I am forever being reminded of the "æsthetic luxury," as I called it above, of living in Rome. To be able to choose of an afternoon for a lounge (respectfully speaking) between St. Peter's and the high precinct you approach by the gate just beyond Villa Medici—counting nothing else—is a proof that if in Rome you may suffer from ennui, at least your ennui has a throbbing soul in it. It is something to say for the Pincio that you don't always choose St. Peter's. Sometimes I lose patience with its parade of eternal idleness, but at others this very idleness is balm to one's conscience. Life on just these terms seems so easy, so monotonously sweet, that you feel it

---

* The grandson of King Victor Emmanuel II.

would be unwise, would be really unsafe, to change. The Roman air is charged with an elixir, the Roman cup seasoned with some insidious drop, of which the action is fatally, yet none the less agreeably, "lowering."

January 26th.—With S. to the Villa Medici—perhaps on the whole the most enchanting place in Rome. The part of the garden called the Boschetto has an incredible, impossible charm; an upper terrace, behind locked gates, covered with a little dusky forest of evergreen oaks. Such a dim light as of a fabled, haunted place, such a soft suffusion of tender grey-green tones, such a company of gnarled and twisted little miniature trunks—dwarfs playing with each other at being giants—and such a shower of golden sparkles drifting in from the vivid west! At the end of the wood is a steep, circular mound, up which the short trees scramble amain, with a long mossy staircase climbing up to a belvedere. This staircase, rising suddenly out of the leafy dusk to you don't see where, is delightfully fantastic. You expect to see an old woman in a crimson petticoat and with a distaff come hobbling down and turn into a fairy and offer you three wishes. I should name for my own first wish that one didn't have to be a Frenchman to come and live and dream and work at the Académie de France. Can there be for a while a happier destiny than that of a young artist conscious of talent and of no errand but to educate, polish and perfect it, transplanted to these sacred shades? One has fancied Plato's Academy—his gleaming colonnades, his blooming gardens and Athenian sky; but was it as good as this one, where Monsieur Hébert* does the Platonic? The blessing in Rome is not that this or that or the other isolated object is so very unsurpassable; but that the general air so contributes to interest, to impressions that are not as any other impressions anywhere in the world. And from this general air the Villa Medici has distilled an essence of its own—walled it in and made it delightfully private. The great façade on the gardens is like an enormous rococo clock-face all incrusted with images and arabesques and tablets. What mornings and afternoons one

* Ernest Hébert (1817–1908), the painter and director of the Académie de France.

might spend there, brush in hand, unpreoccupied, untormented, pensioned, satisfied—either persuading one's self that one would be "doing something" in consequence or not caring if one shouldn't be.

At a later date—middle of March.—A ride with S. W. out of the Porta Pia to the meadows beyond the Ponte Nomentana—close to the site of Phaon's villa where Nero in hiding had himself stabbed. It all spoke as things here only speak, touching more chords than one can *now* really know or say. For these are predestined memories and the stuff that regrets are made of; the mild divine efflorescence of spring, the wonderful landscape, the talk suspended for another gallop. . . . Returning, we dismounted at the gate of the Villa Medici and walked through the twilight of the vaguely perfumed, bird-haunted alleys to H.'s studio, hidden in the wood like a cottage in a fairy tale. I spent there a charming half-hour in the fading light, looking at the pictures while my companion discoursed of her errand. The studio is small and more like a little salon; the painting refined, imaginative, somewhat morbid, full of consummate French ability. A portrait, idealised and etherealised, but a likeness of Mme. de ——— (from last year's Salon) in white satin, quantities of lace, a coronet, diamonds and pearls; a striking combination of brilliant silvery tones. A "Femme Sauvage," a naked dusky girl in a wood, with a wonderfully clever pair of shy, passionate eyes. The author is different enough from any of the numerous American artists. They may be producers, but he's a product as well—a product of influences of a sort of which we have as yet no general command. One of them is his charmed lapse of life in that unprofessional-looking little studio, with his enchanted wood on one side and the plunging wall of Rome on the other.

January 30th.—A drive the other day with a friend to Villa Madama, on the side of Monte Mario; a place like a page out of one of Browning's richest evocations of this clime and civilisation. Wondrous in its haunting melancholy, it might have inspired half "The Ring and the Book"* at a stroke. What a grim commentary on history such a scene—what an irony of

* Robert Browning's narrative poem (1859).

the past! The road up to it through the outer enclosure is almost impassable with mud and stones. At the end, on a terrace, rises the once elegant Casino, with hardly a whole pane of glass in its façade, reduced to its sallow stucco and degraded ornaments. The front away from Rome has in the basement a great loggia, now walled in from the weather, preceded by a grassy belittered platform with an immense sweeping view of the Campagna; the sad-looking, more than sad-looking, evil-looking, Tiber beneath (the colour of gold, the sentimentalists say, the colour of mustard, the realists); a great vague stretch beyond, of various complexions and uses; and on the horizon the ever-iridescent mountains. The place has become the shabbiest farm-house, with muddy water in the old *pièces d'eau* [artificial lakes] and dung-hills on the old parterres. The "feature" is the contents of the loggia: a vaulted roof and walls decorated by Giulio Romano; exquisite stucco-work and still brilliant frescoes; arabesques and figurini, nymphs and fauns, animals and flowers—gracefully lavish designs of every sort. Much of the colour—especially the blues—still almost vivid, and all the work wonderfully ingenious, elegant and charming. Apartments so decorated can have been meant only for the recreation of people greater than any we know, people for whom life was impudent ease and success. Margaret Farnese was the lady of the house, but where she trailed her cloth of gold the chickens now scamper between your legs over rotten straw. It is all inexpressibly dreary. A stupid peasant scratching his head, a couple of critical Americans picking their steps, the walls tattered and befouled breast-high, dampness and decay striking in on your heart, and the scene overbowed by these heavenly frescoes, mouldering there in their airy artistry! It's poignant; it provokes tears; it tells so of the waste of effort. Something human seems to pant beneath the grey pall of time and to implore you to rescue it, to pity it, to stand by it somehow. But you leave it to its lingering death without compunction, almost with pleasure; for the place seems vaguely crime-haunted—paying at least the penalty of some hard immorality. The end of a Renaissance pleasure-house. Endless for the didactic observer the moral, abysmal for the story-seeker the tale.

February 12th.—Yesterday to the Villa Albani. Over-formal

and (as my companion says) too much like a tea-garden; but with beautiful stairs and splendid geometrical lines of immense box-hedge, intersected with high pedestals supporting little antique busts. The light to-day magnificent; the Alban hills of an intenser broken purple than I had yet seen them—their white towns blooming upon it like vague projected lights. It was like a piece of very modern painting, and a good example of how Nature has at times a sort of mannerism which ought to make us careful how we condemn out of hand the more refined and affected artists. The collection of marbles in the Casino (Winckelmann's*) admirable and to be seen again. The famous Antinous crowned with lotus a strangely beautiful and impressive thing. The "Greek manner," on the showing of something now and again encountered here, moves one to feel that even for purely romantic and imaginative effects it surpasses any since invented. If there be not imagination, even in our comparatively modern sense of the word, in the baleful beauty of that perfect young profile there is none in "Hamlet" or in "Lycidas." There is five hundred times as much as in "The Transfiguration." With this at any rate to point to it's not for sculpture not professedly to produce any emotion producible by painting. There are numbers of small and delicate fragments of bas-reliefs of exquisite grace, and a huge piece (two combatants—one, on horseback, beating down another—murder made eternal and beautiful) attributed to the Parthenon and certainly as grandly impressive as anything in the Elgin marbles. S. W. suggested again the Roman villas as a "subject." Excellent if one could find a feast of facts à la Stendhal. A lot of vague ecstatic descriptions and anecdotes wouldn't at all pay. There have been too many already. Enough facts are recorded, I suppose; one should discover them and soak in them for a twelvemonth. And yet a Roman villa, in spite of statues, ideas and atmosphere, affects me as of a scanter human and social *portée* [stature], a shorter, thinner reverberation, than an old English country-house, round which experience seems piled so thick. But this perhaps is either hair-splitting or "racial" prejudice.

* Johann Winckelmann (1817–1886), German archaeologist.

March 9th.—The Vatican is still deadly cold; a couple of hours there yesterday with R. W. E.* Yet he, illustrious and enviable man, fresh from the East, had no overcoat and wanted none. Perfect bliss, I think, would be to live in Rome without thinking of overcoats. The Vatican seems very familiar, but strangely smaller than of old. I never lost the sense before of confusing vastness. *Sancta simplicitas!* [Blessed simplicity!] All my old friends however stand there in undimmed radiance, keeping most of them their old pledges. I am perhaps more struck now with the enormous amount of padding—the number of third-rate, fourth-rate things that weary the eye desirous to approach freshly the twenty and thirty best. In spite of the padding there are dozens of treasures that one passes regretfully; but the impression of the whole place is the great thing—the feeling that through these solemn vistas flows the source of an incalculable part of our present conception of Beauty.

April 10th.—Last night, in the rain, to the Teatro Valle to see a comedy of Goldoni in Venetian dialect—"I Quattro Rustighi." I could but half follow it; enough, however, to be sure that, for all its humanity of irony, it wasn't so good as Molière. The acting was capital—broad, free and natural; the play of talk easier even than life itself; but, like all the Italian acting I have seen, it was wanting in *finesse,* that shade of the shade by which, and by which alone, one really knows art. I contrasted the affair with the evening in December last that I walked over (also in the rain) to the Odéon and saw the "Plaideurs" and the "Malade Imaginaire."† There, too, was hardly more than a handful of spectators; but what rich, ripe, fully representational and above all intellectual comedy, and what polished, educated playing! These Venetians in particular, however, have a marvellous *entrain* [liveliness] of their own; they seem even less than the French to recite. In some of the women—ugly, with red hands and shabby dresses—an extraordinary gift of natural utterance, of seeming to invent joyously as they go.

Later.—Last evening in H.'s box at the Apollo to hear Ernesto Rossi in "Othello." He shares supremacy with Salvini in

* Ralph Waldo Emerson (1803–1882).

† Plays by Racine (1668) and Molière (1673), respectively.

Italian tragedy. Beautiful great theatre with boxes you can walk about in; brilliant audience. The Princess Margaret was there—I have never been to the theatre that she was not—and a number of other princesses in neighbouring boxes. G. G. came in and instructed us that they were the M., the L., the P., &c. Rossi is both very bad and very fine; bad where anything like taste and discretion is required, but "all there," and more than there, in violent passion. The last act reduced too much, however, to mere exhibitional sensibility. The interesting thing to me was to observe the Italian conception of the part—to see how crude it was, how little it expressed the hero's moral side, his depth, his dignity—anything more than his being a creature terrible in mere tantrums. The great point was his seizing Iago's head and whacking it half-a-dozen times on the floor, and then flinging him twenty yards away. It was wonderfully done, but in the doing of it and in the evident relish for it in the house there was I scarce knew what force of easy and thereby rather cheap expression.

April 27th.—A morning with L. B. at Villa Ludovisi, which we agreed that we shouldn't soon forget. The villa now belongs to the King, who has lodged his morganatic wife there. There is nothing so blissfully *right* in Rome, nothing more consummately consecrated to style. The grounds and gardens are immense, and the great rusty-red city wall stretches away behind them and makes the burden of the seven hills seem vast without making *them* seem small. There is everything—dusky avenues trimmed by the clippings of centuries, groves and dells and glades and glowing pastures and reedy fountains and great flowering meadows studded with enormous slanting pines. The day was delicious, the trees all one melody, the whole place a revelation of what Italy and hereditary pomp can do together. Nothing could be more in the grand manner than this garden view of the city ramparts, lifting their fantastic battlements above the trees and flowers. They are all tapestried with vines and made to serve as sunny fruit-walls—grim old defence as they once were; now giving nothing but a splendid buttressed privacy. The sculptures in the little Casino are few, but there are two great ones—the beautiful sitting Mars and the head of the great Juno, the latter thrust into a corner behind a shutter. These things it's almost impossible to praise; we can only mark them well and keep them clear, as we insist on silence to hear great music. . . . If I don't praise Guercino's Aurora in the greater Casino, it's for another reason; this is certainly a very muddy masterpiece. It figures on the ceiling of a small low hall; the painting is coarse and the ceiling too near. Besides, it's unfair to pass straight from the Greek mythology to the Bolognese. We were left to roam at will through the house; the custode shut us in and went to walk in the park. The apartments were all open, and I had an opportunity to reconstruct, from its *milieu* at least, the character of a morganatic queen. I saw nothing to indicate that it was not amiable; but I should have thought more highly of the lady's discrimination if she had had the Juno removed from behind her shutter. In such a house, girdled about with such a park, methinks I could be amiable—and perhaps discriminating too. The Ludovisi Casino is small, but the perfection of the life of ease might surely be led there. There are English houses enough in wondrous parks, but they expose you to too many small needs and observances—to say nothing of a red-faced butler dropping his *h*'s. You are oppressed with the detail of accommodation. Here the billiard-table is old-fashioned, perhaps a trifle crooked; but you have Guercino about your head, and Guercino, after all, is almost as good as Guido. The rooms, I noticed, all pleased by their shape, by a lovely proportion, by a mass of delicate ornamentation on the high concave ceilings. One might live over again in them some deliciously benighted life of a forgotten type—with graceful old *sale,* and immensely thick walls, and a winding stone staircase, and a view from the loggia at the top; a view of twisted parasol-pines balanced, high above a wooden horizon, against a sky of faded sapphire.

May 17th.—It was wonderful yesterday at St. John Lateran. The spring now has turned to perfect summer; there are cascades of verdure over all the walls; the early flowers are a fading memory, and the new grass knee-deep in the Villa Borghese. The winter aspect of the region about the Lateran is one of the best things in Rome; the sunshine is nowhere so golden and the lean shadows nowhere so purple as on the long grassy walk to Santa Croce. But yesterday I seemed to see nothing but green and blue. The expanse before Santa Croce was vivid green; the Campagna rolled away in great green billows, which seemed to break high about the gaunt aqueducts; and the Alban Hills, which in January and February keep shifting and melting along the whole scale of azure, were almost monotonously fresh, and had lost some of their finer modelling. But the sky was ultramarine and everything radiant with light and warmth—warmth which a soft steady breeze kept from excess. I strolled some time about the church, which has a grand air enough, though I don't seize the point of view of Miss ——, who told me the other day how vastly finer she thought it than St. Peter's. But on Miss ——'s lips this seemed a very pretty paradox. The choir and transepts have a sombre splendour, and I like the old vaulted passage with its slabs and monuments behind the choir. The charm of charms at St. John Lateran is the admirable twelfth-century cloister, which was never more charming than yesterday. The shrubs and flowers about the ancient well were blooming away in the intense light, and the twisted pillars and chiselled capitals of the perfect little colonnade seemed to enclose them like the sculptured rim of a precious vase. Standing out among the flowers you may look up and see a section of the summit of the great façade of the church. The robed and mitred apostles, bleached and rain-washed by the ages, rose into the blue air like huge snow figures. I spent at the incorporated museum a subsequent hour of fond vague attention, having it quite to myself. It is rather scantily stocked, but the great cool halls open out impressively one after the other, and the wide spaces between the statues seem to suggest at first that each is a masterpiece. I was in the loving mood of one's last days in Rome, and when I had nothing else to admire I admired the magnificent thickness of the embrasures of the doors and windows. If there were no objects of interest at all in the Lateran the palace would be worth walking through every now and then, to keep up one's idea of solid architecture. I went over to the Scala Santa, where was no one but a very shabby priest sitting like a ticket-taker at the door. But he let me pass, and I ascended one of the profane lateral stairways and treated myself to a glimpse of the Sanctum Sanctorum. Its threshold is crossed but once or twice a year, I believe, by three or four of the most exalted divines, but you may look into it freely enough through a couple of gilded lattices. It is very sombre and splendid, and conveys the impression of a very holy place. And yet somehow it suggested irreverent thoughts; it had to my fancy—perhaps on account of the lattice—an Oriental, a Mahometan note. I expected every moment to see a sultana appear in a silver veil and silken trousers and sit down on the crimson carpet.

Farewell, packing, the sharp pang of going. One would like to be able after five months in Rome to sum up, for tribute and homage, one's experience, one's gains, the whole adventure of one's sensibility. But one has really vibrated too much—the addition of so many items isn't easy. What is simply clear is the sense of an acquired passion for the place and of an incalculable number of gathered impressions. Many of these have been intense and momentous, but one has trodden on the other—there are always the big fish that swallow up the little—and one can hardly say what has become of them. They store themselves noiselessly away, I suppose, in the dim but safe places of memory and "taste," and we live in a quiet faith that they will emerge into vivid relief if life or art should demand them. As for the passion we needn't perhaps trouble ourselves about that. Fifty swallowed palmfuls of the Fountain of Trevi couldn't make us more ardently sure that we shall at any cost come back.

[1873]

．．．．．．．．．．．．．．．．．．．．．．．．．．．．．．．．．

A Few Other Roman Neighbourhoods

If I find my old notes, in all these Roman connections, inevitably bristle with the spirit of the postscript, so I give way to this prompting to the extent of my scant space and with the sense of other occasions awaiting me on which I shall have to do no less. The impression of Rome was repeatedly to renew itself for the author of these now rather antique and artless accents; was to overlay itself again and again with almost heavy thicknesses of experience, the last of which is, as I write, quite fresh to memory; and he has thus felt almost ashamed to drop his subject (though it be one that tends so easily to turn to the infinite) as if the law of change had in all the years had nothing to say to his case. It's of course but of his case alone that he speaks—wondering little what he may make of it for the profit of others by an attempt, however brief, to point the moral of the matter, or in other words compare the musing *mature* visitor's "feeling about Rome" with that of the extremely agitated, even if though extremely inexpert, consciousness reflected in the previous pages. The actual, the current Rome affects him as a world governed by new conditions altogether and ruefully pleading that sorry fact in the ear of the antique wanderer wherever he may yet mournfully turn for some re-capture of what he misses. The city of his first unpremeditated rapture shines to memory, on the other hand, in the manner of a lost paradise the rustle of whose gardens is still just audible enough in the air to make him wonder if some sudden turn, some recovered vista, mayn't lead him back to the thing itself. My genial, my helpful tag, at this point, would doubtless properly resolve itself, for the reader, into a clue toward some such successful ingenuity of quest; a remark I make, I may add, even while reflecting that the Paradise isn't apparently at all "lost" to visitors not of my generation. It is the seekers of *that* remote and romantic tradition who have seen it, from one period of ten, or even of five, years to another, systematically and remorselessly built out from their view. Their helpless plaint, their sense of the generally irrecoverable and unspeakable, is not, however, what I desire here most to express; I should like, on the contrary, with ampler opportunity, positively to enumerate the cases, the cases of contact, impression, experience, in which the cold ashes of a long-chilled passion may fairly feel themselves made to glow again. No one who has ever loved Rome as Rome could be loved in youth and before her poised basketful of the finer appeals to fond fancy was actually upset, wants to stop loving her; so that our bleeding and wounded, though perhaps not wholly moribund, loyalty attends us as a hovering admonitory, anticipatory ghost, one of those magnanimous life-companions who before complete extinction designate to the other member of the union their approved successor. So it is at any rate that I conceive the pilgrim old enough to have become aware in all these later years of what he misses to be counselled and pacified in the interest of recognitions that shall a little make up for it.

It was this wisdom I was putting into practice, no doubt, for instance, when I lately resigned myself to motoring of a splendid June day "out to" Subiaco; as a substitute for a resignation that had anciently taken, alas, but the form of my never getting there at all. Everything that day, moreover, seemed right, surely; everything on certain other days that were like it through their large indebtedness, at this, that and the other point, to the last new thing, seemed so right that they come back to me now, after a moderate interval, in the full light of that unchallenged felicity. I couldn't at all gloriously recall, for instance, as I floated to Subiaco on vast brave wings, how on the occasion of my first visit to Rome, thirty-eight years before, I had devoted certain evenings, evenings of artless "preparation" in my room at the inn, to the perusal of Alphonse Dantier's admirable *Monastères Benedictins d'Italie,* taking piously for granted that I should get myself somehow conveyed to Monte Cassino and to Subiaco at least: such an affront to the passion of curiosity, the generally infatuated state then kindled, would any suspicion of my foredoomed, my all but interminable, privation during visits to come have seemed to me. Fortune, in the event, had never favoured my going, but I was to give myself up at last to the sense of her quite taking me by the hand, and that is how I now think of our splendid June day at Subiaco. The note of the wondrous place itself is conventional "wild" Italy raised to the highest intensity, the ideally, the sublimely conventional and wild, complete and supreme in itself, without a disparity or a flaw; which character of perfect picturesque orthodoxy seemed more particularly to begin for me, I remember, as we passed, on our way, through that indescribable and indestructible Tivoli, where the jumble of the elements of the familiarly and exploitedly, the all too notoriously fair and queer, was more violent and vociferous than ever—so the whole spectacle there seemed at once to rejoice in cockneyfication and to resist it. There at least I had old memories to renew—including that, in especial, from a few years back, of one of the longest, hottest, dustiest return-drives to Rome that the Campagna on a sirocco day was ever to have treated me to.

That was to be more than made up on this later occasion by an hour of early evening, snatched on the run back to Rome, that remains with me as one of those felicities we are wise to leave for ever just as they are, just, that is, where they fell, never attempting to renew or improve them. So happy a chance was it that ensured me at the afternoon's end a solitary stroll through the Villa d'Este, where the day's invasion, whatever it might have been, had left no traces and where I met nobody in the great rococo passages and chambers, and in the prodigious alleys and on the repeated flights of tortuous steps, but the haunting Genius of Style, into whose noble battered old face, as if it had come out clearer in the golden twilight and on recognition of response so deeply moved, I seemed to exhale my sympathy. This was truly, amid a conception and order of things all mossed over from disuse, but still without a form abandoned or a principle disowned, one of the hours that one doesn't forget. The ruined fountains seemed strangely to *wait,* in the stillness and under cover of the approaching dusk, not to begin ever again to play, also, but just only to be tenderly imagined to do so; quite as everything held its breath, at the mystic moment, for the drop of the cruel and garish exposure, for the Spirit of the place to steal forth and go his round. The vistas of the innumerable mighty cypresses ranged themselves, in their files and companies, like beaten heroes for their captain's review; the great artificial "works" of every description, cascades, hemicycles, all graded and grassed and stone-seated as for floral games, mazes and bowers and alcoves and grottos, brave indissoluble unions of the planted and the builded symmetry, with the terraces and staircases that overhang and the arcades and cloisters that underspread, made common cause together as for one's taking up a little, in kindly lingering wonder, the "feeling" out of which they have sprung. One didn't see it, under the actual influence, one wouldn't for the world have seen it, as that they longed to be justified, during a few minutes in the twenty-four hours, of their absurdity of pomp and circumstance—but only that they asked for company, once in a way, as they were so splendidly formed to give it, and that the best company, in a changed world, at the end of time, what could they hope it to be but just the lone, the dawdling person of taste, the visitor with a flicker of fancy, not to speak of a pang of pity, to spare for them? It was in the flicker of fancy, no doubt, that as I hung about the great topmost terrace in especial, and then again took my way through the high gaunt corridors and the square and bare alcoved and recessed saloons, all overscored with such a dim waste of those painted, those delicate and capricious decorations which the loggie of the Vatican promptly borrowed from the ruins of the Palatine, or from whatever other revealed and inspiring ancientries, and which make ghostly confession here of that descent, I gave the rein to my sense of the sinister too, of that vague after-taste as of evil things that lurks so often, for a suspicious sensibility, wherever the terrible game of the life of the Renaissance was played as the Italians played it; wherever the huge tesselated chessboard seems to stretch about us, swept bare, almost always violently swept bare, of its chiselled and shifting figures, of every value and degree, but with this echoing desolation itself representing the long gasp, as it were, of overstrained time, the great after-hush that follows on things too wonderful or dreadful.

I am putting here, however, my cart before my horse, for the hour just glanced at was but a final tag to a day of much brighter curiosity, and which seemed to take its baptism, as we passed through prodigious perched and huddled, adorably scattered and animated and even crowded Tivoli, from the universal happy spray of the drumming Anio waterfalls, all set in their permanent rainbows and Sibylline temples and classic allusions and Byronic quotations; a wondrous romantic jumble of such things and quite others—heterogeneous inns and clamorous *guingettes* [cafés] and factories grabbing at the torrent, to say nothing of innumerable guides and donkeys and white-tied, swallow-tailed waiters dashing out of grottos and from under cataracts, and of the air, on the part of the whole population, of standing about, in the most characteristic *contadino* [peasant] manner, to pounce on you and take you somewhere, snatch you from somebody else, shout something at you, the aqueous and other uproar permitting, and then charge you for it, your innocence aiding. I'm afraid our run the rest of the way to Subiaco remains with me but as an after-sense of that exhilaration, in spite of our rising admirably higher, all the while, and plunging constantly deeper into splendid solitary gravities, supreme romantic solemnities and sublimities, of landscape. The Benedictine convent, which clings to certain more or less vertiginous ledges and slopes of a vast precipitous gorge, constitutes, with the whole perfection of its setting, the very ideal of the tradition of that *extraordinary in the romantic* handed down to us, as the most attaching and inviting spell of Italy, by all the old academic literature of travel and art of the Salvator Rosas and Claudes. This is the main tribute I may pay in a few words to an impression of which a sort of divine rightness of oddity, a pictorial felicity that was almost not of this world, but of a higher degree of distinction altogether, affected me as the leading note; yet about the whole exquisite complexity of which I can't pretend to be informing.

All the elements of the scene melted for me together; even from the pause for luncheon on a grassy wayside knoll, over heaven knows what admirable preparatory headlong slopes and ravines and iridescent distances, under spreading chestnuts and in the high air that was cool and sweet, to the final pedestrian climb of sinuous mountain-paths that the shining limestone and the strong green of shrub and herbage made as white as silver. There the miraculous home of St. Benedict awaited us in the form of a builded and pictured-over maze of chapels and shrines, cells and corridors, stupefying rock-chambers and caves, places all at an extraordinary variety of different levels and with labyrinthine intercommunications; there the spirit of the centuries sat like some invisible icy presence that only permits you to stare and wonder. I stared, I wondered, I went up and down and in and out and lost myself in the fantastic fable of the innumerable hard facts themselves; and whenever I could, above all, I peeped out of small windows and hung over chance terraces for the love of the general outer picture, the splendid fashion in which the fretted mountains of marble, as they might have been, round about, seemed to inlay themselves, for the effect of the "distinction" I speak of, with vegetations of dark emerald. There above all—or at least in what such aspects did further for the prodigy of the Convent, whatever that prodigy might do for *them*—was, to a life-long victim of Italy, almost verily as never before, the operation of the old love-philtre; there were the inexhaustible sources of interest and charm.

These mystic fountains broke out for me elsewhere, again and again, I rejoice to say—and perhaps more particularly, to be frank about it, where the ground about them was pressed with due emphasis of appeal by the firm wheels of the great winged car. I motored, under invitation and protection, repeatedly back into the sense of the other years, that sense of the "old" and comparatively idle Rome of my particular infatuated prime which I was living to see superseded, and this even when the fond vista bristled with innumerable "signs of the times," unmistakable features of the new era, that, by I scarce know what perverse law, succeeded in ministering to a happy effect. Some of these false notes proceed simply from the immense growth of every sort of facilitation—so that people are much more free than of old to come and go and do, to inquire and explore, to pervade and generally "infest"; with a consequent loss, for the fastidious individual, of his blest earlier sense, not infrequent, of having the occasion and the impression, as he used complacently to say, all to himself. We none of us had anything quite all to ourselves during an afternoon at Ostia, on a beautiful June Sunday; it was a different affair, rather, from the long, the comparatively slow and quite unpeopled drive that I was to remember having last taken early in the autumn thirty years before, and which occupied the day—with the aid of a hamper from once supreme old Spillman, the provider for picnics to a vanished world (since I suspect the antique ideal of "a picnic in the Campagna," the fondest conception of a happy day, has lost generally much of its glamour). Our idyllic afternoon, at any rate, left no chord of sensibility that could possibly have been in question untouched—not even that of tea on the shore at Fiumincino, after we had spent an hour among the ruins of Ostia and seen our car ferried across the Tiber, almost saffron-coloured here and swirling towards its mouth, on a boat that was little more than a big rustic raft and that yet bravely resisted the prodigious weight. What shall I say, in the way of the particular, of the general felicity before me, for the sweetness of the hour to which the incident just named, with its strange and amusing juxtapositions of the patriarchally primitive and the insolently supersubtle, the earliest and the latest efforts of restless science, were almost immediately to succeed?

We had but skirted the old gold-and-brown walls of Castel Fusano, where the massive Chigi tower and the immemorial stone-pines and the afternoon sky and the desolate sweetness and concentrated rarity of the picture all kept their appointment, to fond memory, with that especial form of Roman faith, the fine æsthetic conscience in things, that is never, never broken. We had wound through tangled lanes and met handsome sallow country-folk lounging at leisure, as became the Sunday, and ever so pleasantly and garishly clothed, if not quite consistently costumed, as just on purpose to feed our wanton optimism; and then we had addressed ourselves with a soft superficiality to the open, the exquisite little Ostian reliquary, an exhibition of stony vaguenesses half straightened out. The ruins of the ancient port of Rome, the still recoverable identity of streets and habitations and other forms of civil life, are a not inconsiderable handful, though making of the place at best a very small sister to Pompeii; but a soft superficiality is ever the refuge of my shy sense before any ghost of informed reconstitution, and I plead my surrender to it with the less shame that I believe I "enjoy" such scenes even on such futile pretexts as much as it can be appointed them by the invidious spirit of History to *be* enjoyed. It may be said, of course, that enjoyment, question-begging term at best, isn't in these austere connections designated—but rather some principle of appreciation that can at least give a coherent account of itself. On that basis then—as I could, I profess, *but* revel in the looseness of my apprehension, so wide it seemed to fling the gates of vision and divination—I won't pretend to dot, as it were, too many of the i's of my incompetence. I was competent only to have been abjectly interested. On reflection, moreover, I see that no impression of over-much company invaded the picture till the point was exactly reached for its contributing thoroughly to character and amusement; across at Fiumincino, which the age of the bicycle has made, in a small way, the handy Gravesend or Coney Island of Rome, the cafés and *birrerie* [beer halls] were at high pressure, and the bustle all motley and friendly beside the melancholy river, where the waterside life itself had twenty quaint and vivid notes and where a few upstanding objects, ancient or modern, looked eminent and interesting against the delicate Roman sky that dropped down and down to the far-spreading marshes of malaria. Besides which "company" is ever intensely gregarious, hanging heavily together and easily outwitted; so that we had but to proceed a scant distance further and meet the tideless Mediterranean, where it tumbled in a trifle breezily on the sands, to be all to ourselves with our tea-basket, quite as in the good old fashion—only in truth with the advantage that the contemporary tea-basket is so much improved.

I jumble my memories as a tribute to the whole idyll—I give the golden light in which they come back to me for what it is worth; worth, I mean, as allowing that the possibilities of charm of the Witch of the Seven Hills, as we used to call her in magazines, haven't all been vulgarised away. It was precisely there, on such an occasion and in such a place, that this might seem signally to have happened; whereas in fact the mild suburban riot, in which the so gay but so light potations before the array of little houses of entertainment were what struck one as really making most for mildness, was brushed over with a fabled grace, was harmonious, felicitous, distinguished, quite after the fashion of some thoroughly trained chorus or phalanx of opera or ballet. Bicycles were stacked up by the hundred; the youth of Rome are ardent cyclists, with a great taste for flashing about in more or less denuded or costumed athletic and romantic bands and guilds, and on our return cityward, toward evening, along the right bank of the river, the road swarmed with the patient wheels and bent backs of these budding *cives Romani* [Roman citizens] quite to the effect of its finer interest. Such at least, I felt, could only be one's acceptance of almost any feature of a scene bathed in that extraordinarily august air that the waning Roman day is so insidiously capable of taking on when any other element of style happens at all to contribute. Weren't they present, these other elements, in the great classic lines and folds, the fine academic or historic attitudes of the darkening land itself as it hung about the old highway, varying its vague accidents, but achieving always perfect "composition"? I shamelessly add that cockneyfied impression, at all events, to what I have called my jumble; Rome, to which we all swept on together in the wondrous glowing medium, *saved* everything, spreading afar her wide wing and applying after all but her supposed grand gift of the secret of salvation. We kept on and on into the great dim rather sordidly papal streets that approach the quarter of St. Peter's; to the accompaniment, finally, of that markedly felt provocation of fond wonder which had never failed to lie in wait for me under any question of a renewed glimpse of the huge unvisited rear of the basilica. There was no renewed glimpse just then, in the gloaming; but the region I speak of had been for me, in fact, during the previous weeks, less unvisited than ever before, so that I had come to count an occasional walk round and about it as quite of the essence of the convenient small change with which the heterogeneous City may still keep paying you. These frequentations in the company of a sculptor friend had been incidental to our reaching a small artistic foundry of fine metal, an odd and interesting little establishment placed, as who should say in the case of such a mere left-over scrap of a large loose margin, nowhere: it lurked so unsuspectedly, that is, among the various queer things that Rome comprehensively refers to as "behind St. Peter's."

We had passed then, on the occasion of our several pilgrimages, in beneath the great flying, or at least straddling buttresses to the left of the mighty façade, where you enter that great idle precinct of fine dense pavement and averted and sacrificed grandeur, the reverse of the monstrous medal of the front. Here the architectural monster rears its back and shoulders on an equal scale and this whole unregarded world of colossal consistent symmetry and hidden high finish gives you the measure of the vast total treasure of items and features. The outward face of all sorts of inward majesties of utility and ornament here above all correspondingly reproduces itself; the expanses of golden travertine—the freshness of tone, the cleanness of surface, in the sunny air, being extraordinary—climb and soar and spread under the crushing weight of a scheme carried out in every ponderous particular. Never was such a show of *wasted* art, of pomp for pomp's sake, as where all the chapels bulge and all the windows, each one a separate constructional masterpiece, tower above almost grass-grown vacancy; with the full and immediate effect, of course, of reading us a lesson on the value of lawful pride. The pride is the pride of indifference as to whether a greatness so founded be gaped at in all its features or not. My friend and I were alone to gape at them most often while, for the unfailing impression of them, on our way to watch the casting of our figure, we extended our circuit of the place. To which I may add, as another example of that tentative, that appealing twitch of the garment of Roman association of which one kept renewing one's consciousness, the half-hour at the little foundry itself was all charming—with its quite shabby and belittered and ramshackle recall of the old Roman "art-life" of one's early dreams. Everything was somehow in the picture, the rickety sheds, the loose paraphernalia, the sunny, grassy yard where a goat was browsing; then the queer interior gloom of the pits, frilled with little overlooking scaffoldings and bridges, for the sinking fireward of the image that was to take on hardness; and all the pleasantness and quickness, the beguiling refinement, of the three or four light fine "hands" of whom the staff consisted and into whose type and tone one liked to read, with whatever harmless extravagance, so many signs that a lively sense of stiff processes, even in humble life, could still leave untouched the traditional rare feeling for the artistic. How delightful such an occupation in such a general setting—those of my friend, I at such moments irrepressibly moralised; and how one might after such a fashion endlessly go and come and ask nothing better; or if better, only so to the extent of another impression I was to owe to him: that of an evening meal spread, in the warm still darkness that made no candle flicker, on the wide high space of an old loggia that overhung, in one quarter, the great obelisked Square preceding one of the Gates, and in the other the Tiber and the far Trastevere and more things than I can say—above all, as it were, the whole backward past, the mild confused romance of the Rome one had loved and of which one was exactly taking leave under protection of the friendly lanterned and garlanded feast and the commanding, all-embracing roof-garden. It was indeed a reconciling, it was an altogether penetrating, last hour.

[1909]

The Spirit of Rome*

The spirit of the place is what most comes back, in respect to any occasion, for the fond invoker of memories still denounce-able as at their best too meagre; since it is only as holding fast *that* key to all impressions, heterogeneous or other, that one may keep them either together or apart. Was it not, in old days, the special solvent of *all* appearances, *all* encounters, the ele-ment into which they simply melted, so that it mattered comparatively little who or what they individually were—mat-tering, as it did, so very much more, for the mind, that they were part of the general experience of Rome? This experience was in itself so constant and penetrating that almost nobody one might meet, almost nothing one might see, could aspire to any higher dignity than that of a note struck, just sensibly sounded, but made quite humble and relative, for the effect of the symphony. The symphony was a majestic whole, with which the individual would have been ill-advised to take a liberty, so that the greatest celebrities became thus nothing more than placed and waiting fiddles in the mighty orchestra, receiving their cue, as one took one's own explicit order, the sharp rap or recall, from the controlling influence that kept us all in tune. The spirit of the place figured, in fact, the master-conductor of a great harmonious band in which differences were disallowed, so near did one performer come to being as important—in other words as insignificant—as any other. That certainly was the great charm and the great ease—that no one, really, could be a bore about Rome, or even, to any purpose,

* From *William Wetmore Story and His Friends* (1903).

under its cover, about anything else. For nothing practically *existed* but that our conditions met every want, and that we were absolutely in the spirit of them even in trying to name those they failed to supply. This effect was wholly peculiar—an action on the mind, the temper, the life, on speech, manners, intercourse, with which that of no other place could for a moment compete. People might elsewhere be stupid, might elsewhere be vulgar or cross or ugly, for the ways of offence are many; whereas here you cared so little whether they were or not that it was virtually as good as not knowing. They were not, in fact; nobody was any of these things, for the simple reason that nobody could afford, for very shame, to deny the harmonising charm. The truth is even, no doubt, that nobody could grossly dare any such profanity and expect still to live. Something would have happened—something that never did happen, thanks to our cheerful humility and exalted equality. I remember that in days, or rather on evenings, that now seem to me exquisitely dim, I met Matthew Arnold, for the first time, at Palazzo Barberini,* and became conscious then and there—more so at least than I had been before—of the interesting truth I attempt to utter. He had been, in prose and verse, the idol of my previous years, and nothing could have seemed in advance less doubtful than that to encounter him face to face, and under an influence so noble, would have made one fairly stagger with a sense of privilege. What actually happened, however, was that the sense of privilege found itself positively postponed; when I met him again, later on, in London, *then* it had free play. It was, on the Roman evening, as if, for all the world, we were *equally* great and happy, or still more, perhaps, equally nothing and nobody; we were related only to the enclosing fact of Rome, before which every one, it was easy to feel, bore himself with the same good manners.

They then, as it were, the good manners, became the form in which the noble influence was best recognised, so that you could fairly trace it from occasion to occasion, from one consenting victim to another. The victims may very well not have

---

* William Wetmore Story's palazzo was a center of hospitality for American and British visitors to Rome.

been themselves always conscious, but the conscious individual had them all, attentively, imaginatively, at his mercy—drawing precisely from that fact a support in his own submission. He had the rare chance of seeing people kept in order, kept in position before the spectacle, so as to be themselves peculiarly accessible to observation. This faculty had, of course, in the nature of the case, to feed more on their essence and their type than, as it might have done elsewhere, on their extravagance and their overflow; but at least they couldn't elude, impose or deceive, as is always easy in London, Paris, or New York, cities in which the spirit of the place has long since (certainly as an insidious spell) lost any advantage it may ever have practised over the spirit of the person. So, at any rate, fanciful as my plea may appear, I recover the old sense—brave even the imputation of making a mere Rome of words, talking of a Rome of my own which was no Rome of reality. That comes up as exactly the point—that no Rome of reality was concerned in our experience, that the whole thing was a rare state of the imagination, dosed and drugged, as I have already indicated, by the effectual Borgia cup, for the taste of which the simplest as well as the subtlest had a palate. Nothing, verily, used to strike us more than that people of whom, as we said, we wouldn't have expected it, people who had never before shown knowledge, taste or sensibility, had here quite knocked under. They haunted Vatican halls and Palatine gardens; they were detached and pensive on the Pincian; they were silent in strange places; the habit of St. Peter's they clung to as to a vice; the impression of the Campagna they stopped short in attempting to utter. And just as the lowly were brought up, so the mighty were brought down, there being no tribute to the matters in question that was not of the nature of sensibility. Such is the pleasant light with which I see the Barberini drawing-room suffused. It was not that there were not during the same years other interiors on which the benediction also rested; each interior—that was the secret—had its share of the felicity, very much as places of reunion to-day have their share of the electric light. It was virtually "turned on," for instance, during the late hours, that every one *had,* all day, to have been breathing golden air, and that the golden air was exhaled again by the simple fact of any presence. I see, as in a picture, remembered figures sit content or move about in it; I see, fairly, where it prevails, a sweetness in any combination of couples or groups. I listen to the rich voices of young women at the piano and find them all charged with the quality of the day. For there had always *been* a day—a day that, moreover, was never so much of one as when (which was often) there was, for its expectation, to be also an evening. These sequences, these presciences certainly exist by Thames and Seine and Hudson, but quite, as they become familiar, without making us thrill at their touch. Their touch (since we discriminate) is coarse; it was only the Roman touch that was fine—which is the simple moral of my remarks.

[1903]

Florence

·

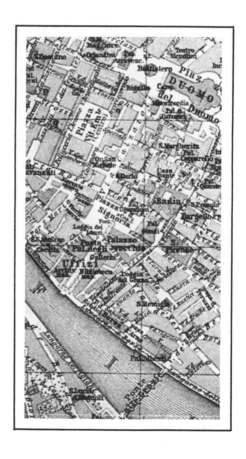

Letters

....

To Mrs. Henry James, Sr., 10/13/1869. Hotel de l'Europe, Florence: If I should ever feel like living a while in Italy I fancy I should choose this place. Not that it strikes me as a particularly cheerful city; its aspect—thanks to the narrowness of many of the streets & the vast cyclopean structure of many of the buildings is rather gloomy than otherwise. But it has the gaity of plenty of business (apparently), plenty of comfort & of strangers & of an unsurpassed collection of art treasures; & then it has on all sides the loveliest *échappés* [vistas] into the beautiful hills among which it lies deposited, like an egg in a nest. I have been spending my days in a regular philosophical appreciation of things. I've gone each morning to the great Uffizi Gallery to commune with the immortals & in the afternoon I have taken a good walk out into the country. I have not yet opened the chapter of churches, having been recently over-churched—save to stare with the proper & inevitable feeling at the magnificent many-colored, marble-plated walls & dome of the Cathedral. I have not even been to see M. Angelo's Medicean statues at St. Lorenzo. I take a rare satisfaction in keeping this adventure in reserve. . . . A journey in Italy moreover, is a great killer of impatience. You learn not only to wait—but in a degree, to like to wait. . . . The great things on the whole, I suppose, are the Rafaels—which give one a feeling distinct from the works of any other painter. More, far more, than any others, he seems to have been a genius pure & simple, unalloyed & unmodified by the struggles of development & the teachings of experience. . . . This beauty seems a direct result of the fact that to Rafael apparently, the world was clear, tranquil & serene—he looked at things & they pleased him.

To ALICE JAMES, 11/7/1869. HOTEL DE ROME: Their beauty [Michelangelo's statues at the Medicean tombs] far surpasses my original conception. As they sit brooding in their dim-lighted chapel, exhaling silence & thought, they form, I imagine, the most impressive work of art in the world. The warrior with the cavernous visage is absolutely terrible: he seems to shed an amount of inarticulate sorrow sufficient to infest the Universe.

To WILLIAM JAMES, 1/1/1870. FLORENCE: What a summer could be spent in a long slow journey of long lingering days between Florence & Rome—every town stopped at—every landscape stared at. . . . The sweetness of Florence restores me to perfect equanimity. I feel once more its delicate charm—I find it the same rounded pearl of cities—cheerful, compact, complete—full of a delicious mixture of beauty & convenience. There is for the moment at least a return of fine weather, but the cold is simply devilish. The streets, the hotels, the churches & galleries all strive to out-freeze each other. I begin to appreciate now the mildness of Rome & Naples. Yesterday, however, the sun was glorious & I got a good warming up in a sweet lone walk beside the rapid Arno to the uttermost end of the charming Cascine, where, sheltered from the north by a magnificent wall of perpetual verdure & basking full in the long-sealed smile of the South, all happy graceful Florence was watching the old year decline into its death-shroud of yellow and pink.

To CHARLES ELIOT NORTON, 3/31/1880. HOTEL DE L'ARNO, FLORENCE: I am sitting at an open window, this perfect spring morning, looking out on the yellow-green Arno with the little overhanging cabins of Ponte Vecchio directly beneath me. . . . I have been here but two days, but the charm of Florence has already taken complete possession of me & assured me that my recollections were not illusions.—I left London a fortnight ago, spent a week in Paris, & then came almost directly here. I am going to Rome & Naples for a fortnight & then coming back here to remain (unless I go to Venice instead!) for some weeks. I find Italy the same old Italy as ever—trying more & more to dis-Italianise herself, but, thank heaven, not succeeding half so well as she would like. The spring is particularly radiant, now that it has begun. . . . I have never seen the views about this place & the glimpses up and down the river, more delicately & divinely beautiful.

To William Dean Howells,* 4/18/1880. Florence: Come back to Italy as soon as you can; but don't come with a masterpiece suspended in the air by the tenderest portions of its texture; or else forbid yourself the pleasure of paying your proper respects to this land of loveliness—I have just come back from a ten day's run to Rome & Naples. . . . Florence is delightful as usual, but I am lacerated with the effect of turning myself away from Rome, where I feared I shouldn't do much work, but which is to Florence, as sunlight unto moonlight.

To Mrs. Edmund Gosse,† 4/14/1887. Villa Bricchiere, Bellosguardo, Florence: I am on a beautiful hill top, in a picturesque, a vast & vaulted old villa, just out of one of the gates of Florence—& the loveliest view on earth lies before & beneath me, while the divine Italian spring, in its first freshness, gives what, if I were affected, I should call an accent to the scene. None the less I languished for your social circle on the 1st, & this is a word to express my vain regret. I languished the more because at that moment I was in Venice, whose pestilent if romantic emanations had made me ill for a month—so that I had a double reason for wishing I might have exchanged the grand for the little canal.‡ Now that I am on terra firma—& high as well as firm—I am quite as well as my perverse nature ever lets me be.

To Edmund Gosse, 4/24/1887. Villa Bricchiere, Bellosguardo, Florence: I sit here making love to Italy. At this divine moment she is perfectly irresistible, & this delicious little Florence

* The American novelist, critic, and editor of the *Atlantic Monthly,* Howells (1837–1920) was an intimate friend and admirer of James.

† Ellen Epps Gosse (1850–1929), the wife of Sir Edmund William Gosse (1849–1928), English essayist and autobiographer, James's supporter and close friend.

‡ The Gosses lived near the Regent's Park Canal in London.

is not the least sovereign of her charms. I am fixed, till June 1st, in a villa which in England would be suburban, but here is supercelestial, whence the most beautiful view on earth hangs before me whenever I lift my head—which is one reason why I can only write short letters.

To Ariana Curtis, 4/24/1887. Villa Bricchiere, Bellosguardo, Florence: Florence is at present quite enchanting. Bellosguardo is still more so—& I am completely restored. I have a vast & vaulted apartment in this old villa & the most beautiful view in the world hangs all day before my eyes. You will answer me with the Palazzo B[arbaro] & *your* views—& I won't contend with you, for I know but too well what you mean. I suppose Venice has begun to glow. . . . I feel all that irradiation even at this distance.

To Robert Underwood Johnson,* 6/13/1887. Palazzo Barbaro, Venice: I love [Italy] about as much as ever. I am stretching out my stay & just now very happy in this effulgent steam bath. I shall probably spend three days in Florence again, before recrossing the Alps. . . . You are right about the bells, the sunsets & every other beauty of Bellosguardo, I was lately there . . . & grew to adore it as a habitation. You don't know what the view is till you live with it—& the bells of Florence talk to you, at a distance, all day long. The *feste* in Florence, for the unveiling of the new façade of the Duomo, were far more interesting than was to be supposed—especially a certain historical procession, of the mounted nobles & burghers, winding through the old palaced streets—very splendid & perfect.

To Grace Norton, 7/3/1890. 1 Via Palestro, Florence: This is a delightful moment to be in Italy & really nowadays the only right one—for the herd of tourists has departed, the scramble at the stations is no more, & one seems alone with the dear old land, who at the same time, seems alone with herself. I am happy to say that I am as fond as ever of this tender little Florence. . . . I should have liked to tell you how fascinating I

* American writer (1853–1937) and editor of *Century Magazine*.

found the Italian Alps & the Tyrol. . . . I never 'sympathised' much with Switzerland—but I can with the Dolomites. When, three mornings ago, I rose early, to take the train for Florence, & in the cool, fresh 7 o'clock light, was rowed through the delicious half-stirred place & the imbroglio of little silent plashing waterways to the station, it was really heartbreaking to come away—to come out into the dust & *banalité* of the rest of the world. (Venice clings closer to one by its dustlessness than perhaps by any other one charm.) But already the sweetness of Florence *tastes*. I am, however, seriously thinking, or rather *dreaming,* of putting my hand on some little cheap permanent refuge in Venice—some little perch over the water, with a bed & a table in it, to call one's own & come away to, without the interposition of luggage & hotels, whenever the weight of London, at certain times, is no longer to be borne.

To Ariana Curtis, 7/7/1890. Villino Rubio, 1 Via Palestro, Florence: I spent yesterday at Vallombrosa & I go this afternoon to Siena for the next three days—but everything happened, & doubtless will happen . . . in the most normal conditions. Quite the most thrilling of my experiences since we parted was to go back to the beautiful empty Barbaro & spend 36 hours there with a grand usurped sense of its being my own. For this is what I had the arrogance to do—I ought long ago to have notified you of it. I arrived at 6 o'clk. with the intention of simply picking up my clothes & sleeping that night. But the next a.m. it was not in human nature to tear itself away! The day was delicious, Angelo & Elise were even more so & your marble halls suffused with the "tender" note of your absence, were most pleasing & irresistable of all. I strutted about in them with a successful effort of self-deception & tasted for once of the fullness of earthly greatness. To say that Angelo was hospitable & that the Tite waited upon me both on my arrival & on my departure, is but faintly to sketch the situation. I spent a good bit of the day with Mrs. Bronson. . . . Stopping however a day at Trent[o] & a couple of days at Verona. Trent[o] was somehow disappointing, & drenched, absolutely reeking, with the electric light. . . . No water . . . I couldn't have a bath! . . . At Verona I collapsed upon my old hotel. . . . It was very hot. . . . Mrs. Jack* having bespoken my company in your mis-appropriated (or at least disappropriated) home for any date that may suit me after the said 1st [of August]—an early date preferred. (I heard from her on the subject a week ago, but have not yet answered her.) This summer aspect of Italy is delightful to me; but my holiday is taking strides to its close & my present prevision is that on August 1st I shall be jogging back to Reality over the Saint-Gothard. I have been in Florence for 6 days—where even after 24 hours the ache of quitting Venice that early morning, in the fresh, cool light, with such a heartbreaking, remonstrating plash—of your oars—down to the station—was somewhat healed & assuaged. For Florence is empty now, & lovely, & "tender" too—& the impression of it infinitely sweet. But it's dusty—& Venice isn't! . . . I start for a little tour in out of the way Tuscany . . . with my friend Baldwin† & an Italian friend of his [who] . . . undertakes to give us, in 5 or 6 days, the inside view of ancient cities & wonderful corners untrodden by tourists & commemorated by Dante. . . . The program involves a good deal of driving & an intimate acquaintance with railway connections. . . . I quite *thirst* for it. But in the meanwhile I go, till the 12th, this afternoon, to Siena. I have, further, for the 17th a room (a rare prize) engaged at the divine Vallombrosa, where by rising at 5 (to go from here,) I got ever so many hours, yesterday, of a lovely day. It struck me as one of the loveliest spots on earth & as deliciously cool & salubrious. . . . The woods, the walks, the views, the excursions, the places to stroll in, & sit, & spend the day in the open air, all being, apparently, exquisite & extremely numerous.

To Ariana Curtis, 5/3/1900. Lamb House. Rye: I'm not—woe is me—coming to Italy . . . I *can't*. . . . I *had* indeed no hope at all of being able to come this spring. . . . It has been but too apparent that I must sit tight in this place. But every whiff of

---

* Isabella Stewart Gardner (1840–1924), American art collector.

† William Wilberforce Baldwin (1850–1910), American doctor and long-time resident of Florence.

Italy is none the less of a joy & a torment. If I *lived* in Italy it is still there [in Florence] I should live—& I fell in love with it 31 years ago, never again really to fall out. Last May, at this moment, Rome didn't come at all up to time—during the weeks I spent there: I felt it too irrecoverably changed. But my little personal Florence was still there in spite of everything: I could manage with it. . . . I live over again, in memory, those divine Barbaro days, as they were for me, in that royal apartment, of last year's April. Every moment of them is delightful to remember.

The Autumn in Florence

Florence too has its "season," not less than Rome, and I have been rejoicing for the past six weeks in the fact that this comparatively crowded parenthesis hasn't yet been opened. Coming here in the first days of October I found the summer still in almost unmenaced possession, and ever since, till within a day or two, the weight of its hand has been sensible. Properly enough, as the city of flowers, Florence mingles the elements most artfully in the spring—during the divine crescendo of March and April, the weeks when six months of steady shiver have still not shaken New York and Boston free of the long Polar reach. But the very quality of the decline of the year as we at present here feel it suits peculiarly the mood in which an undiscourageable gatherer of the sense of things, or taster at least of "charm," moves through these many-memoried streets and galleries and churches. Old things, old places, old people, or at least old races, ever strike us as giving out their secrets most freely in such moist, grey, melancholy days as have formed the complexion of the past fortnight. With Christmas arrives the opera, the only opera worth talking through; the gaiety, the gossip, the reminders in fine of the cosmopolite and watering-place character to which the city of the Medici long ago began to bend her antique temper. Meanwhile it is pleasant enough for the tasters of charm, as I say, and for the makers of invidious distinctions, that the Americans haven't all arrived, however many may be on their way, and that the weather has a monotonous overcast softness in which, apparently, aimless contemplation grows less and less ashamed. There is no crush along the Cascine, as on the sunny days of winter, and the

Arno, wandering away toward the mountains in the haze, seems as shy of being looked at as a good picture in a bad light. No light, to my eyes, nevertheless, could be better than this, which reaches us, all strained and filtered and refined, exquisitely coloured and even a bit conspicuously sophisticated, through the heavy air of the past that hangs about the place forever.

I first knew Florence early enough, I am happy to say, to have heard the change for the worse, the taint of the modern order, bitterly lamented by old haunters, admirers, lovers—those qualified to present a picture of the conditions prevailing under the good old Grand-Dukes, the two last of their line in especial, that, for its blest reflection of sweetness and mildness and cheapness and ease, of every immediate boon in life to be enjoyed quite for nothing, could but draw tears from belated listeners. Some of these survivors from the golden age—just the beauty of which indeed was in the gold, of sorts, that it poured into your lap, and not in the least in its own importunity on that head—have needfully lingered on, have seen the ancient walls pulled down and the compact and belted mass of which the Piazza della Signoria was the immemorial centre expand, under the treatment of enterprising syndics, into an ungirdled organism of the type, as they viciously say, of Chicago; one of those places of which, as their grace of a circumference is nowhere, the dignity of a centre can no longer be predicated. Florence loses itself to-day in dusty boulevards and smart *beaux quartiers* [fine neighborhoods], such as Napoleon III and Baron Haussmann were to set the fashion of to a too mediæval Europe—with the effect of some precious page of antique text swallowed up in a marginal commentary that smacks of the style of the newspaper. So much for what has happened on this side of that line of demarcation which, by an odd law, makes us, with our preference for what we are pleased to call the picturesque, object to such occurrences even *as* occurrences. The real truth is that objections are too vain, and that he would be too rude a critic here, just now, who shouldn't be in the humour to take the thick with the thin and to try at least to read something of the old soul into the new forms.

There is something to be said moreover for your liking a city (once it's a question of your actively circulating) to pretend to comfort you more by its extent than by its limits; in addition to which Florence was anciently, was in her palmy days peculiarly, a daughter of change and movement and variety, of shifting moods, policies and *régimes*—just as the Florentine character, as we have it to-day, is a character that takes all things easily for having seen so many come and go. It saw the national capital, a few years since, arrive and sit down by the Arno, and took no further thought than sufficed for the day; then it saw the odd visitor depart and whistled her cheerfully on her way to Rome. The new boulevards of the Sindaco Peruzzi* come, it may be said, but they don't go; which, after all, it isn't from the æsthetic point of view strictly necessary they should. A part of the essential amiability of Florence, of her genius for making you take to your favour on easy terms everything that in any way belongs to her, is that she has already flung an element of her grace over all their undried mortar and plaster. Such modern arrangements as the Piazza d'Azeglio and the *viale* or Avenue of the Princess Margaret please not a little, I think—for what they are!—and do so even in a degree, by some fine local privilege, just because they are Florentine. The afternoon lights rest on them as if to thank them for not being worse, and their vistas are liberal where they look toward the hills. They carry you close to these admirable elevations, which hang over Florence on all sides, and if in the foreground your sense is a trifle perplexed by the white pavements dotted here and there with a policeman or a nursemaid, you have only to reach beyond and see Fiesole turn to violet, on its ample eminence, from the effect of the opposite sunset.

Facing again then to Florence proper you have local colour enough and to spare—which you enjoy the more, doubtless, from standing off to get your light and your point of view. The elder streets abutting on all this newness bore away into the heart of the city in narrow, dusky perspectives that quite refine, in certain places, by an art of their own, on the romantic appeal. There are temporal and other accidents thanks to

* Boulevards created by the then-current mayor of Florence, Ubaldino Peruzzi.

which, as you pause to look down them and to penetrate the deepening shadows that accompany their retreat, they resemble little corridors leading out from the past, mystical like the ladder in Jacob's dream; so that when you see a single figure advance and draw nearer you are half afraid to wait till it arrives—it must be too much of the nature of a ghost, a messenger from an underworld. However this may be, a place paved with such great mosaics of slabs and lined with palaces of so massive a tradition, structures which, in their large dependence on pure proportion for interest and beauty, reproduce more than other modern styles the simple nobleness of Greek architecture, must ever have placed dignity first in the scale of invoked effect and laid up no great treasure of that ragged picturesqueness—the picturesqueness of large poverty—on which we feast our idle eyes at Rome and Naples. Except in the unfinished fronts of the churches, which, however, unfortunately, are mere ugly blankness, one finds less of the poetry of ancient over-use, or in other words less romantic southern shabbiness, than in most Italian cities. At two or three points, none the less, this sinister grace exists in perfection— just such perfection as so often proves that what is literally hideous may be constructively delightful and what is intrinsically tragic play on the finest chords of appreciation. On the north side of the Arno, between Ponte Vecchio and Ponte Santa Trinità, is a row of immemorial houses that back on the river, in whose yellow flood they bathe their sore old feet. Anything more battered and befouled, more cracked and disjointed, dirtier, drearier, poorer, it would be impossible to conceive. They look as if fifty years ago the liquid mud had risen over their chimneys and then subsided again and left them coated forever with its unsightly slime. And yet forsooth, because the river is yellow, and the light is yellow, and here and there, elsewhere, some mellow mouldering surface, some hint of colour, some accident of atmosphere, takes up the foolish tale and repeats the note—because, in short, it is Florence, it is Italy, and the fond appraiser, the infatuated alien, may have had in his eyes, at birth and afterwards, the micaceous sparkle of brown-stone fronts no more interesting than so much sandpaper, these miserable dwellings, instead of suggesting mental invocations to an enterprising board of health, simply create their own standard of felicity and shamelessly live in it. Lately, during the misty autumn nights, the moon has shone on them faintly and refined their shabbiness away into something ineffably strange and spectral. The turbid stream sweeps along with a sound, and the pale tenements hang above it like a vague miasmatic exhalation. The dimmest back-scene at the opera, when the tenor is singing his sweetest, seems hardly to belong to a world more detached from responsibility.

What it is that infuses so rich an interest into the general charm is difficult to say in a few words; yet as we wander hither and thither in quest of sacred canvas and immortal bronze and stone we still feel the genius of the place hang about. Two industrious English ladies, the Misses Horner, have lately published a couple of volumes of "Walks" by the Arno-side, and their work is a long enumeration of great artistic deeds. These things remain for the most part in sound preservation, and, as the weeks go by and you spend a constant portion of your days among them the sense of one of the happiest periods of human Taste—to put it only at that—settles upon your spirit. It was not long; it lasted, in its splendour, for less than a century; but it has stored away in the palaces and churches of Florence a heritage of beauty that these three enjoying centuries since haven't yet exhausted. This forms a clear intellectual atmosphere into which you may turn aside from the modern world and fill your lungs as with the breath of a forgotten creed. The memorials of the past here address us moreover with a friendliness, win us by we scarcely know what sociability, what equal amenity, that we scarce find matched in other great æsthetically endowed communities and periods. Venice, with her old palaces cracking under the weight of their treasures, is, in her influence, insupportably sad; Athens, with her maimed marbles and dishonoured memories, transmutes the consciousness of sensitive observers, I am told, into a chronic heartache; but in one's impression of old Florence the abiding felicity, the sense of saving sanity, of something sound and human, predominates, offering you a medium still conceivable for life. The reason of this is partly, no doubt, the "sympathetic" nature, the temperate joy, of Florentine art in general—putting the sole Dante, greatest of literary artists, aside; partly the tenderness of time, in its lapse, which, save in a few cases, has been as sparing of injury as if it knew that when it should have dimmed and corroded these charming things it would have nothing so sweet again for its tooth to feed on. If the beautiful Ghirlandaios and Lippis are fading this generation will never know it. The large Fra Angelico in the Academy is as clear and keen as if the good old monk stood there wiping his brushes; the colours seem to *sing,* as it were, like new-fledged birds in June. Nothing is more characteristic of early Tuscan art than the high-reliefs of Luca della Robbia; yet there isn't one of them that, except for the unique mixture of freshness with its wisdom, of candour with its expertness, mightn't have been modelled yesterday.

But perhaps the best image of the absence of stale melancholy or wasted splendour, of the positive presence of what I have called temperate joy, in the Florentine impression and genius, is the bell-tower of Giotto, which rises beside the Cathedral. No beholder of it will have forgotten how straight and slender it stands there, how strangely rich in the common street, plated with coloured marble patterns, and yet so far from simple or severe in design that we easily wonder how its author, the painter of exclusively and portentously grave little pictures, should have fashioned a building which in the way of elaborate elegance, of the true play of taste, leaves a jealous modern criticism nothing to miss. Nothing can be imagined at once more lightly and more pointedly fanciful; it might have been handed over to the city, as it stands, by some Oriental genie tired of too much detail. Yet for all that suggestion it seems of no particular time—not grey and hoary like a Gothic steeple, not cracked and despoiled like a Greek temple; its marbles shining so little less freshly than when they were laid together, and the sunset lighting up its cornice with such a friendly radiance, that you come at last to regard it simply as the graceful, indestructible soul of the place made visible. The Cathedral, externally, for all its solemn hugeness, strikes the same note of would-be reasoned elegance and cheer; it has conventional grandeur, of course, but a grandeur so frank and ingenuous even in its *parti-pris* [bias]. It has seen so much, and outlived so much, and served so many sad purposes, and yet remains in aspect so full of the fine Tuscan geniality, the feeling for life, one may almost say the feeling for amusement, that inspired it. Its vast many-coloured marble walls become at any rate, with this, the friendliest note of all Florence; there is an unfailing charm in walking past them while they lift their great acres of geometrical mosaic higher in the air than you have time or other occasion to look. You greet them from the deep street as you greet the side of a mountain when you move in the gorge—not twisting back your head to keep looking at the top, but content with the minor accidents, the nestling hollows and soft cloud-shadows, the general protection of the valley.

Florence is richer in pictures than we really know till we have begun to look for them in outlying corners. Then, here and there, one comes upon lurking values and hidden gems that it quite seems one might as a good New Yorker quietly "bag" for the so aspiring Museum of that city without their being missed. The Pitti Palace is of course a collection of masterpieces; they jostle each other in their splendour, they perhaps even, in their merciless multitude, rather fatigue our admiration. The Uffizi is almost as fine a show, and together with that long serpentine artery which crosses the Arno and connects them, making you ask yourself, whichever way you take it, what goal can be grand enough to crown such a journey, they form the great central treasure-chamber of the town. But I have been neglecting them of late for love of the Academy, where there are fewer copyists and tourists, above all fewer pictorial lions, those whose roar is heard from afar and who strike us as expecting overmuch to have it their own way in the jungle. The pictures at the Academy are all, rather, doves—the whole impression is less pompously tropical. Selection still leaves one too much to say, but I noted here, on my last occasion, an enchanting Botticelli so obscurely hung, in one of the smaller rooms, that I scarce knew whether most to enjoy or to resent its relegation. Placed, in a mean black frame, where you wouldn't have looked for a masterpiece, it yet gave out to a good glass every characteristic of one. Representing as it does the walk of Tobias with the angel, there are really parts of it that an angel might have painted; but I doubt whether it is observed by half-a-dozen persons a year. That was my excuse for my wanting to know, on the spot, though doubtless all sophistically, what dishonour, could the transfer be artfully accomplished, a strong American light and a brave gilded frame would, comparatively speaking, do it. There and then it would shine with the intense authority that we claim for the fairest things—would exhale its wondrous beauty as a sovereign example. What it comes to is that this master is the most interesting of a great band—the only Florentine save Leonardo and Michael* in whom the impulse was original and the invention rare. His imagination is of things strange, subtle and complicated—things it at first strikes us that we moderns have reason to know, and that it has taken us all the ages to learn; so that we permit ourselves to wonder how a "primitive" could come by them. We soon enough reflect, however, that we ourselves have come by them almost only *through* him, exquisite spirit that he was, and that when we enjoy, or at least when we encounter, in our William Morrises, in our Rossettis and Burne-Joneses, the note of the haunted or over-charged consciousness, we are but treated, with other matters, to repeated doses of diluted Botticelli. He practically set with his own hand almost all the copies to almost all our so-called pre-Raphaelites, earlier and later, near and remote.

Let us at the same time, none the less, never fail of response to the great Florentine geniality at large. Fra Angelico, Filippo Lippi, Ghirlandaio, were not "subtly" imaginative, were not even riotously so; but what other three were ever more gladly observant, more vividly and richly true? If there should some time be a weeding out of the world's possessions the best works of the early Florentines will certainly be counted among the flowers. With the ripest performances of the Venetians—by which I don't mean the over-ripe—we can but take them for the most valuable things in the history of art. Heaven forbid we should be narrowed down to a cruel choice; but if it came to a question of keeping or losing between half-a-dozen Raphaels and half-a-dozen things it would be a joy to pick out at the Academy, I fear that, for myself, the memory of the Transfig-

* Michelangelo.

uration, or indeed of the other Roman relics of the painter, wouldn't save the Raphaels. And yet this was so far from the opinion of a patient artist whom I saw the other day copying the finest of Ghirlandaios—a beautiful Adoration of the Kings at the Hospital of the Innocenti. Here was another sample of the buried art-wealth of Florence. It hangs in an obscure chapel, far aloft, behind an altar, and though now and then a stray tourist wanders in and puzzles awhile over the vaguely-glowing forms, the picture is never really seen and enjoyed. I found an aged Frenchman of modest mien perched on a little platform beneath it, behind a great hedge of altar-candlesticks, with an admirable copy all completed. The difficulties of his task had been well-nigh insuperable, and his performance seemed to me a real feat of magic. He could scarcely move or turn, and could find room for his canvas but by rolling it together and painting a small piece at a time, so that he never enjoyed a view of his *ensemble*. The original is gorgeous with colour and bewildering with decorative detail, but not a gleam of the painter's crimson was wanting, not a curl in his gold arabesques. It seemed to me that if I had copied a Ghirlandaio in such conditions I would at least maintain for my own credit that he was the first painter in the world. "Very good of its kind," said the weary old man with a shrug of reply for my raptures; "but oh how far short of Raphael!" However that may be, if the reader chances to observe this consummate copy in the so commendable Museum devoted in Paris to such works, let him stop before it with a due reverence; it is one of the patient things of art. Seeing it wrought there, in its dusky nook, under such scant convenience, I found no bar in the painter's foreignness to a thrilled sense that the old art-life of Florence isn't yet extinct. It still at least works spells and almost miracles.

[1874]

Florentine Notes

i

Yesterday that languid organism known as the Florentine Carnival put on a momentary semblance of vigour, and decreed a general *corso* [parade and holiday] through the town. The spectacle was not brilliant, but it suggested some natural reflections. I encountered the line of carriages in the square before Santa Croce, of which they were making the circuit. They rolled solemnly by, with their inmates frowning forth at each other in apparent wrath at not finding each other more worth while. There were no masks, no costumes, no decorations, no throwing of flowers or sweetmeats. It was as if each carriageful had privately and not very heroically resolved not to be at costs, and was rather discomfited at finding that it was getting no better entertainment than it gave. The middle of the piazza was filled with little tables, with shouting mountebanks, mostly disguised in battered bonnets and crinolines, offering chances in raffles for plucked fowls and kerosene lamps. I have never thought the huge marble statue of Dante, which overlooks the scene, a work of the last refinement; but, as it stood there on its high pedestal, chin in hand, frowning down on all this cheap foolery, it seemed to have a great moral intention. The carriages followed a prescribed course—through Via Ghibellina, Via del Proconsolo, past the Badia and the Bargello, beneath the great tessellated cliffs of the Cathedral, through Via Tornabuoni and out into ten minutes' sunshine beside the Arno. Much of all this is the gravest and stateliest part of

Florence, a quarter of supreme dignity, and there was an almost ludicrous incongruity in seeing Pleasure leading her train through these dusky historic streets. It was most uncomfortably cold, and in the absence of masks many a fair nose was fantastically tipped with purple. But as the carriages crept solemnly along they seemed to keep a funeral march—to follow an antique custom, an exploded faith, to its tomb. The Carnival is dead, and these good people who had come abroad to make merry were funeral mutes and gravediggers. Last winter in Rome it showed but a galvanised life, yet compared with this humble exhibition it was operatic. At Rome indeed it was too operatic. The knights on horseback there were a bevy of circus-riders, and I'm sure half the mad revellers repaired every night to the Capitol for their twelve sous a day.

I have just been reading over the Letters of the Président de Brosses.* A hundred years ago, in Venice, the Carnival lasted six months; and at Rome for many weeks each year one was free, under cover of a mask, to perpetrate the most fantastic follies and cultivate the most remunerative vices. It's very well to read the President's notes, which have indeed a singular interest; but they make us ask ourselves why we should expect the Italians to persist in manners and practices which we ourselves, if we had responsibilities in the matter, should find intolerable. The Florentines at any rate spend no more money nor faith on the carnivalesque. And yet this truth has a qualification; for what struck me in the whole spectacle yesterday, and prompted these observations, was not at all the more or less of costume of the occupants of the carriages, but the obstinate survival of the merrymaking instinct in the people at large. There could be no better example of it than that so dim a shadow of entertainment should keep all Florence standing and strolling, densely packed for hours, in the cold streets. There was nothing to see that mightn't be seen on the Cascine any fine day in the year—nothing but a name, a tradition, a pretext for sweet staring idleness. The faculty of making much of common things and converting small occasions into great

* *Lettres familières écrites d'Italie en 1739 et 1740* (1799) by Charles de Brosses (1709–1777).

pleasures is, to a son of communities strenuous as ours are strenuous, the most salient characteristic of the so-called Latin civilisations. It charms him and vexes him, according to his mood; and for the most part it represents a moral gulf between his own temperamental and indeed spiritual sense of race, and that of Frenchmen and Italians, far wider than the watery leagues that a steamer may annihilate. But I think his mood is wisest when he accepts the "foreign" easy surrender to *all* the senses as the sign of an unconscious philosophy of life, instilled by the experience of centuries—the philosophy of people who have lived long and much, who have discovered no short cuts to happiness and no effective circumvention of effort, and so have come to regard the average lot as a ponderous fact that absolutely calls for a certain amount of sitting on the lighter tray of the scales. Florence yesterday then took its holiday in a natural, placid fashion that seemed to make its own temper an affair quite independent of the splendour of the compensation decreed on a higher line to the weariness of its legs. That the *corso* was stupid or lively was the shame or the glory of the powers "above"—the fates, the gods, the *forestieri,* the town-councilmen, the rich or the stingy. Common Florence, on the narrow footways, pressed against the houses, obeyed a natural need in looking about complacently, patiently, gently, and never pushing, nor trampling, nor swearing, nor staggering. This liberal margin for festivals in Italy gives the masses a more than man-of-the world urbanity in taking their pleasure.

Meanwhile it occurs to me that by a remote New England fireside an unsophisticated young person of either sex is reading in an old volume of travels or an old romantic tale some account of these anniversaries and appointed revels as old Catholic lands offer them to view. Across the page swims a vision of sculptured palace-fronts draped in crimson and gold and shining in a southern sun; of a motley train of maskers sweeping on in voluptuous confusion and pelting each other with nosegays and love-letters. Into the quiet room, quenching the rhythm of the Connecticut clock, floats an uproar of delighted voices, a medley of stirring foreign sounds, an echo of far-heard music of a strangely alien cadence. But the dusk is falling, and the unsophisticated young person closes the book wearily and wanders to the window. The dusk is falling on the beaten snow. Down the road is a white wooden meeting-house, looking grey among the drifts. The young person surveys the prospect awhile, and then wanders back and stares at the fire. The Carnival of Venice, of Florence, of Rome; colour and costume, romance and rapture! The young person gazes in the firelight at the flickering chiaroscuro of the future, discerns at last the glowing phantasm of opportunity, and determines with a wild heart-beat to go and see it all—twenty years hence!

· · · · · · *ii* · · · · · ·

A couple of days since, driving to Fiesole, we came back by the castle of Vincigliata. The afternoon was lovely; and, though there is as yet (February 10th) no visible revival of vegetation, the air was full of a vague vernal perfume, and the warm colours of the hills and the yellow western sunlight flooding the plain seemed to contain the promise of Nature's return to grace. It's true that above the distant pale blue gorge of Vallombrosa the mountain-line was tipped with snow; but the liberated soul of Spring was nevertheless at large. The view from Fiesole seems vaster and richer with each visit. The hollow in which Florence lies, and which from below seems deep and contracted, opens out into an immense and generous valley and leads away the eye into a hundred gradations of distance. The place itself showed, amid its chequered fields and gardens, with as many towers and spires as a chess-board half cleared. The domes and towers were washed over with a faint blue mist. The scattered columns of smoke, interfused with the sinking sunlight, hung over them like streamers and pennons of silver gauze; and the Arno, twisting and curling and glittering here and there, was a serpent cross-striped with silver.

Vincigliata is a product of the millions, the leisure and the eccentricity, I suppose people say, of an English gentleman— Mr. Temple Leader, whose name should be commemorated. You reach the castle from Fiesole by a narrow road, returning toward Florence by a romantic twist through the hills and passing nothing on its way save thin plantations of cypress and cedar. Upward of twenty years ago, I believe, this gentleman took a fancy to the crumbling shell of a mediæval fortress on a breezy hilltop overlooking the Val d'Arno and forthwith bought it and began to "restore" it. I know nothing of what the original ruin may have cost; but in the dusky courts and chambers of the present elaborate structure this impassioned archæologist must have buried a fortune. He has, however, the compensation of feeling that he has erected a monument which, if it is never to stand a feudal siege, may encounter at least some critical overhauling. It is a disinterested work of art and really a triumph of æsthetic culture. The author has reproduced with minute accuracy a sturdy home-fortress of the fourteenth century, and has kept throughout such rigid terms with his model that the result is literally uninhabitable to degenerate moderns. It is simply a massive facsimile, an elegant museum of archaic images, mainly but most amusingly counterfeit, perched on a spur of the Apennines. The place is most politely shown. There is a charming cloister, painted with extremely clever "quaint" frescoes, celebrating the deeds of the founders of the castle—a cloister that is everything delightful a cloister should be except truly venerable and employable. There is a beautiful castle court, with the embattled tower climbing into the blue far above it, and a spacious loggia with rugged medallions and mild-hued Luca della Robbias fastened unevenly into the walls. But the apartments are the great success, and each of them as good a "reconstruction" as a tale of Walter Scott; or, to speak frankly, a much better one. They are all low-beamed and vaulted, stone-paved, decorated in grave colours and lighted, from narrow, deeply recessed windows, through small leaden-ringed plates of opaque glass.

The details are infinitely ingenious and elaborately grim, and the indoor atmosphere of mediævalism most forcibly revived. No compromising fact of domiciliary darkness and cold is spared us, no producing condition of mediæval manners not glanced at. There are oaken benches round the room, of about six inches in depth and gaunt fauteuils of wrought leather, illustrating the suppressed transitions which, as George Eliot says, unite all contrasts—offering a visible link between the modern conceptions of torture and of luxury. There are fireplaces nowhere but in the kitchen, where a couple of sentry-boxes are inserted on either side of the great hooded chimneypiece, into which people might creep and take their turn at being toasted and smoked. One may doubt whether this dearth of the hearthstone could have raged on such a scale, but it's a happy stroke in the representation of an Italian dwelling of any period. It shows how the graceful fiction that Italy is all "meridional" flourished for some time before being refuted by grumbling tourists. And yet amid this cold comfort you feel the incongruous presence of a constant intuitive regard for beauty. The shapely spring of the vaulted ceilings; the richly figured walls, coarse and hard in substance as they are; the charming shapes of the great platters and flagons in the deep recesses of the quaintly carved black dressers; the wandering hand of ornament, as it were, playing here and there for its own diversion in unlighted corners—such things redress, to our fond credulity, with all sorts of grace, the balance of the picture.

And yet, somehow, with what dim, unillumined vision one fancies even such inmates as those conscious of finer needs than the mere supply of blows and beef and beer would meet passing their heavy eyes over such slender household beguilements! These crepuscular chambers at Vincigliata are a mystery and a challenge; they seem the mere propounding of an answerless riddle. You long, as you wander through them, turning up your coat-collar and wondering whether ghosts can catch bronchitis, to answer it with some positive notion of what people so encaged and situated "did," how they looked and talked and carried themselves, how they took their pains and pleasures, how they counted off the hours. Deadly ennui seems to ooze out of the stones and hang in clouds in the brown corners. No wonder men relished a fight and panted for a fray. "Skull-smashers" were sweet, ears ringing with pain and ribs cracking in a tussle were soothing music, compared with the cruel quietude of the dim-windowed castle. When they came back they could only have slept a good deal and eased their dislocated bones on those meagre oaken ledges. Then they woke up and turned about to the table and ate their portion of roasted sheep. They shouted at each other across the board and flung the wooden plates at the serving-men. They jostled and hustled and hooted and bragged; and then, after gorging and boozing and easing their doublets, they squared their elbows one by one

on the greasy table and buried their scarred foreheads and
dreamed of a good gallop after flying foes. And the women?
They must have been strangely simple—simpler far than any
moral archæologist can show us in a learned restoration. Of
course, their simplicity had its graces and devices; but one
thinks with a sigh that, as the poor things turned away with
patient looks from the viewless windows to the same, same
looming figures on the dusky walls, they hadn't even the consolation of knowing that just this attitude and movement, set
off by their peaked coifs, their falling sleeves and heavily-
twisted trains, would sow the seed of yearning envy—of
sorts—on the part of later generations.

There are moods in which one feels the impulse to enter a
tacit protest against too gross an appetite for pure æsthetics in
this starving and sinning world. One turns half away, mus-
ingly, from certain beautiful useless things. But the healthier
state of mind surely is to lay no tax on any really intelligent
manifestation of the curious and exquisite. Intelligence hangs
together essentially, all along the line; it only needs time to
make, as we say, its connections. The massive *pastiche* of Vincigliata has no superficial use; but, even if it were less complete,
less successful, less brilliant, I should feel a reflective kindness
for it. So disinterested and so expensive a toy is its own justification; it belongs to the heroics of dilettantism.

· · · · · *i i i* . · · · · · ·

One grows to feel the collection of pictures at the Pitti Palace
splendid rather than interesting. After walking through it once
or twice you catch the key in which it is pitched—you know
what you are likely not to find on closer examination; none of
the works of the uncompromising period, nothing from the
half-groping geniuses of the early time, those whose colouring
was sometimes harsh and their outlines sometimes angular.
Vague to me the principle on which the pictures were originally gathered and of the æsthetic creed of the princes who
chiefly selected them. A princely creed I should roughly call
it—the creed of people who believed in things presenting a fine
face to society; who esteemed showy results rather than curious
processes, and would have hardly cared more to admit into

their collection a work by one of the laborious precursors of the full efflorescence than to see a bucket and broom left standing in a state saloon. The gallery contains in literal fact some eight or ten paintings of the early Tuscan School—notably two admirable specimens of Filippo Lippi and one of the frequent circular pictures of the great Botticelli—a Madonna, chilled with tragic prescience, laying a pale cheek against that of a blighted Infant. Such a melancholy mother as this of Botticelli would have strangled her baby in its cradle to rescue it from the future. But of Botticelli there is much to say. One of the Filippo Lippis is perhaps his masterpiece—a Madonna in a small rose-garden (such a "flowery close" as Mr. William Morris loves to haunt), leaning over an Infant who kicks his little human heels on the grass while half-a-dozen curly-pated angels gather about him, looking back over their shoulders with the candour of children in *tableaux vivants,* and one of them drops an armful of gathered roses one by one upon the baby. The delightful earthly innocence of these winged youngsters is quite inexpressible. Their heads are twisted about toward the spectator as if they were playing at leap-frog and were expecting a companion to come and take a jump. Never did "young" art, never did subjective freshness, attempt with greater success to represent those phases. But these three fine works are hung over the tops of doors in a dark back room—the bucket and broom are thrust behind a curtain. It seems to me, nevertheless, that a fine Filippo Lippi is good enough company for an Allori or a Cigoli, and that that too deeply sentient Virgin of Botticelli might happily balance the flower-like irresponsibility of Raphael's "Madonna of the Chair."

Taking the Pitti collection, however, simply for what it pretends to be, it gives us the very flower of the sumptuous, the courtly, the grand-ducal. It is chiefly official art, as one may say, but it presents the fine side of the type—the brilliancy, the facility, the amplitude, the sovereignty of good taste. I agree on the whole with a nameless companion and with what he lately remarked about his own humour on these matters; that, having been on his first acquaintance with pictures nothing if not critical, and held the lesson incomplete and the opportunity slighted if he left a gallery without a headache, he had come,

as he grew older, to regard them more as the grandest of all
pleasantries and less as the most strenuous of all lessons, and to
remind himself that, after all, it is the privilege of art to make
us friendly to the human mind and not to make us suspicious
of it. We do in fact as we grow older unstring the critical bow
a little and strike a truce with invidious comparisons. We work
off the juvenile impulse to heated partisanship and discover
that one spontaneous producer isn't different enough from
another to keep the all-knowing Fates from smiling over our
loves and our aversions. We perceive a certain human solidarity in all cultivated effort, and are conscious of a growing
accommodation of judgment—an easier disposition, the fruit
of experience, to take the joke for what it is worth as it passes.
We have in short less of a quarrel with the masters we don't
delight in, and less of an impulse to pin all our faith on those
in whom, in more zealous days, we fancied that we made out
peculiar meanings. The meanings no longer seem quite so
peculiar. Since then we have arrived at a few in the depths of
our own genius that are not sensibly less striking.

And yet it must be added that all this depends vastly on
one's mood—as a traveller's impressions do, generally, to a
degree which those who give them to the world would do well
more explicitly to declare. We have our hours of expansion and
those of contraction, and yet while we follow the traveller's
trade we go about gazing and judging with unadjusted confidence. We can't suspend judgment; we must take our notes,
and the notes are florid or crabbed, as the case may be. A short
time ago I spent a week in an ancient city on a hill-top, in the
humour, for which I was not to blame, which produces crabbed
notes. I knew it at the time, but couldn't help it. I went through
all the motions of liberal appreciation; I uncapped in all the
churches and on the massive ramparts stared all the views
fairly out of countenance; but my imagination, which I suppose
at bottom had very good reasons of its own and knew perfectly
what it was about, refused to project into the dark old town
and upon the yellow hills that sympathetic glow which forms
half the substance of our genial impressions. So it is that in
museums and palaces we are alternate radicals and conserva-
tives. On some days we ask but to be somewhat sensibly af-

fected; on others, Ruskin-haunted, to be spiritually steadied. After a long absence from the Pitti Palace I went back there the other morning and transferred myself from chair to chair in the great golden-roofed saloons—the chairs are all gilded and covered with faded silk—in the humour to be diverted at any price. I needn't mention the things that diverted me; I yawn now when I think of some of them. But an artist, for instance, to whom my kindlier judgment has made permanent concessions is that charming Andrea del Sarto. When I first knew him, in my cold youth, I used to say without mincing that I didn't like him. *Cet âge est sans pitié* [That age is pitiless]. The fine sympathetic, melancholy, pleasing painter! He has a dozen faults, and if you insist pedantically on your rights the conclusive word you use about him will be the word weak. But if you are a generous soul you will utter it low—low as the mild grave tone of his own sought harmonies. He is monotonous, narrow, incomplete; he has but a dozen different figures and but two or three ways of distributing them; he seems able to utter but half his thought, and his canvases lack apparently some final return on the whole matter—some process which his impulse failed him before he could bestow. And yet in spite of these limitations his genius is both itself of the great pattern and lighted by the air of a great period. Three gifts he had largely: an instinctive, unaffected, unerring grace; a large and rich, and yet a sort of withdrawn and indifferent, sobriety; and best of all, as well as rarest of all, an indescribable property of relatedness as to the moral world. Whether he was aware of the connection or not, or in what measure, I cannot say; but he gives, so to speak, the taste of it. Before his handsome vague-browed Madonnas; the mild, robust young saints who kneel in his foregrounds and look round at you with a conscious anxiety which seems to say that, though in the picture, they are not of it, but of your own sentient life of commingled love and weariness; the stately apostles, with comely heads and harmonious draperies, who gaze up at the high-seated Virgin like early astronomers at a newly seen star—there comes to you the brush of the dark wing of an inward life. A shadow falls for the moment, and in it you feel the chill of moral suffering. Did the Lippis suffer, father or son? Did Raphael suffer? Did Titian? Did Rubens

suffer? Perish the thought—it wouldn't be fair to *us* that they
should have had everything. And I note in our poor second-
rate Andrea an element of interest lacking to a number of
stronger talents.

Interspersed with him at the Pitti hang the stronger and the
weaker in splendid abundance. Raphael is there, strong in
portraiture—easy, various, bountiful genius that he was—and
(strong here isn't the word, but) happy beyond the common
dream in his beautiful "Madonna of the Chair." The general
instinct of posterity seems to have been to treat this lovely
picture as a semi-sacred, an almost miraculous, manifestation.
People stand in a worshipful silence before it, as they would
before a taper-studded shrine. If we suspend in imagination on
the right of it the solid realistic, unidealised portrait of Leo the
Tenth (which hangs in another room) and transport to the left
the fresco of the School of Athens from the Vatican, and then
reflect that these were three separate fancies of a single youthful, amiable genius we recognise that such a producing consciousness must have been a "treat." My companion already
quoted has a phrase that he "doesn't care for Raphael," but
confesses, when pressed, that he was a most remarkable young
man. Titian has a dozen portraits of unequal interest. I never
particularly noticed till lately—it is very ill hung—that portentous image of the Emperor Charles the Fifth. He was a
burlier, more imposing personage than his usual legend figures, and in his great puffed sleeves and gold chains and full-
skirted over-dress he seems to tell of a tread that might
sometimes have been inconveniently resonant. But the *purpose*
to have his way and work his will is there—the great stomach
for divine right, the old monarchical temperament. The great
Titian, in portraiture, however, remains that formidable young
man in black, with the small compact head, the delicate nose
and the irascible blue eye. Who was he? What was he? "*Ri-
tratto virile*" [Portrait of a Man] is all the catalogue is able to call
the picture. "Virile"! Rather! you vulgarly exclaim. You may
weave what romance you please about it, but a romance your
dream must be. Handsome, clever, defiant, passionate, dangerous, it was not his own fault if he hadn't adventures and to
spare. He was a gentleman and a warrior, and his adventures

balanced between camp and court. I imagine him the young orphan of a noble house, about to come into mortgaged estates. One wouldn't have cared to be his guardian, bound to paternal admonitions once a month over his precocious transactions with the Jews or his scandalous abduction from her convent of such and such a noble maiden.

The Pitti Gallery contains none of Titian's golden-toned groups; but it boasts a lovely composition by Paul Veronese, the dealer in silver hues—a Baptism of Christ. W—— named it to me the other day as the picture he most enjoyed, and surely painting seems here to have proposed to itself to discredit and annihilate—and even on the occasion of such a subject—everything but the loveliness of life. The picture bedims and enfeebles its neighbours. We ask ourselves whether painting as such can go further. It is simply that here at last the art stands complete. The early Tuscans, as well as Leonardo, as Raphael, as Michael, saw the great spectacle that surrounded them in beautiful sharp-edged elements and parts. The great Venetians felt its indissoluble unity and recognised that form and colour and earth and air were equal members of every possible subject; and beneath their magical touch the hard outlines melted together and the blank intervals bloomed with meaning. In this beautiful Paul Veronese of the Pitti everything is part of the charm—the atmosphere as well as the figures, the look of radiant morning in the white-streaked sky as well as the living human limbs, the cloth of Venetian purple about the lions of the Christ as well as the noble humility of his attitude. The relation to Nature of the other Italian schools differs from that of the Venetian as courtship—even ardent courtship—differs from marriage.

····· *i v* .······

I went the other day to the secularised Convent of San Marco, paid my franc at the profane little wicket which creaks away at the door—no less than six custodians, apparently, are needed to turn it, as if it may have a recusant conscience—passed along the bright, still cloister and paid my respects to Fra Angelico's Crucifixion, in that dusky chamber in the basement. I looked long; one can hardly do otherwise. The fresco deals with the pathetic on the grand scale, and after taking in its beauty you feel as little at liberty to go away abruptly as you would to leave church during the sermon. You may be as little of a formal Christian as Fra Angelico was much of one; you yet feel admonished by spiritual decency to let so yearning a view of the Christian story work its utmost will on you. The three crosses rise high against a strange completely crimson sky, which deepens mysteriously the tragic expression of the scene, though I remain perforce vague as to whether this lurid background be a fine intended piece of symbolism or an effective accident of time. In the first case the extravagance quite triumphs. Between the crosses, under no great rigour of composition, are scattered the most exemplary saints—kneeling, praying, weeping, pitying, worshipping. The swoon of the Madonna is depicted at the left, and this gives the holy presences, in respect to the case, the strangest historical or actual air. Everything is so real that you feel a vague impatience and almost ask yourself how it was that amid the army of his consecrated servants our Lord was permitted to suffer. On reflection you see that the painter's design, so far as coherent, has been simply to offer an immense representation of Pity, and all with such concentrated truth that his colours here seem dissolved in tears that drop and drop, however softly, through all time. Of this single yearning consciousness the figures are admirably expressive. No later painter learned to render with deeper force than Fra Angelico the one state of the spirit he could conceive—a passionate pious tenderness. Immured in his quiet convent, he apparently never received an intelligible impression of evil; and his conception of human life was a perpetual sense of sacredly loving and being loved. But how, immured in his quiet convent, away from the streets and the studios, did he become that genuine, finished, perfectly professional painter? No one is less of a mere mawkish amateur. His range was broad, from this really heroic fresco to the little trumpeting seraphs, in their opaline robes, enamelled, as it were, on the gold margins of his pictures.

I sat out the sermon and departed, I hope, with the gentle preacher's blessing. I went into the smaller refectory, near by, to refresh my memory of the beautiful Last Supper of Domenico Ghirlandaio. It would be putting things coarsely to say that I adjourned thus from a sermon to a comedy, though Ghirlandaio's theme, as contrasted with the blessed Angelico's, was the dramatic, spectacular side of human life. How keenly he observed it and how richly he rendered it, the world about him of colour and costume, of handsome heads and pictorial groupings! In his admirable school there is no painter one enjoys—*pace* Ruskin—more sociably and irresponsibly. Lippo Lippi is simpler, quainter, more frankly expressive; but we retain before him a remnant of the sympathetic discomfort provoked by the masters whose conceptions were still a trifle too large for their means. The pictorial vision in their minds seems to stretch and strain their undeveloped skill almost to a sense of pain. In Ghirlandaio the skill and the imagination are equal, and he gives us a delightful impression of enjoying his own resources. Of all the painters of his time he affects us least as positively not of ours. He enjoyed a crimson mantle spreading and tumbling in curious folds and embroidered with needlework of gold, just as he enjoyed a handsome well-rounded head, with vigorous dusky locks, profiled in courteous adoration. He enjoyed in short the various reality of things, and had the good fortune to live in an age when reality flowered into a thousand amusing graces—to speak only of those. He was not especially addicted to giving spiritual hints; and yet how hard and meagre they seem, the professed and finished realists of our own day, with the spiritual *bonhomie* or candour that makes half Ghirlandaio's richness left out! The Last Supper at San Marco is an excellent example of the natural reverence of an artist of that time with whom reverence was not, as one may say, a specialty. The main idea with him has been the variety, the material bravery and positively social charm of the scene, which finds expression, with irrepressible generosity, in the accessories of the background. Instinctively he imagines an opulent garden—imagines it with a good faith which quite tides him over the reflection that Christ and his disciples were poor men and unused to sit at meat in palaces. Great full-fruited orange-trees peep over the wall before which the table is spread, strange birds fly through the air, while a peacock perches on the edge of the partition and looks down on the sacred repast. It is striking that, without any at all intense religious purpose, the figures, in their varied naturalness, have a dignity and sweetness of attitude that admits of numberless reverential constructions. I should call all this the happy tact of a robust faith.

On the staircase leading up to the little painted cells of the Beato Angelico, however, I suddenly faltered and paused. Somehow I had grown averse to the intenser zeal of the Monk of Fiesole. I wanted no more of him that day. I wanted no more macerated friars and spear-gashed sides. Ghirlandaio's elegant way of telling his story had put me in the humour for something more largely intelligent, more profanely pleasing. I departed, walked across the square, and found it in the Academy, standing in a particular spot and looking up at a particular high-hung picture. It is difficult to speak adequately, perhaps even intelligibly, of Sandro Botticelli. An accomplished critic—Mr. Pater, in his *Studies on the History of the Renaissance*—has lately paid him the tribute of an exquisite, a supreme, curiosity. He was rarity and distinction incarnate, and of all the multitudinous masters of his group incomparably the most interesting, the one who detains and perplexes and fascinates us most. Exquisitely fine his imagination—infinitely audacious and adventurous his fancy. Alone among the painters of his time he strikes us as having invention. The glow and thrill of expanding observation—this was the feeling that sent his comrades to their easels; but Botticelli's moved him to reactions and emotions of which they knew nothing, caused his faculty to sport and wander and explore on its own account. These impulses have fruits often so ingenious and so lovely that it would be easy to talk nonsense about them. I hope it is not nonsense, however, to say that the picture to which I just alluded (the "Coronation of the Virgin," with a group of life-sized saints below and a garland of miniature angels above) is one of the supremely beautiful productions of the human mind. It is hung so high that you need a good glass to see it; to say nothing of the unprecedented delicacy of the work. The lower half is of moderate interest; but the dance of hand-clasped angels round the heavenly couple above has a beauty newly exhaled from the deepest sources of inspiration. Their perfect little hands are locked with ineffable elegance; their blowing robes are tossed into folds of which each line is a study; their charming feet have the relief of the most delicate sculpture. But, as I have already noted, of Botticelli there is much, too much to say—besides which Mr. Pater has said all. Only add thus to his inimitable grace of design that the exquisite pictorial force driving him goes a-Maying not on wanton errands of its own, but on those of some mystic superstition which trembles forever in his heart.

· · · · · *v* · · · · · ·

The more I look at the old Florentine domestic architecture the more I like it—that of the great examples at least; and if I ever am able to build myself a lordly pleasure-house I don't see how in conscience I can build it different from these. They are sombre and frowning, and look a trifle more as if they were meant to keep people out than to let them in; but what equally "important" type—if there be an equally important—is more expressive of domiciliary dignity and security and yet attests them with a finer æsthetic economy? They are impressively "handsome," and yet contrive to be so by the simplest means. I don't say at the smallest pecuniary cost—that's another matter. There is money buried in the thick walls and diffused through the echoing excess of space. The merchant nobles of the fifteenth century had deep and full pockets, I suppose, though the present bearers of their names are glad to let out their palaces in suites of apartments which are occupied by the commercial aristocracy of another republic. One is told of fine old mouldering chambers of which possession is to be enjoyed for a sum not worth mentioning. I am afraid that behind these so gravely harmonious fronts there is a good deal of dusky discomfort, and I speak now simply of the large serious faces themselves as you can see them from the street; see them ranged cheek to cheek in the grey historic light of Via dei Bardi, Via Maggio, Via degli Albizzi. The force of character, the familiar severity and majesty, depend on a few simple features: on the great iron-caged windows of the rough-hewn basement; on the noble stretch of space between the summit of one high, round-topped window and the bottom of that above;

on the high-hung sculptured shield at the angle of the house; on the flat far-projecting roof; and, finally, on the magnificent tallness of the whole building, which so dwarfs our modern attempts at size. The finest of these Florentine palaces are, I imagine, the tallest habitations in Europe that are frankly and amply habitations—not mere shafts for machinery of the American grain-elevator pattern. Some of the creations of M. Haussmann* in Paris may climb very nearly as high; but there is all the difference in the world between the impressiveness of a building which takes breath, as it were, some six or seven times, from storey to storey, and of one that erects itself to an equal height in three long-drawn pulsations. When a house is ten windows wide and the drawing-room floor is as high as a chapel it can afford but three floors. The spaciousness of some of those ancient drawing-rooms is that of a Russian steppe. The "family circle," gathered anywhere within speaking distance, must resemble a group of pilgrims encamped in the desert on a little oasis of carpet. Madame Gryzanowska,† living at the top of a house in that dusky, tortuous old Borgo Pinti, initiated me the other evening most good-naturedly, lamp in hand, into the far-spreading mysteries of her apartment. Such quarters seem a translation into space of the old-fashioned idea of leisure. Leisure and "room" have been passing out of our manners together, but here and there, being of stouter structure, the latter lingers and survives.

Here and there, indeed, in this blessed Italy, reluctantly modern in spite alike of boasts and lamentations, it seems to have been preserved for curiosity's and fancy's sake, with a vague, sweet odour of the embalmer's spices about it. I went the other morning to the Corsini Palace. The proprietors obviously are great people. One of the ornaments of Rome is their great white-faced palace in the dark Trastevere and its voluminous gallery, none the less delectable for the poorness of the pictures. Here they have a palace on the Arno, with another

---

* Baron George Eugène Haussmann (1809–1891), French civic official and city planner.

† The wife of a Polish diplomat whom James met through his friends Elizabeth and Frances Boott, neighbors of the Gryzanowskis in Florence.

large, handsome, respectable and mainly uninteresting collection. It contains indeed three or four fine examples of early Florentines. It was not especially for the pictures that I went, however; and certainly not for the pictures that I stayed. I was under the same spell as the inveterate companion with whom I walked the other day through the beautiful private apartments of the Pitti Palace and who said: "I suppose I care for nature, and I know there have been times when I have thought it the greatest pleasure in life to lie under a tree and gaze away at blue hills. But just now I had rather lie on that faded sea-green satin sofa and gaze down through the open door at that retreating vista of gilded, deserted, haunted chambers. In other words I prefer a good 'interior' to a good landscape. The impression has a greater intensity—the thing itself a more complex animation. I like fine old rooms that have been occupied in a fine old way. I like the musty upholstery, the antiquated knick-knacks, the view out of the tall deep-embrasured windows at garden cypresses rocking against a grey sky. If you don't know why I'm afraid I can't tell you." It seemed to me at the Palazzo Corsini that I did know why. In places that have been lived in so long and so much and in such a fine old way, as my friend said—that is under social conditions so multifold and to a comparatively starved and democratic sense so curious—the past seems to have left a sensible deposit, an aroma, an atmosphere. This ghostly presence tells you no secrets, but it prompts you to try and guess a few. What has been done and said here through so many years, what has been ventured or suffered, what has been dreamed or despaired of? Guess the riddle if you can, or if you think it worth your ingenuity. The rooms at Palazzo Corsini suggest indeed, and seem to recall, but a monotony of peace and plenty. One of them imaged such a noble perfection of a home-scene that I dawdled there until the old custodian came shuffling back to see whether possibly I was trying to conceal a Caravaggio about my person: a great crimson-draped drawing-room of the amplest and yet most charming proportions; walls hung with large dark pictures, a great concave ceiling frescoed and moulded with dusky richness, and half-a-dozen south windows looking out on the Arno, whose swift yellow tide sends up the light in a cheerful flicker.

I fear that in my appreciation of the particular effect so achieved I uttered a monstrous folly—some momentary willingness to be maimed or crippled all my days if I might pass them in such a place. In fact half the pleasure of inhabiting this spacious saloon would be that of using one's legs, of strolling up and down past the windows, one by one, and making desultory journeys from station to station and corner to corner. Near by is a colossal ball-room, domed and pilastered like a Renaissance cathedral, and superabundantly decorated with marble effigies, all yellow and grey with the years.

· · · · · *v i .* · · · · · ·

In the Carthusian Monastery outside the Roman Gate, mutilated and profaned though it is, one may still snuff up a strong if stale redolence of old Catholicism and old Italy. The road to it is ugly, being encumbered with vulgar waggons and fringed with tenements suggestive of an Irish-American suburb. Your interest begins as you come in sight of the convent perched on its little mountain and lifting against the sky, around the bell-tower of its gorgeous chapel, a coronet of clustered cells. You make your way into the lower gate, through a clamouring press of deformed beggars who thrust at you their stumps of limbs, and you climb the steep hillside through a shabby plantation which it is proper to fancy was better tended in the monkish time. The monks are not totally abolished, the government having the grace to await the natural extinction of the half-dozen old brothers who remain, and who shuffle doggedly about the cloisters, looking, with their white robes and their pale blank old faces, quite anticipatory ghosts of their future selves. A prosaic, profane old man in a coat and trousers serves you, however, as custodian. The melancholy friars have not even the privilege of doing you the honours of their dishonour. One must imagine the pathetic effect of their former silent pointings to this and that conventual treasure under stress of the feeling that such pointings were narrowly numbered. The convent is vast and irregular—it bristles with those picture-making arts and accidents which one notes as one lingers and passes, but which in Italy the overburdened memory learns to resolve into broadly general images. I rather deplore its position at the gates of a bustling city—it ought rather to be lodged in some lonely fold of the Apennines. And yet to look out from the shady porch of one of the quiet cells upon the teeming vale of the Arno and the clustered towers of Florence must have deepened the sense of monastic quietude.

The chapel, or rather the church, which is of great proportions and designed by Andrea Orcagna, the primitive painter, refines upon the consecrated type or even quite glorifies it. The massive cincture of black sculptured stalls, the dusky Gothic roof, the high-hung, deep-toned pictures and the superb pavement of verd-antique and dark red marble, polished into glassy lights, must throw the white-robed figures of the gathered friars into the highest romantic relief. All this luxury of worship has nowhere such value as in the chapels of monasteries, where we find it contrasted with the otherwise so ascetic economy of the worshippers. The paintings and gildings of their church, the gem-bright marbles and fantastic carvings, are really but the monastic tribute to sensuous delight—an imperious need for which the fond imagination of Rome has officiously opened the door. One smiles when one thinks how largely a fine starved sense for the forbidden things of earth, if it makes the most of its opportunities, may gratify this need under cover of devotion. Nothing is too base, too hard, too sordid for real humility, but nothing too elegant, too amiable, too caressing, caressed, caressable, for the exaltation of faith. The meaner the convent cell the richer the convent chapel. Out of poverty and solitude, inanition and cold, your honest friar may rise at his will into a Mahomet's Paradise of luxurious analogies.

There are further various dusky subterranean oratories where a number of bad pictures contend faintly with the friendly gloom. Two or three of these funereal vaults, however, deserve mention. In one of them, side by side, sculptured by Donatello in low relief, lie the white marble effigies of the three members of the Accaiuoli family who founded the convent in the thirteenth century. In another, on his back, on the pavement, rests a grim old bishop of the same stout race by the same honest craftsman. Terribly grim he is, and scowling as if in his stony sleep he still dreamed of his hates and his hard ambitions. Last and best, in another low chapel, with the trodden pavement for its bed, shines dimly a grand image of a later bishop— Leonardo Buonafede, who, dying in 1545, owes his monument to Francesco di San Gallo. I have seen little from this artist's hand, but it was clearly of the cunningest. His model here was a very sturdy old prelate, though I should say a very genial old man. The sculptor has respected his monumental ugliness, but has suffused it with a singular homely charm—a look of confessed physical comfort in the privilege of paradise. All these figures have an inimitable reality, and their lifelike marble seems such an incorruptible incarnation of the genius of the place that you begin to think of it as even more reckless than cruel on the part of the present public powers to have begun to pull the establishment down, morally speaking, about their ears. They are lying quiet yet awhile; but when the last old friar dies and the convent formally lapses, won't they rise on their stiff old legs and hobble out to the gates and thunder forth anathemas before which even a future and more enterprising régime may be disposed to pause?

Out of the great central cloister open the snug little detached dwellings of the absent fathers. When I said just now that the Certosa in Val d'Ema gives you a glimpse of old Italy I was thinking of this great pillared quadrangle, lying half in sun and half in shade, of its tangled garden-growth in the centre, surrounding the ancient customary well, and of the intense blue sky bending above it, to say nothing of the indispensable old white-robed monk who pokes about among the lettuce and parsley. We have seen such places before; we have visited them in that divinatory glance which strays away into space for a moment over the top of a suggestive book. I don't quite know whether it's more or less as one's fancy would have it that the monkish cells are no cells at all, but very tidy little *appartements complets,* consisting of a couple of chambers, a sitting-room and a spacious loggia, projecting out into space from the cliff-like wall of the monastery and sweeping from pole to pole the loveliest view in the world. It's poor work, however, taking notes on views, and I will let this one pass. The little chambers are terribly cold and musty now. Their odour and atmosphere are such as one used, as a child, to imagine those of the school-room during Saturday and Sunday.

····· *vii.* ······

In the Roman streets, wherever you turn, the façade of a church in more or less degenerate flamboyance is the principal feature of the scene; and if, in the absence of purer motives, you are weary of æsthetic trudging over the corrugated surface of the Seven Hills, a system of pavement in which small cobble-stones anomalously endowed with angles and edges are alone employed, you may turn aside at your pleasure and take a reviving sniff at the pungency of incense. In Florence, one soon observes, the churches are relatively few and the dusky house-fronts more rarely interrupted by specimens of that extraordi-nary architecture which in Rome passes for sacred. In Florence, in other words, ecclesiasticism is less cheap a commodity and not dispensed in the same abundance at the street-corners. Heaven forbid, at the same time, that I should undervalue the Roman churches, which are for the most part treasure-houses of history, of curiosity, of promiscuous and associational inter-est. It is a fact, nevertheless, that, after Saint Peter's, I know but one really beautiful church by the Tiber, the enchanting basil-ica of Saint Mary Major. Many have structural character, some a great *allure,* but as a rule they all lack the dignity of the best of the Florentine temples. Here, the list being immeasurably shorter and the seed less scattered, the principal churches are all beautiful. And yet I went into the Annunziata the other day and sat there for half-an-hour because, forsooth, the gildings and the marbles and the frescoed dome and the great rococo shrine near the door, with its little black jewelled fetish, re-minded me so poignantly of Rome. Such is the city properly styled eternal—since it is eternal, at least, as regards the con-sciousness of the individual. One loves it in its sophistications—though for that matter isn't it all rich and precious sophistication?—better than other places in their purity.

Coming out of the Annunziata you look past the bronze statue of the Grand Duke Ferdinand I (whom Mr. Browning's heroine used to watch for—in the poem of "The Statue and the Bust"—from the red palace near by), and down a street vista of enchanting picturesqueness. The street is narrow and dusky and filled with misty shadows, and at its opposite end rises the vast bright-coloured side of the Cathedral. It stands up in very much the same mountainous fashion as the far-shining mass of the bigger prodigy at Milan, of which your first glimpse as you leave your hotel is generally through another such dark avenue; only that, if we talk of mountains, the white walls of Milan must be likened to snow and ice from their base, while those of the Duomo of Florence may be the image of some mighty hillside enamelled with blooming flowers. The big bleak interior here has a naked majesty which, though it may fail of its effect at first, becomes after a while extraordinarily touching. Originally disconcerting, it soon inspired me with a passion. Externally, at any rate, it is one of the loveliest works of man's hands, and an overwhelming proof into the bargain that when elegance belittles grandeur you have simply had a bungling artist.

Santa Croce within not only triumphs here, but would triumph almost anywhere. "A trifle naked if you like," said my irrepressible companion, "but that's what I call architecture, just as I don't call bronze or marble clothes (save under urgent stress of portraiture) statuary." And indeed we are far enough away from the clustering odds and ends borrowed from every art and every province without which the ritually builded thing doesn't trust its spell to work in Rome. The vastness, the lightness, the open spring of the arches at Santa Croce, the beautiful shape of the high and narrow choir, the impression made as of mass without weight and the gravity yet reigning without gloom—these are my frequent delight, and the interest grows with acquaintance. The place is the great Florentine Valhalla, the final home or memorial harbour of the native illustrious dead, but that consideration of it would take me far. It must be confessed moreover that, between his coarsely-imagined statue out in front and his horrible monument in one of the aisles, the author of *The Divine Comedy,* for instance, is just hereabouts rather an extravagant figure. "Ungrateful Florence," declaims Byron. Ungrateful indeed—would she were more so! the susceptible spirit of the great exile may be still aware enough to exclaim; in common, that is, with most of the other immortals sacrificed on so very large a scale to current Florentine "plastic" facility. In explanation of which remark, however, I must confine myself to noting that, as almost all the old monuments at Santa Croce are small, comparatively small, and interesting and exquisite, so the modern, well nigh without exception, are disproportionately vast and pompous, or in other words distressingly vague and vain. The aptitude of hand, the compositional assurance, with which such things are nevertheless turned out, constitutes an anomaly replete with suggestion for an observer of the present state of the arts on the soil and in the air that once befriended them, taking them all together, as even the soil and the air of Greece scarce availed to do. But on this head, I repeat, there would be too much to say; and I find myself checked by the same warning at the threshold of the church in Florence really interesting beyond Santa Croce, beyond all others. Such, of course, easily, is Santa Maria Novella, where the chapels arc lined and plated with wonderful figured and peopled fresco-work even as most of those in Rome with precious inanimate substances. These overscored retreats of devotion, as dusky, some of them, as eremitic caves swarming with importunate visions, have kept me divided all winter between the love of Ghirlandaio and the fear of those seeds of catarrh to which their mortal chill seems propitious till far on into the spring. So I pause here just on the praise of that delightful painter—as to the spirit of whose work the reflections I have already made are but confirmed by these examples. In the choir at Santa Maria Novella, where the incense swings and the great chants resound, between the gorgeous coloured window and the florid grand altar, he still "goes in," with all his might, for the wicked, the amusing world, the world of faces and forms and characters, of every sort of curious human and rare material thing.

····· *v i i i .* ······

I had always felt the Boboli Gardens charming enough for me to "haunt" them; and yet such is the interest of Florence in every quarter that it took another *corso* of the same cheap pattern as the last to cause me yesterday to flee the crowded streets, passing under that archway of the Pitti Palace which might almost be the gate of an Etruscan city, so that I might spend the afternoon among the mouldy statues that compose with their screens of cypress, looking down at our clustered towers and our background of pale blue hills vaguely freckled with white villas. These pleasure-grounds of the austere Pitti pile, with its inconsequent charm of being so rough-hewn and yet somehow so elegantly balanced, plead with a voice all their own the general cause of the ample enclosed, planted, culti-vated private preserve—preserve of tranquillity and beauty and immunity—in the heart of a city; a cause, I allow, for that matter, easy to plead anywhere, once the pretext is found, the large, quiet distributed town-garden, with the vague hum of big grudging boundaries all about it, but with everything worse excluded, being of course the most insolently-pleasant thing in the world. In addition to which, when the garden is in the Italian manner, with flowers rather remarkably omitted, as too flimsy and easy and cheap, and without lawns that are too smart, paths that are too often swept and shrubs that are too closely trimmed, though with a fanciful formalism giving style to its shabbiness, and here and there a dusky ilex-walk, and here and there a dried-up fountain, and every-where a piece of mildewed sculpture staring at you from a green alcove, and just in the right place, above all, a grassy amphitheatre curtained behind with black cypresses and slop-ing downward in mossy marble steps—when, I say, the place possesses these attractions, and you lounge there of a soft Sun-day afternoon, the racier spectacle of the streets having made your fellow-loungers few and left you to the deep stillness and the shady vistas that lead you wonder where, left you to the insidious irresistible mixture of nature and art, nothing too much of either, only a supreme happy resultant, a divine *ter-tium quid* [unclassifiable element]: under these conditions, it need scarce be said, the revelation invoked descends upon you.

The Boboli Gardens are not large—you wonder how com-pact little Florence finds room for them within her walls. But they are scattered, to their extreme, their all-romantic advan-tage and felicity, over a group of steep undulations between the rugged and terraced palace and a still-surviving stretch of city wall, where the unevenness of the ground much adds to their apparent size. You may cultivate in them the fancy of their solemn and haunted character, of something faint and dim and even, if you like, tragic, in their prescribed, their functional smile; as if they borrowed from the huge monument that over-hangs them certain of its ponderous memories and regrets. This course is open to you, I mention, but it isn't enjoined, and will doubtless indeed not come up for you at all if it isn't your habit, cherished beyond any other, to spin your impressions to the last tenuity of fineness. Now that I bethink myself I must always have happened to wander here on grey and melancholy days. It remains none the less true that the place contains, thank goodness—or at least thank the grave, the infinitely-distinguished traditional *taste* of Florence—no cheerful, trivial object, neither parterres, nor pagodas, nor peacocks, nor swans. They have their famous amphitheatre already referred to, with its degrees or stone benches of a thoroughly aged and mottled complexion and its circular wall of evergreens behind, in which small cracked images and vases, things that, according to as-sociation, and with the law of the same quite indefinable, may make as much on one occasion for exquisite dignity as they may make on another for (to express it kindly) nothing at all. Something was once done in this charmed and forsaken cir-cle—done or meant to be done; what was it, dumb statues, who saw it with your blank eyes? Opposite stands the huge flat-roofed palace, putting forward two great rectangular arms and looking, with its closed windows and its foundations of almost unreduced rock, like some ghost of a sample of a ruder Baby-lon. In the wide court-like space between the wings is a fine old white marble fountain that never plays. Its dusty idleness com-pletes the general air of abandonment. Chancing on such a cluster of objects in Italy—glancing at them in a certain light and a certain mood—I get (perhaps on too easy terms, you may think) a sense of *history* that takes away my breath. Generations of Medici have stood at these closed windows, embroidered and brocaded according to their period, and held *fêtes cham-pêtres* [village holidays] and floral games on the greensward, beneath the mouldering hemicycle. And the Medici were great people! But what remains of it all now is a mere tone in the air, a faint sigh in the breeze, a vague expression in things, a passive—or call it rather, perhaps, to be fair, a shyly, pathetically responsive—accessibility to the yearning guess. Call it much or call it little, the ineffaceability of this deep stain of experience, it is the interest of old places and the bribe to the brooding analyst. Time has devoured the doers and their doings, but there still hangs about some effect of their passage. We can "lay out" parks on virgin soil, and cause them to bristle with the most expensive importations, but we unfortunately can't scatter abroad again this seed of the eventual human soul of a place—that comes but in its time and takes too long to grow. There is nothing like it when it *has* come.

[1874]

....

From Italy Revisited

I had never known Florence more charming than I found her for a week in that brilliant October. She sat in the sunshine beside her yellow river like the little treasure-city that she has always seemed, without commerce, without other industry than the manufacture of mosaic paper-weights and alabaster Cupids, without actuality, or energy, or earnestness, or any of those rugged virtues which in most cases are deemed indispensable for civic robustness; with nothing but the little unaugmented stock of her mediæval memories, her tender-coloured mountains, her churches and palaces, pictures and statues. There were very few strangers; one's detested fellow-pilgrim was infrequent; the native population itself seemed scanty; the sound of wheels in the streets was but occasional; by eight o'clock at night, apparently, every one had gone to bed, and the wandering tourist, still wandering, had the place to himself—had the thick shadow-masses of the great palaces, and the shafts of moonlight striking the polygonal paving-stones, and the empty bridges, and the silvered yellow of the Arno, and the stillness broken only by a homeward step, accompanied by a snatch of song from a warm Italian voice. My room at the inn looked out on the river, and was flooded all day with sunshine. There was an absurd orange-coloured paper on the walls; the Arno, of a hue not altogether different, flowed beneath; and on the other side of it rose a line of sallow houses, of extreme antiquity, crumbling and mouldering, bulging and protruding over the stream. (I seem to speak of their fronts; but what I saw was their shabby backs, which were exposed to the cheerful flicker of the river, while the fronts stood for ever in the deep, damp shadow of a narrow mediæval street.) All this brightness and yellowness was a perpetual delight; it was a part of that indefinably charming colour which Florence always seems to wear as you look up and down at it from the river, from the bridges and quays. This is a kind of grave brilliancy—a harmony of high tints—which I know not how to describe. There are yellow walls and green blinds and red roofs, and intervals of brilliant brown and natural-looking blue; but the picture is not spotty nor gaudy, thanks to the colours being distributed in large and comfortable masses, and to its being washed over, as it were, by some happy softness of sunshine. The river-front of Florence is, in short, a delightful composition. Part of its charm comes, of course, from the generous aspect of those high-based Tuscan palaces which a renewal of acquaintance with them has again commended to me as the most dignified dwellings in the world. Nothing can be finer than that look of giving up the whole immense ground-floor to simple purposes of vestibule and staircase, of court and high-arched entrance; as if this were all but a massive pedestal for the real habitation, and people were not properly housed unless, to begin with, they should be lifted fifty feet above the pavement. The great blocks of the basement; the great intervals, horizontally and vertically, from window to window (telling of the height and breadth of the rooms within); the armorial shield hung forward at one of the angles; the wide-brimmed roof, overshadowing the narrow street; the rich old browns and yellows of the walls—these definite elements are put together with admirable art.

Take one of these noble structures out of its oblique situation in the town; call it no longer a palace, but a villa; set it down upon a terrace, on one of the hills that encircle Florence, with a row of high-waisted cypresses beside it, a grassy courtyard, and a view of the Florentine towers and the valley of the Arno, and you will think it perhaps even more worthy of your esteem. It was a Sunday noon, and brilliantly warm, when I arrived in Florence; and after I had looked from my windows a while at that quietly-basking river-front I have spoken of, I took my way across one of the bridges and then out of one of the gates—that immensely tall Roman Gate, in which the space from the top of the arch to the cornice (except that there is scarcely a cornice, it is all a plain, massive piece of wall) is as great (or seems to be) as that from the ground to the former point. Then I climbed a steep and winding way—much of it a little dull, if one likes, being bounded by mottled, mossy garden-walls—to a villa on a hill-top, where I found various things that touched me with almost too fine a point. Seeing them again, often, for a week, both by sunlight and moonshine, I never quite learned not to covet them; not to feel that not being a part of them was somehow to miss an exquisite chance. What a tranquil, contented life it seemed, with romantic beauty as a part of its daily texture!—the sunny terrace, with its tangled *podere* [farm] beneath it; the bright grey olives against the bright blue sky; the long, serene, horizontal lines of other villas, flanked by their upward cypresses, disposed upon the neighbouring hills; the richest little city in the world in a softly-scooped hollow at one's feet, and beyond it the most appealing of views, the most majestic, yet the most familiar. Within the villa was a great love of art and a painting-room full of successful work, so that if human life there seemed very tranquil, the tranquillity meant simply contentment and devoted occupation. A beautiful occupation in that beautiful position, what could possibly be better? That is what I spoke just now of envying—a way of life that is not afraid of a little isolation and tolerably quiet days. When such a life presents itself in a dull or an ugly place, we esteem it, we admire it, but we do not feel it to be the ideal of good fortune. When, however, the people who lead it move as figures in an ancient, noble landscape, and their walks and contemplations are like a turning of the leaves of history, we seem to have before us an admirable case of virtue made easy; meaning here by virtue, contentment and concentration, the love of privacy and study. One need not be exacting if one lives among local conditions that are of themselves constantly suggestive. It is true, indeed, that I might, after a certain time, grow weary of a regular afternoon stroll among the Florentine lanes; of sitting on low parapets, in intervals of flower-topped wall, and looking across at Fiesole, or down the rich-hued valley of the Arno; of pausing at the open gates of villas and wondering at the height of cypresses and the depth of loggias; of walking home in the fading light and noting on a dozen westward-looking surfaces the glow of the opposite sunset. But for a week or so all this was delightful. The villas are innumerable, and if one is a stranger half the talk is about villas. This one has a story; that one has another; they all look as if they had stories. Most of them are offered to rent (many of them for sale) at prices unnaturally low; you may have a tower and a garden, a chapel and an expanse of thirty windows, for five hundred dollars a year. In imagination, you hire three or four; you take possession, and settle, and live there. About the finest there is something very grave and stately; about two or three of the best there is something even solemn and tragic. From what does this latter impression come? You gather it as you stand there in the early dusk, looking at the long, pale-brown façade, the enormous windows, the iron cages fastened upon the lower ones. Part of the brooding expression of these great houses comes, even when they have not fallen into decay, from their look of having outlived their original use. Their extraordinary largeness and massiveness are a satire upon their present fate. They were not built with such a thickness of wall and depth of embrasure, such a solidity of staircase and superfluity of stone, simply to afford an economical winter residence to English and American families. I know not whether it was the appearance of these stony old villas, which seemed so dumbly conscious of a change of manners, that threw a tinge of melancholy over the general prospect; certain it is that, having always found this plaintive note in the view of Florence, it seemed to me now particularly distinct. "Lovely, lovely, but it makes me blue," the fanciful stranger could not but murmur to himself as, in the late afternoon, he looked at the landscape from over one of the low parapets, and then, with his hands in his pockets, turned away indoors to candles and dinner.

· · · · · *v* · · · · · ·

Below, in the city, in wandering about in the streets and churches and museums, it was impossible not to have a good deal of the same feeling; but here the impression was more easy to analyse. It came from a sense of the perfect separateness of all the great productions of the Renaissance from the present and the future of the place, from the actual life and manners, the native ideal. I have already spoken of the way in which the great aggregation of beautiful works of art in the Italian cities strikes the visitor nowadays (so far as present Italy is concerned) as the mere stock-in-trade of an impecunious but thrifty people. It is this metaphysical desertedness and loneliness of the great works of architecture and sculpture that deposits a certain weight upon the heart; when we see a great tradition broken we feel something of the pain with which we hear a stifled cry. But regret is one thing and resentment is another. Seeing one morning, in a shop-window, the series of *Mornings in Florence,* published a few years since by Mr. Ruskin, I made haste to enter and purchase these amusing little books, some passages of which I remembered formerly to have read. I could not turn over many pages without observing that the "separateness" of the new and old which I just mentioned had produced in their author the liveliest irritation. With the more acute phases of this sentiment it was difficult to sympathise, for the simple reason, it seems to me, that it savours of arrogance to demand of any people, as a right of one's own, that they shall be artistic. "Be artistic yourselves!" is the very natural reply that young Italy has at hand for English critics and censors. When a people produces beautiful statues and pictures it gives us something more than is set down in the bond, and we must thank it for its generosity; and when it stops producing them or caring for them we may cease thanking, but we hardly have a right to begin and abuse it. The wreck of Florence, says Mr. Ruskin, "is now too ghastly and heart-breaking to any human soul that remembers the days of old"; and these desperate words are an allusion to the fact that the little square in front of the cathedral, at the foot of Giotto's Tower, with the grand Baptistery on the other side, is now the resort of a number of hackney-coaches and omnibuses. This fact is doubtless lamentable, and it would be a hundred times more agreeable to see among people who have been made the heirs of so priceless a work of art as the sublime campanile some such feeling about it as would keep it free even from the danger of defilement. A cab-stand is a very ugly and dirty thing, and Giotto's Tower should have nothing in common with such conveniences. But there is more than one way of taking such things, and a quiet traveller, who has been walking about for a week with his mind full of the sweetness and suggestiveness of a hundred Florentine places, may feel at last, in looking into Mr. Ruskin's little tracts, that, discord for discord, there is not much to choose between the importunity of the author's personal ill-humour and the incongruity of horse-pails and bundles of hay. And one may say this without being at all a partisan of the doctrine of the inevitableness of new desecrations. For my own part, I believe there are few things in this line that the new Italian spirit is not capable of, and not many, indeed, that we are not destined to see. Pictures and buildings will not be completely destroyed, because in that case foreigners with full pockets would cease to visit the country, and the turn-stiles at the doors of the old palaces and convents, with the little patented slit for absorbing your half-franc, would grow quite rusty, and creak with disuse. But it is safe to say that the new Italy, growing into an old Italy again, will continue to take her elbow-room wherever she finds it.

I am almost ashamed to say what I did with Mr. Ruskin's little books. I put them into my pocket and betook myself to Santa Maria Novella. There I sat down, and after I had looked about for a while at the beautiful church, I drew them forth one by one, and read the greater part of them. Occupying one's self with light literature in a great religious edifice is perhaps as bad a piece of profanation as any of those rude dealings which Mr. Ruskin justly deplores; but a traveller has to make the most of odd moments, and I was waiting for a friend in whose company I was to go and look at Giotto's beautiful frescoes in the cloister of the church. My friend was a long time coming, so that I had an hour with Mr. Ruskin, whom I called just now a light *littérateur,* because in these little Mornings in Florence he is for ever making his readers laugh. I remembered, of course, where I was; and, in spite of my latent hilarity, I felt that I had rarely got such a snubbing. I had really been enjoying the good old city of Florence; but I now learned from Mr. Ruskin that this was a scandalous waste of charity. I should have gone about with an imprecation on my lips, I should have worn a face three yards long. I had taken great pleasure in certain frescoes by Ghirlandaio, in the choir of that very church; but it appeared from one of the little books that these frescoes were as naught. I had much admired Santa Croce, and I had thought the Duomo a very noble affair; but I had now the most positive assurance I knew nothing about it. After a while, if it was only ill-humour that was needed for doing honour to the city of the Medici, I felt that I had risen to a proper level; only now it was Mr. Ruskin himself I had lost patience with, and not the stupid Brunelleschi and the vulgar Ghirlandaio. Indeed, I lost patience altogether, and asked myself by what right this informal votary of form pretended to run riot through a quiet traveller's relish for the noblest of pleasures—his wholesome enjoyment of the loveliest of cities. The little books seemed invidious and insane, and it was only when I remembered that I had been under no obligation to buy them that I checked myself in repenting of having done so. Then, at last, my friend arrived, and we passed together out of the church, and through the first cloister beside it, into a smaller enclosure, where we stood a while to look at the tomb of the Marchesa Strozzi-Ridolfi, upon which the great Giotto has painted four superb little pictures. It was easy to see the pictures were superb; but I drew forth one of my little books again, for I had observed that Mr. Ruskin spoke of them. Hereupon I recovered my tolerance; for what could be better in this case, I asked myself, than Mr. Ruskin's remarks? They are, in fact, excellent and charming, and full of appreciation of the deep and simple beauty of the great painter's work. I read them aloud to my companion; but my companion was rather, as the phrase is, "put off" by them. One of the frescoes (it is a picture of the birth of the Virgin) contains a figure coming through a door. "Of ornament," I quote, "there is only the entirely simple outline of the vase which the servant carries; of colour two or three masses of sober red and pure white, with brown and grey. That is all," Mr. Ruskin continues. "And if you are pleased with this you can see Florence. But if not, by all means amuse yourself there, if you find it amusing, as long as you like; you can never see it." *You can never see it.* This seemed to my friend insufferable, and I had to shuffle away the book again, so that we might look at the fresco with the unruffled geniality it deserves.

We agreed afterwards, when in a more convenient place I read aloud a good many more passages from Mr. Ruskin's tracts, that there are a great many ways of seeing Florence, as there are of seeing most beautiful and interesting things, and that it is very dry and pedantic to say that the happy vision depends upon our squaring our toes with a certain particular chalk-mark. We see Florence wherever and whenever we enjoy it, and for enjoying it we find a great many more pretexts than Mr. Ruskin seems inclined to allow. My friend and I agreed also, however, that the little books were an excellent purchase, on account of the great charm and felicity of much of their incidental criticism; to say nothing, as I hinted just now, of their being extremely amusing. Nothing, in fact, is more comical than the familiar asperity of the author's style and the pedagogic fashion in which he pushes and pulls his unhappy pupils about, jerking their heads toward this, rapping their knuckles for that, sending them to stand in corners, and giving them Scripture texts to copy. But it is neither the felicities nor the aberrations of detail, in Mr. Ruskin's writings, that are the main affair for most readers; it is the general tone that, as I have said, puts them off or draws them on. For many persons he will never bear the test of being read in this rich old Italy, where art, so long as it really lived at all, was spontaneous, joyous, irresponsible. If the reader is in daily contact with those beautiful Florentine works which do still, in a way, force themselves into notice through the vulgarity and cruelty of modern profanation, it will seem to him that Mr. Ruskin's little books are pitched in the strangest falsetto key. "One may read a hundred pages of this sort of thing," said my friend, "without ever dreaming that he is talking about *art*. You can say nothing worse about it than that." And that is very true. Art is the one corner of human life in which we may take our ease. To justify our presence there the only thing that is demanded of us is that we shall have a passion for representation. In other places our passions are conditioned and embarrassed; we are allowed to have only so many as are consistent with those of our neighbours; with their convenience and well-being, with their convictions and prejudices, their rules and regulations. Art means an escape from all this. Wherever her brilliant standard floats the need for apologies and exonerations is over; there it is enough simply that we please or that we are pleased. There the tree is judged only by its fruits. If these are sweet, one is welcome to pluck them.

One may read a great many pages of Mr. Ruskin without getting a hint of this delightful truth; a hint of the not unimportant fact that art, after all, is made for us, and not we for art. This idea of the value of a work of art being the amount of illusion it yields is conspicuous by its absence. And as for Mr. Ruskin's world of art being a place where we may take life easily, woe to the luckless mortal who enters it with any such disposition. Instead of a garden of delight, he finds a sort of assize-court, in perpetual session. Instead of a place in which human responsibilities are lightened and suspended, he finds a region governed by a kind of Draconic legislation. His responsibilities, indeed, are tenfold increased; the gulf between truth and error is for ever yawning at his feet; the pains and penalties of this same error are advertised, in apocalyptic terminology, upon a thousand sign-posts; and the poor wanderer soon begins to look back with infinite longing to the lost paradise of the artless. There can be no greater want of tact in dealing with those things with which men attempt to ornament life than to be perpetually talking about "error." A truce to all rigidities is the law of the place; the only thing that is absolute there is sensible charm. The grim old bearer of the scales excuses herself; she feels that this is not her province. Differences here are not iniquity and righteousness; they are simply variations of temperament and of point of view. We are not under theological government.

····· *v i* ·······

It was very charming, in the bright, warm days, to wander from one corner of Florence to another, paying one's respects again to remembered masterpieces. It was pleasant also to find that memory had played no tricks, and that the beautiful things of an earlier year were as beautiful as ever. To enumerate these beautiful things would take a great deal of space; for I never had been more struck with the mere quantity of brilliant Florentine work. Even giving up the Duomo and Santa Croce to Mr. Ruskin as very ill-arranged edifices, the list of the Florentine treasures is almost inexhaustible. Those long outer galleries of the Uffizi had never seemed to me more delectable; sometimes there were not more than two or three figures standing there, Baedeker in hand, to break the charming perspective. One side of this upstairs-portico, it will be remembered, is entirely composed of glass; a continuity of old-fashioned windows, draped with white curtains of rather primitive fashion, which hang there till they acquire a perceptible "tone." The light, passing through them, is softly filtered and diffused; it rests mildly upon the old marbles—chiefly antique Roman busts—which stand in the narrow intervals of the casements. It is projected upon the numerous pictures that cover the opposite wall, and that are not by any means, as a general thing, the gems of the great collection; it imparts a faded brightness to the old ornamental arabesques upon the painted wooden ceiling, and it makes a great soft shining upon the marble floor, in which, as you look up and down, you see the strolling tourists and the motionless copyists almost reflected. I don't know why I should find all this very pleasant, but, in fact, I have seldom gone into the Uffizi without walking the length of this third-story cloister, between the (for the most part) third-rate pictures and the faded cotton curtains. Why is it that in Italy we see a charm in things in regard to which in other countries we always take vulgarity for granted? If in the city of New York a great museum of the arts were to be provided, by way of decoration, with a species of verandah inclosed on one side by a series of small-paned windows, draped in dirty linen, and furnished on the other with an array of pictorial feebleness, the place being surmounted by a thinly-painted wooden roof, strongly suggestive of summer heat, of winter cold, of frequent leakage, those amateurs who had had the advantage of foreign travel would be at small pains to conceal their contempt. Contemptible or respectable, to the judicial mind, this quaint old loggia of the Uffizi admitted me into twenty chambers where I found as great a number of ancient favourites. I do not know that I had a warmer greeting for any old friend than for

Andrea del Sarto, that most touching of painters who is not one of the first. But it was on the other side of the Arno that I found him in force, in those dusky drawing-rooms of the Pitti Palace, to which you take your way along the tortuous tunnel that wanders through the houses of Florence, and is supported by the little goldsmiths' booths on the Ponte Vecchio. In the rich, insufficient light of these beautiful rooms, where, to look at the pictures, you sit in damask chairs and rest your elbows on tables of malachite, Andrea del Sarto becomes peculiarly effective. Before long you feel a real affection for him. But the great pleasure, after all, was to revisit the earlier masters, in those specimens of them chiefly that bloom so unfadingly on the big, plain walls of the Academy. Fra Angelico and Filippo Lippi, Botticelli, and Lorenzo di Credi are the sweetest and best of all painters; as I sat for an hour in their company, in the cold great hall of the institution I have mentioned—there are shabby rafters above and an immense expanse of brick tiles below, and many bad pictures as well as good ones—it seemed to me more than ever that if one really had to choose one could not do better than choose here. You may sit very quietly and comfortably at the Academy, in this big first room—at the upper end, especially, on the left—because more than many other places it savours of old Florence. More for instance, in reality, than the Bargello, though the Bargello makes great pretensions. Beautiful and picturesque as the Bargello is, it smells too strongly of restoration, and, much of old Italy as still lurks in its furbished and renovated chambers, it speaks even more distinctly of the ill-mannered young kingdom that has (as unavoidably as you please) lifted down a hundred delicate works of sculpture from the convent-walls where their pious authors placed them. If the early Tuscan painters are exquisite, I can think of no praise generous enough for the sculptors of the same period, Donatello and Luca della Robbia, Matteo Civitale and Mino da Fiesole, who, as I refreshed my memory of them, seemed to me to leave absolutely nothing to be desired in the way of purity of inspiration and grace of invention. The Bargello is full of early Tuscan sculpture, most of the pieces of which have come from suppressed convents; and even if the visitor be an ardent liberal, he is uncomfortably conscious of the rather brutal process by which it has been collected. One can hardly envy young Italy the number of disagreeable things she has had to do.

The railway journey from Florence to Rome has been altered both for the better and for the worse; for the better, in that it has been shortened by a couple of hours; for the worse, inasmuch as, when about half the distance has been traversed, the train deflects to the west, and leaves the beautiful old cities of Assisi, Perugia, Terni, Narni, unvisited. Of old, it was possible to visit these places, in a manner, from the window of the train; even if you did not stop, as you probably could not, every time you passed, the picturesque fashion in which, like a loosened belt on an aged and shrunken person, their old red walls held them easily together was something well worth noting. Now, however, by way of compensation, the express train to Rome stops at Orvieto, and in consequence . . . In consequence what? What is the consequence of an express train stopping at Orvieto? As I glibly wrote that sentence I suddenly paused, with a sense of the queer stuff I was uttering. That an express train would graze the base of the horrid purple mountain from the apex of which this dark old Catholic city uplifts the glittering front of its cathedral—that might have been foretold by a keen observer of contemporary manners. But that it would really have the grossness to stop there, this is a fact over which, as he records it, a sentimental chronicler may well make what is vulgarly called an ado. The train does stop at Orvieto, not very long, it is true, but long enough to let you out. The same phenomenon takes place on the following day, when, having visited the city, you get in again. I availed myself of both of these occasions, having formerly neglected to drive to Orvieto in a post-chaise. And really, the railway-station being in the plain, and the town on the summit of an extraordinary hill, you have time to forget all about the triumphs of steam, while you wind upwards to the city-gate. The position of Orvieto is superb; it is worthy of the "middle distance" of a last-century landscape. But, as every one knows, the beautiful cathedral is the proper attraction of the place, which, indeed, save for this fine monument, and for its craggy and crumbling ramparts, is a meanly arranged and, as Italian cities go, not particularly impressive little town. I spent a beautiful Sunday there, and I looked at the charming church. I looked at it a great deal—a great deal considering that on the whole I found it inferior to its fame. Intensely brilliant, however, is the densely carved front; densely covered with the freshest-looking mosaics. The old white marble of the sculptured portions is as softly yellow as ancient ivory; the large, exceedingly bright pictures above them flashed and twinkled in the splendid weather. Very beautiful and interesting are the theological frescoes of Luca Signorelli, though I have seen pictures that struck me as more attaching. Very enchanting, finally, are the clear-faced saints and seraphs, in robes of pink and azure, whom Fra Angelico has painted upon the ceiling of the great chapel, along with a noble sitting figure—more expressive of movement than most of the creations of this pictorial peace-maker—of Christ in judgment. But the interest of the cathedral of Orvieto is mainly not the visible result, but the historical process that lies behind it; those three hundred years of devoted popular labour of which an American scholar has written an admirable account.*

[1878]

* Charles Eliot Norton: *Study and Travel in Italy*. [James's footnote.]

*B*ay of Naples

.

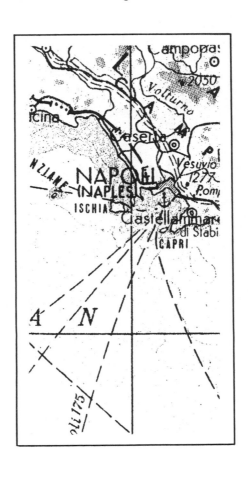

L *etters*

....

To Grace Norton, 12/25/1869. Rome: My stay [in Naples] abbreviated by the wretched weather. . . . I saw neither Vesuvius nor Sorrento. I made two vain attempts on the latter. . . . So I saw Naples without sunshine—but still I saw it.

To Grace Norton, 4/9/1880. Sorrento: I wish I could send you . . . , a patch of the blue sea that stretches away to Naples & Capri—a few square feet of the pale purple that covers the gentle-looking flanks of Vesuvius—or even a bunch of the deep-coloured oranges that are hung, like Chinese lamps, in all the gardens & orchards, amid the tangle that their own foliage makes with the silvery dusk of the olives. I see these things—most of them—as I sit writing to you. I have a big window which stands open & directly overhangs the Sea. It is early in the morning. . . . The bay of Naples lies before me like a vast pale-blue floor, streaked in all sorts of fantastic ways with currents both of lighter & darker colour. The opposite coast—Posilippo, Baiae, etc.—is wonderfully distinct in the clear still light, & I can almost see the shapes of the villas, & the boats pulled up along the strand. Vesuvius sits there on my right, looking wonderfully serene as he smokes his morning pipe, & just beneath my window a boatful of fishermen in red caps send up a murmur of lazy sounds which mingles with the clash of little waves at the base of the cliff on which the hotel is planted. . . . I drove yesterday afternoon from Castellamare to this, along the famous & beautiful road which winds among the orchards of orange & olive & overhangs the sea. . . . I spend but today here . . . & then return to Rome & Florence. Rome has much of the old charm, but it had not all of it. The air of the modern watering-place has invaded it to a very sensible degree, & the government are doing everything that the most diabolical ingenuity can suggest to destroy the dear old purely Roman quality. The enormous crowds, the new streets, the horse-cars (you might think yourself in Brattle Street [Boston])! the ruination of the Coliseum, the hideous iron bridge over the Tiber, the wholesale desecration of the Pincio, etc., are all so many death-blows to the picturesque. Nevertheless, of a lovely spring day, the place is still capable of exciting an agreeable emotion. . . . Florence seems to me on the whole less spoiled than Rome.

....

The Saint's Afternoon and Others

Before and above all was the sense that, with the narrow limits of past adventure, I had never yet had such an impression of what the summer could be in the south or the south in the summer; but I promptly found it, for the occasion, a good fortune that my terms of comparison were restricted. It was really something, at a time when the stride of the traveller had become as long as it was easy, when the seven-league boots positively hung, for frequent use, in the closet of the most sedentary, to have kept one's self so innocent of strange horizons that the Bay of Naples in June might still seem quite final. That picture struck me—a particular corner of it at least, and for many reasons—as the last word; and it is this last word that comes back to me, after a short interval, in a green, grey northern nook, and offers me again its warm, bright golden meaning before it also inevitably catches the chill. Too precious, surely, for us not to suffer it to help us as it may is the faculty of putting together again in an order the sharp minutes and hours that the wave of time has been as ready to pass over as the salt sea to wipe out the letters and words your stick has traced in the sand. Let me, at any rate, recover a sufficient number of such signs to make a sort of sense.

..... *i* ......

Far aloft on the great rock was pitched, as the first note, and indeed the highest, of the wondrous concert, the amazing creation of the friend who had offered me hospitality, and whom, more almost than I had ever envied any one anything, I envied the privilege of being able to reward a heated, artless pilgrim with a revelation of effects so incalculable. There was none but the loosest prefigurement as the creaking and puffing little boat, which had conveyed me only from Sorrento, drew closer beneath the prodigious island—beautiful, horrible and haunted—that does most, of all the happy elements and accidents, towards making the Bay of Naples, for the study of composition, a lesson in the grand style. There was only, above and below, through the blue of the air and sea, a great confused shining of hot cliffs and crags and buttresses, a loss, from nearness, of the splendid couchant outline and the more comprehensive mass, and an opportunity—oh, not lost, I assure you—to sit and meditate, even moralise, on the empty deck, while a happy brotherhood of American and German tourists, including, of course, many sisters, scrambled down into little waiting, rocking tubs and, after a few strokes, popped systematically into the small orifice of the Blue Grotto. There was an appreciable moment when they were all lost to view in that receptacle, the daily "psychological" moment during which it must so often befall the recalcitrant observer on the deserted deck to find himself aware of how delightful it might be if none of them should come out again. The charm, the fascination of the idea is not a little—though also not wholly—in the fact that, as the wave rises over the aperture, there is the most encouraging appearance that they perfectly may not. There it is. There is no more of them. It is a case to which nature has, by the neatest stroke and with the best taste in the world, just quietly attended.

Beautiful, horrible, haunted: that is the essence of what, about itself, Capri says to you—dip again into your Tacitus and see why; and yet, while you roast a little under the awning and in the vaster shadow, it is not because the trail of Tiberius is ineffaceable that you are most uneasy. The trail of Germanicus in Italy to-day ramifies further and bites perhaps even deeper; a proof of which is, precisely, that his eclipse in the Blue Grotto is inexorably brief, that here he is popping out again, bobbing enthusiastically back and scrambling triumphantly back. The spirit, in truth, of his effective appropriation of Capri has a broad-faced candour against which there is no standing up, supremely expressive as it is of the well-known "love that kills," of Germanicus's fatal susceptibility. If I were to let myself, however, incline to *that* aspect of the serious case of Capri I should embark on strange depths. The straightness and simplicity, the classic, synthetic directness of the German passion for Italy, make this passion probably the sentiment in the world that is in the act of supplying enjoyment in the largest, sweetest mouthfuls; and there is something unsurpassably marked in the way that on this irresistible shore it has seated itself to ruminate and digest. It keeps the record in its own loud accents; it breaks out in the folds of the hills and on the crests of the crags into every manner of symptom and warning. Huge advertisements and portents stare across the bay; the acclivities bristle with breweries and "restorations" and with great ugly Gothic names. I hasten, of course, to add that some such general consciousness as this may well oppress, under any sky, at the century's end, the brooding tourist who makes himself a prey by staying anywhere, when the gong sounds, "behind." It is behind, in the track and the reaction, that he least makes out the end of it all, perceives that to visit any one's country for any one's sake is more and more to find some one quite other in possession. No one, least of all the brooder himself, is in his own.

····· *i i* ·······

I certainly, at any rate, felt the force of this truth when, on scaling the general rock with the eye of apprehension, I made out at a point much nearer its summit than its base the gleam of a dizzily-perched white sea-gazing front which I knew for my particular landmark and which promised so much that it would have been welcome to keep even no more than half. Let me instantly say that it kept still more than it promised, and by no means least in the way of leaving far below it the worst of the outbreak of restorations and breweries. There is a road at present to the upper village, with which till recently communication was all by rude steps cut in the rock and diminutive donkeys scrambling on the flints; one of those fine flights of construction which the great road-making "Latin races" take, wherever they prevail, without advertisement or bombast; and even while I followed along the face of the cliff its climbing consolidated ledge, I asked myself how I could think so well of it without consistently thinking better still of the temples of beer so obviously destined to enrich its terminus. The perfect answer to that was of course that the brooding tourist is never bound to be consistent. What happier law for him than this very one, precisely, when on at last alighting, high up in the blue air, to stare and gasp and almost disbelieve, he embraced little by little the beautiful truth particularly, on this occasion, reserved for himself, and took in the stupendous picture? For here above all had the thought and the hand come from far away—even from *ultima Thule* [the most distant place], and yet were in possession triumphant and acclaimed. Well, all one could say was that the way they had felt their opportunity, the divine conditions of the place, spoke of the advantage of some such intellectual perspective as a remote original standpoint alone perhaps can give. If what had finally, with infinite patience, passion, labour, taste, got itself done there, was like some supreme reward of an old dream of Italy, something perfect after long delays, was it not verily in *ultima Thule* that the vow would have been piously enough made and the germ tenderly enough nursed? For a certain art of asking of Italy all she can give, you must doubtless either be a rare *raffiné* [cultivated person] or a rare genius, a sophisticated Norseman or just a Gabriele d'Annunzio.

All she can give appeared to me, assuredly, for that day and the following, gathered up and enrolled there: in the wondrous cluster and dispersal of chambers, corners, courts, galleries, arbours, arcades, long white ambulatories and vertiginous points of view. The greatest charm of all perhaps was that, thanks to the particular conditions, she seemed to abound, to overflow, in directions in which I had never yet enjoyed the chance to find her so free. The indispensable thing was therefore, in observation, in reflection, to press the opportunity hard, to recognise that as the abundance was splendid, so, by the same stroke, it was immensely suggestive. It dropped into one's

lap, naturally, at the end of an hour or two, the little white
flower of its formula: the brooding tourist, in other words,
could only continue to brood till he had made out in a measure,
as I may say, what was so wonderfully the matter with him. He
was simply then in the presence, more than ever yet, of the
possible poetry of the personal and social life of the south, and
the fun would depend much—as occasions are fleeting—on his
arriving in time, in the interest of that imagination which is his
only field of sport, at adequate new notations of it. The sense
of all this, his obscure and special fun in the general bravery,
mixed, on the morrow, with the long, human hum of the
bright, hot day and filled up the golden cup with questions and
answers. The feast of St. Antony, the patron of the upper town,
was the one thing in the air, and of the private beauty of the
place, there on the narrow shelf, in the shining, shaded loggias
and above the blue gulfs, all comers were to be made free.

····· *i i i* . ······

The church-feast of its saint is of course for Anacapri, as for
any self-respecting Italian town, the great day of the year, and
the smaller the small "country," in native parlance, as well as
the simpler, accordingly, the life, the less the chance for leakage, on other pretexts, of the stored wine of loyalty. This pure
fluid, it was easy to feel overnight, had not sensibly lowered its
level; so that nothing indeed, when the hour came, could well
exceed the outpouring. All up and down the Sorrentine promontory the early summer happens to be the time of the saints,
and I had just been witness there of a week on every day of
which one might have travelled, through kicked-up clouds
and other demonstrations, to a different hot holiday. There
had been no bland evening that, somewhere or other, in the
hills or by the sea, the white dust and the red glow didn't rise
to the dim stars. Dust, perspiration, illumination, conversation—these were the regular elements. "They're very civilised,"
a friend who knows them as well as they can be known had
said to me of the people in general; "plenty of fireworks and
plenty of talk—that's all they ever want." That they were
"civilised"—on the side on which they were most to show—
was therefore to be the word of the whole business, and noth-

ing could have, in fact, had more interest than the meaning that for the thirty-six hours I read into it.

Seen from below and diminished by distance, Anacapri makes scarce a sign, and the road that leads to it is not traceable over the rock; but it sits at its ease on its high, wide table, of which it covers—and with picturesque southern culture as well—as much as it finds convenient. As much of it as possible was squeezed all the morning, for St. Antony, into the piazzetta before the church, and as much more into that edifice as the robust odour mainly prevailing there allowed room for. It was the odour that was in prime occupation, and one could only wonder how so many men, women and children could cram themselves into so much smell. It was surely the smell, thick and resisting, that was least successfully to be elbowed. Meanwhile the good saint, before he could move into the air, had, among the tapers and the tinsel, the opera-music and the pulpit poundings, bravely to snuff it up. The shade outside was hot, and the sun was hot; but we waited as densely for him to come out, or rather to come "on," as the pit at the opera waits for the great tenor. There were people from below and people from the mainland and people from Pomerania and a brass band from Naples. There were other figures at the end of longer strings—strings that, some of them indeed, had pretty well given way and were now but little snippets trailing in the dust. Oh, the queer sense of the good old Capri of artistic legend, of which the name itself was, in the more benighted years—years of the contadina [peasant] and the pifferaro [piper]—a bright evocation! Oh, the echo, on the spot, of each romantic tale. Oh, the loafing painters, so bad and so happy, the conscious models, the vague personalities! The "beautiful Capri girl" was of course not missed, though not perhaps so beautiful as in her ancient glamour, which none the less didn't at all exclude the probable presence—with *his* legendary light quite undimmed—of the English lord in disguise who will at no distant date marry her. The whole thing was there; one held it in one's hand.

The saint comes out at last, borne aloft in long procession and under a high canopy: a rejoicing, staring, smiling saint, openly delighted with the one happy hour in the year on which he may take his own walk. Frocked and tonsured, but not at

all macerated, he holds in his hand a small wax puppet of an
infant Jesus and shows him to all their friends, to whom he
nods and bows: to whom, in the dazzle of the sun he literally
seems to grin and wink, while his litter sways and his banners
flap and every one gaily greets him. The ribbons and draperies
flutter, and the white veils of the marching maidens, the music
blares and the guns go off and the chants resound, and it is all
as holy and merry and noisy as possible. The procession—
down to the delightful little tinselled and bare-bodied babies,
miniature St. Antonys irrespective of sex, led or carried by
proud papas or brown grandsires—includes so much of the
population that you marvel there is such a muster to look
on—like the charades given in a family in which every one
wants to act. But it is all indeed in a manner one house, the
little high-niched island community, and nobody therefore,
even in the presence of the head of it, puts on an air of solemnity. Singular and suggestive before everything else is the absence of any approach to our notion of the posture of respect,
and this among people whose manners in general struck one as
so good and, in particular, as so cultivated. The office of the
saint—of which the festa is but the annual reaffirmation—
involves not the faintest attribute of remoteness or mystery.

While, with my friend, I waited for him, we went for coolness into the second church of the place, a considerable and
bedizened structure, with the rare curiosity of a wondrous
pictured pavement of majolica, the garden of Eden done in
large coloured tiles or squares, with every beast, bird and river,
and a brave *diminuendo,* in especial, from portal to altar, of
perspective, so that the animals and objects of the foreground
are big and those of the successive distances differ with much
propriety. Here in the sacred shade the old women were knitting, gossiping, yawning, shuffling about; here the children
were romping and "larking"; here, in a manner, were the open
parlour, the nursery, the kindergarten and the conversazione
of the poor. This is everywhere the case by the southern sea. I
remember near Sorrento a wayside chapel that seemed the
scene of every function of domestic life, including cookery and
others. The odd thing is that it all appears to interfere so little
with that special civilised note—the note of manners—which is

so constantly touched. It is barbarous to expectorate in the temple of your faith, but that doubtless is an extreme case. Is civilisation really measured by the number of things people do respect? There would seem to be much evidence against it. The oldest societies, the societies with most traditions, are naturally not the least ironic, the least *blasées,* and the African tribes who take so many things into account that they fear to quit their huts at night are not the fine flower.

····· *i v* . ······

Where, on the other hand, it was impossible not to feel to the full all the charming *riguardi* [considerations]—to use their own good word—in which our friends *could* abound, was, that afternoon, in the extraordinary temple of art and hospitality that had been benignantly opened to me. Hither, from three o'clock to seven, all the world, from the small in particular to the smaller and the smallest, might freely flock, and here, from the first hour to the last, the huge straw-bellied flasks of purple wine were tilted for all the thirsty. They were many, the thirsty, they were three hundred, they were unending; but the draughts they drank were neither countable nor counted. This boon was dispensed in a long, pillared portico, where everything was white and light save the blue of the great bay as it played up from far below or as you took it in, between shining columns, with your elbows on the parapet. Sorrento and Vesuvius were over against you; Naples furthest off, melted, in the middle of the picture, into shimmering vagueness and innocence; and the long arm of Posilippo and the presence of the other islands, Procida, the stricken Ischia,* made themselves felt to the left. The grand air of it all was in one's very nostrils and seemed to come from sources too numerous and too complex to name. It was antiquity in solution, with every brown, mild figure, every note of the old speech, every tilt of the great flask, every shadow cast by every classic fragment, adding its touch to the impression. What was the secret of the surprising amenity?—to the

* A destructive earthquake had occurred on the island of Ischia in July 1883.

essence of which one got no nearer than simply by feeling afresh the old story of the deep interfusion of the present with the past. You had felt that often before, and all that could, at the most, help you now was that, more than ever yet, the present appeared to become again really classic, to sigh with strange elusive sounds of Virgil and Theocritus. Heaven only knows how little they would in truth have had to say to it, but we yield to these visions as we must, and when the imagination fairly turns in its pain almost any soft name is good enough to soothe it.

It threw such difficulties but a step back to say that the secret of the amenity was "style"; for what in the world was the secret of style, which you might have followed up and down the abysmal old Italy for so many a year only to be still vainly calling for it? Everything, at any rate, that happy afternoon, in that place of poetry, was bathed and blessed with it. The castle of Barbarossa had been on the height behind; the villa of black Tiberius had overhung the immensity from the right; the white arcades and the cool chambers offered to every step some sweet old "piece" of the past, some rounded porphyry pillar supporting a bust, some shaft of pale alabaster upholding a trellis, some mutilated marble image, some bronze that had roughly resisted. Our host, if we came to that, had the secret; but he could only express it in grand practical ways. One of them was precisely this wonderful "afternoon tea," in which tea only—*that,* good as it is, has never the note of style—was not to be found. The beauty and the poetry, at all events, were clear enough, and the extraordinary uplifted distinction; but where, in all this, it may be asked, was the element of "horror" that I have spoken of as sensible?—what obsession that was not charming could find a place in that splendid light, out of which the long summer squeezes every secret and shadow? I'm afraid I'm driven to plead that these evils were exactly in one's imagination, a predestined victim always of the cruel, the fatal historic sense. To make so much distinction, how much history had been needed!—so that the whole air still throbbed and ached with it, as with an accumulation of ghosts to whom the very climate was pitiless, condemning them to blanch for ever in the general glare and grandeur, offering them no dusky northern nook, no place at the friendly fireside, no shelter of legend or song.

· · · · · · *v* · · · · · ·

My friend had, among many original relics, in one of his white galleries—and how he understood the effect and the "value" of whiteness!—two or three reproductions of the finest bronzes of the Naples museum, the work of a small band of brothers whom he had found himself justified in trusting to deal with their problem honourably and to bring forth something as different as possible from the usual compromise of commerce. They had brought forth, in especial, for him, a copy of the young resting, slightly-panting Mercury which it was a pure delight to live with, and they had come over from Naples on St. Antony's eve, as they had done the year before, to report themselves to their patron, to keep up good relations, to drink Capri wine and to join in the tarantella. They arrived late, while we were at supper; they received their welcome and their billet, and I am not sure it was not the conversation and the beautiful manners of these obscure young men that most fixed in my mind for the time the sense of the side of life that, all around, was to come out strongest. It would be artless, no doubt, to represent them as high types of innocence or even of energy—at the same time that, weighing them against *some* ruder folk of our own race, we might perhaps have made bold to place their share even of these qualities in the scale. It was an impression indeed never infrequent in Italy, of which I might, in these days, first have felt the force during a stay, just earlier, with a friend at Sorrento—a friend who had good-naturedly "had in," on his wondrous terrace, after dinner, for the pleasure of the gaping alien, the usual local quartette, violins, guitar and flute, the musical barber, the musical tailor, sadler, joiner, humblest sons of the people and exponents of Neapolitan song. Neapolitan song, as we know, has been blown well about the world, and it is late in the day to arrive with a ravished ear for it. That, however, was scarcely at all, for me, the question: the question, on the Sorrento terrace, so high up in the cool Capri night, was of the present outlook, in the world, for the races with whom it has been a tradition, in intercourse, positively to please.

The personal civilisation, for intercourse, of the musical barber and tailor, of the pleasant young craftsmen of my other friend's company, was something that could be trusted to make the brooding tourist brood afresh—to say more to him in fact, all the rest of the second occasion, than everything else put together. The happy address, the charming expression, the indistinctive discretion, the complete eclipse, in short, of vulgarity and brutality—these things easily became among these people the supremely suggestive note, begetting a hundred hopes and fears as to the place that, with the present general turn of affairs about the globe, is being kept for them. They are perhaps what the races politically feeble have still most to contribute—but what appears to be the happy prospect for the races politically feeble? And so the afternoon waned, among the mellow marbles and the pleasant folk—the purple wine flowed, the golden light faded, song and dance grew free and circulation slightly embarrassed. But the great impression remained and finally was exquisite. It was all purple wine, all art and song, and nobody a grain the worse. It was fireworks and conversation—the former, in the piazzetta, were to come later; it was civilisation and amenity. I took in the greater picture, but I lost nothing else; and I talked with the contadini about antique sculpture. No, nobody was a grain the worse; and I had plenty to think of. So it was I was quickened to remember that we others, we of my own country, as a race politically *not* weak, had—by what I had somewhere just heard—opened "three hundred 'saloons' " at Manilla.*

····· *v i*. ······

The "other" afternoons I here pass on to—and I may include in them, for that matter, various mornings scarce less charmingly sacred to memory—were occasions of another and a later year; a brief but all felicitous impression of Naples itself, and of the approach to it from Rome, as well as of the return

* As a result of the American victory in the Spanish-American War (1898), American troops were now occupying the Philippines.

to Rome by a different wonderful way, which I feel I shall be wise never to attempt to "improve on." Let me muster assurance to confess that this comparatively recent and superlatively rich reminiscence gives me for its first train of ineffable images those of a motor-run that, beginning betimes of a splendid June day, and seeing me, with my genial companions, blissfully out of Porta San Paolo, hung over us thus its benediction till the splendour had faded in the lamplit rest of the Chiaja. "We'll go by the mountains," my friend, of the winged chariot, had said, "and we'll come back, after three days, by the sea"; which handsome promise flowered into such flawless performance that I could but feel it to have closed and rounded for me, beyond any further rehandling, the long-drawn rather indeed than thick-studded chaplet of my visitations of Naples—from the first, seasoned with the highest sensibility of youth, forty years ago, to this last the other day. I find myself noting with interest—and just to be able to emphasise it is what inspires me with these remarks—that, in spite of the milder and smoother and perhaps, pictorially speaking, considerably emptier, Neapolitan face of things, things in general, of our later time, I recognised in my final impression a grateful, a beguiling serenity. The place is at the best wild and weird and sinister, and yet seemed on this occasion to be seated more at her ease in her immense natural dignity. My disposition to feel that, I hasten to add, was doubtless my own secret; my three beautiful days, at any rate, filled themselves with the splendid harmony, several of the minor notes of which ask for a place, such as it may be, just here.

Wondrously, it was a clean and cool and, as who should say, quiet and amply interspaced Naples—in tune with itself, no harsh jangle of *forestieri* vulgarising the concert. I seemed in fact, under the blaze of summer, the only stranger—though the blaze of summer itself was, for that matter, everywhere but a higher pitch of light and colour and tradition, and a lower pitch of everything else; even, it struck me, of sound and fury. The appeal in short was genial, and, faring out to Pompeii of a Sunday afternoon, I enjoyed there, for the only time I can recall, the sweet chance of a late hour or two, the hour of the lengthening shadows, absolutely alone. The impression remains ineffaceable—it was to supersede half-a-dozen other mixed memories, the sense that had remained with me, from far back, of a pilgrimage always here beset with traps and shocks and vulgar importunities, achieved under fatal discouragements. Even Pompeii, in fine, haunt of *all* the cockneys of creation, burned itself, in the warm still eventide, as clear as glass, or as the glow of a pale topaz, and the particular cockney who roamed without a plan and at his ease, but with his feet on Roman slabs, his hands on Roman stones, his eyes on the Roman void, his consciousness really at last of some good to him, could open himself as never before to the fond luxurious fallacy of a close communion, a direct revelation. With which there were other moments for him not less the fruit of the slow unfolding of time; the clearest of these again being those enjoyed on the terrace of a small island-villa—the island a rock and the villa a wondrous little rock-garden, unless a better term would be perhaps rock-salon, just off the extreme point of Posilippo and where, thanks to a friendliest hospitality, he was to hang ecstatic, through another sublime afternoon, on the wave of a magical wand. Here, as happened, were charming wise, original people even down to delightful amphibious American children, enamelled by the sun of the Bay as for figures of miniature Tritons and Nereids on a Renaissance plaque; and above all, on the part of the general prospect, a demonstration of the grand style of composition and effect that one was never to wish to see bettered. The way in which the Italian scene on such occasions as this seems to purify itself to the transcendent and perfect *idea* alone—idea of beauty, of dignity, of comprehensive grace, with all accidents merged, all defects disowned, all experience outlived, and to gather itself up into the mere mute eloquence of what has just incalculably *been,* remains forever the secret and the lesson of the subtlest daughter of History. All one could do, at the heart of the overarching crystal, and in presence of the relegated City, the far-trailing Mount, the grand Sorrentine headland, the islands incomparably stationed and related, was to wonder what may well become of the so many other elements of any poor human and social complexus, what might become of any successfully-working or only struggling and floundering civilisation at all, when high Natural Elegance proceeds to take such exclusive charge and recklessly assume, as it were, *all* the responsibilities.

····· *v i i* · ······

This indeed had been quite the thing I was asking myself all the wondrous way down from Rome, and was to ask myself afresh, on the return, largely within sight of the sea, as our earlier course had kept to the ineffably romantic inland valleys, the great decorated blue vistas in which the breasts of the mountains shine vaguely with strange high-lying city and castle and church and convent, even as shoulders of no diviner line might be hung about with dim old jewels. It was odd, at the end of time, long after those initiations, of comparative youth, that had then struck one as extending the very field itself of felt charm, as exhausting the possibilities of fond surrender, it was odd to have positively a new basis of enjoyment, a new gate of triumphant passage, thrust into one's consciousness and opening to one's use; just as I confess I have to brace myself a little to call by such fine names our latest, our ugliest and most monstrous aid to motion. It is true of the monster, as we have known him up to now, that one can neither quite praise him nor quite blame him without a blush—he reflects so the nature of the company he's condemned to keep. His splendid easy power addressed to noble aims make him assuredly on occasion a purely beneficient creature. I parenthesise at any rate that I know him in no other light—counting out of course the acquaintance that consists of a dismayed arrest in the road, with back flattened against wall or hedge, for the dusty, smoky, stenchy shock of his passage. To no end is his easy power more blest than to that of ministering to the ramifications, as it were, of curiosity, or to that, in other words, of achieving for us, among the kingdoms of the earth, the grander and more genial, the comprehensive and *complete* introduction. Much as was ever to be said for our old forms of pilgrimage—and I am convinced that they are far from wholly superseded—they left, they had to leave, dreadful gaps in our yearning, dreadful lapses in our knowledge, dreadful failures in our energy; there were always things off and beyond, goals of delight and dreams of desire, that dropped as a matter of course into the unattainable, and over to which our wonder-working agent now flings the firm straight bridge. Curiosity has lost, under this amazing extension, its salutary renouncements perhaps; contemplation has become one with action and satisfaction one with desire—speaking always in the spirit of the inordinate lover of an enlightened use of our eyes. That may represent, for all I know, an insolence of advantage on which there will be eventual heavy charges, as yet obscure and incalculable, to pay, and I glance at the possibility only to avoid all thought of the lesson of the long run, and to insist that I utter this dithyramb but in the immediate flush and fever of the short. For such a beat of time as our fine courteous and contemplative advance upon Naples, and for such another as our retreat northward under the same fine law of observation and homage, the bribed consciousness could only decline to question its security. The sword of Damocles suspended over that presumption, the skeleton at the banquet of extravagant ease, would have been that even at our actual inordinate rate—leaving quite apart "improvements" to come—such savings of trouble begin to use up the world; some hard grain of difficulty being always a necessary part of the composition of pleasure. The hard grain in our old comparatively pedestrian mixture, before this business of our learning not so much even to fly (which might indeed involve trouble) as to be mechanically and prodigiously flown, quite another matter, was the element of uncertainty, effort and patience; the handful of silver nails which, I admit, drove many an impression home. The seated motorist misses the silver nails, I fully acknowledge, save in so far as his æsthetic (let alone his moral) conscience may supply him with some artful subjective substitute; in which case the thing becomes a precious secret of his own.

However, I wander wild—by which I mean I look too far ahead; my intention having been only to let my sense of the merciless June beauty of Naples Bay at the sunset hour and on the island terrace associate itself with the whole inexpressible taste of our two motor-days' feast of scenery. That queer question of the exquisite grand manner as the most emphasised *all* of things—of what it may, seated so predominant in nature, insidiously, through the centuries, let generations and populations "in for," hadn't in the least waited for the special emphasis I speak of to hang about me. I must have found myself more or less consciously entertaining it by the way—since how couldn't it be of the very essence of the truth, constantly and intensely before us, that Italy is really so much the most beautiful country in the world, taking all things together, that others must stand off and be hushed while she speaks? Seen thus in great comprehensive iridescent stretches, it is the incomparable wrought *fusion,* fusion of human history and mortal passion with the elements of earth and air, of colour, composition and form, that constitute her appeal and give it the supreme heroic grace. The chariot of fire favours fusion rather than promotes analysis, and leaves much of that first June picture for me, doubtless, a great accepted blur of violet and silver. The various hours and successive aspects, the different strong passages of our reverse process, on the other hand, still figure for me even as some series of sublime landscape-frescoes—if the great Claude, say, had ever used that medium—in the immense gallery of a palace; the homeward run by Capua, Terracina, Gaeta and its storied headland fortress, across the deep, strong, indescribable Pontine Marshes, white-cattled, strangely pastoral, sleeping in the afternoon glow, yet stirred by the near sea-breath. Thick somehow to the imagination as some full-bodied sweetness of syrup is thick to the palate the atmosphere of that region—thick with the sense of history and the very taste of time; as if the haunt and home (which indeed it is) of some great fair bovine aristocracy attended and guarded by halberdiers in the form of the mounted and long-lanced herdsmen, admirably congruous with the whole picture at every point, and never more so than in their manner of gaily taking up, as with bell-voices of golden bronze, the offered wayside greeting.

There had been this morning among the impressions of our first hour an unforgettable specimen of that general type—the image of one of those human figures on which our perception of the romantic so often pounces in Italy as on the genius of the scene personified; with this advantage, that as the scene there has, at its best, an unsurpassable distinction, so the physiognomic representative, standing for it all, and with an animation, a complexion, an expression, a fineness and fulness of humanity that appear to have gathered it in and to sum it up, becomes beautiful by the same simple process, very much, that makes the heir to a great capitalist rich. Our early start, our round-about descent from Posilippo by shining Baiae for avoidance of the city, had been an hour of enchantment beyond any notation I can here recover; all lustre and azure, yet all composition and classicism, the prospect developed and spread, till after extraordinary upper reaches of radiance and horizons of pearl we came at the turn of a descent upon a stalwart young game-keeper, or perhaps substantial young farmer, who, well-appointed and blooming, had unslung his gun and, resting on it beside a hedge, just lived for us, in the rare felicity of his whole look, during that moment and while, in recognition, or almost, as we felt, in homage, we instinctively checked our speed. He pointed, as it were, the lesson, giving the supreme right accent or final exquisite turn to the immense magnificent phrase; which from those moments on, and on and on, resembled doubtless nothing so much as a page written, by a consummate verbal economist and master of style, in the noblest of all tongues. Our splendid human plant by the wayside had flowered thus into style—and there wasn't to be, all day, a lapse of eloquence, a wasted word or a cadence missed.

These things are personal memories, however, with the logic of certain insistences of that sort often difficult to seize. Why should I have kept so sacredly uneffaced, for instance, our small afternoon wait at tea-time or, as we made it, coffee-time, in the little brown piazzetta of Velletri, just short of the final push on through the flushed Castelli Romani and the drop and home-stretch across the darkening Campagna? We had been dropped into the very lap of the ancient civic family, after the inveterate fashion of one's sense of such stations in small Italian towns. There was a narrow raised terrace, with steps, in front of the best of the two or three local cafés, and in the soft enclosed, the warm waning light of June various benign contemplative worthies sat at disburdened tables and, while they smoked long black weeds, enjoyed us under those probable workings of subtlety with which we invest so many quite unimaginably blank (I dare say) Italian simplicities. The charm was, as always in Italy, in the tone and the air and the happy hazard of things, which made any positive pretension or claimed importance a comparatively trifling question. We slid, in the steep little place, more or less down hill; we wished, stomachically, we had rather addressed ourselves to a tea-basket; we suffered importunity from unchidden infants who swarmed about our chairs and romped about our feet; we stayed no long time, and "went to see" nothing; yet we communicated to intensity, we lay at our ease in the bosom of the past, we practised intimacy, in short, an intimacy so much greater than the mere accidental and ostensible: the difficulty for the right and grateful expression of which makes the old, the familiar tax on the luxury of loving Italy.

[1910]

On the Road to and Within Italy

·

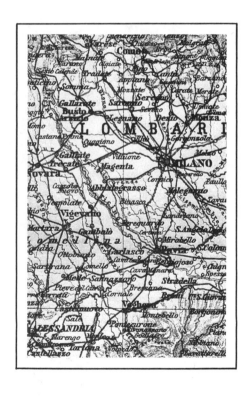

Letters

....

To William James, 12/28/1869. Assisi: I have been taking a deep delicious bath of mediævalism. I left Rome this morning by the 6:40 A.M. train & under a villainous cloudy sky, & came along in a mortally slow train (all the better to see from) thro' the great romantic country which leads up to Florence. Anything *more* romantic—more deeply & darkly dyed with the picturesque & the happy chiaroscuro of song & story, it would be impossible to conceive. . . . I've seen such passages of color & composition—such bits—such effects—as can only be reproduced by a moan of joy. It's *dramatic* landscape. The towns are all built alike, perched on a mountain summit & huddled together within the dark-belted circuit of their walls. At 2.30, after a long morning of delight . . . I arrived at this famous little spot—famous as the birthplace of St. Francis & the seat of that vast wondrous double church. . . . The town lies away up on the mountain & the church is built sheer upon its side. I got the one little *carriole* [light carriage] at the station to convey me thither, & found to my delight that I had time to see it tolerably well & get a hasty ramble through the terrific little city before dark. I have made a magnificent afternoon of it. . . . The church is a vast & curious edifice of a great deal of beauty & even more picturesqueness—a dark cavernous solemn sanctuary below—& above it another, high, aspiring & filled with light—& with various sadly decayed frescoes of Giotto. The position is glorious. A great aerial portico winds about it & commands a tremendous view. The whole thing is intensely mediæval. . . . & if such is the church—what are the strange, tortuous, hill-scaling little streets of the city? Never have I seen local color laid on so thick.

To Henry James, Sr., 1/18/1870. Grand Hotel, Nice: The drive [in Italy toward France along the Cornice Road] is said to be the most beautiful part of the Riviera. . . . It leaves the shore & climbs & winds aloft among the mountains, giving you on one side a succession of the grandest masses of hill-scenery, all clad in purple & spotted & streaked with broken lights—& on the other, seen thro' the open portals of shady seaward gorges, the vast blue glitter of the Mediterranean. But it lacks the lovely swarming detail—the lingering clinging *Italianism* of the earlier portions of the road. . . . Here Italy quite gives it up & Imperial France reigns supreme—France which I used to love—but somehow love no more. That passion is dead & buried. —But what *shall* I tell you of this transcendent journey? Great heavens! That while he has breath in his body & a brain in his head a man should [never] leave that land of the immortal gods! Never never never have I got such a sense of the essential enchantment—the incomparable 'distinction' of Italy. . . . No, one has not *lived* unless one has left Italy by the Cornice, in the full mid-glow of enjoyment. . . . I have been journeying . . . thro' a belt of eternal spring. It has been a revelation of the possible kindness of nature. . . . The country is a land of universal olive—a foliage as gentle & tender as the feathers on the breast of a dove—of olives & lusty cacti & fierce fantastic date-palms, perfect debauches of light & heat. Two moments stand out beyond the rest in my memory of the last three days—the night I spent at Oneghi—& the two sweet morning hours I passed at San Remo, yesterday. The first had a peculiar sanctity from the fact that it was my last night on Italian soil. I still had a good long hour of day-light after arriving & well I used it to roam thro' the little sea-side town. But it was the moon-light which set its stamp on the event . . . a few pale stars looking on & the Mediterranean beneath, a sheet of murmurous silver. At San Remo, as the Italian coast draws to a close, it gathers up on its lovely bosom the scattered elements of its beauty & heart-broken at ceasing to be that land of lands, it exhales towards the blind insensate heavens a rapturous smile, more poignant than any reproach. There is something hideous in having at such a place to get back into one's carriage. The color of the Mediterranean there is something unutterable—as blue as one has dreamed the skies of heaven —as one's seen the Rhone at Geneva. There, too, the last sweet remnant of the beautiful Italian race looks at you with kindly dark-eyed wonder as you take your way to the stupid unlovely North.

To GRACE NORTON, 5/18/1890. HOTEL DE GENES, GENOA: I came straight to Milan by the St. Gothard (a lovely day & a road that survives somehow the outrage of the railway & tunnel;) spent at Milan a couple of delightful fresh, hot Italian days, & came on thence to this place this morning. The air is warm & full of colour & noise; my window is open on a great chattering square, & the sense of Italy is in everything. . . . Pisa . . . Florence . . . Siena. . . . The 1st day of June I go to Venice for the rest of that month . . . the prospect of several clear & irresponsible weeks of Italy at a lovely season is delightful to me. . . . I shall return by the 10th of August.

To CARY & ALICE JAMES,* 5/20/1890. HOTEL DE GENES, GENOA: I quitted London & its overwhelming bustle only 6 days ago, & I have been in constant movement ever since. This bustling picturesque port of Genoa is my second stopping place. I have come to Italy to spend 10 weeks or so, after which I go back to England, where I expect to be quietly at home during the empty weeks of August, September, & October, when every one else is away. I hope that some day each of you will be able to see this dear old land of Italy, which is so full of beauty & historic interest that it makes other countries seem pale & tame. The summer has begun here; the air is full of light & colour, the sunshine golden, the Mediterranean as blue as Alice's best bonnet, or Cary's best necktie, & the whole feeling of the place soothing & sympathetic. One feels, comparatively, out of the rush & crush of the modern world, & one wants only to stroll about & look at splendid old palaces & pictures & smoke cigarettes. I think even Alice would

---

* Henry James's nephew and niece, Cary (Joseph Cary James, 1874–1925) and Alice James (1875–1925), were the children of Henry's brother Garth Wilkinson James.

take to them (I mean to the cigarettes) & I wish my dear children, I had a wishing cap that I could put on & transport you & your dear Mother for a little while to scenes so refreshing & in a sort of way, consoling.

To Frederick Macmillan,* 5/29/1890. Villino Rubio, 1, Via Palaestro, Florence: I am rejoicing in Italy & in hot weather & in a simplified life. This truly amiable country seems to me more faithful to characters. I am afraid I am not the least little bit homesick for London—but I expect suddenly to become so about August 1st. . . . I go on Saturday for a fortnight to Palazzo Barbaro.

To Charles Eliot Norton, 7/4/1892. Hotel de Sienne, Siena: A singularly charming month that I have been spending in this most lovable old city. . . . But I believe I shouldn't love Siena any better even if I knew it better. I am very happy indeed to feel that—as I grow older—many things come & go, but Italy remains. I have been here many times—regularly every year or almost, for many years now, but the spell, the charm, the magic is still in the air. I always try, between May & August, to give London a wide berth, & I find these parts far & away most pleasant when summer has begun & the barbarians have fled. As one stays & stays on here—I mean on *this* spot—one feels how untouched Siena really is by the modern hand. . . . You remember well enough of course—though to such a far-away world your Siena summer must seem to belong—the rich loveliness, at this moment, of this exquisite old Tuscany. One can't say enough about it, & the way the great sea of growing things—the corn & the vines & the olives—breaks in green surges at the very foot of the old golden-brown ramparts, is one of the most enchanting features of Siena. There is still never a suburb to speak of save in the quarter of the railway-station, & everywhere you look out of back-windows & back-doors & off terraces & over parapets straight down into the golden grain & tangled *poderi* [farms]. Every evening we have gone to walk in

---

* The eventual heir to the Macmillan publishing house, Frederick Macmillan (1851–1936) was James's publisher and friend.

the Lizza* & hang over the bastions of the Castello; where the near views & the far, & the late afternoons & the sunsets & the mountains have made us say again & again that we could never, never go away. But we are coming back.

To Ariana Curtis, 7/3/?1894. Hotel du Parc, Lugano [Ticino]: I proceeded, last Wednesday, on a headlong course from one ancient city to another, which culminated last evening in my arrival at this lovely spot, where I shall probably spend several days. . . . I have visited in the last four days the romantic towns of Vincenza, Mantua, Cremona, Brescia & Bergamo—& a considerable part of the lake of Como—so that you won't have it on your conscience that I have been—or that I was for the moment—made soft & lax by the delightful influence with which you surrounded me [in Venice]. You wouldn't have thought this had you seen me struggling with the fleas of Mantua & the beef steak of Brescia. I encountered a good deal of rain, a good deal of heat, a good deal of dirt—to say nothing of a good deal of danger of rushing straight back to Venice. How I should have dreamed of you if I had slept! But the nights were vocal as well as sensible. I skipped Verona for Mantua, & was infinitely beskipped for my pains. Mantua is dreary & pestilential. . . . But the old Palazzo della Corte has wondrous (exquisite) ceilings, & a strange haunted, wicked look. . . . I returned to Brescia to revisit the beautiful Asonza Victory of the Museum, & was again of my old opinion that she is really second only to the Venus of Milo. And she has wings—& such beauties—which the Venus hasn't. Bergamo—the old town on the mountain—is admirable, with its brown walls & shady ramparts, hanging gardens & splendid views. I came thence to Lecco, on the lake of Como, & so across, in a few hours, by boat & a really very pretty little narrow-gauge railway, to this place, which is lovely, empty & very hot. The heat however isn't intolerable, the hotel is excellent & has *2* big gardens, with *real* shade, & as many nightingales as at Vescovano, & my window looks out on all kinds of sublimities & bluenesses. I shall stay here a few days & then go for a week to Stresa, on the Lago Mag-

* A public park.

giore. . . . I shall [then] go rapidly back to London—to spend, contentedly but still rather nostalgically, the rest of the summer. How I shall welcome the revolving year. I foresee that Venice will have become for me an annual need.

To Grace Norton, 1/20/1870. Nice. I have said nothing about the main feature of my journey after all—I mean my *sentiments*. Ah the way Italy keeps tugging at my heart! Will I know her the better for leaving her thus? I know myself the better at least. I know I really care for her. But for herself she puts in a heavy chain on my future. Already I feel my bows beneath her weight settle comfortably into the water.

To Grace Norton, 12/13/1891. Hotel de l'Europe, Dresden: The dreams of my youth come back to me—& I want to end my days in Italy.

E ssays

....

From Chambéry to Milan

Your truly sentimental tourist will never take it from any occasion that there is absolutely nothing for him, and it was at Chambéry—but four hours from Geneva—that I accepted the situation and decided there might be mysterious delights in entering Italy by a whizz through an eight-mile tunnel, even as a bullet through the bore of a gun. I found my reward in the Savoyard landscape, which greets you betimes with the smile of anticipation. If it is not so Italian as Italy it is at least more Italian than anything *but* Italy—more Italian, too, I should think, than can seem natural and proper to the swarming red-legged soldiery who so publicly proclaim it of the empire of M. Thiers.* The light and the complexion of things had to my eyes not a little of that mollified depth last loved by them rather further on. It was simply perhaps that the weather was hot and the mountains drowsing in that iridescent haze that I have seen nearer home than at Chambéry. But the vegetation, assuredly, had an all but Transalpine twist and curl, and the classic wayside tangle of corn and vines left nothing to be desired in the line of careless grace. Chambéry as a town, however, constitutes no foretaste of the monumental cities. There is shabbiness and shabbiness, the fond critic of such things will tell you; and that of the ancient capital of Savoy lacks style. I found a better pastime, however, than strolling through the dark dull streets in quest of effects that were not forthcoming. The first urchin you meet will show you the way

---

* As French territory; Adolphe Thiers (1797–1877), French politician, journalist, and historian, became president of the Republic in 1871.

to Les Charmettes and the Maison Jean-Jacques.* A very pleasant way it becomes as soon as it leaves the town—a winding,
climbing by-road, bordered with such a tall and sturdy hedge
as to give it the air of an English lane—if you can fancy an
English lane introducing you to the haunts of a Madame de
Warens.†

The house that formerly sheltered this lady's singular mé-
nage stands on a hillside above the road, which a rapid path
connects with the little grass-grown terrace before it. It is a
small shabby, homely dwelling, with a certain reputable solidity, however, and more of internal spaciousness than of outside
promise. The place is shown by an elderly competent dame
who points out the very few surviving objects which you may
touch with the reflection—complacent in whatsoever degree
suits you—that they have known the familiarity of Rousseau's
hand. It was presumably a meagrely-appointed house, and I
wondered that on such scanty features so much expression
should linger. But the structure has an ancient ponderosity, and
the dust of the eighteenth century seems to lie on its worm-
eaten floors, to cling to the faded old *papiers à ramages* [flow-
ered wallpaper] on the walls and to lodge in the crevices of the
brown wooden ceilings. Madame de Warens's bed remains,
with the narrow couch of Jean-Jacques as well, his little warped
and cracked yellow spinet, and a battered, turnip-shaped silver
timepiece, engraved with its master's name—its primitive tick
as extinct as his passionate heart-beats. It cost me, I confess, a
somewhat pitying acceleration of my own to see this intimately
personal relic of the *genius loci*—for it had dwelt in his
waistcoat-pocket, than which there is hardly a material point in
space nearer to a man's consciousness—tossed so irreverently
upon the table on which you deposit your fee, beside the dog's-
eared visitors' record or *livre de cuisine* [household accounts]
recently denounced by Madame George Sand. In fact the place
generally, in so far as some faint ghostly presence of its famous
inmates seems to linger there, is by no means exhilarating.

* The home of Jean-Jacques Rousseau from 1731 to 1741.

† Rousseau's mistress and patroness, Louise Eleanore de Warens (1700–
1762).

Coppet and Ferney* tell, if not of pure happiness, at least of prosperity and honour, wealth and success. But Les Charmettes is haunted by ghosts unclean and forlorn. The place tells of poverty, perversity, distress. A good deal of clever modern talent in France has been employed in touching up the episode of which it was the scene and tricking it out in idyllic love-knots. But as I stood on the charming terrace I have mentioned—a little jewel of a terrace, with grassy flags and a mossy parapet, and an admirable view of great swelling violet hills—stood there reminded how much sweeter Nature is than man, the story looked rather wan and unlovely beneath these literary decorations, and I could pay it no livelier homage than is implied in perfect pity. Hero and heroine have become too much creatures of history to take up attitudes as part of any poetry. But, not to moralise too sternly for a tourist between trains, I should add that, as an illustration, to be inserted mentally in the text of the "Confessions," a glimpse of Les Charmettes is pleasant enough. It completes the rare charm of good autobiography to behold with one's eyes the faded and battered background of the story; and Rousseau's narrative is so incomparably vivid and forcible that the sordid little house at Chambéry seems of a hardly deeper shade of reality than so many other passages of his projected truth.

If I spent an hour at Les Charmettes, fumbling thus help-lessly with the past, I recognised on the morrow how strongly the Mont Cenis Tunnel smells of the time to come. As I passed along the Saint-Gothard highway a couple of months since, I perceived, half up the Swiss ascent, a group of navvies at work in a gorge beneath the road. They had laid bare a broad surface of granite and had punched in the centre of it a round black cavity, of about the dimensions, as it seemed to me, of a soup-plate. This was to attain its perfect development some eight years hence. The Mont Cenis may therefore be held to have set a fashion which will be followed till the highest Himalaya is but the ornamental apex or snow-capped gable-tip of some resounding fuliginous corridor. The tunnel differs but in

* Both towns on Lake Geneva, associated with Mme. de Staël and with Voltaire.

length from other tunnels; you spend half an hour in it. But
you whirl out into the blest peninsula, and as you look back
seem to see the mighty mass shrug its shoulders over the line,
the mere turn of a dreaming giant in his sleep. The tunnel is
certainly not a poetic object, but there is no perfection without
its beauty; and as you measure the long rugged outline of the
pyramid of which it forms the base you accept it as the perfection of a short cut. Twenty-four hours from Paris to Turin
is speed for the times—speed which may content us, at any
rate, until expansive Berlin has succeeded in placing itself at
thirty-six from Milan.

To enter Turin then of a lovely August afternoon was to
find a city of arcades, of pink and yellow stucco, of innumerable cafés, of blue-legged officers, of ladies draped in the North-
Italian mantilla. An old friend of Italy coming back to her finds
an easy waking for dormant memories. Every object is a reminder and every reminder a thrill. Half an hour after my
arrival, as I stood at my window, which overhung the great
square, I found the scene, within and without, a rough epitome
of every pleasure and every impression I had formerly gathered
from Italy: the balcony and the Venetian-blind, the cool floor
of speckled concrete, the lavish delusions of frescoed wall and
ceiling, the broad divan framed for the noonday siesta, the
massive mediæval Castello in mid-piazza, with its shabby rear
and its pompous Palladian front, the brick campaniles beyond,
the milder, yellower light, the range of colour, the suggestion
of sound. Later, beneath the arcades, I found many an old
acquaintance: beautiful officers, resplendent, slow-strolling,
contemplative of female beauty; civil and peaceful dandies,
hardly less gorgeous, with that religious faith in moustache and
shirt-front which distinguishes the *belle jeunesse* [attractive
young people] of Italy; ladies with heads artfully shawled in
Spanish-looking lace, but with too little art—or too much
nature at least—in the region of the bodice; well-conditioned
young *abbati* [priests] with neatly drawn stockings. These indeed are not objects of first-rate interest, and with such Turin
is rather meagrely furnished. It has no architecture, no
churches, no monuments, no romantic street-scenery. It has the
great votive temple of the Superga, which stands on a high

hilltop above the city, gazing across at Monte Rosa and lifting its own fine dome against the sky with no contemptible art. But when you have seen the Superga from the quay beside the Po, a skein of a few yellow threads in August, despite its frequent habit of rising high and running wild, and said to yourself that in architecture position is half the battle, you have nothing left to visit but the Museum of pictures. The Turin Gallery, which is large and well arranged, is the fortunate owner of three or four masterpieces; a couple of magnificent Vandycks and a couple of Paul Veroneses; the latter a Queen of Sheba and a Feast at the House of Levi—the usual splendid combination of brocades, grandees and marble colonnades dividing those skies *de turquoise malade* [of sickly-looking purple] to which Théophile Gautier is fond of alluding. The Veroneses are fine, but with Venice in prospect the traveller feels at liberty to keep his best attention in reserve. If, however, he has the proper relish for Vandyck, let him linger long and fondly here; for that admiration will never be more potently stirred than by the adorable group of the three little royal highnesses, sons and the daughter of Charles I. All the purity of childhood is here, and all its soft solidity of structure, rounded tenderly beneath the spangled satin and contrasted charmingly with the pompous rigidity. Clad respectively in crimson, white and blue, these small scions stand up in their ruffs and fardingales in dimpled serenity, squaring their infantine stomachers at the spectator with an innocence, a dignity, a delightful grotesqueness, which make the picture a thing of close truth as well as of fine decorum. You might kiss their hands, but you certainly would think twice before pinching their cheeks—provocative as they are of this tribute of admiration—and would altogether lack presumption to lift them off the ground or the higher level or dais on which they stand so sturdily planted by right of birth. There is something inimitable in the paternal gallantry with which the painter has touched off the young lady. She was a princess, yet she was a baby, and he has contrived, we let ourselves fancy, to interweave an intimation that she was a creature whom, in her teens, the lucklessly smitten—even as he was prematurely—must vainly sigh for. Though the work is a masterpiece of execution its merits under this head may be emulated, at a distance; the lovely modulations of colour in the three contrasted and harmonised little satin petticoats, the solidity of the little heads, in spite of all their prettiness, the happy, unexaggerated squareness and maturity of *pose,* are, severally, points to study, to imitate, and to reproduce with profit. But the taste of such a consummate thing is its great secret as well as its great merit—a taste which seems one of the lost instincts of mankind. Go and enjoy this supreme expression of Vandyck's fine sense, and admit that never was a politer production.

Milan speaks to us of a burden of felt life of which Turin is innocent, but in its general aspect still lingers a northern reserve which makes the place rather perhaps the last of the prose capitals than the first of the poetic. The long Austrian occupation perhaps did something to Germanise its physiognomy; though indeed this is an indifferent explanation when one remembers how well, temperamentally speaking, Italy held her own in Venetia. Milan, at any rate, if not bristling with the æsthetic impulse, opens to us frankly enough the thick volume of her past. Of that volume the Cathedral is the fairest and fullest page—a structure not supremely interesting, not logical, not even, to some minds, commandingly beautiful, but grandly curious and superbly rich. I hope, for my own part, never to grow too particular to admire it. If it had no other distinction it would still have that of impressive, immeasurable achievement. As I strolled beside its vast indented base one evening, and felt it, above me, rear its grey mysteries into the starlight while the restless human tide on which I floated rose no higher than the first few layers of street-soiled marble, I was tempted to believe that beauty in great architecture is almost a secondary merit, and that the main point is mass—such mass as may make it a supreme embodiment of vigorous effort. Viewed in this way a great building is the greatest conceivable work of art. More than any other it represents difficulties mastered, resources combined, labour, courage and patience. And there are people who tell us that art has nothing to do with morality! Little enough, doubtless, when it is concerned, even ever so little, in painting the roof of Milan Cathedral within to represent carved stone-work. Of this famous roof every one has heard—how good it is, how bad, how perfect a delusion, how transparent an artifice. It is the first thing your cicerone shows you on entering the church. The occasionally accommodating art-lover may accept it philosophically, I think; for the interior, though admirably effective as a whole, has no great sublimity, nor even purity, of pitch. It is splendidly vast and dim; the altar-lamps twinkle afar through the incense-thickened air like fog-lights at sea, and the great columns rise straight to the roof, which hardly curves to meet them, with the girth and altitude of oaks of a thousand years; but there is little refinement of design—few of those felicities of proportion which the eye caresses, when it finds them, very much as the memory retains and repeats some happy line of poetry or some haunting musical phrase. Consistently brave, none the less, is the result produced, and nothing braver than a certain exhibition that I privately enjoyed of the relics of St. Charles Borromeus. This holy man lies at his eternal rest in a small but gorgeous sepulchral chapel, beneath the boundless pavement and before the high altar; and for the modest sum of five francs you may have his shrivelled mortality unveiled and gaze at it with whatever reserves occur to you. The Catholic Church never renounces a chance of the sublime for fear of a chance of the ridiculous—especially when the chance of the sublime may be the very excellent chance of five francs. The performance in question, of which the good San Carlo paid in the first instance the cost, was impressive certainly, but as a monstrous matter or a grim comedy may still be. The little sacristan, having secured his audience, whipped on a white tunic over his frock, lighted a couple of extra candles and proceeded to remove from above the altar, by means of a crank, a sort of sliding shutter, just as you may see a shop-boy do of a morning at his master's window. In this case too a large sheet of plate-glass was uncovered, and to form an idea of the *étalage* [window display] you must imagine that a jeweller, for reasons of his own, has struck an unnatural partnership with an undertaker. The black mummified corpse of the saint is stretched out in a glass coffin, clad in his mouldering canonicals, mitred, crosiered and gloved, glittering with votive jewels. It is an extraordinary mixture of death and life; the desiccated clay, the ashen rags, the hideous little black mask and skull, and the living, glowing, twinkling splendour of diamonds, emeralds and sapphires. The collection is really fine, and many great historic names are attached to the different offerings. Whatever may be the better opinion as to the future of the Church, I can't help thinking she will make a figure in the world so long as she retains this great fund of precious "properties," this prodigious capital decoratively invested and scintillating throughout Christendom at effectively-scattered points. You see I am forced to agree after all, in spite of the sliding shutter and the profane swagger of the sacristan, that a certain pastoral majesty saved the situation, or at least made irony gape. Yet it was from a natural desire to breathe a sweeter air that I immediately afterwards undertook the interminable climb to the roof of the cathedral. This is another world of wonders, and one which enjoys due renown, every square inch of wall on the winding stairways being bescribbled with a traveller's name. There is a great glare from the far-stretching slopes of marble, a confusion (like the masts of a navy or the spears of an army) of image-capped pinnacles, biting the impalpable blue, and, better than either, the good-liest view of level Lombardy sleeping in its rich transalpine light and resembling, with its white-walled dwellings and the spires on its horizon, a vast green sea spotted with ships. After two months of Switzerland the Lombard plain is a rich rest to the eye, and the yellow, liquid, free-flowing light—as if on favoured Italy the vessels of heaven were more widely opened—had for mine a charm which made me think of a great opaque mountain as a blasphemous invasion of the atmospheric spaces.

I have mentioned the cathedral first, but the prime treasure of Milan at the present hour is the beautiful, tragical Leonardo.* The cathedral is good for another thousand years, but we ask whether our children will find in the most majestic and most luckless of frescoes much more than the shadow of a shadow. Its fame has been for a century or two that, as one may say, of an illustrious invalid whom people visit to see how he lasts, with leave-taking sighs and almost death-bed or tiptoe

* The Last Supper.

precautions. The picture needs not another scar or stain, now, to be the saddest work of art in the world; and battered, defaced, ruined as it is, it remains one of the greatest. We may really compare its anguish of decay to the slow conscious ebb of life in a human organism. The production of the prodigy was a breath from the infinite, and the painter's conception not immeasurably less complex than the scheme, say, of his own mortal constitution. There has been much talk lately of the irony of fate, but I suspect fate was never more ironical than when she led the most scientific, the most calculating of all painters to spend fifteen long years in building his goodly house upon the sand. And yet, after all, may not the playing of that trick represent but a deeper wisdom, since if the thing enjoyed the immortal health and bloom of a first-rate Titian we should have lost one of the most pertinent lessons in the history of art? We know it as hearsay, but here is the plain proof, that there is no limit to the amount of "stuff" an artist may put into his work. Every painter ought once in his life to stand before the Cenacolo and decipher its moral. Mix with your colours and mess on your palette every particle of the very substance of your soul, and this lest perchance your "prepared surface" shall play you a trick! Then, and then only, it will fight to the last—it will resist even in death. Raphael was a happier genius; you look at his lovely "Marriage of the Virgin" at the Brera, beautiful as some first deep smile of conscious inspiration, but to feel that he foresaw no complaint against fate, and that he knew the world he wanted to know and charmed it into never giving him away. But I have left no space to speak of the Brera, nor of that paradise of bookworms with an eye for their background—if such creatures exist—the Ambrosian Library; nor of that mighty basilica of Saint Ambrose, with its spacious atrium and its crudely solemn mosaics, in which it is surely your own fault if you don't forget Dr. Strauss and M. Renan* and worship as grimly as a Christian of the ninth century.

---

* David Strauss (1808–1874), German theologian, and Ernest Renan (1823–1892), French author, both of whom denied the historical validity of Christian biblical events, particularly the deity of Jesus.

It is part of the sordid prose of the Mont Cenis road that, unlike those fine old unimproved passes, the Simplon, the Splügen and—yet awhile longer—the Saint-Gothard, it denies you a glimpse of that paradise adorned by the four lakes even that of uncommented Scripture by the rivers of Eden. I made, however, an excursion to the Lake of Como, which, though brief, lasted long enough to suggest to me that I too was a hero of romance with leisure for a love-affair, and not a hurrying tourist with a Bradshaw* in his pocket. The Lake of Como has figured largely in novels of "immoral" tendency—being commonly the spot to which inflamed young gentlemen invite the wives of other gentlemen to fly with them and ignore the restrictions of public opinion. But even the Lake of Como has been revised and improved; the fondest prejudices yield to time; it gives one somehow a sense of an aspiringly high tone. I should pay a poor compliment at least to the swarming inmates of the hotels which now alternate attractively by the water-side with villas old and new were I to read the appearances more cynically. But if it is lost to florid fiction it still presents its blue bosom to most other refined uses, and the unsophisticated tourist, the American at least, may do any amount of private romancing there. The pretty hotel at Cadenabbia offers him, for instance, in the most elegant and assured form, the so often precarious adventure of what he calls at home summer board. It is all so unreal, so fictitious, so elegant and idle, so framed to undermine a rigid sense of the chief end of man not being to float forever in an ornamental boat, beneath an awning tasselled like a circus-horse, impelled by an affable Giovanni or Antonio from one stately stretch of lake-laved villa steps to another, that departure seems as harsh and unnatural as the dream-dispelling note of some punctual voice at your bedside on a dusky winter morning. Yet I wondered, for my own part, where I had seen it all before—the pink-walled villas gleaming through their shrubberies of orange and oleander, the mountains shimmering in the hazy light like so many breasts of doves, the constant presence of the melodious Italian voice. Where indeed but at the Opera when

* A monthly railroad guide published in England.

the manager has been more than usually regardless of expense? Here in the foreground was the palace of the nefarious barytone, with its banqueting-hall opening as freely on the stage as a railway buffet on the platform; beyond, the delightful back scene, with its operatic gamut of colouring; in the middle the scarlet-sashed *barcaiuoli* [boatmen], grouped like a chorus, hat in hand, awaiting the conductor's signal. It was better even than being in a novel—this being, this fairly wallowing, in a libretto.

[1872]

....

The Old Saint-Gothard: Leaves from a Note-Book

Berne, September, 1873. —In Berne again, some eleven weeks after having left it in July. I have never been in Switzerland so late, and I came hither innocently supposing the last Cook's tourist* to have paid out his last coupon and departed. But I was lucky, it seems, to discover an empty cot in an attic and a very tight place at a table d'hôte. People are all flocking out of Switzerland, as in July they were flocking in, and the main channels of egress are terribly choked. I have been here several days, watching them come and go; it is like the march-past of an army. It gives one, for an occasional change from darker thoughts, a lively impression of the numbers of people now living, and above all now moving, at extreme ease in the world. Here is little Switzerland disgorging its tens of thousands of honest folk, chiefly English, and rarely, to judge by their faces and talk, children of light in any eminent degree; for whom snow-peaks and glaciers and passes and lakes and chalets and sunsets and a *café complet,* "including honey," as the coupon says, have become prime necessities for six weeks every year. It's not so long ago that lords and nabobs monopolised these pleasures; but nowadays a month's tour in Switzerland is no more a *jeu de prince* [princely adventure] than a Sunday excursion. To watch this huge Anglo-Saxon wave ebbing through Berne suggests, no doubt most fallaciously, that the common

---

* Thomas Cook (1808–1892) founded in 1841 the most successful Victorian travel agency.

lot of mankind isn't after all so very hard and that the masses have reached a high standard of comfort. The view of the Oberland chain, as you see it from the garden of the hotel, really butters one's bread most handsomely; and here are I don't know how many hundred Cook's tourists a day looking at it through the smoke of their pipes. Is it really the "masses," however, that I see every day at the table d'hôte? They have rather too few h's to the dozen, but their good-nature is great. Some people complain that they "vulgarise" Switzerland; but as far as I am concerned I freely give it up to them and offer them a personal welcome and take a peculiar satisfaction in seeing them here. Switzerland is a "show country"—I am more and more struck with the bearings of that truth; and its use in the world is to reassure persons of a benevolent imagination when they begin to wish for the drudging millions a greater supply of elevating amusement. Here is amusement for a thousand years, and as elevating certainly as mountains five miles high can make it. I expect to live to see the summit of Monte Rosa heated by steam-tubes and adorned with a hotel setting three tables d'hôte a day.

I have been walking about the arcades, which used to bestow a grateful shade in July, but which seem rather dusky and chilly in these shortening autumn days. I am struck with the way the English always speak of them—with a shudder, as gloomy, as dirty, as evil-smelling, as suffocating, as freezing, as anything and everything but admirably picturesque. I take us Americans for the only people who, in travelling, judge things on the first impulse—when we do judge them at all—not from the standpoint of simple comfort. Most of us, strolling forth into these bustling basements, are, I imagine, too much amused, too much diverted from the sense of an alienable right to public ease, to be conscious of heat or cold, of thick air, or even of the universal smell of strong *charcuterie*. If the visible romantic were banished from the face of the earth I am sure the idea of it would still survive in some typical American heart. . . .

Lucerne, September.—Berne, I find, has been filling with tourists at the expense of Lucerne, which I have been having almost to myself. There are six people at the table d'hôte; the excellent dinner denotes on the part of the *chef* the easy leisure in which true artists love to work. The waiters have nothing to do but lounge about the hall and chink in their pockets the fees of the past seasons. The day has been lovely in itself, and pervaded, to my sense, by the gentle glow of a natural satisfaction at my finding myself again on the threshold of Italy. I am lodged *en prince,* in a room with a balcony hanging over the lake—a balcony on which I spent a long time this morning at dawn, thanking the mountain-tops, from the depths of a landscape-lover's heart, for their promise of superbly fair weather. There were a great many mountain-tops to thank, for the crags and peaks and pinnacles tumbled away through the morning mist in an endless confusion of grandeur. I have been all day in better humour with Lucerne than ever before—a forecast reflection of Italian moods. If Switzerland, as I wrote the other day, is so furiously a show-place, Lucerne is certainly one of the biggest booths at the fair. The little quay, under the trees, squeezed in between the decks of the steamboats and the doors of the hotels, is a terrible medley of Saxon dialects—a jumple of pilgrims in all the phases of devotion, equipped with book and staff, alpenstock and Baedeker. There are so many hotels and trinket-shops, so many omnibuses and steamers, so many Saint-Gothard *vetturini* [cab drivers], so many ragged urchins poking photographs, minerals and Lucernese English at you, that you feel as if lake and mountains themselves, in all their loveliness, were but a part of the "enterprise" of landlords and pedlars, and half expect to see the Righi and Pilatus* and the fine weather figure as items on your hotel-bill between the *bougie* [candle] and the *siphon* [sparkling water]. Nature herself assists you to this conceit; there is something so operatic and suggestive of footlights and scene-shifters in the view on which Lucerne looks out. You are one of five thousand—fifty thousand—"accommodated" spectators; you have taken your season-ticket and there is a responsible impresario somewhere behind the scenes. There is such a luxury of beauty in the prospect—such a redundancy of composition and effect—so many more peaks and pinnacles than are needed to make one heart happy or regale the vision of one quiet observer, that you

* Mountain peaks.

finally accept the little Babel on the quay and the looming masses in the clouds as equal parts of a perfect system, and feel as if the mountains had been waiting so many ages for the hotels to come and balance the colossal group, that they show a right, after all, to have them big and numerous. The scene-shifters have been at work all day long, composing and dis-composing the beautiful background of the prospect—massing the clouds and scattering the light, effacing and reviving, mak-ing play with their wonderful machinery of mist and haze. The mountains rise, one behind the other, in an enchanting grada-tion of distances and of melting blues and greys; you think each successive tone the loveliest and haziest possible till you see another loom dimly behind it. I couldn't enjoy even *The Swiss Times,* over my breakfast, till I had marched forth to the office of the Saint-Gothard service of coaches and demanded the banquette for to-morrow. The one place at the disposal of the office was taken, but I might possibly *m'entendre* [come to an agreement] with the conductor for his own seat—the conduc-tor being generally visible, in the intervals of business, at the post-office. To the post-office, after breakfast, I repaired, over the fine new bridge which now spans the green Reuss and gives such a woeful air of country-cousinship to the crooked old wooden structure which did sole service when I was here four years ago. The old bridge is covered with a running hood of shingles and adorned with a series of very quaint and vivid little paintings of the "Dance of Death," quite in the Holbein manner; the new sends up a painful glare from its white lime-stone, and is ornamented with candelabra in a meretricious imitation of platinum. As an almost professional cherisher of the quaint I ought to have chosen to return at least by the dark and narrow way; but mark how luxury unmans us. I was already demoralised. I crossed the threshold of the timbered portal, took a few steps, and retreated. It *smelt badly!* So I marched back, counting the lamps in their fine falsity. But the other, the crooked and covered way, smelt very badly indeed; and no good American is without a fund of accumulated sen-sibility to the odour of stale timber.

Meanwhile I had spent an hour in the great yard of the post-office, waiting for my conductor to turn up and seeing the yellow malles-postes [mail coaches] pushed to and fro. At last, being told my man was at my serivce, I was brought to speech of a huge, jovial, bearded, delightful Italian, clad in the blue coat and waistcoat, with close, round silver buttons, which are a heritage of the old postilions. No, it was not he; it was a friend of his; and finally the friend was produced, *en costume de ville* [in everyday clothes], but equally jovial, and Italian enough—a brave Lucernese, who had spent half of his life between Bellinzona and Camerlata. For ten francs this worthy man's perch behind the luggage was made mine as far as Bellinzona, and we separated with reciprocal wishes for good weather on the morrow. To-morrow is so manifestly deter-mined to be as fine as any other 30th of September since the weather became on this planet a topic of conversation that I have had nothing to do but stroll about Lucerne, staring, loaf-ing and vaguely intent on regarding the fact that, whatever happens, my place is paid to Milan. I loafed into the immense new Hôtel National and read the *New York Tribune* on a blue satin divan; after which I was rather surprised, on coming out, to find myself staring at a green Swiss lake and not at the Broadway omnibuses. The Hôtel National is adorned with a perfectly appointed Broadway bar—one of the "prohibited" ones seeking hospitality in foreign lands after the manner of an old-fashioned French or Italian refugee.

Milan, October.—My journey hither was such a pleasant piece of traveller's luck that I feel a delicacy for taking it to pieces to see what it was made of. Do what we will, however, there remains in all deeply agreeable impressions a charming something we can't analyse. I found it agreeable even, given the rest of my case, to turn out of bed, at Lucerne, by four o'clock, into the chilly autumn darkness. The thick-starred sky was cloudless, and there was as yet no flush of dawn; but the lake was wrapped in a ghostly white mist which crept halfway up the mountains and made them look as if they too had been lying down for the night and were casting away the vaporous tissues of their bedclothes. Into this fantastic fog the little steamer went creaking away, and I hung about the deck with the two or three travellers who had known better than to believe it would save them francs or midnight sighs—over those debts you "pay with your person"—to go and wait for the diligence at the Poste at Flüelen, or yet at the Guillaume Tell. The dawn came sailing up over the mountain-tops, flushed but unperturbed, and blew out the little stars and then the big ones, as a thrifty matron after a party blows out her candles and lamps; the mist went melting and wandering away into the duskier hollows and recesses of the mountains, and the summits defined their profiles against the cool soft light.

At Flüelen, before the landing, the big yellow coaches were actively making themselves bigger, and piling up boxes and bags on their roofs in a way to turn nervous people's thoughts to the sharp corners of the downward twists of the great road. I climbed into my own banquette, and stood eating peaches—half-a-dozen women were hawking them about under the horses' legs—with an air of security that might have been offensive to the people scrambling and protesting below between coupé and intérieur. They were all English and all had false alarms about the claim of somebody else to their place, the place for which they produced their ticket, with a declaration in three or four different tongues of the inalienable right to it given them by the expenditure of British gold. They were all serenely confuted by the stout, purple-faced, many-buttoned conductors, patted on the backs, assured that their bath-tubs had every advantage of position on the top, and stowed away according to their dues. When once one has fairly started on a journey and has but to go and go by the impetus received, it is surprising what entertainment one finds in very small things. We surrender to the gaping traveller's mood, which surely isn't the unwisest the heart knows. I don't envy people, at any rate, who have outlived or outworn the simple sweetness of feeling settled to go somewhere with bag and umbrella. If we are settled on the top of a coach, and the "somewhere" contains an element of the new and strange, the case is at its best. In this matter wise people are content to become children again. We don't turn about on our knees to look out of the omnibus-window, but we indulge in very much the same round-eyed contemplation of accessible objects. Responsibility is left at home or at the worst packed away in the valise, relegated to quite another part of the diligence with the clean shirts and the writing-case. I sucked in the gladness of gaping, for this occasion, with the somewhat acrid juice of my indifferent peaches; it made me think them very good. This was the first of a series of kindly services it rendered me. It made me agree next, as we started, that the gentleman at the booking-office at Lucerne had but played a harmless joke when he told me the regular seat in the banquette was taken. No one appeared to claim it; so the conductor and I reversed positions, and I found him quite as conversible as the usual Anglo-Saxon.

He was trolling snatches of melody and showing his great yellow teeth in a jovial grin all the way to Bellinzona—and this in face of the sombre fact that the Saint-Gothard tunnel is scraping away into the mountain, all the while, under his nose, and numbering the days of the many-buttoned brotherhood. But he hopes, for long service's sake, to be taken into the employ of the railway; *he* at least is no cherisher of quaintness and has no romantic perversity. I found the railway coming on, however, in a manner very shocking to mine. About an hour short of Andermatt they have pierced a huge black cavity in the mountain, around which has grown up a swarming, digging, hammering, smoke-compelling colony. There are great barracks, with tall chimneys, down in the gorge that bristled the other day but with natural graces, and a wonderful increase of wine-shops in the little village of Göschenen above. Along the breast of the mountain, beside the road, come wandering several miles of very handsome iron pipes, of a stupendous girth—a conduit for the water-power with which some of the machinery is worked. It lies at its mighty length among the rocks like an immense black serpent, and serves, as a mere detail, to give one the measure of the central enterprise. When at the end of our long day's journey, well down in warm Italy, we came upon the other aperture of the tunnel, I could but uncap with a grim reverence. Truly Nature is great, but she seems to me to stand in very much the shoes of my poor friend the conductor. She is being superseded at her strongest points, successively, and nothing remains but for her to take humble service with her master. If she can hear herself think amid that din of blasting and hammering she must be reckoning up the years to elapse before the cleverest of Ober-Ingénieurs decides that mountains are mere obstructive matter and has the Jung-frau melted down and the residuum carried away in balloons and dumped upon another planet.

The Devil's Bridge, with the same failing apparently as the good Homer, was decidedly nodding. The volume of water in the torrent was shrunken, and I missed the thunderous uproar and far-leaping spray that have kept up a miniature tempest in the neighbourhood on my other passages. It suddenly occurs to me that the fault is not in the good Homer's inspiration, but simply in the big black pipes above-mentioned. They dip into the rushing stream higher up, presumably, and pervert its fine frenzy to their prosaic uses. There could hardly be a more vivid reminder of the standing quarrel between use and beauty, and of the hard time poor beauty is having. I looked wistfully, as we rattled into dreary Andermatt, at the great white zigzags of the Oberalp road, which climbed away to the left. Even on one's way to Italy one may spare a throb of desire for the beautiful vision of the castled Grisons. Dear to me the memory of my day's drive last summer through that long blue avenue of mountains, to queer little mouldering Ilanz, visited before supper in the ghostly dusk. At Andermatt a sign over a little black doorway flanked by two dunghills seemed to me toler-ably comical: *Minéraux, Quadrupèdes, Oiseaux, Œufs, Tableaux Antiques* [minerals, quadrupeds, birds, eggs, antique paintings]. We bundled in to dinner and the American gentleman in the banquette made the acquaintance of the Irish lady in the coupé, who talked of the weather as *foine* and wore a Persian scarf twisted about her head. At the other end of the table sat an Englishman, out of the intérieur, who bore an extraordinary resemblance to the portraits of Edward VI's and Mary's reigns. He was a walking, a convincing Holbein. The impression was of value to a cherisher of quaintness, and he must have won-dered—not knowing me for such a character—why I stared at him. It wasn't him I was staring at, but some handsome Sey-mour or Dudley or Digby with a ruff and a round cap and plume.

From Andermatt, through its high, cold, sunny valley, we passed into rugged little Hospenthal, and then up the last stages of the ascent. From here the road was all new to me.

Among the summits of the various Alpine passes there is little to choose. You wind and double slowly into keener cold and deeper stillness; you put on your overcoat and turn up the collar; you count the nestling snow-patches and then you cease to count them; you pause, as you trudge before the lumbering coach, and listen to the last-heard cow-bell tinkling away below you in kindlier herbage. The sky was tremendously blue, and the little stunted bushes on the snow-streaked slopes were all dyed with autumnal purples and crimsons. It was a great display of colour. Purple and crimson too, though not so fine, were the faces thrust out at us from the greasy little double casements of a barrack beside the road, where the horses paused before the last pull. There was one little girl in particular, beginning to *lisser* [smooth] her hair, as civilisation approached, in a manner not to be described, with her poor little blue-black hands. At the summit are the two usual grim little stone taverns, the steel-blue tarn, the snow-white peaks, the pause in the cold sunshine. Then we begin to rattle down with two horses. In five minutes we are swinging along the famous zigzags. Engineer, driver, horses—it's very handsomely done by all of them. The road curves and curls and twists and plunges like the tail of a kite; sitting perched in the banquette, you see it making below you and in mid-air certain bold gyrations which bring you as near as possible, short of the actual experience, to the philosophy of that immortal Irishman who wished that his fall from the house-top would only last. But the zigzags last no more than Paddy's fall, and in due time we were all coming to our senses over café au lait in the little inn at Faido. After Faido the valley, plunging deeper, began to take thick afternoon shadows from the hills, and at Airolo we were fairly in the twilight. But the pink and yellow houses shimmered through the gentle gloom, and Italy began in broken syllables to whisper that she was at hand. For the rest of the way to Bellinzona her voice was muffled in the grey of evening, and I was half vexed to lose the charming sight of the changing vegetation. But only half vexed, for the moon was climbing all the while nearer the edge of the crags that overshadowed us, and a thin magical light came trickling down into the winding, murmuring gorges. It was a most enchanting business. The chestnut-trees loomed up with double their daylight stature; the vines began to swing their low festoons like nets to trip up the fairies. At last the ruined towers of Bellinzona stood gleaming in the moonshine, and we rattled into the great post-yard. It was eleven o'clock and I had risen at four; moonshine apart I wasn't sorry.

All that was very well; but the drive next day from Bellinzona to Como is to my mind what gives its supreme beauty to this great pass. One can't describe the beauty of the Italian lakes, nor would one try if one could; the floweriest rhetoric can recall it only as a picture on a fireboard recalls a Claude. But it lay spread before me for a whole perfect day: in the long gleam of the Major, from whose head the diligence swerves away and begins to climb the bosky hills that divide it from Lugano; in the shimmering, melting azure of the southern slopes and masses; in the luxurious tangle of nature and the familiar amenity of man; in the lawn-like inclinations, where the great grouped chestnuts make so cool a shadow in so warm a light; in the rusty vineyards, the littered cornfields and the tawdry wayside shrines. But most of all it's the deep yellow light that enchants you and tells you where you are. See it come filtering down through a vine-covered trellis on the red handkerchief with which a ragged contadina has bound her hair, and all the magic of Italy, to the eye, makes an aureole about the poor girl's head. Look at a brown-breasted reaper eating his chunk of black bread under a spreading chestnut; nowhere is shadow so charming, nowhere is colour so charged, nowhere has accident such grace. The whole drive to Lugano was one long loveliness, and the town itself is admirably Italian. There was a great unlading of the coach, during which I wandered under certain brown old arcades and bought for six sous, from a young woman in a gold necklace, a hatful of peaches and figs. When I came back I found the young man holding open the door of the second diligence, which had lately come up, and beckoning to me with a despairing smile. The young man, I must note, was the most amiable of Ticinese; though he wore no buttons he was attached to the diligence in some amateurish capacity, and had an eye to the mail-bags and other valuables in the boot. I grumbled at Berne over the want of soft curves in the Swiss temperament; but the children of the tangled Tessin are cast in the Italian mould. My friend had as many quips and cranks as a Neapolitan; we walked together for an hour under the chestnuts, while the coach was plodding up from Bellinzona, and he never stopped singing till we reached a little wine-house where he got his mouth full of bread and cheese. I looked into his open door, à la Sterne,* and saw the young woman sitting rigid and grim, staring over his head and with a great pile of bread and butter in her lap. He had only informed her most politely that she was to be transferred to another diligence and must do him the favour to descend; but she evidently knew of but one way for a respectable young insulary of her sex to receive the politeness of a foreign adventurer guilty of an eye betraying latent pleasantry. Heaven only knew what he was saying! I told her, and she gathered up her parcels and emerged. A part of the day's great pleasure perhaps was my grave sense of being an instrument in the hands of the powers toward the safe consignment of this young woman and her boxes. When once you have really bent to the helpless you are caught; there is no such steel trap, and it holds you fast. My rather grim Abigail was a neophyte in foreign travel, though doubtless cunning enough at her trade, which I inferred to be that of making up those prodigious chignons worn mainly by English ladies. Her mistress had gone on a mule over the mountains to Cadenabbia, and she herself was coming up with the wardrobe, two big boxes and a bath-tub. I had played my part, under the powers, at Bellinzona, and had interposed between the poor girl's frightened English and the dreadful Ticinese French of the functionaries in the post-yard. At the custom-house on the Italian frontier I was of peculiar service; there was a kind of fateful fascination in it. The wardrobe was voluminous; I exchanged a paternal glance with my charge as the *douanier* [customs officer] plunged his brown fists into it. Who was the lady at Cadenabbia? What was she to me or I to her? She wouldn't know, when she rustled down to dinner next day, that it was I who had guided the frail skiff of her

* As in Laurence Sterne's (1713–1768) *A Sentimental Journey Through France and Italy* (1768).

public basis of vanity to port. So unseen but not unfelt do we cross each other's orbits. The skiff however may have foundered that evening in sight of land. I disengaged the young woman from among her fellow-travellers and placed her boxes on a hand-cart in the picturesque streets of Como, within a stone's-throw of that lovely striped and toned cathedral which has the façade of cameo medallions. I could only make the *facchino* [porter] swear to take her to the steamboat. He too was a jovial dog, but I hope he was polite with precautions.

[1874]

....

A Chain of Cities

One day in midwinter, some years since, during a journey from Rome to Florence perforce too rapid to allow much wayside sacrifice to curiosity, I waited for the train at Narni. There was time to stroll far enough from the station to have a look at the famous old bridge of Augustus, broken short off in mid-Tiber. While I stood admiring the measure of impression was made to overflow by the gratuitous grace of a white-cowled monk who came trudging up the road that wound to the gate of the town. Narni stood, in its own presented felicity, on a hill a good space away, boxed in behind its perfect grey wall, and the monk, to oblige me, crept slowly along and disappeared within the aperture. Everything was distinct in the clear air, and the view exactly as like the bit of background by an Umbrian master as it ideally should have been. The winter is bare and brown enough in southern Italy and the earth reduced to more of a mere anatomy than among ourselves, for whom the very *crânerie* [swagger] of its exposed state, naked and unashamed, gives it much of the robust serenity, not of a fleshless skeleton, but of a fine nude statue. In these regions, at any rate, the tone of the air, for the eye, during the brief desolation, has often an extraordinary charm: nature still smiles as with the deputed and provisional charity of colour and light, the duty of not ceasing to cheer man's heart. Her whole behaviour, at the time, cast such a spell on the broken bridge, the little walled town and the trudging friar, that I turned away with the impatient vow and the fond vision of how I would take the journey again and pause to my heart's content at Narni, at Spoleto, at Assisi, at Perugia, at Cortona, at Arezzo.

But we have generally to clip our vows a little when we come to fulfil them; and so it befell that when my blest springtime arrived I had to begin as resignedly as possible, yet with comparative meagreness, at Assisi.

I suppose enjoyment would have a simple zest which it often lacks if we always did things at the moment we want to, for it's mostly when we can't that we're thoroughly sure we *would,* and we can answer too little for moods in the future conditional. Winter at least seemed to me to have put something into these seats of antiquity that the May sun had more or less melted away—a desirable strength of tone, a depth upon depth of queerness and quaintness. Assisi had been in the January twilight, after my mere snatch at Narni, a vignette out of some brown old missal. But you'll have to be a fearless explorer now to find of a fine spring day any such cluster of curious objects as doesn't seem made to match before anything else Mr. Baedeker's polyglot estimate of its chief recommendations. This great man was at Assisi in force, and a brand-new inn for his accommodation has just been opened cheek by jowl with the church of St. Francis. I don't know that even the dire discomfort of this harbourage makes it seem less impertinent; but I confess I sought its protection, and the great view seemed hardly less beautiful from my window than from the gallery of the convent. This view embraces the whole wide reach of Umbria, which becomes as twilight deepens a purple counterfeit of the misty sea. The visitor's first errand is with the church; and it's fair furthermore to admit that when he has crossed that threshold the position and quality of his hotel cease for the time to be matters of moment. This twofold temple of St. Francis is one of the very sacred places of Italy, and it would be hard to breathe anywhere an air more heavy with holiness. Such seems especially the case if you happen thus to have come from Rome, where everything ecclesiastical is, in aspect, so very much of this world—so florid, so elegant, so full of accommodations and excrescences. The mere site here makes for authority, and they were brave builders who laid the foundation-stones. The thing rises straight from a steep mountain-side and plunges forward on its great substructure of arches even as a crowned headland may frown over the main.

Before it stretches a long, a grassy piazza, at the end of which you look up a small grey street, to see it first climb a little way the rest of the hill and then pause and leave a broad green slope, crested, high in the air, with a ruined castle. When I say before it I mean before the upper church; for by way of doing something supremely handsome and impressive the sturdy architects of the thirteenth century piled temple upon temple and bequeathed a double version of their idea. One may imagine them to have intended perhaps an architectural image of the relation between heart and head. Entering the lower church at the bottom of the great flight of steps which leads from the upper door, you seem to push at least into the very heart of Catholicism.

For the first minutes after leaving the clearer gloom you catch nothing but a vista of low black columns closed by the great fantastic cage surrounding the altar, which is thus placed, by your impression, in a sort of gorgeous cavern. Gradually you distinguish details, become accustomed to the penetrating chill, and even manage to make out a few frescoes; but the general effect remains splendidly sombre and subterranean. The vaulted roof is very low and the pillars dwarfish, though immense in girth, as befits pillars supporting substantially a cathedral. The tone of the place is a triumph of mystery, the richest harmony of lurking shadows and dusky corners, all relieved by scattered images and scintillations. There was little light but what came through the windows of the choir over which the red curtains had been dropped and were beginning to glow with the downward sun. The choir was guarded by a screen behind which a dozen venerable voices droned vespers; but over the top of the screen came the heavy radiance and played among the ornaments of the high fence round the shrine, casting the shadow of the whole elaborate mass forward into the obscured nave. The darkness of vaults and side-chapels is overwrought with vague frescoes, most of them by Giotto and his school, out of which confused richness the terribly distinct little faces characteristic of these artists stare at you with a solemn formalism. Some are faded and injured, and many so ill-lighted and ill-placed that you can only glance at them with decent conjecture; the great group, however—four paintings by Giotto on the ceiling above the altar—may be examined with some success. Like everything of that grim and beautiful master they deserve examination; but with the effect ever of carrying one's appreciation in and in, as it were, rather than of carrying it out and out, off and off, as happens for us with those artists who have been helped by the process of "evolution" to grow wings. This one, "going in" for emphasis at any price, stamps hard, as who should say, on the very spot of his idea—thanks to which fact he has a concentration that has never been surpassed. He was in other words, in proportion to his means, a genius supremely expressive; he makes the very shade of an intended meaning or a represented attitude so unmistakable that his figures affect us at moments as creatures all too suddenly, too alarmingly, too menacingly met. Meagre, primitive, undeveloped, he yet is immeasurably strong; he even suggests that if he had lived the due span of years later Michael Angelo might have found a rival. Not that he is given, however, to complicated postures or superhuman flights. The something strange that troubles and haunts us in his work spring rather from a kind of fierce familiarity.

It is part of the wealth of the lower church that it contains an admirable primitive fresco by an artist of genius rarely encountered, Pietro Cavallini, pupil of Giotto. This represents the Crucifixion; the three crosses rising into a sky spotted with the winged heads of angels while a dense crowd presses below. You will nowhere see anything more direfully lugubrious, or more approaching for direct force, though not of course for amplitude of style, Tintoretto's great renderings of the scene in Venice. The abject anguish of the crucified and the straddling authority and brutality of the mounted guards in the foreground are contrasted in a fashion worthy of a great dramatist. But the most poignant touch is the tragic grimaces of the little angelic heads that fall like hailstones through the dark air. It is genuine realistic weeping, the act of irrepressible "crying," that the painter has depicted, and the effect is pitiful at the same time as grotesque. There are many more frescoes besides; all the chapels on one side are lined with them, but these are chiefly interesting in their general impressiveness—as they people the dim recesses with startling presences, with apparitions out of scale. Before leaving the place I lingered long near the door, for I was sure I shouldn't soon again enjoy such a feast of scenic composition. The opposite end glowed with subdued colour; the middle portion was vague and thick and brown, with two or three scattered worshippers looming through the obscurity; while, all the way down, the polished pavement, its uneven slabs glittering dimly in the obstructed light, was of the very essence of expensive picture. It is certainly desirable, if one takes the lower church of Saint Francis to represent the human heart, that one should find a few bright places there. But if the general effect is of brightness terrorised and smothered, is the symbol less valid? For the contracted, prejudiced, passionate heart let it stand.

One thing at all events we can say, that we should rejoice to boast as capacious, symmetrical and well-ordered a head as the upper sanctuary. Thanks to these merits, in spite of a brave array of Giottesque work which has the advantage of being easily seen, it lacks the great character of its counterpart. The frescoes, which are admirable, represent certain leading events in the life of Saint Francis, and suddenly remind you, by one of those anomalies that are half the secret of the consummate *mise-en-scène* of Catholicism, that the apostle of beggary, the saint whose only tenement in life was the ragged robe which barely covered him, is the hero of this massive structure. Church upon church, nothing less will adequately shroud his consecrated clay. The great reality of Giotto's designs adds to the helpless wonderment with which we feel the passionate pluck of the Hero, the sense of being separated from it by an impassable gulf, the reflection on all that has come and gone to make morality at that vertiginous pitch impossible. There are no such high places of humility left to climb to. An observant friend who has lived long in Italy lately declared to me, however, that she detested the name of this moralist, deeming him chief propagator of the Italian vice most trying to the would-be lover of the people, the want of personal self-respect. There is a solidarity in the use of soap, and every cringing beggar, idler, liar and pilferer flourished for her under the shadow of the great Franciscan indifference to it. She was possibly right; at Rome, at Naples, I might have admitted she was right; but at

Assisi, face to face with Giotto's vivid chronicle, we admire too much in its main subject the exquisite play of that subject's genius—we don't remit to him, and this for very envy, a single throb of his consciousness. It took in, that human, that divine embrace, everything *but* soap.

I should find it hard to give an orderly account of my next adventures or impressions at Assisi, which couldn't well be anything more than mere romantic *flânerie* [strolling]. One may easily plead as the final result of a meditation at the shrine of Saint Francis a great and even an amused charity. This state of mind led me slowly up and down for a couple of hours through the steep little streets, and at last stretched itself on the grass with me in the shadow of the great ruined castle that decorates so grandly the eminence above the town. I remember edging along the sunless side of the small mouldy houses and pausing very often to look at nothing in particular. It was all very hot, very hushed, very resignedly but very persistently old. A wheeled vehicle in such a place is an event, and the *forestiero's* [stranger's] interrogative tread in the blank sonorous lanes has the privilege of bringing the inhabitants to their doorways. Some of the better houses, however, achieve a sombre stillness that protests against the least curiosity as to what may happen in any such century as this. You wonder, as you pass, what lingering old-world social types vegetate there, but you won't find out; albeit that in one very silent little street I had a glimpse of an open door which I have not forgotten. A long-haired peddler who must have been a Jew, and who yet carried without prejudice a burden of mass-books and rosaries, was offering his wares to a stout old priest. The priest had opened the door rather stingily and appeared half-heartedly to dismiss him. But the peddler held up something I couldn't see; the priest wavered with a timorous concession to profane curiosity and then furtively pulled the agent of sophistication, or whatever it might be, into the house. I should have liked to enter with that worthy.

I saw later some gentlemen of Assisi who also seemed bored enough to have found entertainment in his tray. They were at the door of the café on the Piazza, and were so thankful to me for asking them the way to the cathedral that, answering all in chorus, they lighted up with smiles as sympathetic as if I had done them a favour. Of that type were my mild, my delicate adventures. The Piazza has a fine old portico of an ancient Temple of Minerva—six fluted columns and a pediment, of beautiful proportions, but sadly battered and decayed. Goethe, I believe, found it much more interesting than the mighty mediæval church, and Goethe, as a cicerone, doubtless could have persuaded one that it was so; but in the humble society of Murray we shall most of us find a richer sense in the later monument. I found quaint old meanings enough in the dark yellow façade of the small cathedral as I sat on a stone bench by the oblong green stretched before it. This is a pleasing piece of Italian Gothic and, like several of its companions at Assisi, has an elegant wheel window and a number of grotesque little carvings of creatures human and bestial. If with Goethe I were to balance anything against the attractions of the double church I should choose the ruined castle on the hill above the town. I had been having glimpses of it all the afternoon at the end of steep street-vistas, and promising myself half-an-hour beside its grey walls at sunset. The sun was very late setting, and my half-hour became a long lounge in the lee of an abutment which arrested the gentle uproar of the wind. The castle is a splendid piece of ruin, perched on the summit of the mountain to whose slope Assisi clings and dropping a pair of stony arms to enclose the little town in its embrace. The city wall, in other words, straggles up the steep green hill and meets the crumbling skeleton of the fortress. On the side off from the town the mountain plunges into a deep ravine, the opposite face of which is formed by the powerful undraped shoulder of Monte Subasio, a fierce reflector of the sun. Gorge and mountain are wild enough, but their frown expires in the teeming softness of the great vale of Umbria. To lie aloft there on the grass, with silver-grey ramparts at one's back and the warm rushing wind in one's ears, and watch the beautiful plain mellow into the tones of twilight, was as exquisite a form of repose as ever fell to a tired tourist's lot.

Perugia too has an ancient stronghold, which one must speak of in earnest as that unconscious humourist the classic American traveller is supposed invariably to speak of the Colosseum:

it will be a very handsome building when it's finished. Even Perugia is going the way of all Italy—straightening out her streets, preparing her ruins, laying her venerable ghosts. The castle is being completely *remis à neuf* [renovated]—a Massachusetts school-house couldn't cultivate a "smarter" ideal. There are shops in the basement and fresh putty on all the windows; so that the only thing proper to a castle it has kept is its magnificent position and range, which you may enjoy from the broad platform where the Perugini assemble at eventide. Perugia is chiefly known to fame as the city of Raphael's master; but it has a still higher claim to renown and ought to figure in the gazetteer of fond memory as the little City of the infinite View. The small dusky, crooked place tries by a hundred prompt pretensions, immediate contortions, rich mantling flushes and other ingenuities, to waylay your attention and keep it at home; but your consciousness, alert and uneasy from the first moment, is all abroad even when your back is turned to the vast alternative or when fifty house-walls conceal it, and you are forever rushing up by-streets and peeping round corners in the hope of another glimpse or reach of it. As it stretches away before you in that eminent indifference to limits which is at the same time at every step an eminent homage to style, it is altogether too free and fair for compasses and terms. You can only say, and rest upon it, that you prefer it to any other visible fruit of position or claimed empire of the eye that you are anywhere likely to enjoy.

For it is such a wondrous mixture of blooming plain and gleaming river and wavily-multitudinous mountain vaguely dotted with pale grey cities, that, placed as you are, roughly speaking, in the centre of Italy, you all but span the divine peninsula from sea to sea. Up the long vista of the Tiber you look—almost to Rome; past Assisi, Spello, Foligno, Spoleto, all perched on their respective heights and shining through the violet haze. To the north, to the east, to the west, you see a hundred variations of the prospect, of which I have kept no record. Two notes only I have made: one—though who hasn't made it over and over again?—on the exquisite elegance of mountain forms in this endless play of the excrescence, it being exactly as if there were variation of sex in the upheaved mass, with the effect here mainly of contour and curve and complexion determined in the feminine sense. It further came home to me that the command of such an outlook on the world goes far, surely, to give authority and centrality and experience, those of the great seats of dominion, even to so scant a cluster of attesting objects as here. It must deepen the civic consciousness and take off the edge of ennui. It performs this kindly office, at any rate, for the traveller who may overstay his curiosity as to Perugino and the Etruscan relics. It continually solicits his wonder and praise—it reinforces the historic page. I spent a week in the place, and when it was gone I had had enough of Perugino, but hadn't had enough of the View.

I should perhaps do the reader a service by telling him just how a week at Perugia may be spent. His first care must be to ignore the very dream of haste, walking everywhere very slowly and very much at random, and to impute an esoteric sense to almost anything his eye may happen to encounter. Almost everything in fact lends itself to the historic, the romantic, the æsthetic fallacy—almost everything has an antique queerness and richness that ekes out the reduced state; that of a grim and battered old adventuress, the heroine of many shames and scandals, surviving to an extraordinary age and a considerable penury, but with ancient gifts of princes and other forms of the wages of sin to show, and the most beautiful garden of all the world to sit and doze and count her beads in and remember. He must hang a great deal about the huge Palazzo Pubblico, which indeed is very well worth any acquaintance you may scrape with it. It masses itself gloomily above the narrow street to an immense elevation, and leads up the eye along a cliff-like surface of rugged wall, mottled with old scars and new repairs, to the loggia dizzily perched on its cornice. He must repeat his visit to the Etruscan Gate, by whose immemorial composition he must indeed linger long to resolve it back into the elements originally attending it. He must uncap to the irrecoverable, the inimitable style of the statue of Pope Julius III before the cathedral, remembering that Hawthorne fabled his Miriam,* an air of romance from

* In *The Marble Faun* (1860).

which we are well-nigh as far to-day as from the building of
Etruscan gates, to have given rendezvous to Kenyon at its base.
Its material is a vivid green bronze, and the mantle and tiara
are covered with a delicate embroidery worthy of a silversmith.

Then our leisurely friend must bestow on Perugino's frescoes in the Exchange, and on his pictures in the University, all
the placid contemplation they deserve. He must go to the theatre every evening, in an orchestra-chair at twenty-two soldi,
and enjoy the curious didacticism of Amore senza Stima, Se-
verità e Debolezza, La Società Equivoca, and other popular
specimens of contemporaneous Italian comedy—unless indeed
the last-named be not the edifying title applied, for peninsular
use, to "Le Demi-Monde" of the younger Dumas. I shall be
very much surprised if, at the end of a week of this varied
entertainment, he hasn't learnt how to live, not exactly in, but
with, Perugia. His strolls will abound in small accidents and
mercies of vision, but of which a dozen pencil-strokes would be
a better memento than this poor word-sketching. From the hill
on which the town is planted radiate a dozen ravines, down
whose sides the houses slide and scramble with an alarming
indifference to the cohesion of their little rugged blocks of
flinty red stone. You ramble really nowhither without emerging on some small court or terrace that throws your view across
a gulf of tangled gardens or vineyards and over to a cluster of
serried black dwellings which have to hollow in their backs to
keep their balance on the opposite ledge. On archways and
street-staircases and dark alleys that bore through a density of
massive basements, and curve and climb and plunge as they go,
all to the truest mediæval tune, you may feast your fill. These
are the local, the architectural, the compositional commonplaces. Some of the little streets in out-of-the-way corners are
so rugged and brown and silent that you may imagine them
passages long since hewn by the pick-axe in a deserted stone-
quarry. The battered black houses, of the colour of buried
things—things buried, that is, in accumulations of time, closer
packed, even as such are, than spadefuls of earth—resemble
exposed sections of natural rock; none the less so when, beyond
some narrow gap, you catch the blue and silver of the sublime
circle of landscape.

But I oughtn't to talk of mouldy alleys, or yet of azure distances, as if they formed the main appeal to taste in this accomplished little city. In the Sala del Cambio, where in ancient days the money-changers rattled their embossed coin and figured up their profits, you may enjoy one of the serenest æsthetic pleasures that the golden age of art anywhere offers us. Bank parlours, I believe, are always handsomely appointed, but are even those of Messrs. Rothschild such models of mural bravery as this little counting-house of a bygone fashion? The bravery is Perugino's own; for, invited clearly to do his best, he left it as a lesson to the ages, covering the four low walls and the vault with scriptural and mythological figures of extraordinary beauty. They are ranged in artless attitudes round the upper half of the room—the sybils, the prophets, the philosophers, the Greek and Roman heroes—looking down with broad serene faces, with small mild eyes and sweet mouths that commit them to nothing in particular unless to being comfortably and charmingly alive, at the incongruous proceedings of a Board of Brokers. Had finance a very high tone in those days, or were genius and faith then simply as frequent as capital and enterprise are among ourselves? The great distinction of the Sala del Cambio is that it has a friendly Yes for both these questions. There was a rigid transactional probity, it seems to say; there was also a high tide of inspiration. About the artist himself many things come up for us—more than I can attempt in their order; for he was not, I think, to an attentive observer, the mere smooth and entire and devout spirit we at first are inclined to take him for. He has that about him which leads us to wonder if he may not, after all, play a proper part enough here as the patron of the money-changers. He is the delight of a million of young ladies; but who knows whether we shouldn't find in his works, might we "go into" them a little, a trifle more of manner than of conviction and of system than of deep sincerity?

This, I allow, would put no great affront on them, and one speculates thus partly but because it's a pleasure to hang about him on any pretext, and partly because his immediate effect is to make us quite inordinately embrace the pretext of his lovely soul. His portrait, painted on the wall of the Sala (you may see

it also in Rome and Florence) might at any rate serve for the
likeness of Mr. Worldly-Wiseman in Bunyan's allegory.* He
was fond of his glass, I believe, and he made his art lucrative.
This tradition is not refuted by his preserved face, and after
some experience—or rather after a good deal, since you can't
have a *little* of Perugino, who abounds wherever old masters
congregate, so that one has constantly the sense of being "in"
for all there is—you may find an echo of it in the uniform type
of his creatures, their monotonous grace, their prodigious in-
variability. He may very well have wanted to produce figures
of a substantial, yet at the same time of an impeccable innocence; but we feel that he had taught himself *how* even beyond
his own belief in them, and had arrived at a process that acted
at last mechanically. I confess at the same time that, so interpreted, the painter affects me as hardly less interesting, and one
can't but become conscious of one's style when one's style has
become, as it were, so conscious of one's, or at least of its own,
fortune. If he was the inventor of a remarkably calculable
facture [treatment], a calculation that never fails is in its way a
grace of the first order, and there are things in this special
appearance of perfection of practice that make him the fore-
runner of a mighty and more modern race. More than any of
the early painters who strongly charm, you may take all his
measure from a single specimen. The other samples infallibly
match, reproduce unerringly the one type he had mastered, but
which had the good fortune to be adorably fair, to seem to have
dawned on a vision unsullied by the shadows of earth. Which
truth, moreover, leaves Perugino all delightful as composer and
draughtsman; he has in each of these characters a sort of spacious neatness which suggests that the whole conception has
been washed clean by some spiritual chemistry the last thing
before reaching the canvas; after which it has been applied to
that surface with a rare economy of time and means. Giotto
and Fra Angelico, beside him, are full of interesting waste and
irrelevant passion. In the sacristy of the charming church of
San Pietro—a museum of pictures and carvings—is a row of
small heads of saints formerly covering the frame of the artist's

* In *The Pilgrim's Progress,* Part I (1678).

Ascension, carried off by the French. It is almost miniature work, and here at least Perugino triumphs in sincerity, in apparent candour, as well as in touch. Two of the holy men are reading their breviaries, but with an air of infantine innocence quite consistent with their holding the book upside down.

Between Perugia and Cortona lies the large weedy water of Lake Thrasymene, turned into a witching word forever by Hannibal's recorded victory over Rome. Dim as such records have become to us and remote such realities, he is yet a passionless pilgrim who doesn't, as he passes, of a heavy summer's day, feel the air and the light and the very faintness of the breeze all charged and haunted with them, all interfused as with the wasted ache of experience and with the vague historic haze. Processions of indistinguishable ghosts bore me company to Cortona itself, most sturdily ancient of Italian towns. It must have been a seat of ancient knowledge even when Hannibal and Flaminius came to the shock of battle, and have looked down afar from its grey ramparts on the contending swarm with something of the philosophic composure suitable to a survivor of Pelasgic and Etruscan revolutions. These grey ramparts are in great part still visible, and form the chief attraction of Cortona. It is perched on the very pinnacle of a mountain, and I wound and doubled interminably over the face of the great hill, while the jumbled roofs and towers of the arrogant little city still seemed nearer to the sky than to the railway-station. "Rather rough," Murray pronounces the local inn; and rough indeed it was; there was scarce a square foot of it that you would have cared to stroke with your hand. The landlord himself, however, was all smoothness and the best fellow in the world; he took me up into a rickety old loggia on the tip-top of his establishment and played showman as to half the kingdoms of the earth. I was free to decide at the same time whether my loss or my gain was the greater for my seeing Cortona through the medium of a festa. On the one hand the museum was closed (and in a certain sense the smaller and obscurer the town the more I like the museum); the churches —an interesting note of manners and morals—were impenetrably crowded, though, for that matter, so was the café, where I found neither an empty stool nor the edge of a table. I missed a sight of the famous painted Muse, the art-treasure of Cortona and supposedly the most precious, as it falls little short of being the only, sample of the Greek painted picture that has come down to us. On the other hand, I saw—but this is what I saw.

A part of the mountain-top is occupied by the church of St. Margaret, and this was St. Margaret's day. The houses pause roundabout it and leave a grassy slope, planted here and there with lean black cypresses. The contadini from near and far had congregated in force and were crowding into the church or winding up the slope. When I arrived they were all kneeling or uncovered; a bedizened procession, with banners and censers, bearing abroad, I believe, the relics of the saint, was re-entering the church. The scene made one of those pictures that Italy still brushes in for you with an incomparable hand and from an inexhaustible palette when you find her in the mood. The day was superb—the sky blazed overhead like a vault of deepest sapphire. The grave brown peasantry, with no great accent of costume, but with sundry small ones—decked, that is, in cheap fineries of scarlet and yellow—made a mass of motley colour in the high wind-stirred light. The procession halted in the pious hush, and the lovely land around and beneath us melted away, almost to either sea, in tones of azure scarcely less intense than the sky. Behind the church was an empty crumbling citadel, with half-a-dozen old women keeping the gate for coppers. Here were views and breezes and sun and shade and grassy corners to the heart's content, together with one couldn't say what huge seated mystic melancholy presence, the after-taste of everything the still open maw of time had consumed. I chose a spot that fairly combined all these advantages, a spot from which I seemed to look, as who should say, straight down the throat of the monster, no dark passage now, but with all the glorious day playing into it, and spent a good part of my stay at Cortona lying there at my length and observing the situation over the top of a volume that I must have brought in my pocket just for that especial wanton luxury of the resource provided and slighted. In the afternoon I came down and hustled awhile through the crowded little streets, and then strolled forth under the scorching sun and made the outer circuit of the wall. There I found tremendous uncemented blocks; they glared and twinkled in the powerful light, and I had to put on a blue eye-glass in order to throw into its proper perspective the vague Etruscan past, obtruded and magnified in such masses quite as with the effect of inadequately-withdrawn hands and feet in photographs.

I spent the next day at Arezzo, but I confess in very much the same uninvestigating fashion—taking in the "general impression," I dare say, at every pore, but rather systematically leaving the dust of the ages unfingered on the stored records: I should doubtless, in the poor time at my command, have fingered it to so little purpose. The seeker for the story of things has moreover, if he be worth his salt, a hundred insidious arts; and in that case indeed—by which I mean when his sensibility has come duly to adjust itself—the story assaults him but from too many sides. He even feels at moments that he must sneak along on tiptoe in order not to have too much of it. Besides which the case all depends on the kind of use, the range of application, his tangled consciousness, or his intelligible genius, say, may come to recognize for it. At Arezzo, however this might be, one was far from Rome, one was well within genial Tuscany, and the historic, the romantic decoction seemed to reach one's lips in less stiff doses. There at once was the "general impression"—the exquisite sense of the scarce expressible Tuscan quality, which makes immediately, for the whole pitch of one's perception, a grateful, a not at all strenuous difference, attaches to almost any coherent group of objects, to any happy aspect of the scene, for a main note, some mild recall, through pleasant friendly colour, through settled ample form, through something homely and economic too at the very heart of "style," of an identity of temperament and habit with those of the divine little Florence that one originally knew. Adorable Italy in which, for the constant renewal of interest, of attention, of affection, these refinements of variety, these so harmoniously-grouped and individually-seasoned fruits of the great garden of history, keep presenting themselves! It seemed to fall in with the cheerful Tuscan mildness for instance—sticking as I do to that ineffectual expression of the Tuscan charm, of the yellow-brown Tuscan dignity at large—that the ruined castle on the hill (with which agreeable feature Arezzo is no less furnished than Assisi and Cortona) had been converted into a great blooming, and I hope all profitable, podere or market-garden. I lounged away the half hours there under a spell as potent as the "wildest" forecast of propriety—propriety to all the particular conditions—could have figured it. I had seen Santa Maria della Pieve and its campanile of quaint colonnades, the stately, dusky cathedral—grass-plotted and residenced about almost after the fashion of an English "close"—and John of Pisa's elaborate marble shrine; I had seen the museum and its Etruscan vases and majolica platters. These were very well, but the old pacified citadel somehow, through a day of soft saturation, placed me most in relation. Beautiful hills surrounded it, cypresses cast straight shadows at its corners, while in the middle grew a wondrous Italian tangle of wheat and corn, vines and figs, peaches and cabbages, memories and images, anything and everything.

   [1874]

....

The Shades of Siena*

Siena ... is peopled for us to-day with wandering shades—
impalpable phantoms of lightly-dressed precursors† that melt,
for every sense, into the splendid summer light, when, on the
chance of making them confess by some weak sign to acquaintance, we take our way out of one of the open gates (great
mouths in the old walls, overbrowed as with high pink foreheads) to the region of the haunted villas. How can one hope
to find the right word for the sense of rest and leisure that must
in olden summers have awaited here the consenting victims of
Italy, among ancient things all made sweet by their age, and
with Nature helping Time very much as a tender, unwearied,
ingenious sister waits upon a brother, heavy of limb and dim of
sight, who sits with his back against a sun-warmed wall. The
lurking shades at present, on the spot, in the places they occupied and that must have changed ever so little, melt, for
every sense, into the actual splendid light, the mere happy,
indifferent, oblivious luxuriance of garden, vineyard and podere, into the shimmer of olive-slopes, the tangle of orchards
and cornfields and long-armed flowers, springing up like em-
bracing girls—the blaze of blue, the glow of tawny yellow and
iridescence of far away violet. Strange and special the effect, in
Italy, of the empty places (and there are many) that we stand
and wonder in to-day for the sake of the vanished, the English
poets; the irresistible reconstruction, to the all but baffled vi-

---

* From *William Wetmore Story and His Friends* (1903).

† Nineteenth-century English and American artists and writers who lived
in Italy, such as the poet Robert Browning.

sion, of irrecoverable presences and aspects, the conscious, shining, mocking void, sad somehow with excess of serenity. There is positively no great difference between the impression of the Lerici of Shelley, that of the Ravenna of Byron, that of the painted chamber of Keats by the Spanish Steps in Rome, and the great, bright, vacant, yet all so solemn smile with which, one July morning, not long ago, the cluster of Sienese villas met my unanswerable questions. These questions—which were, for one's self, about William Story and Robert Browning and Walter Savage Landor,* and other spirits of the general scene not here to be named—renewed, in their vanity, renewed, on the high terraces meant for soft evenings and in the cool bare echoing rooms where shutters were pulled open for me to violet views, that pang, not so much of accepted loss as of resented exclusion, of which the other more or less violated shrines had pressed the spring. There they still stand, at any rate, the old cool houses—Meschatelli, Belvedere, Spanocchi-Sergardi, Alberti, Gori, Borghese—on their communicating slopes, behind their overclambered walls and their winding, accommodating lanes; there they stand in the gladness of their gardens (congruous haunts of delightfully-named young gardeners, Adone and Narciso) and in that wondrous mountain ring which seems to contract and expand as, with the time of day and the state of the air, colour deepens or swoons. And there, at its distance, on its admirable deep-plunging ramparts—a presence as felt, perpetually, as marked for your spiritual economy as that of some great reduced personage on a prolonged visit to you would be for your domestic and social—stands the hard old fighting, painting, dwindling city, even yet as embattled for the eye, even yet as buttressed and bristling and frowning, with its tallest sharp tower in the sky, as some girt and armoured warrior who forever shakes his spear.

[1903]

* Walter Savage Landor (1775–1864), an English poet and essayist, lived in Italy from 1815 to 1835.

....

Siena Early and Late

Florence being oppressively hot and delivered over to the mosquitoes, the occasion seemed to favour that visit to Siena which I had more than once planned and missed. I arrived late in the evening, by the light of a magnificent moon, and while a couple of benignantly-mumbling old crones were making up my bed at the inn strolled forth in quest of a first impression. Five minutes brought me to where I might gather it unhindered as it bloomed in the white moonshine. The great Piazza of Siena is famous, and though in this day of multiplied photographs and blunted surprises and profaned revelations none of the world's wonders can pretend, like Wordsworth's phantom of delight, really to "startle and waylay," yet as I stepped upon the waiting scene from under a dark archway I was conscious of no loss of the edge of a precious presented sensibility. The waiting scene, as I have called it, was in the shape of a shallow horse-shoe—as the untravelled reader who has turned over his travelled friends' portfolios will respectfully remember; or, better, of a bow in which the high wide face of the Palazzo Pubblico forms the cord and everything else the arc. It was void of any human presence that could figure to me the current year; so that, the moonshine assisting, I had half-an-hour's infinite vision of mediæval Italy. The Piazza being built on the side of a hill—or rather, as I believe science affirms, in the cup of a volcanic crater—the vast pavement converges downwards in slanting radiations of stone, the spokes of a great wheel, to a point directly before the Palazzo, which may mark the hub, though it is nothing more ornamental than the mouth of a drain. The great monument stands on the lower side and might seem, in spite of its goodly mass and its embattled cornice, to be rather defiantly out-countenanced by vast private constructions occupying the opposite eminence. This *might* be, without the extraordinary dignity of the architectural gesture with which the huge high-shouldered pile asserts itself.

On the firm edge of the palace, from bracketed base to grey-capped summit against the sky, there grows a tall slim tower which soars and soars till it has given notice of the city's greatness over the blue mountains that mark the horizon. It rises as slender and straight as a pennoned lance planted on the steel-shod toe of a mounted knight, and keeps all to itself in the blue air, far above the changing fashions of the market, the proud consciousness or rare arrogance once built into it. This beautiful tower, the finest thing in Siena and, in its rigid fashion, as permanently fine thus as a really handsome nose on a face of no matter what accumulated age, figures there still as a Declaration of Independence beside which such an affair as ours, thrown off at Philadelphia, appears to have scarce done more than helplessly give way to time. Our Independence has become a dependence on a thousand such dreadful things as the incorrupt declaration of Siena strikes us as looking for ever straight over the level of. As it stood silvered by the moonlight, while my greeting lasted, it seemed to speak, all as from soul to soul, very much indeed as some ancient worthy of a lower order, button-holing one on the coveted chance and at the quiet hour, might have done, of a state of things long and vulgarly superseded, but to the pride and power, the once prodigious vitality, of which who could expect any one effect to testify more incomparably, more indestructibly, quite, as it were, more immortally? The gigantic houses enclosing the rest of the Piazza took up the tale and mingled with it their burden. "We are very old and a trifle weary, but we were built strong and piled high, and we shall last for many an age. The present is cold and heedless, but we keep ourselves in heart by brooding over our store of memories and traditions. We are haunted houses in every creaking timber and aching stone." Such were the gossiping connections I established with Siena before I went to bed.

Since that night I have had a week's daylight knowledge of the surface of the subject at least, and don't know how I can better present it than simply as another and a vivider page of the lesson that the ever-hungry artist has only to *trust* old Italy for her to feed him at every single step from her hand—and if not with one sort of sweetly-stale grain from that wondrous mill of history which during so many ages ground finer than any other on earth, why then always with something else. Siena has at any rate "preserved appearances"—kept the greatest number of them, that is, unaltered for the eye—about as consistently as one can imagine the thing done. Other places perhaps may treat you to as drowsy an odour of antiquity, but few exhale it from so large an area. Lying massed within her walls on a dozen clustered hilltops, she shows you at every turn in how much greater a way she once lived; and if so much of the grand manner is extinct the receptacle of the ashes still solidly rounds itself. This heavy general stress of all her emphasis on the past is what she constantly keeps in your eyes and your ears, and if you be but a casual observer and admirer the generalised response is mainly what you give her. The casual observer, however beguiled, is mostly not very learned, not over-equipped in advance with data; he hasn't specialised, his notions are necessarily vague, the chords of his imagination, for all his good-will, are inevitably muffled and weak. But such as it is, his received, his welcome impression serves his turn so far as the life of sensibility goes, and reminds him from time to time that even the lore of German doctors is but the shadow of satisfied curiosity. I have been living at the inn, walking about the streets, sitting in the Piazza; these are the simple terms of my experience. But streets and inns in Italy are the vehicles of half one's knowledge; if one has no fancy for their lessons one may burn one's note-book. In Siena everything is Sienese. The inn has an English sign over the door—a little battered plate with a rusty representation of the lion and the unicorn; but advance hopefully into the mouldy stone alley which serves as vestibule and you will find local colour enough. The landlord, I was told, had been servant in an English family, and I was curious to see how he met the probable argument of the casual Anglo-Saxon after the latter's first twelve hours in his establishment. As he failed to appear I asked the waiter if he weren't at home. "Oh," said the latter, "he's a *piccolo grasso vecchiotto* [little fat old man] who doesn't like to move." I'm afraid this little fat old man has simply a bad conscience. It's no small burden for one who likes the Italians—as who doesn't, under this restriction?—to have so much indifference even to rudimentary purifying processes to dispose of. What is the real philosophy of dirty habits, and are foul surfaces merely superficial? If unclean manners have in truth the moral meaning which I suspect in them we must love Italy better than consistency. This a number of us are prepared to do, but while we are making the sacrifice it is as well as we should be aware.

We may plead moreover for these impecunious heirs of the past that even if it were easy to be clean in the midst of their mouldering heritage it would be difficult to appear so. At the risk of seeming to flaunt the silly superstition of restless renovation for the sake of renovation, which is but the challenge of the infinitely precious principle of duration, one is still moved to say that the prime result of one's contemplative strolls in the dusky alleys of such a place is an ineffable sense of disrepair. Everything is cracking, peeling, fading, crumbling, rotting. No young Sienese eyes rest upon anything youthful; they open into a world battered and befouled with long use. Everything has passed its meridian except the brilliant façade of the cathedral, which is being diligently retouched and restored, and a few private palaces whose broad fronts seem to have been lately furbished and polished. Siena was long ago mellowed to the pictorial tone; the operation of time is now to deposit shabbiness upon shabbiness. But it's for the most part a patient, sturdy, sympathetic shabbiness, which soothes rather than irritates the nerves, and has in many cases doubtless as long a career to run as most of our pert and shallow freshnesses. It projects at all events a deeper shadow into the constant twilight of the narrow streets—that vague historic dusk, as I may call it, in which one walks and wonders. These streets are hardly more than sinuous flagged alleys, into which the huge black houses, between their almost meeting cornices, suffer a meagre light to filter down over rough-hewn stone, past windows often of graceful Gothic form, and great pendent iron

rings and twisted sockets for torches. Scattered over their
many-headed hill, they suffer the roadway often to incline to
the perpendicular, becoming so impracticable for vehicles that
the sound of wheels is only a trifle less anomalous than it would
be in Venice. But all day long there comes up to my window
an incessant shuffling of feet and clangour of voices. The
weather is very warm for the season, all the world is out of
doors, and the Tuscan tongue (which in Siena is reputed to
have a classic purity) wags in every imaginable key. It doesn't
rest even at night, and I am often an uninvited guest at concerts
and *conversazioni* at two o'clock in the morning. The concerts
are sometimes charming. I not only don't curse my wakeful-
ness, but go to my window to listen. Three men come carolling
by, trolling and quavering with voices of delightful sweetness,
or a lonely troubadour in his shirt-sleeves draws such artful
love-notes from his clear, fresh tenor, that I seem for the moment to be behind the scenes at the opera, watching some
Rubini or Mario go "on" and waiting for the round of ap-
plause. In the intervals a couple of friends or enemies stop—
Italians always make their points in conversation by pulling up,
letting you walk on a few paces, to turn and find them standing
with finger on nose and engaging your interrogative eye—they
pause, by a happy instinct, directly under my window, and
dispute their point or tell their story or make their confidence.
One scarce is sure which it may be; everything has such an
explosive promptness, such a redundancy of inflection and action. But everything for that matter takes on such dramatic life
as *our* lame colloquies never know—so that almost any uttered
communications here become an acted play, improvised, mim-
icked, proportioned and rounded, carried bravely to its *dénoûment*. The speaker seems actually to establish his stage and
face his foot-lights, to create by a gesture a little scenic circum-
scription about him; he rushes to and fro and shouts and stamps
and postures, he ranges through every phase of his inspiration.
I noted the other evening a striking instance of the spontaneity
of the Italian gesture, in the person of a small Sienese of I
hardly know what exact age—the age of inarticulate sounds
and the experimental use of a spoon. It was a Sunday evening,
and this little man had accompanied his parents to the café.

The Caffè Greco at Siena is a most delightful institution; you get a capital *demi-tasse* for three sous, and an excellent ice for eight, and while you consume these easy luxuries you may buy from a little hunchback the local weekly periodical, the *Vita Nuova,* for three centimes (the two centimes left from your sou, if you are under the spell of this magical frugality, will do to give the waiter). My young friend was sitting on his father's knee and helping himself to the half of a strawberry-ice with which his mamma had presented him. He had so many misadventures with his spoon that this lady at length confiscated it, there being nothing left of the ice but a little crimson liquid which he might dispose of by the common instinct of childhood. But he was no friend, it appeared, to such freedoms; he was a perfect little gentleman and he resented its being expected of him that he should drink down his remnant. He protested therefore, and it was the manner of his protest that struck me. He didn't cry audibly, though he made a very wry face. It was no stupid squall, and yet he was too young to speak. It was a penetrating concord of inarticulately pleading, accusing sounds, accompanied by gestures of the most exquisite propriety. These were perfectly mature; he did everything that a man of forty would have done if he had been pouring out a flood of sonorous eloquence. He shrugged his shoulders and wrinkled his eye-brows, tossed out his hands and folded his arms, obtruded his chin and bobbed about his head—and at last, I am happy to say, recovered his spoon. If I had had a solid little silver one I would have presented it to him as a testimonial to a perfect, though as yet unconscious, artist.

My actual tribute to him, however, has diverted me from what I had in mind—a much weightier matter—the great private palaces which are the massive majestic syllables, sentences, periods, of the strange message the place addresses to us. They are extraordinarily spacious and numerous, and one wonders what part they can play in the meagre economy of the actual city. The Siena of to-day is a mere shrunken semblance of the rabid little republic which in the thirteenth century waged triumphant war with Florence, cultivated the arts with splendour, planned a cathedral (though it had ultimately to curtail the design) of proportions almost unequalled, and contained a population of two hundred thousand souls. Many of these dusky piles still bear the names of the old mediæval magnates the vague mild occupancy of whose descendants has the effect of armour of proof worn over "pot" hats and tweed jackets and trousers. Half-a-dozen of them are as high as the Strozzi and Riccardi palaces in Florence; they couldn't well be higher. The very essence of the romantic and the scenic is in the way these colossal dwellings are packed together in their steep streets, in the depths of their little enclosed, agglomerated city. When we, in our day and country, raise a structure of half the mass and dignity, we leave a great space about it in the manner of a pause after a showy speech. But when a Sienese countess, as things are here, is doing her hair near the window, she is a wonderfully near neighbour to the cavalier opposite, who is being shaved by his valet. Possibly the countess doesn't object to a certain chosen publicity at her toilet; what does an Italian gentleman assure me but that the aristocracy make very free with each other? Some of the palaces are shown, but only when the occupants are at home, and now they are in *villeggiatura*. Their villeggiatura lasts eight months of the year, the waiter at the inn informs me, and they spend little more than the carnival in the city. The gossip of an inn-waiter ought perhaps to be beneath the dignity of even such thin history as this; but I confess that when, as a story-seeker always and ever, I have come in from my strolls with an irritated sense of the dumbness of stones and mortar, it has been to listen with avidity, over my dinner, to the proffered confidences of the worthy man who stands by with a napkin. His talk is really very fine, and he prides himself greatly on his cultivated tone, to which he calls my attention. He has very little good to say about the Sienese nobility. They are "proprio d'origine egoista" [of a very selfish nature]—whatever that may be—and there are many who can't write their names. This may be calumny; but I doubt whether the most blameless of them all could have spoken more delicately of a lady of peculiar personal appearance who had been dining near me. "She's too fat," I grossly said on her leaving the room. The waiter shook his head with a little sniff: "È troppo materiale [and all too physical]." This lady and her companion were the party whom, thinking I might relish a little company—I had been dining alone for a week—he gleefully announced to me as newly arrived Americans. They were Americans, I found, who wore, pinned to their heads in permanence, the black lace veil or mantilla, conveyed their beans to their mouth with a knife, and spoke a strange raucous Spanish. They were in fine compatriots from Montevideo. The genius of old Siena, however, would make little of any stress of such distinctions; one representative of a far-off social platitude being about as much in order as another as he stands before the great loggia of the Casino di Nobili, the club of the best society. The nobility, which is very numerous and very rich, is still, says the apparently competent native I began by quoting, perfectly feudal and uplifted and separate. Morally and intellectually, behind the walls of its palaces, the fourteenth century, it's thrilling to think, hasn't ceased to hang on. There is no bourgeoisie to speak of; immediately after the aristocracy come the poor people, who are very poor indeed. My friend's account of these matters made me wish more than ever, as a lover of the preserved social specimen, of type at almost any price, that one weren't, a helpless victim of the historic sense, reduced simply to staring at black stones and peeping up stately staircases; and that when one had examined the street-face of the palace, Murray in hand, one might walk up to the great drawing-room, make one's bow to the master and mistress, the old abbé and the young count, and invite them to favour one with a sketch of their social philosophy or a few first-hand family anecdotes.

The dusky labyrinth of the streets, we must in default of such initiations content ourselves with noting, is interrupted by two great candid spaces: the fan-shaped piazza, of which I just now said a word, and the smaller square in which the cathedral erects its walls of many-coloured marble. Of course since paying the great piazza my compliments by moonlight I have strolled through it often at sunnier and shadier hours. The market is held there, and wherever Italians buy and sell, wherever they count and chaffer—as indeed you hear them do right and left, at almost any moment, as you take your way among them—the pulse of life beats fast. It has been doing so on the spot just named, I suppose, for the last five hundred years, and during that time the cost of eggs and earthen pots has been grad-ually but inexorably increasing. The buyers nevertheless wrestle over their purchases as lustily as so many fourteenth-century burghers suddenly waking up in horror to current prices. You have but to walk aside, however, into the Palazzo Pubblico really to feel yourself a thrifty old mediævalist. The state affairs of the Republic were formerly transacted here, but it now gives shelter to modern law-courts and other prosy business. I was marched through a number of vaulted halls and chambers, which, in the intervals of the administrative sessions held in them, are peopled only by the great mouldering archaic fres-coes—anything but inanimate these even in their present ruin—that cover the walls and ceiling. The chief painters of the Sienese school lent a hand in producing the works I name, and you may complete there the connoisseurship in which, possibly, you will have embarked at the Academy. I say "possibly" to be very ju-dicial, my own observation having led me no great length. I have rather than otherwise cherished the thought that the Sienese school suffers one's eagerness peacefully to slumber—benig-nantly abstains in fact from whipping up a languid curiosity and a tepid faith. "A formidable rival to the Florentine," says some book—I forget which—into which I recently glanced. Not a bit of it thereupon boldly say I; the Florentines may rest on their laurels and the lounger on his lounge. The early painters of the two groups have indeed much in common; but the Florentines had the good fortune to see their efforts gathered up and applied by a few pre-eminent spirits, such as never came to the rescue of the groping Sienese. Fra Angelico and Ghirlandaio said all their feebler *confrères* dreamt of and a great deal more beside, but the inspiration of Simone Memmi and Ambrogio Lorenzetti and Sano di Pietro has a painful air of never efflorescing into a maximum. Sodoma and Beccafumi are to my taste a rather abor-tive maximum. But one should speak of them all gently—and I do, from my soul; for their labour, by their lights, has wrought a precious heritage of still-living colour and rich figure-peopled shadow for the echoing chambers of their old civic fortress. The faded frescoes cover the walls like quaintly-storied tapestries; in one way or another they cast their spell. If one owes a large debt of pleasure to pictorial art one comes to think tenderly and easily of its whole evolution, as of the conscious experience of a single mysterious, striving spirit, and one shrinks from saying rude things about any particular phase of it, just as one would from referring without precautions to some error or lapse in the life of a person one esteemed. You don't care to remind a grizzled veteran of his defeats, and why should we linger in Siena to talk about Beccafumi? I by no means go so far as to say, with an amateur with whom I have just been discussing the matter, that "Sodoma is a precious poor painter and Beccafumi no painter at all"; but, opportunity being limited, I am willing to let the remark about Beccafumi pass for true. With regard to Sodoma, I remember seeing four years ago in the choir of the Cathedral of Pisa a certain small dusky specimen of the painter—an Abraham and Isaac, if I am not mistaken—which was charged with a gloomy grace. One rarely meets him in general collections, and I had never done so till the other day. He was not prolific, apparently; he had however his own elegance, and his rarity is a part of it.

Here in Siena are a couple of dozen scattered frescoes and three or four canvases; his masterpiece, among others, an harmonious Descent from the Cross. I wouldn't give a fig for the equilibrium of the figures or the ladders; but while it lasts the scene is all intensely solemn and graceful and sweet—too sweet for so bitter a subject. Sodoma's women are strangely sweet; an imaginative sense of morbid appealing attitude—as notably in the sentimental, the pathetic, but the none the less pleasant, "Swooning of Saint Catherine," the great Sienese heroine, at San Domenico—seems to me the author's finest accomplishment. His frescoes have all the same almost appealing evasion of difficulty, and a kind of mild melancholy which I am inclined to think the sincerest part of them, for it strikes me as practically the artist's depressed suspicion of his own want of force. Once he determined, however, that if he couldn't be strong he would make capital of his weakness, and painted the Christ bound to the Column, of the Academy. Here he got much nearer and I have no doubt mixed his colours with his tears; but the result can't be better described than by saying that it is, pictorially, the first of the modern Christs. Unfortunately it hasn't been the last.

The main strength of Sienese art went possibly into the erection of the Cathedral, and yet even here the strength is not of the greatest strain. If, however, there are more interesting temples in Italy, there are few more richly and variously scenic and splendid, the comparative meagreness of the architectural idea being overlaid by a marvellous wealth of ingenious detail. Opposite the church—with the dull old archbishop's palace on one side and a dismantled residence of the late Grand Duke of Tuscany on the other—is an ancient hospital with a big stone bench running all along its front. Here I have sat awhile every morning for a week, like a philosophic convalescent, watching the florid façade of the cathedral glitter against the deep blue sky. It has been lavishly restored of late years, and the fresh white marble of the densely clustered pinnacles and statues and beasts and flowers flashes in the sunshine like a mosaic of jewels. There is more of this goldsmith's work in stone than I can remember or describe; it is piled up over three great doors with immense margins of exquisite decorative sculpture—still in the ancient cream-coloured marble—and beneath three sharp pediments embossed with images relieved against red marble and tipped with golden mosaics. It is in the highest degree fantastic and luxuriant—it is on the whole very lovely. As a triumph of the many-hued it prepares you for the interior, where the same parti-coloured splendour is endlessly at play—a confident complication of harmonies and contrasts and of the minor structural refinements and braveries. The internal surface is mainly wrought in alternate courses of black and white marble; but as the latter has been dimmed by the centuries to a fine mild brown the place is all a concert of relieved and dispersed glooms. Save for Pinturicchio's brilliant frescoes in the Sacristy there are no pictures to speak of; but the pavement is covered with many elaborate designs in black and white mosaic after cartoons by Beccafumi. The patient skill of these compositions makes them a rare piece of decoration; yet even here the friend whom I lately quoted rejects this over-ripe fruit of the Sienese school. The designs are nonsensical, he declares, and all his admiration is for the cunning artisans who have imitated the hatchings and shadings and hair-strokes of the pencil by the finest curves of inserted black stone. But the true romance of handiwork at Siena is to be seen in the wondrous stalls of the choir, under the coloured light of the great wheel-window. Wood-carving has ever been a cherished craft of the place, and the best masters of the art during the fifteenth century lavished themselves on this prodigious task. It is the frost-work on one's window-panes interpreted in polished oak. It would be hard to find, doubtless, a more moving illustration of the peculiar patience, the sacred candour, of the great time. Into such artistry as this the author seems to put more of his personal substance than into any other; he has to wrestle not only with his subject, but with his material. He is richly fortunate when his subject is charming—when his devices, inventions and fantasies spring lightly to his hand; for in the material itself, after age and use have ripened and polished and darkened it to the richness of ebony and to a greater warmth there is something surpassingly delectable and venerable. Wander behind the altar at Siena when the chanting is over and the incense has faded, and look well at the stalls of the Barili.*

[1874]

····· *i i* .······

I leave the impression noted in the foregoing pages to tell its own small story, but have it on my conscience to wonder, in this connection, quite candidly and publicly and by way of due penance, at the scantness of such first-fruits of my sensibility. I was to see Siena repeatedly in the years to follow, I was to know her better, and I would say that I was to do her an ampler justice didn't that remark seem to reflect a little on my earlier poor judgment. This judgment strikes me to-day as having fallen short—true as it may be that I find ever a value, or at least an interest, even in the moods and humours and lapses of any brooding, musing or fantasticating observer to whom the finer sense of things is *on the whole* not closed. If he has on a given occasion nodded or stumbled or strayed, this fact by itself speaks to me of him—speaks to me, that is, of his faculty and his idiosyncrasies, and I care nothing for the ap-

* Sixteenth-century wood carving done by the brothers Antonio and Giovanni Barili.

plication of his faculty unless it be, first of all, in itself interesting. Which may serve as my reply to any objection here
breaking out—on the ground that if a spectator's languors are
evidence, of a sort, about that personage, they are scarce evidence about the case before him, at least if the case be important. I let my perhaps rather weak expression of the sense of
Siena stand, at any rate—for the sake of what I myself read
into it; but I should like to amplify it by other memories, and
would do so eagerly if I might here enjoy the space. The
difficulty for these rectifications is that if the early vision has
failed of competence or of full felicity, if initiation has thus
been slow, so, with renewals and extensions, so, with the larger
experience, one hindrance is exchanged for another. There is
quite such a possibility as having lived into a relation too much
to be able to make a statement of it.

I remember on one occasion arriving very late of a summer
night, after an almost unbroken run from London, and the
note of that approach—I was the only person alighting at the
station below the great hill of the little fortress city, under
whose at once frowning and gaping gate I must have passed, in
the warm darkness and the absolute stillness, very much after
the felt fashion of a person of importance about to be enor-
mously incarcerated—gives me, for preservation thus belated,
the pitch, as I may call it, at various times, though always at one
season, of an almost systematised æsthetic use of the place. It
wasn't to be denied that the immensely better "accommodations" instituted by the multiplying, though alas more bustling,
years had to be recognised as supplying a basis, comparatively
prosaic if one would, to that luxury. No sooner have I written
which words, however, than I find myself adding that one
"wouldn't," that one doesn't—doesn't, that is, consent now to
regard the then "new" hotel (pretty old indeed by this time) as
anything but an aid to a free play of perception. The strong and
rank old Arme d'Inghilterra, in the darker street, had passed
away; but its ancient rival the Aquila Nera put forth claims to
modernisation, and the Grand Hotel, the still fresher flower of
modernity near the gate by which you enter from the station,
takes on to my present remembrance a mellowness as of all
sorts of comfort, cleanliness and kindness. The particular facts,

those of the visit I began here by alluding to and those of still others, at all events, inveterately made in June or early in July, enter together into a fusion as of hot golden-brown objects seen through the practicable crevices of shutters drawn upon high, cool, darkened rooms where the scheme of the scene involved longish days of quiet work, with late afternoon emergence and contemplation waiting on the better or the worse conscience. I thus associate the compact world of the admirable hilltop, the world of a predominant golden-brown, with a general invocation of sensibility and fancy, and think of myself as going forth into the lingering light of summer evenings all attuned to intensity of the idea of compositional beauty, or in other words, freely speaking, to the question of colour, to intensity of picture. To communicate with Siena in this charming way was thus, I admit, to have no great margin for the prosecution of inquiries, but I am not sure that it wasn't, little by little, to feel the whole combination of elements better than by a more exemplary method, and this from beginning to end of the scale.

More of the elements indeed, for memory, hang about the days that were ushered in by that straight flight from the north than about any other series—if partly, doubtless, but because of my having then stayed longest. I specify it at all events for fond reminiscence as the year, the only year, at which I was present at the Palio, the earlier one, the series of furious horse-races between elected representatives of different quarters of the town taking place toward the end of June, as the second and still more characteristic exhibition of the same sort is appointed to the month of August; a spectacle that I am far from speaking of as the finest flower of my old and perhaps even a little faded cluster of impressions, but which smudges that special sojourn as with the big thumb-mark of a slightly soiled and decidedly ensanguined hand. For really, after all, the great loud gaudy romp or heated frolic, simulating ferocity if not achieving it, that is the annual pride of the town, was not intrinsically, to my view, extraordinarily impressive—in spite of its bristling with all due testimony to the passionate Italian clutch of any pretext for costume and attitude and utterance, for mumming and masquerading and raucously representing; the vast cheap vividness rather somehow refines itself, and the swarm and hub-

bub of the immense square melt, to the uplifted sense of a very
high-placed balcony of the overhanging Chigi palace, where
everything was superseded but the intenser passage, across the
ages, of the great Renaissance tradition of architecture and the
infinite sweetness of the waning golden day. The Palio, indu-
bitably, was *criard* [loud]—and the more so for quite monop-
olising, at Siena, the note of crudity; and much of it demanded
doubtless of one's patience a due respect for the long local
continuity of such things; it drops into its humoured position,
however, in any retrospective command of the many brave
aspects of the prodigious place. Not that I am pretending here,
even for rectification, to take these at all in turn; I only go on
a little with my rueful glance at the marked gaps left in my
original report of sympathies entertained.

I bow my head for instance to the mystery of my not having
mentioned that the coolest and freshest flower of the day was
ever that of one's constant renewal of a charmed homage to
Pinturicchio, coolest and freshest and signally youngest and
most matutinal (as distinguished from merely primitive or crepuscular) of painters, in the library or sacristy of the Cathedral.
Did I *always* find time before work to spend half-an-hour of
immersion, under that splendid roof, in the clearest and tenderest, the very cleanest and "straightest," as it masters our
envious credulity, of all storied fresco-worlds? This wondrous
apartment, a monument in itself to the ancient pride and power
of the Church, and which contains an unsurpassed treasure of
gloriously illuminated missals, psalters and other vast parchment folios, almost each of whose successive leaves gives the
impression of rubies, sapphires and emeralds set in gold and
practically embedded in the page, offers thus to view, after a
fashion splendidly sustained, a pictorial record of the career of
Pope Pius II, Æneas Sylvius of the Siena Piccolomini (who
gave him for an immediate successor a second of their name),
most profanely literary of Pontiffs and last of would-be Cru-
saders, whose adventures and achievements under Pinturicchio's brush smooth themselves out for us very much to the
tune of the "stories" told by some fine old man of the world, at
the restful end of his life, to the cluster of his grandchildren.
The end of Æneas Sylvius was not restful; he died at Ancona

in troublous times, preaching war, and attempting to make it, against the then terrific Turk; but over no great worldly personal legend, among those of men of arduous affairs, arches a fairer, lighter or more pacific memorial vault than the shining Libreria of Siena. I seem to remember having it and its unfrequented enclosing precinct so often all to myself that I must indeed mostly have resorted to it for a prompt benediction on the day. Like no other strong solicitation, among artistic appeals to which one may compare it up and down the whole wonderful country, is the felt neighbouring presence of the overwrought Cathedral in its little proud possessive town: you may so often feel by the week at a time that it stands there really for your own personal enjoyment, your romantic convenience, your small wanton æsthetic use. In such a light shines for me, at all events, under such an accumulation and complication of tone flushes and darkens and richly recedes for me, across the years, the treasure-house of many-coloured marbles in the untrodden, the drowsy, empty Sienese square. One could positively do, in the free exercise of any responsible fancy or luxurious taste, what one would with it.

But that proposition holds true, after all, for almost any mild pastime of the incurable student of loose meanings and stray relics and odd references and dim analogies in an Italian hill-city bronzed and seasoned by the ages. I ought perhaps, for justification of the right to talk, to have plunged into the Siena archives of which, on one occasion, a kindly custodian gave me, in rather dusty and stuffy conditions, as the incident vaguely comes back to me, a glimpse that was like a moment's stand at the mouth of a deep, dark mine. I didn't descend into the pit; I did, instead of this, a much idler and easier thing: I simply went every afternoon, my stint of work over, I like to recall, for a musing stroll upon the Lizza*—the Lizza which had its own unpretentious but quite insidious art of meeting the lover of old stories half-way. The great and subtle thing, if you are not a strenuous specialist, in places of a heavily charged historic consciousness, is to profit by the sense of that consciousness—or in other words to cultivate a relation with the oracle—after the

* A public park.

fashion that suits yourself; so that if the general after-taste of experience, experience at large, the fine distilled essence of the matter, seems to breathe, in such a case, from the very stones and to make a thick strong liquor of the very air, you may thus gather as you pass what is most to your purpose; which is more the indestructible mixture of lived things, with its concentrated lingering odour, than any interminable list of numbered chapters and verses. Chapters and verses, literally scanned, refuse coincidence, mostly, with the divisional proprieties of your own pile of manuscript—which is but another way of saying, in short, that if the Lizza is a mere fortified promontory of the great Sienese hill, serving at once as a stronghold for the present military garrison and as a planted and benched and band-standed walk and recreation-ground for the citizens, so I could never, toward close of day, either have enough of it or yet feel the vaguest saunterings there to be vain. They were vague with the qualification always of that finer massing, as one wandered off, of the bronzed and seasoned element, the huge rock pedestal, the bravery of walls and gates and towers and palaces and loudly asserted dominion; and then of that pervaded or mildly infested air in which one feels the experience of the ages, of which I just spoke, to be exquisitely in solution; and lastly of the wide, strange, sad, beautiful horizon, a rim of far mountains that always pictured, for the leaner on old rubbed and smoothed parapets at the sunset hour, a country not exactly blighted or deserted, but that had had its life, on an immense scale, and had gone, with all its memories and relics, into rather austere, in fact into almost grim and misanthropic, retirement. This was a manner and a mood, at any rate, in all the land, that favoured in the late afternoons the divinest landscape blues and purples—not to speak of its favouring still more my practical contention that the whole guarded headland in question, with the immense ramparts of golden brown and red that dropped into vineyards and orchards and cornfields and all the rustic elegance of the Tuscan *podere* [farm], was knitting for me a chain of unforgettable hours; to the justice of which claim let these divagations testify.

It wasn't, however, that one mightn't without disloyalty to that scheme of profit seek impressions further afield—though indeed I may best say of such a matter as the long pilgrimage to the pictured convent of Monte Oliveto that it but played on the same fine chords as the overhanging, the far-gazing Lizza. What it came to was that one simply put to the friendly test, as it were, the mood and manner of the country. This remembrance is precious, but the demonstration of that sense as of a great heaving region stilled by some final shock and returning thoughtfully, in fact tragically, on itself, couldn't have been more pointed. The long-drawn rural road I refer to, stretching over hill and dale and to which I devoted the whole of the longest day of the year—I was in a small single-horse conveyance, of which I had already made appreciative use, and with a driver as disposed as myself ever to sacrifice speed to contemplation—is doubtless familiar now with the rush of the motor-car; the thought of whose free dealings with the solitude of Monte Oliveto makes me a little ruefully reconsider, I confess, the spirit in which I have elsewhere in these pages, on behalf of the lust, the landscape lust, of the eyes, acknowledged our general increasing debt to that vehicle. For that we met nothing whatever, as I seem at this distance of time to recall, while we gently trotted and trotted through the splendid summer hours and a dry desolation that yet somehow smiled and smiled, was part of the charm and the intimacy of the whole impression—the impression that culminated at last, before the great cloistered square, lonely, bleak and stricken, in the almost aching vision, more frequent in the Italy of to-day than anywhere in the world, of the uncalculated waste of a myriad forms of piety, forces of labour, beautiful fruits of genius. However, one gaped above all things for the impression, and what one mainly asked was that it should be strong of its kind. That was the case, I think I couldn't but feel, at every moment of the couple of hours I spent in the vast, cold, empty shell, out of which the Benedictine brotherhood sheltered there for ages had lately been turned by the strong arm of a secular State. There was but one good brother left, a very lean and tough survivor, a dusky, elderly, friendly Abbate, of an indescribable type and a perfect manner, of whom I think I felt immediately thereafter that I should have liked to say much, but as to whom I must have yielded to the fact that ingenious and vivid com-

memoration was even then in store for him. Literary portraiture had marked him for its own, and in the short story of *Un
Saint*, one of the most finished of contemporary French *nou-
velles*, the art and the sympathy of Monsieur Paul Bourget*
preserve his interesting image. He figures in the beautiful tale,
the Abbate of the desolate cloister and of those comparatively
quiet years, as a clean, clear type of sainthood; a circumstance
this in itself to cause a fond analyst of other than "Latin" race
(model and painter in this case having their Latinism so
strongly in common) almost endlessly to meditate. Oh, the
unutterable differences in any scheme or estimate of physiognomic values, in any range of sensibility to expressional association, among observers of different, of inevitably more or less
opposed, traditional and "racial" points of view! One had heard
convinced Latins—or at least I had!—speak of situations of
trust and intimacy in which they couldn't have endured near
them a Protestant or, as who should say for instance, an Anglo-
Saxon; but I was to remember my own private attempt to
measure such a change of sensibility as might have permitted
the prolonged close approach of the dear dingy, half-starved,
very possibly all heroic, and quite ideally urbane Abbate. The
depth upon depth of things, the cloud upon cloud of associations, on one side and the other, that would have had to change
first!

To which I may add nevertheless that since one ever supremely invoked intensity of impression and abundance of
character, I feasted my fill of it at Monte Oliveto, and that for
that matter this would have constituted my sole refreshment in
the vast icy void of the blighted refectory if I hadn't bethought
myself of bringing with me a scrap of food, too scantly apportioned, I recollect—very scantly indeed, since my *cocchiere*
[coach driver] was to share with me—by my purveyor at Siena.
Our tragic—even if so tenderly tragic—entertainer had nothing to give us; but the immemorial cold of the enormous monastic interior in which we smilingly fasted would doubtless
not have had for me without that such a wealth of reference.

* A popular but minor French novelist, Bourget (1852–1935) and James
became friends in the mid-1880s and spent time together in Italy.

I was to have "liked" the whole adventure, so I must somehow have liked that; by which remark I am recalled to the special treasure of the desecrated temple, those extraordinarily strong and brave frescoes of Luca Signorelli and Sodoma that adorn, in admirable condition, several stretches of cloister wall. These creations in a manner took care of themselves; aided by the blue of the sky above the cloister-court they glowed, they insistently lived; I remember the frigid prowl through all the rest of the bareness, including that of the big dishonoured church and that even of the Abbate's abysmally resigned testimony to his mere human and personal situation; and then, with such a force of contrast and effect of relief, the great sheltered sun-flares and colour-patches of scenic composition and design where a couple of hands centuries ago turned to dust had so wrought the defiant miracle of life and beauty that the effect is of a garden blooming among ruins. Discredited somehow, since they all would, the destroyers themselves, the ancient piety, the general spirit and intention, but still bright and assured and sublime—practically, enviably immortal—the other, the still subtler, the all æsthetic good faith.

[1909]

Ravenna

I write these lines on a cold Swiss mountain-top, shut in by an intense white mist from any glimpse of the under-world of lovely Italy; but as I jotted down the other day in the ancient capital of Honorius and Theodoric the few notes of which they are composed, I let the original date stand for local colour's sake. Its mere look, as I transcribe it, emits a grateful glow in the midst of the Alpine rawness, and gives a depressed imagination something tangible to grasp while awaiting the return of fine weather. For Ravenna was glowing, less than a week since, as I edged along the narrow strip of shadow binding one side of the empty, white streets. After a long, chill spring the summer this year descended upon Italy with a sudden jump and an ominous hot breath. I stole away from Florence in the night, and even on top of the Apennines, under the dull star-light and in the rushing train, one could but sit and pant perspiringly.

At Bologna I found a festa, or rather two festas, a civil and a religious, going on in mutual mistrust and disparagement. The civil, that of the Statuto, was the one fully national Italian holiday as by law established—the day that signalises every-where over the land at once its achieved and hard-won unifi-cation; the religious was a jubilee of certain local churches. The latter is observed by the Bolognese parishes in couples, and comes round for each couple but once in ten years—an ar-rangement by which the faithful at large insure themselves a liberal recurrence of expensive processions. It wasn't my busi-ness to distinguish the sheep from the goats, the pious from the profane, the prayers from the scoffers; it was enough that, melting together under the scorching sun, they filled the admirably solid city with a flood of spectacular life. The combination at one point was really dramatic. While a long procession of priests and young virgins in white veils, bearing tapers, marshalled itself in one of the streets, a review of the King's troops went forward outside the town. On its return a large detachment of cavalry passed across the space where the incense was burning, the pictured banners swaying and the litany being droned, and checked the advance of the little ecclesiastical troop. The long vista of the street, between the porticoes, was festooned with garlands and scarlet and tinsel; the robes and crosses and canopies of the priests, the clouds of perfumed smoke and the white veils of the maidens, were resolved by the hot bright air into a gorgeous medley of colour, across which the mounted soldiers rattled and flashed as if it had been a conquering army trampling on an embassy of propitiation. It was, to tell the truth, the first time an Italian festa had really exhibited to my eyes the genial glow and the romantic particulars promised by song and story; and I confess that those eyes found more pleasure in it than they were to find an hour later in the picturesque on canvas as one observes it in the Pinacoteca. I found myself scowling most unmercifully at Guido and Domenichino.

For Ravenna, however, I had nothing but smiles—grave, reflective, philosophic smiles, I hasten to add, such as accord with the historic dignity, not to say the mortal sunny sadness, of the place. I arrived there in the evening, before, even at drowsy Ravenna, the festa of the Statuto had altogether put itself to bed. I immediately strolled forth from the inn, and found it sitting up awhile longer on the piazza, chiefly at the café door, listening to the band of the garrison by the light of a dozen or so of feeble tapers, fastened along the front of the palace of the Government. Before long, however, it had dispersed and departed, and I was left alone with the grey illumination and with an affable citizen whose testimony as to the manners and customs of Ravenna I had aspired to obtain. I had, borrowing confidence from prompt observation, suggested deferentially that it wasn't the liveliest place in the world, and my friend admitted that it was in fact not a seat of ardent life.

But had I seen the Corso? Without seeing the Corso one didn't exhaust the possibilities. The Corso of Ravenna, of a hot summer night, had an air of surprising seclusion and repose. Here and there in an upper closed window glimmered a light; my companion's footsteps and my own were the only sounds; not a creature was within sight. The suffocating air helped me to believe for a moment that I walked in the Italy of Boccaccio, hand-in-hand with the plague, through a city which had lost half its population by pestilence and the other half by flight. I turned back into my inn profoundly satisfied. This at last was the old-world dullness of a prime distillation; this at last was antiquity, history, repose.

The impression was largely confirmed and enriched on the following day; but it was obliged at an early stage of my visit to give precedence to another—the lively perception, namely, of the thinness of my saturation with Gibbon and the other sources of legend. At Ravenna the waiter at the café and the coachman who drives you to the Pine-Forest allude to Galla Placidia and Justinian as to any attractive topic of the hour; wherever you turn you encounter some fond appeal to your historic presence of mind. For myself I could only attune my spirit vaguely to so ponderous a challenge, could only feel I was breathing an air of prodigious records and relics. I conned my guide-book and looked up at the great mosaics, and then fumbled at poor Murray again for some intenser light on the court of Justinian; but I can imagine that to a visitor more intimate with the originals of the various great almond-eyed mosaic portraits in the vaults of the churches these extremely curious works of art may have a really formidable interest. I found in the place at large, by daylight, the look of a vast straggling depopulated village. The streets with hardly an exception are grass-grown, and though I walked about all day I failed to encounter a single wheeled vehicle. I remember no shop but the little establishment of an urbane photographer, whose views of the Pineta, the great legendary pine-forest just without the town, gave me an irresistible desire to seek that refuge. There was no architecture to speak of; and though there are a great many large domiciles with aristocratic names they stand cracking and baking in the sun in no very comfortable fashion. The houses have for the most part an all but rustic rudeness; they are low and featureless and shabby, as well as interspersed with high garden walls over which the long arms of tangled vines hang motionless into the stagnant streets. Here and there in all this dreariness, in some particularly silent and grassy corner, rises an old brick church with a front more or less spoiled by cheap modernisation, and a strange cylindrical campanile pierced with small arched windows and extremely suggestive of the fifth century. These churches constitute the palpable interest of Ravenna, and their own principal interest, after thirteen centuries of well-intentioned spoliation, resides in their unequalled collection of early Christian mosaics. It is an interest simple, as who should say, almost to harshness, and leads one's attention along a straight and narrow way. There are older churches in Rome, and churches which, looked at as museums, are more variously and richly informing; but in Rome you stumble at every step on some curious pagan memorial, often beautiful enough to make your thoughts wander far from the strange stiff primitive Christian forms.

Ravenna, on the other hand, began with the Church, and all her monuments and relics are harmoniously rigid. By the middle of the first century she possessed an exemplary saint, Apollinaris, a disciple of Peter, to whom her two finest places of worship are dedicated. It was to one of these, jocosely entitled the "new," that I first directed my steps. I lingered outside awhile and looked at the great red, barrel-shaped bell-towers, so rusty, so crumbling, so archaic, and yet so resolute to ring in another century or two, and then went in to the coolness, the shining marble columns, the queer old sculptured slabs and sarcophagi and the long mosaics that scintillated, under the roof, along the wall of the nave. San Apollinare Nuovo, like most of its companions, is a magazine of early Christian odds and ends; fragments of yellow marble encrusted with quaint sculptured emblems of primitive dogma; great rough troughs, containing the bones of old bishops; episcopal chairs with the marble worn narrow by centuries of pressure from the solid episcopal person; slabs from the fronts of old pulpits, covered with carven hieroglyphics of an almost Egyptian abstruseness—lambs and stags and fishes and beasts of theological affinities even less apparent. Upon all these strange things the strange figures in the great mosaic panorama look down, with coloured cheeks and staring eyes, lifelike enough to speak to you and answer your wonderment and tell you in bad Latin of the decadence that it was in such and such a fashion they believed and worshipped. First, on each side, near the door, are houses and ships and various old landmarks of Ravenna; then begins a long procession, on one side, of twenty-two white-robed virgins and three obsequious magi, terminating in a throne bearing the Madonna and Child, surrounded by four angels; on the other side, of an equal number of male saints (twenty-five, that is) holding crowns in their hands and leading to a Saviour enthroned between angels of singular expressiveness. What it is these long slim seraphs express I cannot quite say, but they have an odd, knowing, sidelong look out of the narrow ovals of their eyes which, though not without sweetness, would certainly make me murmur a defensive prayer or so were I to find myself alone in the church towards dusk. All this work is of the latter part of the sixth century and brilliantly preserved. The gold backgrounds twinkle as if they had been inserted yesterday, and here and there a figure is executed almost too much in the modern manner to be interesting; for the charm of mosaic work is, to my sense, confined altogether to the infancy of the art. The great Christ, in the series of which I speak, is quite an elaborate picture, and yet he retains enough of the orthodox stiffness to make him impressive in the simpler, elder sense. He is clad in a purple robe, even as an emperor, his hair and beard are artfully curled, his eyebrows arched, his complexion brilliant, his whole aspect such a one as the popular mind may have attributed to Honorius or Valentinian. It is all very Byzantine, and yet I found in it much of that interest which is inseparable, to a facile imagination, from all early representations of our Lord. Practically they are no more authentic than the more or less plausible inventions of Ary Scheffer and Holman Hunt;* in spite of which they borrow a certain value, factitious perhaps but irresistible, from the

* Scheffer (1785–1858), a minor French painter, and Hunt (1827–1910), an English pre-Raphaelite painter.

mere fact that they are twelve or thirteen centuries less distant from the original. It is something that this was the way the people in the sixth century imagined Jesus to have looked; the image has suffered by so many the fewer accretions. The great purple-robed monarch on the wall of Ravenna is at least a very potent and positive Christ, and the only objection I have to make to him is that though in this character he must have had a full apportionment of divine foreknowledge he betrays no apprehension of Dr. Channing and M. Renan.* If one's preference lies, for distinctness' sake, between the old plainness and the modern fantasy, one must admit that the plainness has here a very grand outline.

I spent the rest of the morning in charmed transition between the hot yellow streets and the cool grey interiors of the churches. The greyness everywhere was lighted up by the scintillation, on vault and entablature, of mosaics more or less archaic, but always brilliant and elaborate, and everywhere too by the same deep amaze of the fact that, while centuries had worn themselves away and empires risen and fallen, these little cubes of coloured glass had stuck in their allotted places and kept their freshness. I have no space for a list of the various shrines so distinguished, and, to tell the truth, my memory of them has already become a very generalised and undiscriminated record. The total aspect of the place, its sepulchral stillness, its absorbing perfume of evanescence and decay and mortality, confounds the distinctions and blurs the details. The Cathedral, which is vast and high, has been excessively modernised, and was being still more so by a lavish application of tinsel and cotton-velvet in preparation for the centenary feast of Saint Apollinaris, which befalls next month. Things on this occasion are to be done handsomely, and a fair Ravennese informed me that a single family had contributed three thousand francs towards a month's vesper-music. It seemed to me hereupon that I should like in the August twilight to wander into the quiet nave of San Apollinare, and look up at the great

* William Ellery Channing (1780–1842), the founder of American Unitarianism, and Joseph Renan (1823–1892), the French author of a controversial life of Jesus.

mosaics through the resonance of some fine chanting. I remember distinctly enough, however, the tall basilica of San Vitale, of octagonal shape, like an exchange or custom-house—modelled, I believe, upon Saint Sophia at Constantinople. It has a great span of height and a great solemnity, as well as a choir densely pictured over on arch and apse with mosaics of the time of Justinian. These are regular pictures, full of movement, gesture and perspective, and just enough sobered in hue by time to bring home their remoteness. In the middle of the church, under the great dome, sat an artist whom I envied, making at an effective angle a study of the choir and its broken lights, its decorated altar and its encrusted twinkling walls. The picture, when finished, will hang, I suppose, on the library wall of some person of taste; but even if it is much better than is probable—I didn't look at it—all his taste won't tell the owner, unless he has been there, in just what a soundless, mouldering, out-of-the-way corner of old Italy it was painted. An even better place for an artist fond of dusky architectural nooks, except that here the dusk is excessive and he would hardly be able to tell his green from his red, is the extraordinary little church of the Santi Nazaro e Celso, otherwise known as the mausoleum of Galla Placidia. This is perhaps on the whole the spot in Ravenna where the impression is of most sovereign authority and most thrilling force. It consists of a narrow low-browed cave, shaped like a Latin cross, every inch of which except the floor is covered with dense symbolic mosaics. Before you and on each side, through the thick brown light, loom three enormous barbaric sarcophagi, containing the remains of potentates of the Lower Empire. It is as if history had burrowed under ground to escape from research and you had fairly run it to earth. On the right lie the ashes of the Emperor Honorius, and in the middle those of his sister, Galla Placidia, a lady who, I believe, had great adventures. On the other side rest the bones of Constantius III. The place might be a small natural grotto lined with glimmering mineral substances, and there is something quite tremendous in being shut up so closely with these three imperial ghosts. The shadow of the great Roman name broods upon the huge sepulchres and abides forever within the narrow walls.

But still other memories hang about than those of primitive bishops and degenerate emperors. Byron lived here and Dante died here, and the tomb of the one poet and the dwelling of the other are among the advertised appeals. The grave of Dante, it must be said, is anything but Dantesque, and the whole precinct is disposed with that odd vulgarity of taste which distinguishes most modern Italian tributes to greatness. The author of *The Divine Comedy* commemorated in stucco, even in a slumbering corner of Ravenna, is not "sympathetic." Fortunately of all poets he least needs a monument, as he was preeminently an architect in diction and built himself his temple of fame in verses more solid than Cyclopean blocks. If Dante's tomb is not Dantesque, so neither is Byron's house Byronic, being a homely, shabby, two-storied dwelling, directly on the street, with as little as possible of isolation and mystery. In Byron's time it was an inn, and it is rather a curious reflection that "Cain" and the "Vision of Judgement" should have been written at an hotel. The fact supplies a commanding precedent for self-abstraction to tourists at once sentimental and literary. I must declare indeed that my acquaintance with Ravenna considerably increased my esteem for Byron and helped to renew my faith in the sincerity of his inspiration. A man so much *de son temps* [of his own time] as the author of the above-named and other pieces can have spent two long years in this stagnant city only by the help of taking a great deal of disinterested pleasure in his own genius. He had indeed a notable pastime—the various churches are adorned with monuments of ancestral Guicciolis—but it is none the less obvious that Ravenna, fifty years ago, would have been an intolerably dull residence to a foreigner of distinction unequipped with intellectual resources. The hour one spends with Byron's memory then is almost compassionate. After all, one says to one's self as one turns away from the grandiloquent little slab in front of his house and looks down the deadly provincial vista of the empty, sunny street, the author of so many superb stanzas asked less from the world than he gave it. One of his diversions was to ride in the Pineta, which, beginning a couple of miles from the city, extends some twenty-five miles along the sands of the Adriatic. I drove out to it for Byron's sake, and

Dante's, and Boccaccio's, all of whom have interwoven it with their fictions, and for that of a possible whiff of coolness from the sea. Between the city and the forest, in the midst of malarious rice-swamps, stands the finest of the Ravennese churches, the stately temple of San Apollinare in Classe. The Emperor Augustus constructed hereabouts a harbour for fleets, which the ages have choked up, and which survives only in the title of this ancient church. Its extreme loneliness makes it doubly impressive. They opened the great doors for me, and let a shaft of heated air go wander up the beautiful nave between the twenty-four lustrous, pearly columns of cipollino marble, and mount the wide staircase of the choir and spend itself beneath the mosaics of the vault. I passed a memorable half-hour sitting in this wave of tempered light, looking down the cool grey avenue of the nave, out of the open door, at the vivid green swamps, and listening to the melancholy stillness. I rambled for an hour in the Wood of Associations, between the tall smooth, silvery stems of the pines, and beside a creek which led me to the outer edge of the wood and a view of white sails, gleaming and gliding behind the sand-hills. It was infinitely, it was nobly "quaint," but, as the trees stand at wide intervals and bear far aloft in the blue air but a little parasol of foliage, I suppose that, of a glaring summer day, the forest itself was only the more characteristic of its clime and country for being perfectly shadeless.

[1874]

Tuscan Cities

....

The cities I refer to are Leghorn, Pisa, Lucca and Pistoia, among which I have been spending the last few days. The most striking fact as to Leghorn, it must be conceded at the outset, is that, being in Tuscany, it should be so scantily Tuscan. The traveller curious in local colour must content himself with the deep blue expanse of the Mediterranean. The streets, away from the docks, are modern, genteel and rectangular; Liverpool might acknowledge them if it weren't for their clean-coloured, sun-bleached stucco. They are the offspring of the new industry which is death to the old idleness. Of interesting architecture, fruit of the old idleness or at least of the old leisure, Leghorn is singularly destitute. It has neither a church worth one's attention, nor a municipal palace, nor a museum, and it may claim the distinction, unique in Italy, of being the city of no pictures. In a shabby corner near the docks stands a statue of one of the elder Grand-Dukes of Tuscany, appealing to posterity on grounds now vague—chiefly that of having placed certain Moors under tribute. Four colossal negroes, in very bad bronze, are chained to the base of the monument, which forms with their assistance a sufficiently fantastic group; but to patronise the arts is not the line of the Livornese, and for want of the slender annuity which would keep its precinct sacred this curious memorial is buried in dockyard rubbish. I must add that on the other hand there is a very well-conditioned and, in attitude and gesture, extremely natural and familiar statue of Cavour in one of the city squares, and in another a couple of effigies of recent Grand-Dukes, represented, that is dressed, or rather undressed, in the character of heroes of Plutarch. Leghorn is a city of magnificent spaces, and it was so long a journey from the sidewalk to the pedestal of these images that I never took the time to go and read the inscriptions. And in truth, vaguely, I bore the originals a grudge, and wished to know as little about them as possible; for it seemed to me that as *patres patriæ* [fathers of their country], in their degree, they might have decreed that the great blank, ochre-faced piazza should be a trifle less ugly. There is a distinct amenity, however, in any experience of Italy almost anywhere, and I shall probably in the future not be above sparing a light regret to several of the hours of which the one I speak of was composed. I shall remember a large cool bourgeois villa in the garden of a noiseless suburb—a middle-aged Villa Franco (I owe it as a genial pleasant *pension* the tribute of recognition), roomy and stony, as an Italian villa should be. I shall remember that, as I sat in the garden and, looking up from my book, saw through a gap in the shrubbery the red house-tiles against the deep blue sky and the grey underside of the ilex-leaves turned up by the Mediterranean breeze, it was all still quite Tuscany, if Tuscany in the minor key.

If you should naturally desire, in such conditions, a higher intensity, you have but to proceed, by a very short journey, to Pisa—where, for that matter, you will seem to yourself to have hung about a good deal already, and from an early age. Few of us can have had a childhood so unblessed by contact with the arts as that one of its occasional diversions shan't have been a puzzled scrutiny of some alabaster model of the Leaning Tower under a glass cover in a back-parlour. Pisa and its monuments have, in other words, been industriously vulgarised, but it is astonishing how well they have survived the process. The charm of the place is in fact of a high order and but partially foreshadowed by the famous crookedness of its campanile. I felt it irresistibly and yet almost inexpressibly the other afternoon, as I made my way to the classic corner of the city through the warm drowsy air which nervous people come to inhale as a sedative. I was with an invalid companion who had had no sleep to speak of for a fortnight. "Ah! stop the carriage," she sighed, or yawned, as I could feel, deliciously, "in the shadow of this old slumbering palazzo, and let me sit here and close my eyes, and taste for an hour of oblivion." Once strolling over the grass, however, out of which the quartette of marble monuments rises, we awaked responsively enough to the present hour. Most people remember the happy remark of tasteful, old-fashioned Forsyth* (who touched a hundred other points in his "Italy" scarce less happily) as to the fact that the four famous objects are "fortunate alike in their society and their solitude." It must be admitted that they are more fortunate in their society than we felt ourselves to be in ours; for the scene presented the animated appearance for which, on any fine spring day, all the choicest haunts of ancient quietude in Italy are becoming yearly more remarkable. There were clamorous beggars at all the sculptured portals, and bait for beggars, in abundance, trailing in and out of them under convoy of loquacious ciceroni. I forget just how I apportioned the responsibility of intrusion, for it was not long before fellow-tourists and fellow-countrymen became a vague, deadened, muffled presence, that of the dentist's last words when he is giving you ether. They suffered mystic disintegration in the dense, bright, tranquil air, so charged with its own messages. The Cathedral and its companions are fortunate indeed in everything—fortunate in the spacious angle of the grey old city-wall which folds about them in their sculptured elegance like a strong protecting arm; fortunate in the broad greensward which stretches from the marble base of Cathedral and cemetery to the rugged foot of the rampart; fortunate in the little vagabonds who dot the grass, plucking daisies and exchanging Italian cries; fortunate in the pale-gold tone to which time and the soft sea-damp have mellowed and darkened their marble plates; fortunate, above all, in an indescribable grace of grouping, half hazard, half design, which insures them, in one's memory of things admired, very much the same isolated corner that they occupy in the charming city.

Of the smaller cathedrals of Italy I know none I prefer to that of Pisa; none that, on a moderate scale, produces more the impression of a great church. It has without so modest a measurability, represents so clean and compact a mass, that you are startled when you cross the threshold at the apparent space it encloses. An architect of genius, for all that he works with

* Joseph Forsyth (1763–1815), *Remarks on Antiquities, Arts, and Letters, During an Excursion into Italy, 1802–1803* (1813).

colossal blocks and cumbrous pillars, is certainly the most cunning of conjurors. The front of the Duomo is a small pyramidal screen, covered with delicate carvings and chasings, distributed over a series of short columns upholding narrow arches. It might be a sought imitation of goldsmith's work in stone, and the area covered is apparently so small that extreme fineness has been prescribed. How it is therefore that on the inner side of this façade the wall should appear to rise to a splendid height and to support one end of a ceiling as remote in its gilded grandeur, one could almost fancy, as that of St. Peter's; how it is that the nave should stretch away in such solemn vastness, the shallow transepts emphasise the grand impression and the apse of the choir hollow itself out like a dusky cavern fretted with golden stalactites, is all matter for exposition by a keener architectural analyst than I. To sit somewhere against a pillar where the vista is large and the incidents cluster richly, and vaguely revolve these mysteries without answering them, is the best of one's usual enjoyment of a great church. It takes no deep sounding to conclude indeed that a gigantic Byzantine Christ in mosaic, on the concave roof of the choir, contributes largely to the particular impression here as of very old and choice and original and individual things. It has even more of stiff solemnity than is common to works of its school, and prompts to more wonder than ever on the nature of the human mind at a time when such unlovely shapes could satisfy its conception of holiness. Truly pathetic is the fate of these huge mosaic idols, thanks to the change that has overtaken our manner of acceptance of them. Strong the contrast between the original sublimity of their pretensions and the way in which they flatter that free sense of the grotesque which the modern imagination has smuggled even into the appreciation of religious forms. They were meant to yield scarcely to the Deity itself in grandeur, but the only part they play now is to stare helplessly at our critical, our æsthetic patronage of them. The spiritual refinement marking the hither end of a progress hadn't, however, to wait for *us* to signalise it; it found expression three centuries ago in the beautiful specimen of the painter Sodoma on the wall of the choir. This latter, a small Sacrifice of Isaac, is one of the best examples of its exquisite author, and perhaps, as chance has it, the most perfect opposition that could be found in the way of the range of taste to the effect of the great mosaic. There are many painters more powerful than Sodoma—painters who, like the author of the mosaic, attempted and compassed grandeur; but none has a more persuasive grace, none more than he was to sift and chasten a conception till it should affect one with the sweetness of a perfectly distilled perfume.

Of the patient successive efforts of painting to arrive at the supreme refinement of such a work as the Sodoma the Campo Santo hard by offers a most interesting memorial. It presents a long, blank marble wall to the relative profaneness of the Cathedral close, but within it is a perfect treasure-house of art. This quadrangular defence surrounds an open court where weeds and wild roses are tangled together and a sunny stillness seems to rest consentingly, as if Nature had been won to consciousness of the precious relics committed to her. Something in the quality of the place recalls the collegiate cloisters of Oxford, but it must be added that this is the handsomest compliment to that seat of learning. The open arches of the quadrangles of Magdalen and Christ Church are not of mellow Carrara marble, nor do they offer to sight columns, slim and elegant, that seem to frame the unglazed windows of a cathedral. To be buried in the Campo Santo of Pisa, I may however further qualify, you need only be, or to have more or less anciently been, illustrious, and there is a liberal allowance both as to the character and degree of your fame. The most obtrusive object in one of the long vistas is a most complicated monument to Madame Catalani,* the singer, recently erected by her possibly too-appreciative heirs. The wide pavement is a mosaic of sepulchral slabs, and the walls, below the base of the paling frescoes, are encrusted with inscriptions and encumbered with urns and antique sarcophagi. The place is at once a cemetery and a museum, and its especial charm is its strange mixture of the active and the passive, of art and rest, of life and death. Originally its walls were one vast continuity of closely pressed frescoes; but now the great capricious scars and stains

* Angelica Catalani (1780–1849).

have come to outnumber the pictures, and the cemetery has grown to be a burial-place of pulverised masterpieces as well as of finished lives. The fragments of painting that remain are fortunately the best; for one is safe in believing that a host of undimmed neighbours would distract but little from the two great works of Orcagna. Most people know the "Triumph of Death" and the "Last Judgment" from descriptions and engravings; but to measure the possible good faith of imitative art one must stand there and see the painter's howling potentates dragged into hell in all the vividness of his bright hard colouring; see his feudal courtiers, on their palfreys, hold their noses at what they are so fast coming to; see his great Christ, in judgment, refuse forgiveness with a gesture commanding enough, really inhuman enough, to make virtue merciless forever. The charge that Michael Angelo borrowed his cursing Saviour from this great figure of Orcagna is more valid than most accusations of plagiarism; but of the two figures one at least could be spared. For direct, triumphant expressiveness these two superb frescoes have probably never been surpassed. The painter aims at no very delicate meanings, but he drives certain gross ones home so effectively that for a parallel to his process one must look to the art of the actor, the emphasising "point"-making mime. Some of his female figures are superb— they represent creatures of a formidable temperament.

There are charming women, however, on the other side of the cloister—in the beautiful frescoes of Benozzo Gozzoli. If Orcagna's work was appointed to survive the ravage of time it is a happy chance that it should be balanced by a group of performances of such a different temper. The contrast is the more striking that in subject the inspiration of both painters is strictly, even though superficially, theological. But Benozzo cares, in his theology, for nothing but the story, the scene and the drama—the chance to pile up palaces and spires in his backgrounds against pale blue skies cross-barred with pearly, fleecy clouds, and to scatter sculptured arches and shady trellises over the front, with every incident of human life going forward lightly and gracefully beneath them. Lightness and grace are the painter's great qualities, marking the hithermost limit of unconscious elegance, after which "style" and science and the wisdom of the serpent set in. His charm is natural fineness; a little more and we should have refinement—which is a very different thing. Like all *les délicats* [refined souls] of this world, as M. Renan calls them, Benozzo has suffered greatly. The space on the walls he originally covered with his Old Testament stories is immense; but his exquisite handiwork has peeled off by the acre, as one may almost say, and the latter compartments of the series are swallowed up in huge white scars, out of which a helpless head or hand peeps forth like those of creatures sinking into a quicksand. As for Pisa at large, although it is not exactly what one would call a mouldering city—for it has a certain well-aired cleanness and brightness, even in its supreme tranquillity—it affects the imagination very much in the same way as the Campo Santo. And, in truth, a city so ancient and deeply historic as Pisa is at every step but the burial-ground of a larger life than its present one. The wide empty streets, the goodly Tuscan palaces—which look as if about all of them there were a genteel private understanding, independent of placards, that they are to be let extremely cheap—the delicious relaxing air, the full-flowing yellow river, the lounging Pisani, smelling, metaphorically, their poppy-flowers, seemed to me all so many admonitions to resignation and oblivion. And this is what I mean by saying that the charm of Pisa (apart from its cluster of monuments) is a charm of a high order. The architecture has but a modest dignity; the lions are few; there are no fixed points for stopping and gaping. And yet the impression is profound; the charm is a moral charm. If I were ever to be incurably disappointed in life, if I had lost my health, my money, or my friends, if I were resigned forever-more to pitching my expectations in a minor key, I should go and invoke the Pisan peace. Its quietude would seem something more than a stillness—a hush. Pisa may be a dull place to live in, but it's an ideal place to wait for death.

Nothing could be more charming than the country between Pisa and Lucca—unless possibly the country between Lucca and Pistoia. If Pisa is dead Tuscany Lucca is Tuscany still living and enjoying, desiring and intending. The town is a charming mixture of antique "character" and modern inconsequence; and not only the town, but the country—the blooming romantic country which you admire from the famous promenade on the city-wall. The wall is of superbly solid and intensely "toned" brickwork and of extraordinary breadth, and its summit, planted with goodly trees and swelling here and there into bastions and outworks and little open gardens, surrounds the city with a circular lounging-place of a splendid dignity. This well-kept, shady, ivy-grown rampart reminded me of certain mossy corners of England; but it looks away to a prospect of more than English loveliness—a broad green plain where the summer yields a double crop of grain, and a circle of bright blue mountains speckled with high-hung convents and profiled castles and nestling villas, and traversed by valleys of a deeper and duskier blue. In one of the deepest and shadiest of these recesses one of the most "sympathetic" of small watering-places is hidden away yet awhile longer from easy invasion—the Baths to which Lucca has lent its name. Lucca is pre-eminently a city of churches; ecclesiastical architecture being indeed the only one of the arts to which it seems to have given attention. There are curious bits of domestic architecture, but no great palaces, and no importunate frequency of pictures. The Cathedral, however, sums up the merits of its companions and is a singularly noble and interesting church. Its peculiar boast is a wonderful inlaid front, on which horses and hounds and hunted beasts are lavishly figured in black marble over a white ground. What I chiefly appreciated in the grey solemnity of the nave and transepts was the superb effect of certain second-story Gothic arches—those which rest on the pavement being Lombard. These arches are delicate and slender, like those of the cloister at Pisa, and they play their part in the dusky upper air with real sublimity.

At Pistoia there is of course a Cathedral, and there is nothing unexpected in its being, externally at least, highly impressive; in its having a grand campanile at its door, a gaudy baptistery, in alternate layers of black and white marble, across the way, and a stately civic palace on either side. But even had I the space to do otherwise I should prefer to speak less of the particular objects of interest in the place than of the pleasure I found it to lounge away in the empty streets the quiet hours of a warm afternoon. To say where I lingered longest would be to tell of a little square before the hospital, out of which you look up at the beautiful frieze in coloured earthenware by the brothers Della Robbia, which runs across the front of the building. It represents the seven orthodox offices of charity and, with its brilliant blues and yellows and its tender expressiveness, brightens up amazingly, to the sense and soul, this little grey corner of the mediæval city. Pistoia is still mediæval. How grass-grown it seemed, how drowsy, how full of idle vistas and melancholy nooks! If nothing was supremely wonderful, everything was delicious.

[1874]

Other Tuscan Cities

..... i ....

I had scanted charming Pisa even as I had scanted great Siena in my original small report of it, my scarce more than stammering notes of years before; but even if there had been meagreness of mere gaping vision—which there in fact hadn't been—as well as insufficiency of public tribute, the indignity would soon have ceased to weigh on my conscience. For to this affection I was to return again still oftener than to the strong call of Siena; my eventual frequentations of Pisa, all merely impressionistic and amateurish as they might be—and I pretended, up and down the length of the land, to none other— leave me at the hither end of time with little more than a confused consciousness of exquisite *quality* on the part of the small sweet scrap of a place of ancient glory; a consciousness so pleadingly content to be general and vague that I shrink from pulling it to pieces. The Republic of Pisa fought with the Republic of Florence, through the ages, so ferociously and all but invincibly that what is so pale and languid in her to-day may well be the aspect of any civil or, still more, military creature bled and bled and bled at the "critical" time of its life. She has verily a just languor and is touchingly anæmic; the past history, or at any rate the present perfect acceptedness, of which condition hangs about her with the last grace of weakness, making her state in this particular the very secret of her irresistible appeal. I was to find the appeal, again and again, one of the sweetest, tenderest, even if not one of the fullest and richest impressions possible; and if I went back whenever I could it was very much as one doesn't indecently neglect a gentle invalid friend. The couch of the invalid friend, beautifully, appealingly resigned, has been wheeled, say, for the case, into the warm still garden, and your visit but consists of your sitting beside it with kind, discreet, testifying silences. Such is the figurative form under which the once rugged enemy of Florence, stretched at her length by the rarely troubled Arno, today presents herself; and I find my analogy complete even to my sense of the mere mild *séance,* the inevitably tacit communion or rather blank interchange, between motionless cripple and hardly more incurable admirer.

The terms of my enjoyment of Pisa scarce departed from that ideal—slow contemplative perambulations, rather late in the day and after work done mostly in the particular decent inn-room that was repeatedly my portion; where the sunny flicker of the river played up from below to the very ceiling, which, by the same sign, anciently and curiously raftered and hanging over my table at a great height, had been colour-pencilled into ornament as fine (for all practical purposes) as the page of a missal. I add to this, for remembrance, an inveteracy of evening idleness and of reiterated ices in front of one of the quiet cafés—quiet as everything at Pisa is quiet, or will certainly but in these latest days have ceased to be; one in especial so beautifully, so mysteriously void of bustle that almost always the neighbouring presence and admirable chatter of some group of the local University students would fall upon my ear, by the half-hour at a time, not less as a privilege, frankly, than as a clear-cut image of the young Italian mind and life, by which I lost nothing. I use such terms as "admirable" and "privilege," in this last most casual of connections—which was moreover no connection at all but what my attention made it—simply as an acknowledgment of the interest that might play there through some inevitable thoughts. These were, for that matter, intensely in keeping with the ancient scene and air: they dealt with the exquisite difference between that tone and type of ingenuous adolescence—in the mere relation of charmed *audition*—and other forms of juvenility of whose mental and material accent one had elsewhere met the assault. Civilised, charmingly civilised, were my loquacious neighbours—as how hadn't they to be, one asked oneself, through the use of a medium of speech that is in itself a sovereign saturation? *There* was the beautiful congruity of the happily-caught impression; the fact of my young men's general Tuscanism of tongue, which related them so on the spot to the whole historic consensus of things. It wasn't dialect—as it of course easily might have been elsewhere, at Milan, at Turin, at Bologna, at Naples; it was the clear Italian in which all the rest of the surrounding story was told, all the rest of the result of time recorded; and it made them delightful, prattling, unconscious men of the particular little constituted and bequeathed world which everything else that was charged with old meanings and old beauty referred to—all the more that their talk was never by any chance of romping games or deeds of violence, but kept flowering, charmingly and incredibly, into eager ideas and literary opinions and philosophic discussions and, upon my honour, vital questions.

They have taken me too far, for so light a reminiscence; but I claim for the loose web of my impressions at no point a heavier texture. Which comes back to what I was a moment ago saying—that just in proportion as you "feel" the morbid charm of Pisa you press on it gently, and this somehow even under stress of whatever respectful attention. I found this last impulse, at all events, so far as I was concerned, quite contentedly spend itself in a renewed sense of the simple large pacified felicity of such an afternoon aspect as that of the Lung' Arno, taken up or down its course; whether to within sight of small Santa Maria della Spina, the tiny, the delicate, the exquisite Gothic chapel perched where the quay drops straight, or, in the other direction, toward the melting perspective of the narrow local pleasure-ground, the rather thin and careless bosky grace of which recedes, beside the stream whose very turbidity pleases, to a middle distance of hot and tangled and exuberant rural industry and a proper blue horizon of Carrara mountains. The Pisan Lung' Arno is shorter and less featured and framed than the Florentine, but it has the fine accent of a marked curve and is quite as bravely Tuscan; witness the type of river-fronting palace which, in half-a-dozen massive specimens, the last word of the anciently "handsome," are of the essence of the physiognomy of the place. In the glow of which retrospective admission I ask myself how I came, under my first flush, reflected in other pages, to fail of justice to so much proud domestic architecture—in the very teeth moreover of the fact that I was forever paying my compliments, in a wistful, wondering way, to the fine Palazzo Lanfranchi, occupied in 1822 by the migratory Byron, and whither Leigh Hunt, as commemorated in the latter's Autobiography, came out to join him in an odd journalistic scheme.

Of course, however, I need scarcely add, the centre of my daily revolution—quite thereby on the circumference—was the great Company of Four in their sequestered corner; objects of regularly recurrent pious pilgrimage, if for no other purpose than to see whether each would each time again so inimitably carry itself as one of a group of wonderfully-worked old ivories. Their charm of relation to each other and to everything else that concerns them, that of the quartette of monuments, is more or less inexpressible all round; but not the least of it, ever, is in their beautiful secret for taking at different hours and seasons, in different states of the light, the sky, the wind, the weather—in different states, even, it used verily to seem to me, of an admirer's imagination or temper or nerves—different complexional appearances, different shades and pallors, different glows and chills. I have seen them look almost viciously black, and I have seen them as clear and fair as pale gold. And these things, for the most part, off on the large grassy carpet spread for them, and with the elbow of the old city-wall, not elsewhere erect, respectfully but protectingly crooked about, to the tune of a usual unanimity save perhaps in the case of the Leaning Tower—so abnormal a member of any respectable family this structure at best that I always somehow fancied its three companions, the Cathedral, the Baptistery and the Campo Santo, capable of quiet common understandings, for the major or the minor effect, into which their odd fellow, no hint thrown out to him, was left to enter as he might. If one haunted the place one ended by yielding to the conceit that, beautifully though the others of the group may be said to behave about him, one sometimes caught them in the act of tacitly combining to ignore him—as if he had, after so long, begun to give on their nerves. Or is that absurdity but my shamefaced form of admission that, for all the wonder of him, he finally gave on mine? Frankly—I would put it at such moments—he becomes at last an optical bore or *bêtise* [foolishness].

····· *ii* ······

To Lucca I was not to return often—I was to return only once; when that compact and admirable little city, the very model of a small *pays de Cocagne* [utopia], overflowing with everything that makes for ease, for plenty, for beauty, for interest and good example, renewed for me, in the highest degree, its genial and robust appearance. The perfection of this renewal must indeed have been, at bottom, the ground of my rather hanging back from possible excess of acquaintance—with the instinct that so right and rich and rounded a little impression had better be left than endangered. I remember positively saying to myself the second time that no brown-and-gold Tuscan city, even, could *be* as happy as Lucca looked—save always, exactly, Lucca; so that, on the chance of any shade of human illusion in the case, I wouldn't, as a brooding analyst, go within fifty miles of it again. Just so, I fear I must confess, it was this mere face-value of the place that, when I went back, formed my sufficiency; I spent all my scant time—or the greater part, for I took a day to drive over to the Bagni—just gaping at its visible attitude. This may be described as that of simply sitting there, through the centuries, at the receipt of perfect felicity; on its splendid solid seat of russet masonry, that is—for its great republican ramparts of long ago still lock it tight—with its wide garden-land, its ancient appanage or hereditary domain, teeming and blooming with everything that is good and pleasant for man, all about, and with a ring of graceful and noble, yet comparatively unbeneficed uplands and mountains watching it, for very envy, across the plain, as a circle of bigger boys, in the playground, may watch a privileged or pampered smaller one munch a particularly fine apple. Half smothered thus in oil and wine and corn and all the fruits of the earth, Lucca seems fairly to laugh for good-humour, and it's as if one can't say more for her than that, thanks to her putting forward for you a temperament somehow still richer than her heritage, you forgive her at every turn her fortune. She smiles up at you her greeting as you dip into her wide lap, out of which you may select almost any rare morsel whatever. Looking back at my own choice indeed I see it must have suffered a certain embarrassment—that of the sense of too many things; for I scarce remember choosing at all, any more than I recall having had to go hungry. I turned into all the churches—taking care, however, to pause before one of them, though before which I now irrecoverably forget, for verification of Ruskin's so characteristically magnified rapture over the high and rather narrow and obscure hunting-frieze on its front*—and in the Cathedral paid my respects at every turn to the greatest of Lucchesi, Matteo Civitale, wisest, sanest, homeliest, kindest of *quattro-cento* sculptors, to whose works the Duomo serves almost as a museum. But my nearest approach to anything so invidious as a discrimination or a preference, under the spell of so felt an equilibrium, must have been the act of engaging a carriage for the Baths.

That inconsequence once perpetrated, let me add, the impression was as right as any other—the impression of the drive through the huge general tangled and fruited *podere* of the countryside; that of the pair of jogging hours that bring the visitor to where the wideish gate of the valley of the Serchio opens. The question after this became quite other; the narrowing, though always more or less smiling gorge that draws you on and on is a different, a distinct proposition altogether, with its own individual grace of appeal and association. It is the association, exactly, that would even now, on this page, beckon me forward, or perhaps I should rather say backward—weren't more than a glance at it out of the question—to a view of that easier and not so inordinately remote past when "people spent the summer" in these perhaps slightly stuffy shades. I speak of that age, I think of it at least, as easier than ours, in spite of the fact that even as I made my pilgrimage the mark of modern change, the railway in construction, had begun to be distinct, though the automobile was still pretty far in the future. The relations and proportions

---

* In *The Stones of Venice,* Vol. I (1851).

of everything are of course now altered—I indeed, I confess, wince at the vision of the cloud of motor-dust that must in the fine season hang over the whole connection. That represents greater promptness of approach to the bosky depths of Ponte-a-Serraglio and the Bagni Caldi, but it throws back the other time, that of the old jogging relation, of the Tuscan grand-ducal "season" and the small cosmopolite sociability, into quite Arcadian air and the comparatively primitive scale. The "easier" Italy of our infatuated precursors there wears its glamour of facility not through any question of "the development of communications," but through the very absence of the dream of that boon, thanks to which every one (among the infatuated) lived on terms of so much closer intercourse with the general object of their passion. After we had crossed the Serchio that beautiful day we passed into the charming, the amiably tortuous, the thickly umbrageous, valley of the Lima, and then it was that I seemed fairly to remount the stream of time; figuring to myself wistfully, at the small scattered centres of entertainment—modest inns, pensions and other places of convenience clustered where the friendly torrent is bridged or the forested slopes adjust themselves—what the summer days and the summer rambles and the summer dreams must have been, in the blest place, when "people" (by which I mean the contingent of beguiled barbarians) didn't know better, as we say, than to content themselves with such a mild substitute, such a soft, sweet and essentially elegant apology, for adventure. One wanted not simply to hang about a little, but really to live back, as surely one might have done by staying on, into the so romantically strong, if mechanically weak, Italy of the associations of one's youth. It was a pang to have to revert to the present even in the form of Lucca—which says everything.

· · · · · *i i i* · · · · · ·

If undeveloped communications were to become enough for me at those retrospective moments, I might have felt myself supplied to my taste, let me go on to say, at the hour of my making, with great resolution, an attempt on high-seated and quite grandly out-of-the way Volterra: a reminiscence associated with quite a different year and, I should perhaps sooner

have bethought myself, with my fond experience of Pisa—
inasmuch as it was during a pause under that bland and motionless wing that I seem to have had to organise in the
darkness of a summer dawn my approach to the old Etruscan
stronghold. The railway then existed, but I rose in the dim
small hours to take my train; moreover, so far as that might too
much savour of an incongruous facility, the fault was in due
course quite adequately repaired by an apparent repudiation of
any awareness of such false notes on the part of the town. I may
not invite the reader to penetrate with me by so much as a step
the boundless backward reach of history to which the more
massive of the Etruscan gates of Volterra, the Porta all' Arco,
forms the solidest of thresholds; since I perforce take no step
myself, and am even exceptionally condemned here to impressionism unashamed. My errand was to spend a Sunday with an
Italian friend, a native in fact of the place, master of a house
there in which he offered me hospitality; who, also arriving
from Florence the night before, had obligingly come on with
me from Pisa, and whose consciousness of a due urbanity,
already rather overstrained, and still well before noon, by the
accumulation of our matutinal vicissitudes and other grounds
for patience, met all ruefully at the station the supreme shock
of an apparently great desolate world of volcanic hills, of blank,
though "engineered," undulations, as the emergence of a road
testified, unmitigated by the smallest sign of a wheeled vehicle.
The station, in other words, looked out at that time (and I
daresay the case hasn't strikingly altered) on a mere bare huge
hill-country, by some remote mighty shoulder of which the
goal of our pilgrimage, so questionably "served" by the railway, was hidden from view. Served as well by a belated om-
nibus, a four-in-hand of lame and lamentable quality, the place,
I hasten to add, eventually put forth some show of being; after
a complete practical recognition of which, let me at once further mention, all the other, the positive and sublime, connections of Volterra established themselves for me without my
lifting a finger.

The small shrunken, but still lordly prehistoric city i⸱
perched, when once you have rather painfully zigzagged ⸱
within sight of it, very much as an eagle's eyrie, oversweep⸱

the land and the sea; and to that type of position, the ideal of the airy peak of vantage, with all accessories and minor features a drop, a slide and a giddiness, its individual items and elements strike you at first as instinctively conforming. This impression was doubtless after a little modified for me; there were levels, there were small stony practicable streets, there were walks and strolls, outside the gates and roundabout the cyclopean wall, to the far end of downward-tending protrusions and promontories, natural buttresses and pleasant terrene headlands, friendly suburban spots (one would call them if the word had less detestable references) where games of bowls and overtrellised wine-tables could put in their note; in spite of which however my friend's little house of hospitality, clean and charming and oh so immemorially Tuscan, was as perpendicular and ladder-like as so compact a residence could be; it kept up for me beautifully—as regards posture and air, though humanly and socially it rather cooed like a dovecote—the illusion of the vertiginously "balanced" eagle's nest. The air, in truth, all the rest of that splendid day, must have been the key to the promptly-produced intensity of one's relation to every aspect of the charming episode; the light, cool, keen air of those delightful high places, in Italy, that tonically correct the ardours of July, and which at our actual altitude could but affect me as the very breath of the grand local legend. I might have "had" the little house, our particular eagle's nest, for the summer, and even on such touching terms; and I well remember the force of the temptation to take it, if only other complications had permitted; to spend the series of weeks with that admirable *interesting* freshness in my lungs: interesting, I especially note as the strong appropriate medium in which a continuity with the irrecoverable but still effective past had been so robustly preserved. I couldn't yield, alas, to the conceived felicity, which had half-a-dozen appealing aspects; I could only, while thus feeling how the atmospheric medium itself made for a positively initiative exhilaration, enjoy my illusion till the morrow. The exhilaration therefore supplies to memory the whole light in which, for the too brief time, I went out "seeing" Volterra; so that my glance at the seated splen-ur reduces itself, as I have said, to the merest impressionism;

nothing more was to be looked for, on the stretched surface of consciousness, from one breezy wash of the brush. I find there the clean strong image simplified to the three or four unforgettable particulars of the vast rake of the view; with the Maremma, of evil fame,* more or less immediately below, but with those islands of the sea, Corsica and Elba, the names of which are sharply associational beyond any others, dressing the far horizon in the grand manner, and the Ligurian coast-line melting northward into beauty and history galore; with colossal uncemented blocks of Etruscan gates and walls plunging you—and by their very interest—into a sweet surrender of any privilege of appreciation more crushing than your general synthetic stare; and with the rich and perfectly arranged museum, an unsurpassed exhibition of monumental treasure from Etruscan tombs, funereal urns mainly, reliquaries of an infinite power to move and charm us still, contributing to this same so resigned, but somehow at the same time so inspired, collapse of the historic imagination under too heavy a pressure, or abeyance of "private judgment" in too unequal a relation.

· · · · · *i v* · · · · · · ·

I remember recovering private judgment indeed in the course of two or three days following the excursion I have just noted; which must have shaped themselves in some sort of consonance with the idea that as we were hereabouts in the very middle of dim Etruria a common self-respect prescribed our somehow profiting by the fact. This kindled in us the spirit of exploration, but with results of which I here attempt no record, so utterly does the whole impression swoon away, for present memory, into vagueness, confusion and intolerable heat. Our self-respect was of the common order, but the blaze of the July sun was, even for Tuscany, of the uncommon; so that the project of a trudging quest for Etruscan tombs in shadeless wastes yielded to its own temerity. There comes back to me nevertheless at the same time, from the mild misadventure, and quite as through this positive humility of failure, the sense of a supremely intimate revelation of Italy in undress, so

---

* Notorious for its malarial swamps.

to speak (the state, it seemed, in which one would most fondly, most ideally, enjoy her); Italy no longer in winter starch and sobriety, with winter manners and winter prices and winter excuses, all addressed to the *forestieri* and the philistines; but lolling at her length, with her graces all relaxed, and thereby only the more natural; the brilliant performer, in short, *en famille,* the curtain down and her salary stopped for the season—thanks to which she is by so much more the easy genius and the good creature as she is by so much less the advertised *prima donna.* She received us nowhere more sympathetically, that is with less ceremony or self-consciousness, I seem to recall, than at Montepulciano, for instance—where it was indeed that the recovery of private judgment I just referred to couldn't help taking place. What we were doing, or what we expected to do, at Montepulciano I keep no other trace of than is bound up in a present quite tender consciousness that I wouldn't for the world not have been there. I think my reason must have been largely just in the beauty of the name (for could any beauty be greater?), reinforced no doubt by the fame of the local vintage and the sense of how we should quaff it on the spot. Perhaps we quaffed it too constantly; since the romantic picture reduces itself for me but to two definite appearances; that of the more priggish discrimination so far reasserting itself as to advise me that Montepulciano was dirty, even remarkably dirty; and that of its being not much else besides but perched and brown and queer and crooked, and noble withal (which is what almost any Tuscan city more easily than not acquits herself of); all the while she may on such occasions figure, when one looks off from her to the end of dark street-vistas or catches glimpses through high arcades, some big battered, blistered, overladen, overmasted ship, swimming in a violet sea.

If I have lost the sense of what we were doing, that could at all suffer commemoration, at Montepulciano, so I sit helpless before the memory of small stewing Torrita, which we must somehow have expected to yield, under our confidence, a view of shy charms, but which didn't yield, to my recollection, even anything that could fairly be called a breakfast or a dinner.

There may have been in the neighbourhood a rumour of Etruscan tombs; the neighbourhood, however, was vast, and that possibility not to be verified, in the conditions, save after due refreshment. Then it was, doubtless, that the question of refreshment so beckoned us, by a direct appeal, straight across country, from Perugia, that, casting consistency, if not to the winds, since alas there were none, but to the lifeless air, we made the sweltering best of our way (and it took, for the distance, a terrible time) to the Grand Hotel of that city. This course shines for me, in the retrospect, with a light even more shameless than that in which my rueful conscience then saw it; since we thus exchanged again, at a stroke, the tousled *bonne fille* [good-hearted girl] of our vacational Tuscany for the formal and figged-out presence of Italy on her good behaviour. We had never seen her conform more to all the proprieties, we felt, than under this aspect of lavish hospitality to that now apparently quite inveterate swarm of pampered *forestieri,* English and Americans in especial, who, having had Roman palaces and villas deliciously to linger in, break the northward journey, when once they decide to take it, in the Umbrian paradise. They were, goodness knows, within their rights, and we profited, as any one may easily and cannily profit at that time, by the sophistications paraded for them; only I feel, as I pleasantly recover it all, that though we had arrived perhaps at the most poetical of watering-places we had lost our finer clue. (The difference from other days was immense, all the span of evolution from the ancient malodorous inn which somehow didn't matter, to that new type of polyglot caravanserai which everywhere insists on mattering—mattering, even in places where other interests abound, so much more than anything else.) That clue, the finer as I say, I would fain at any rate to-day pick up for its close attachment to another Tuscan city or two—for a felt pull from strange little San Gimignano delle belle Torre in especial; by which I mean from the memory of a summer Sunday spent there during a stay at Siena. But I have already superabounded, for mere love of my general present rubric—the real thickness of experience having a good deal evaporated, so that the Tiny Town of the Many Towers hangs before me, not to say, rather, far behind me, after the manner of an object directly meeting the wrong or diminishing lens of one's telescope.

It did everything, on the occasion of that pilgrimage, that it was expected to do, presenting itself more or less in the guise of some rare silvery shell, washed up by the sea of time, cracked and battered and dishonoured, with its mutilated marks of adjustment to the extinct type of creature it once harboured figuring against the sky as maimed gesticulating arms flourished in protest against fate. If the centuries, however, had pretty well cleaned out, vulgarly speaking, this amazing little fortress-town, it wasn't that a mere aching void was bequeathed us, I recognise as I consult a somewhat faded impression; the whole scene and occasion come back to me as the exhibition, on the contrary, of a stage rather crowded and agitated, of no small quantity of sound and fury, of concussions, discussions, vociferations, hurryings to and fro, that could scarce have reached a higher pitch in the old days of the siege and the sortie. San Gimignano affected me, to a certainty, as not dead, I mean, but as inspired with that strange and slightly sinister new life that is now, in case after case, up and down the peninsula, and even in presence of the dryest and most scattered bones, producing the miracles of resurrection. The effect is often—and I find it strikingly involved in this particular reminiscence—that of the buried hero himself positively waking up to show you his bones for a fee, and almost capering about in his appeal to your attention. What has become of the soul of San Gimignano who shall say?—but, of a genial modern Sunday, it is as if the heroic skeleton, risen from the dust, were in high activity, officious for your entertainment and your detention, clattering and changing plates at the informal friendly inn, personally conducting you to a sight of the admirable Santa Fina of Ghirlandaio, as I believe is supposed, in a dim chapel of the Collegiata church; the poor young saint, on her low bed, in a state of ecstatic vision (the angelic apparition is given), accompanied by a few figures and accessories of the most beautiful and touching truth. This image is what has most vividly remained with me, of the day I thus so ineffectually recover; the precious ill-set gem or domestic treasure of

Santa Fina, and then the wonderful drive, at eventide, back to Siena: the progress through the darkening land that was like a dense fragrant garden, all fireflies and warm emanations and dimly-seen motionless festoons, extravagant vines and elegant branches intertwisted for miles, with couples and companies of young countryfolk almost as fondly united and raising their voices to the night as if superfluously to sing out at you that they were happy, and above all were Tuscan. On reflection, and to be just, I connect the slightly incongruous loudness that hung about me under the Beautiful Towers with the really too coarse competition for my favour among the young vetturini [cab driver] who lay in wait for my approach, and with an eye to my subsequent departure, on my quitting, at some unre-membered spot, the morning train from Siena, from which point there was then still a drive. That onset was of a fine mediæval violence, but the subsiding echoes of it alone must have afterwards borne me company; mingled, at the worst, with certain reverberations of the animated rather than con-centrated presence of sundry young sketchers and copyists of my own nationality, which element in the picture conveyed beyond anything else how thoroughly it was all to sit again henceforth in the eye of day. My final vision perhaps was of a sacred reliquary not so much rudely as familiarly and "humor-ously" torn open. The note had, with all its references, its own interest; but I never went again.

[1909]

Index

....

About the Editor

FRED KAPLAN is a Distinguished Professor of English and American Literature at Queens College and the Graduate Center of the City University of New York. He is the author of *Henry James: The Imagination of Genius: A Biography* (1992) and *Dickens: A Biography* (1988). His *Thomas Carlyle: A Biography* (1983) was nominated for the National Book Critics' Circle Award and was a jury-nominated finalist for the Pulitzer Prize. His *Sacred Tears: Sentimentality in Victorian Literature* (1987), *Dickens and Mesmerism: The Hidden Springs of Fiction* (1975), and *Miracles of Rare Device: The Poet's Sense of Self in Nineteenth-Century Poetry* (1972) are significant contributions to the study of Romantic and Victorian literature and culture. He has held Guggenheim and National Endowment for the Humanities Fellowships and been a Fellow of the National Humanities Center, the Rockefeller Foundation, and the Huntington Library.